D1796490

In the Shadow of a Conflict

In the Shadow of a Conflict

*Crisis in Zimbabwe and its effects in
Mozambique, South Africa and Zambia*

Edited by Bill Derman and Randi Kaarhus

Published in 2013
by

Weaver Press
PO Box A1922
Avondale
Harare
Zimbabwe
www.weaverpress.co.zw

Cover design: Danes Design, Harare
Typeset by forzalibro designs, Harare
Printed by Sable Press, Harare

ISBN 978-1-77922-217-6

Contents

List of Maps and Illustrations   vii

List of Tables   viii

Acknowledgements   ix

Contributors' details   xi

1

Introduction   1

Crisis in Zimbabwe and its regional effects

Bill Derman and Randi Kaarhus

2

Reflections on National Dynamics, Responses   29
and Discourses in a Regional Context

Randi Kaarhus, Bill Derman and Espen Sjaastad

3

Poverty, Shelter and Opportunities   67

Zimbabweans' experiences in Mozambique

Randi Kaarhus

4

Settling for Less?   92

Zimbabwean farmers and commercial farming in Mozambique

Amanda Hammar

5

Reversing the Flows of People, Skills and Goods   121

Rural livelihood changes in central Mozambique

Alex Bolding, with Rodriguez Lino Piloto

6

Governing the South African/Zimbabwean Border   146

Immigration, criminalization and human rights

Bill Derman

7

Hierarchies, Violence, Gender 180
Narratives from Zimbabwean migrants on South African farms
Ruth Hall

8

Finding Shelter and Work in the Communal Areas of Limpopo 207
Zimbabweans in rural South Africa
Bill Derman, Anne Hellum and Shirhami Shirinda

9

Factions in the Field 236
Social divisions and gendered survival strategies
on a South African border farm
Lincoln Addison

10

Farms as Camps 260
Displaced Zimbabweans on commercial farms
in Limpopo Province, South Africa
Poul Wisborg

11

Home away from Home 285
Land, identity and community on the Mkushi Farm Block
Espen Sjaastad, Thomson Kalinda and Fabian Maimbo

12

The Impact of the Zimbabwean Crisis on Informal 309
Cross-Border Trade with Zambia
Thomson Kalinda, Diana Banda, Priscilla Hamukwala,
Fabian Maimbo and Espen Sjaastad

Bibliography 327

List of Maps, Illustrations and Tables

Maps

1. SADC countries, with Zimbabwean border crossing points covered in the book ... 28
2. Manica Province in Mozambique and Beira corridor ... 70
3. Border Area Manicaland, Zimbabwe – Manica Province, Mozambique ... 124
4. Limpopo Province, South Africa ... 156
5. Communal areas/former homelands, Limpopo Province ... 210
6. Study sites in Vhembe District, Limpopo Province ... 268
7. Mkushi District in Central Province, Zambia ... 286

Colour Plates

1. Billboard encouraging Zimbabweans in South Africa to go home to vote in 2008.
2. Billboard in South Africa commenting on the fear that the Zimbabwean election of 2008 will be 'stolen'.
3. South African Home Affairs Refugee Officer in Musina calling the names of people receiving permits to stay in RSA.
4. The porous high-security border between South Africa and Zimbabwe close to Musina – damaged by seasonal rains.
5. Farm workers during a short break in orange harvesting on a South African border farm.
6. A headman in Nzhelele communal area talks about the Zimbabweans in his district.
7. Part of the research team interviewing in a farm worker villages.
8. At the water tap in a farm workers' village on a commercial farm, Limpopo, South Africa.
9. The 'invisible' green revolution in a Mozambican border area: Zimbabwean ideals and technology in Pandagoma, Manica Province, Mozambique.
10. Mobile street vendors from Zimbabwe in Vila de Manica, Mozambique, 2008.
11. Crossing the border on foot: a 'scud runner' on his way from Mozambique back to Zimbabwe with rice and cooking oil in 2008.

12. Informal cross-border traders in Zambia preparing to return home to Zimbabwe
13. Large- and small-scale cross-border trade between Zambia and Zimbabwe
14. Looking into the future? At the Zimbabwean border with South Africa

Tables

1. Dominant population fluxes and their drivers   125
2. Age of respondents   215
3. Socio-demographic characteristics of sampled cross-border traders   314

Acknowledgements

This book is a result of a long-standing collaboration among six institutions, including the Department of International Environment and Development Studies (Noragric at the Norwegian University of the Life Sciences, the Institute for Poverty, Land and Agrarian Studies (PLAAS) at the University of the Western Cape, the University of Zambia, Wageningen University, the Catholic University of Mozambique, and the Nordic Africa Institute (NAI). The book is based on an interdisciplinary research project, which in the end proved to be more productive than problematic! First of all, the editors and all the contributors recognize the contributions of so many people we worked with in the field, whose knowledge, experience and insights form a core part of the research process. We would also thank the Research Council of Norway, and more specifically the Poverty and Peace Programme. Through their funding of the research project 'In the Shadow of a Conflict' they provided the financial basis for several years of multi-sited, fieldwork-based data collection.

We would also like to acknowledge the Norwegian government for funding and the Norwegian Center for Human Rights for co-ordinating the South Africa programme, which enabled part of the PLAAS-Noragric collaboration, under which field research on farm workers and farm dwellers was carried out. NAI furthermore funded part of Amanda Hammar's research in Mozambique for Chapter 4. The editors would like to thank the two reviewers for each chapter who gave of their time and their knowledge to improve the quality of the individual papers, and in this way significantly assisted the work of editing the book; in particular we must mention Blair Rutherford, Michael Walker, Lincoln Addison, Bjørn Bertelsen, Steefan Dondeyne, James Bannerman, Marja Spierenburg and Helge Rønning.

In addition, the editors would like to thank Noragric whose administrative staff facilitated the entire project, and provided additional funding for the publication. Lastly, we would like to thank Weaver Press for their unflinching support for the project and high-quality efforts in bringing the project to a successful conclusion.

Contributors' details

Lincoln Addison is a PhD candidate in the Department of Anthropology at Rutgers University. Since 2005, he has conducted research with Zimbabwean farm workers in northern Limpopo province, South Africa. This research informs his dissertation currently titled 'Delegated Despotism: Frontiers of Agrarian Labor on a South African Border Farm.'

Diana Banda is a Lecturer in the Department of Agricultural Economics and Extension at the University of Zambia. She is a rural sociologist who has undertaken several research and consultancy studies on issues in customary and leasehold tenure and women's access to agricultural land in Zambia. She is currently working on a collaborative research project examining poverty dynamics among Zambian smallholder farmers.

Alex Bolding is an Associate Professor at the Irrigation and Water Engineering group, Wageningen University. His field of specialisation is irrigation and water governance in southern Africa. His PhD was based on research in eastern Zimbabwe on water governance at field, irrigation scheme and river catchment levels. Since then he has been involved in research on furrow irrigators and shifts in water governance in central and southern Mozambique and capacity building programmes in the fields of participatory irrigation design and integrated water resources management in both Mozambique and South Africa.

Bill Derman is currently Professor Emeritus at Michigan State University and the Department of International Environment and Development Studies at the Norwegian University of Life Sciences. He holds a PhD in Anthropology from the University of Michigan and has carried out long term field work in west and southern Africa. He is currently engaged in research on land restitution in South Africa and in water governance, human rights, gender and integrated water resources management in Zimbabwe. He is currently editing (with Anne Hellum and Kristin B. Sandvik) a volume entitled *Human Rights: Ambiguities of Rights Claiming in Africa.*

Amanda Hammar is a Professor at the Centre for African Studies at the University of Copenhagen. Recent publications include edited special issues of the *Journal of Southern African Studies* (2010) on 'The Zimbabwe Crisis Through the Lens of Displacement', and the *Journal of Contemporary African Studies* (2008) on 'Political Economies of Displacement in Southern Africa'. She co-edited *Zimbabwe's Unfinished Business: Rethinking Land, State and Nation in the Context of Crisis* (Harare: Weaver Press, 2003), and is currently editing a volume entitled *Displacement Economies in Africa: Paradoxes of Crisis and Creativity* (forthcoming with Zed Press and Nordic Africa Institute).

Priscilla Hamukwala is a Lecturer in the Department of Agricultural Economics and Extension at the University of Zambia. Her research focus has mainly been in the area of agricultural marketing and economic development. Since 2005, she has been part of a collaborative research project examining new market development and marketing strategies for sorghum and millet farmers. She has also been the lead researcher in a sorghum and millet seed value chain study. She is currently working on two other collaborative research projects; one on poverty dynamics among Zambian smallholder farmers and the other on economic valuation of land in Zambia.

Anne Hellum is a Professor at the Department of Public and International Law at the University of Oslo. She is director of the Institute of Women's Law, Child Law, Discrimination and Equality Law. Her research cuts across human rights law, discrimination law and the anthropology of law. She has written extensively on the relationship between women's human rights and legal pluralism in Zimbabwe, South Africa, and Norway, including (with Julie Stewart and Amy Tsanga) *Human Rights, Gendered Realities and Plural Legalities: Paths are Made by Walking* (Harare: Weaver Press, 2007).

Randi Kaarhus is currently Head of Research at the Department of International Environment and Development Studies (Noragric) at the Norwegian University of Life Sciences. Holding a PhD in Social Anthropology from the University of Oslo, she has carried out research both in South America and south-eastern Africa, focusing on Mozambique, Malawi and Tanzania. Recent publications analyse local conceptions of rights and gender, food and livelihoods, and address conflicts over land and natural resources.

Thomson Kalinda is a Senior Lecturer and Chair of the Department of Agricultural Economics and Extension at the University of Zambia. His PhD thesis examined smallholder farmers' access to resources in Southern Province, Zambia. He has been involved in research on issues related to rural development, food security, and agricultural growth and investment options for poverty reduction. He has also been recently involved in research and on cultural practices and the spread of HIV and AIDS in rural communities in Zambia.

Fabian Maimbo is a Senior Lecturer at the Department of Agricultural Economics and Extension, University of Zambia. He formerly served as a Research Fellow at the University's Rural Development Studies Bureau. He has done extensive research work in the area of rural development with specific focus on marketing and rural-urban terms of trade, and has done consultancy work for a number of international organizations.

Rodriguez Lino Piloto was born in Moatize, Mozambique. During a long and wide-ranging career he performed jobs as farm labourer in Malawi and Zimbabwe, before becoming a clerk at the Zimbabwean Agricultural Extension Service (Agritex) in the early 1980s. In 2004 he returned to Mozambique where he became a research assistant for Alex Bolding. Since 2009 he has worked for Resiliençia Lda, a private NGO based in Chimoio that engages in participatory irrigation design and rehabilitation programmes in central Mozambique.

Espen Sjaastad is a Professor at the Department of International Environment and Development Studies at the Norwegian University of Life Sciences. He specialises in resource economics and institutional economics. His main research interests include land tenure evolution, land rights formalisation, rural livelihoods, rural exchange systems and poverty measurement.

Poul Wisborg is a researcher in development studies based at the Department of International Environment and Development Studies at the Norwegian University of Life Sciences, and is currently researching large-scale land acquisition in Africa. His PhD thesis examined human rights and land tenure reform in Namaqualand, South Africa, and his academic interests include land and agrarian studies, development, human rights, social justice, gender and political ecology.

1. Billboard encouraging Zimbabweans in South Africa to go home to vote in 2008 (*Photo: R. Hall*)
2. Billboard in South Africa commenting on the fear that the Zimbabwean election of 2008 will be 'stolen' (*Photo: R. Hall*)

Pl 1

3. South African Home Affairs Refugee Officer in Musina calling the names of people receiving permits to stay in South Africa (*Photo: B. Derman*)

4. The porous high-security border between South Africa and Zimbabwe close to Musina – damaged by seasonal rains (*Photo: B. Derman*)

Pl 2

5. Farm workers during a short break in orange harvesting on a South African border farm (*Photo: B. Derman*)

Pl 3

6. A headman in Nzhelele communal area talks about the Zimbaweans in his district. (*Photo: B. Derman*)

7. Part of the research team interviewing in a farm worker villages. (*Photo: R. Hall*)

Pl 4

8. At the water tap in a farm workers' village on a commercial farm, Limpopo, South Africa (*Photo: B. Derman*)

9. The 'invisible' green revolution in a Mozambican border area: Zimbabwean ideals and technology in Pandagoma, Manica Province, Mozambique (*Photo: A. Bolding*)

Pl 5

10. Mobile street vendors from Zimbabwe in Vila de Manica, Mozambique, 2008 (*Photo: A. Bolding*)
11. Crossing the border on foot: a 'scud runner' on his way from Mozambique back to Zimbabwe with rice and cooking oil in 2008 (*Photo: A. Bolding*)

Pl 6

12. Informal cross-border traders in Zambia preparing to return home to Zimbabwe (*Photo: T. Kalinda*)

13. Large and small-scale cross-border trade between Zambia and Zimbabwe (*Photo: T. Kalinda*)

Pl 7

14. Looking into the future? At the Zimbabwean border with South Africa (*Photo: R. Hall*)

Pl 8

1

Introduction
Crisis in Zimbabwe and its Regional Effects

Bill Derman and Randi Kaarhus[1]

Introduction

Zimbabwe has cast a powerful regional and international shadow since it became independent in 1980 and more recently, through the crises of the first decade of the twenty-first century. The 2000s were a decade of combined political, economic and social crises in Zimbabwe following what had been a relatively successful twenty years of independence since 1980. The scale, depth and severity of the crises evolving since 2000 have been as dramatic as they have been unexpected. Our point of departure in this book is that while there has been substantial coverage of the internal consequences of Zimbabwe's crises less attention has been paid to its regional and cross-border consequences.[2] In explaining the ongoing processes stemming from the crises, we have selected three neighboring countries – Mozambique, South Africa and Zambia – to depict how, over time, they have experienced and interpreted events in Zimbabwe, how they have dealt with Zimbabweans entering their territories, and how they have or have not formulated policies and developed practices to cope with the arrival of new and mainly undocumented Zimbabwean immigrants. While much attention, both popular and academic, has been devoted to Zimbabwe's 'Fast Track'[3] land reform – its causes, manifestations and impacts – less has been written about the fates of those who left the country in the wake of its implementation. In particular, little is known about the processes by which they entered and settled into rural communities and farms in neighboring countries. Most of the focus has been upon urban contexts and what has been labeled as xenophobic violence towards Zimbabweans and other 'foreigners' in South Africa (Hassim, Kupe and Worby, 2008). We augment these accounts through concentrating on the rural dimensions of the Zimbabwean diaspora.

This book presents the findings of a three-and-a-half-year collaborative study on the regional consequences of Zimbabwe's crises in Mozambique, South Africa and Zambia. We present the stories of those Zimbabweans who have sought work, shelter and exile from their home, how they have fared, and in some cases under what conditions they would return to Zimbabwe and home. We further analyze the differences in policies and strategies followed by the governments of Mozambique, South Africa and Zambia as they have faced the ongoing political, economic and humanitarian crises in Zimbabwe as well as those within their own borders. In addition, we explore how Zimbabwean migrants' needs and interests have been articulated with local politics and pressures on land and related natural resources, and how these have intersected with changing agrarian dynamics in their host countries and communities.

The chapters are based upon sustained fieldwork at multiple sites in the three nations from 2007 to 2010. Methodologies employed by different researchers included scheduled interviews, open-ended interviews, life histories, document collection, interviews with government officials, multilateral organizations and NGOs, and recording of public debates in national media. The main emphasis was upon gaining insights into the experiences and understandings of Zimbabweans in the three countries, and the effects of their presence in this new context. We emphasize that there are long patterns of migration in southern Africa, ranging from oscillating labour migration (First, 1983; Murray, 1981; Lubkemann, 2008) to forced displacement associated with wars of national liberation. The mines, fields and homes of whites in South Africa, in particular, became dependent upon black labour from Zimbabwe (Southern Rhodesia), Lesotho, Swaziland, Mozambique, Malawi and South Africa itself. Much of the labour came from rural areas where the men left their families to cope at home. In this book we contend that the multiple crises in Zimbabwe since 2000 have introduced new dynamics and patterns into earlier flows and livelihood strategies.

The book contributes to debates on the following issues in southern Africa: the challenges posed to the three countries by the effects of the crises in Zimbabwe; migration as a strategy and opportunity for coping with displacement, violence, poverty and vulnerability; the depth of desperation among Zimbabwean migrants caused by the economic decline in Zimbabwe; the importance of rural livelihoods and the degree to which they are weakened or strengthened through employment in larger scale commercial agriculture; the nature of labour and social relations between people of different nationalities on commercial farms in the border areas; and the complex relationships between national policies (or the deliberate lack thereof) and how Zimbabweans have fared in the region. Lastly, the highly gendered nature of these processes is explored in almost all chapters. While it is an obvious point, the chapters seek to give a nuanced account of the human conditions of the Zimbabweans whom we encountered in the course of our study, and to emphasize how they have sought to keep their dignity in often extraordinarily difficult circumstances.

In general, no matter what the broader analysis and policies, the perspective of migrants will focus on their own opportunities and difficulties. And while we will emphasize the many complex political, economic, social and cultural issues embedded in migration, the issue of migration will be viewed from the perspective of the migrant, in contrast to that of the multiple authorities seeking to control the movement of Zimbabweans out of the country and into others. We have sought to keep the intentions of Zimbabwean migrants foregrounded while holding the perspective that in the decade since 2000 it has been a genuine survival strategy for Zimbabwean individuals and families.

The Zimbabwe Context

Zimbabwe accentuates deep theoretical and political differences in understanding and explaining post-colonial Africa, especially in relationship to its governance and land reform programmes. Its independence in 1980, negotiated after a bitter armed struggle, serves as both a real and imagined beginning for debates about the post-colonial state. There have been the analyses describing how Marxist guerrillas and spirit mediums worked together (Lan, 1985), the popular and progressive nature of the revolution (Martin and Johnson, 1981), and how the post-2000 land reform continued revolutionary ideals (Moyo and Yeros, 2005). There has been an equally intense discussion on reassessing issues of violence and the role of the state under the ruling party, following the Zimbabwean army campaign against Matabeleland, under suspicion that there were links between the apartheid regime in South Africa and dissidents from the Zimbabwe African People's Union (ZAPU) (Alexander et al., 2000; CCJP, 1997). The initial post-independence policies of racial reconciliation which were the explicit policies of ZANU when they took power in 1980 have been altered since the constitutional referendum and the parliamentary elections in 2000, when ZANU-PF argued that whites were trying to recolonize Zimbabwe (Hammar et al., 2003; Raftopoulos and Savage, 2004; Hellum and Derman, 2004). In a return to the use of state violence in 2000, the ruling

3

party[4] claims that it is simply continuing the liberation war (the *chimurenga*) because of continued colonial efforts to re-subjugate Zimbabwe (Raftopoulos, 2004).[5]

Contested Versions of Zimbabwe's Post-independence History

Zimbabwe's history resonates in contemporary debates about the nature of the country's crises. Through armed struggle against the white-dominated Rhodesian government from 1965–1979, the armies based upon the two major political formations (ZANU's Zimbabwe African National Liberation Army (ZANLA) and ZAPU's Zimbabwe Peoples' Revolutionary Army (ZIPRA)) paved the way for black majority rule. In the first free election in 1980, ZANU, led by Robert Mugabe, won a decisive electoral victory over ZAPU (led by Joshua Nkomo) and smaller parties. In a compromise constitution many white interests were protected; significantly, for the first decade, land could not be nationalized or acquired without the permission of the owner. However, while land reform was restricted by the new constitution much land became available as white owners had abandoned or left their farms. The government responded to land need by initiating a programme which involved the resettlement of approximately 40,000 households on over 2.2 million hectares of land (Cusworth, 2000: 26). Thus in the period from 1982 to 1987 nine per cent of the country's land area became resettlement areas, based on a variety of models. Model A included family based holdings with specific areas set aside for residences, fields (called arables) and village grazing areas.[6] Model B comprised collective co-operatives; Model C, satellite producers linked to centralized commercial crop and livestock production and processing (this was rarely used), and Model D, for livestock-keeping in the drier parts of the country, now also a rarity (Kinsey 2000). Education, health, agricultural extension, and agricultural production were government priorities until the early 1990s. Due to a combination of government borrowing, expensive social programmes, corruption, import restrictions, and the vagaries of global markets, Zimbabwe adopted its own modified structural adjustment programme. Reduced social spending led to increasing popular dissatisfaction with the government in the late 1990s.

With the end of the first decade of independence, the moratorium on forcible land acquisition also ended, and a land acquisition act was passed which gave the government the right of 'first refusal' on all properties available for sale.[7]

Little use was made of this potentially powerful tool. Government supporters contended that there were insufficient funds to enter the land market. However, during the 1990s, land and land reform were not major national issues in Zimbabwe in comparison to the growing economic difficulties.[8] Rather, the poor (rural and urban) were being ignored as the political leadership used the levers of state power to enrich itself. In general the defence budget was second only to education in terms of expenditures (Dashwood, 2000; Compagnon, 2011). These policies were legitimized through notions of the indigenization of the economy, which became the slogan for the 1990s, and has intensified through 2012. Indigenization, however, has so far been applied selectively, and to benefit narrow circles of business people and the political elite (Bayart, 2009; Bond, 1998; Carmody and Taylor, 2003; Compagnon, 2011; Dashwood 2000).

In 1998 Zimbabwe sent its armed forces into the Democratic Republic of Congo. Typical of western assessment of this intervention was the following comment from a BBC reporter:

Zimbabwe's expensive involvement in the civil war in the Democratic Republic of Congo continues despite opposition at home, and no obvious strategic advantage. A war which is increasingly unpopular with Zimbabweans has been cited as one of the reasons for the massive swing towards the opposition in June's election. An estimated 11,000 Zimbabwean soldiers form the mainstay of support for President Laurent Kabila's government in his war against rebels backed by Rwanda and Uganda.

In the middle of Zimbabwe's worst economic crisis since independence in 1980, President Robert Mugabe's government is reported to be spending millions of dollars each month on the war. Zimbabwe does not share a common boundary with the DR Congo, and is under no strategic threat from within the country. Instead, there are signs that Harare is pouring money into the war with the hope of reaping longer-term financial rewards from its relationship with DR Congo.[9]

In addition to the war, economic demands by the Zimbabwe National Liberation War Veterans Association (ZNLWVA) contributed to a rapid depletion of the treasury. According to some analysts the economy began its generalized plunge in 1997 when the Zimbabwe dollar lost 74 per cent of its value (Bond and Manyanya 2002). In turn, the accelerating economic crisis of 1997 led to unprecedented strikes, food riots and intensified pressures from civil society for opening up the political space.[10]

Dissatisfaction with the ruling party led to the formation of the National Constitutional Assembly (NCA), a civil society organization which campaigned for a new constitution, and subsequently the formation of a new political party, the Movement for Democratic Change (MDC), led by the labour leader Morgan Tsvangirai, head of the Zimbabwe Congress of Trade Unions (ZCTU). In response, the government formed its own constitutional commission and drafted its own new constitution.

In 2000, a referendum was held and the government's draft constitution was defeated. ZANU-PF blamed white farmers, and civil society, along with its own weak organization, for this defeat. To salvage popular support in the parliamentary elections of June 2000, ZANU-PF turned to what it claimed was the unfinished business of the liberation era – the land issue and colonialism.[11] It characterized the political opposition as agents of foreign powers working to overthrow the successful revolution, and generated the Third Chimurenga. The parliamentary elections of June 2000 were accompanied by electoral violence and large-scale farm invasions, initially organized by the war veterans' organization – led by Chenjerai Hunzvi[12] – and ZANU-PF.[13]

While questions of violence have now faded there is much debate about the successes and failures of Zimbabwe's 'radical' land reform. There are ongoing academic and political considerations about how land reform was carried out, who benefited, who lost, what have been the outcomes for agricultural production, who received farms and in general how one assesses the successes or failures of past 12 years. Its significant to recall that not just farm owners and managers were forced from their farms, but the farm workers as well. They were driven not just from employment but also from their homes.[14] And nationwide, substantial violence was visited upon members and supporters of the MDC in communal and urban areas. There are different understandings of the post-referendum land invasions. One strand of scholarship sees the invasions as part of a racialized discourse of citizenship and belonging constituted around the land question and the ZANU-PF contribution to the liberation struggle (Hammar et al., 2003; Derman and Hellum, 2007; Alexander, 2006; Raftopoulos, 2009; and summarized by Sachikonye, 2011). The other strand, represented by Sam Moyo emphasizes the continuities with the popular occupations taking place in the 1980s and 1990s (Moyo, 2001) or as the leading edge of a new alliance between workers and peasants (Moyo and Yeros, 2005).[15]

Since 2000, Zimbabwe has seen massive internal displacement and migration.[16] The government's eviction campaign of Operation Murambatsvina in

2005 displaced around 700,000 urban Zimbabweans, while Fast Track has displaced an unknown number of farm workers (Tibaijuka, 2005; Vambe, 2008; Potts, 2010). Operation Murambatsvina was carried out, according to the government, to arrest 'disorderly or chaotic urbanization, stopping illegal market transactions and reversing environmental damage caused by inappropriate urban agricultural practices' (Tibaijuka 2005: 20).[17] Yet Tibaijuka's report for the United Nations provides a wide range of other reasons including political motivations such as retribution directed at an electorate that voted against ZANU-PF. Potts (2010) observes that one major reason was to push urban residents out of the city and back into rural areas. Although it might have served to discourage rural-urban migration, the operation caused massive suffering in several of Zimbabwe's cities and increased the impoverishment of Zimbabweans.

If we fast-forward to 2008, we arrive at a combined parliamentary and presidential election which took place on 29 March after mediation by the Southern African Development Community (SADC) and President Mbeki to resolve Zimbabwe's political crisis. The South African president had assisted in negotiating a new Electoral Act in Zimbabwe in 2008, an act which included mechanisms of transparency such as displaying local election results at each polling station. And when the first results of the 2008 elections were divulged, they appeared to represent a dramatic change in the post-independence political landscape (International Crisis Group, 2008:1). The counting of ballots showed that ZANU-PF had lost their majority in Parliament to the MDC.[18] It was consequently expected that Robert Mugabe, after 28 years in power, would also lose the presidency to the opposition candidate Morgan Tsvangirai. The combined elections were held on 29 March and the results released over the next couple of days. It was claimed by the Zimbabwe Electoral Commission that there were problems with the releasing of the results of the presidential poll. On 2 May, the Chief Elections Officer Lovemore Sekeramayi announced that Tsvangirai had received 47.9 per cent, Mugabe had received 43.2 per cent and therefore there would have to be a run-off. ZANU-PF and Mugabe deployed the army and militias across the country.[19] The run-off date was announced as 27 June; Tsvangirai withdrew due to extreme violence against MDC members and supporters, and this resulted in a victory for the sitting president. Human Rights Watch released a report on 12 August 2008 in which it said that at least 163 people had been killed by ZANU-PF supporters throughout the election period and up to the time of the report; 32 of these deaths, according to the report, occurred after the second round, and two of them had occurred after the start of negotiations. The report also said that 5,000 people had been beaten and tortured, and it described criminal charges against 12 elected MDC Members of Parliament as 'politically motivated'.[20] There was little international recognition of the results and SADC pressured the government to accept a new set of conditions and a government of national unity. The two factions of MDC entered into a Government of National Unity (GNU) with ZANU-PF.[21] Based on this Global Political Agreement (GPA) of 2009 Mugabe continued as president while Morgan Tsvangirai became Prime Minister and cabinet ministers were divided between the two parties. However, the security sector (police, military, etc.) remained in the firm control of ZANU-PF.

What had been described as a relatively successful post-independence government with indicators of education, levels of agricultural production, income, and life expectancy rising, now exhibits dramatic if uneven decline in all these areas.[22] There are numerous ways to capture Zimbabwe's descent, among which are high levels of malnutrition and hunger, the amount of food aid required to keep the population alive, the numbers of Zimbabweans who have left the country, extremely high levels of unemployment, the shrinkage of the gross domestic product, and the number of people tortured and women raped in political violence. Perhaps it is most dramatically summed up by the Human Development Index for 2010 which placed Zimbabwe last in the world (169th of 169 nations).

The overwhelming decline in living standards and physical security has meant the flight of large, if unknown, numbers of its citizens. Certainly labour migration itself is not new, and this collection emphasizes some of the continuities in patterns of farm employment back and forth across the northern border of South Africa as well as the longer history of labour migration in the region. However, the scale and form of such movement has changed substantially in the past decade. Our conclusion is that leaving, for most Zimbabweans, was coerced or forced migration caused by the decline of Zimbabwe's economy, which was stripped of formal sector jobs on the farms, in the factories, as well as in tourism – three sectors that had been the pillars of the country's pre-2000 economy. Those who stayed at home sought alternatives through the growing informal economy and by creating new modes of exchange using barter and other mechanisms to cope with hyperinflation in the period prior to 2008. The hyperinflation was not ended until the Government of National Unity was installed and the Zimbabwe dollar was replaced by currencies including the

U.S. dollar, the Botswana Pula and the South African Rand.[23]

Although Zimbabwe has not officially been at war,[24] the flight of its population rivals that of countries at war. The primary driver of this flight is economic decline, which includes growing unemployment, high rates of inflation, and the decline in education, health, and other government services. In addition, the electoral campaigns of 2000, 2002, 2005 and 2008 were accompanied by high levels of violence, the politicization of food aid, agricultural inputs and other government benefits. Lastly, the Fast Track Land Reform, which saw the number of white farmers reduced from around 4,500 to less than 300 between 2000 and 2012, has led to a substantial decline in agricultural production and agricultural exports in key areas, previously one of the main sources of foreign currency.[25]

Fast Track Land Reform

In the year 2000, Zimbabwe embarked on what has become known as its Fast Track Land Reform programme. Widespread farm occupations began as a political response to the electoral defeat of a new draft constitution in Zimbabwe's first national referendum.[26] The initial goals of Fast Track were consistent with the long-term government goals for the acquisition of five million hectares of commercial farmland. However, this goal was abandoned in favour of forcing almost all white farmers from the land they occupied. Part of our book explores what happened to those who started farming in the neighboring countries of Mozambique and Zambia (Chapters 4 and 11).

Zimbabwe's aggressive and often violent process of forcing farmers and farm workers off the land has led to a series of significant debates about the process, the means that were used, who received the land and the degree to which to which it was 'successful'. Behind the notion of 'successful' rests a series of other empirical, ideological, political and human rights considerations. Moreover, because the issue has been extremely racialized it has been difficult to attempt to be impartial and objective. In this book we will simply note the importance and heatedness of the debates rather than set out our own views and perspectives.[27]

There are some features of contemporary Zimbabwe that are uncontested: most white farmers and black farm workers have been forced off the farms that they owned or worked.[28] Poorly paid farm workers were the largest sector of formal paid labour in Zimbabwe until Fast Track. Yet they were neglected in the resettlement plans that transpired in the 1980s and have repeatedly emerged as victims in ongoing conflicts between government, white farmers, and the Movement for Democratic Change (Rutherford, 2001, 2003; Magaramombe 2010). For many years commercial farms were presented as unpopulated landscapes with insufficient attention paid to the work forces that made them profitable businesses. If attention was given, it was simply to point to exploited labour and claims that farm workers were non-Zimbabweans.[29] Many farm workers never obtained their citizenship papers for a range of reasons, including failure to register children at birth, thus later were unable to meet bureaucratic requirements; many were denied registration by government representatives, many never attempted to obtain citizenship while some married Zimbabwean men or women and their children attained citizenship through that route. In general there is a lack of good statistical data on farm workers and it will not be possible to recapture the past. Moreover, the government sought to repress their vote in 2000 since it was judged that they would most likely vote for the MDC.

There were approximately 350,000 black farm workers employed on large-scale commercial farms before Fast Track.[30] Farm workers were considered opponents of ZANU-PF policies, and frequently resisted the takeovers. Often they were successful in forcing the occupiers off the farms, but typically the war veterans and associated supporters returned with reinforcements, weapons, police and local political personalities (Holtzclaw, 2004). The Utete Report (GoZ, 2003) estimated that five per cent of the new farms had been given to former farm workers, while Sachikonye (2003a, b, c) Mabvurira et al. (2012) and Magaramombe (2001, 2010) report widespread victimization, displacement and deepening poverty. Many conflicts remain between the recipients of farms and farm workers because the new 'owners' cannot afford official wages. In addition, many new farmers occupied the homes of farm workers thus forcing them out of their residences. The UNDP (2008) estimated that at least one million people – 200,000 farm workers and their families – were homeless as a result of the Fast Track Land Reform.

Citizenship

The Citizenship Amendment Act passed in 2001 prohibited Zimbabweans from holding dual citizenship. It was directed at white Zimbabweans who often had a second passport (usually British) but was also aimed at farm workers. Few farm workers, despite their eligibility, had obtained citizenship and a passport and now they were considered to have dual nationality. Malawi, Mozambique, and Zambia did not consider Zimbabwean-born farm workers as their citizens, and did not have procedures in place for farm workers to renounce their possible dual citizenship and thus gain a Zimbabwean one. It fell to individual farm workers to renounce their so-called foreign citizenship and prove to the Zimbabwean government that they had done so in order to gain Zimbabwean citizenship. Many could do neither and thus became 'stateless'. While farm workers have often been victims of violent dispossession, they have tended not to leave Zimbabwe and have tended to stay around the farms where they had their homes and work.[31] We had expected to find more former farm workers on the farms in South Africa, but they were few in number.[32] On the Mozambican border with Zimbabwe, in northern Manica province, however, we did identify former farm workers who were establishing their own smaller-scale farms or working on others' land (Chapter 6).

Zimbabwean Migrants

An analysis of the experiences of migrants, and of the regional responses to Zimbabwe's crises, highlights important and often unexplored processes and consequences of Zimbabwe's unresolved issues. In the broad debates around the nature of the regime of President Mugabe and of the Government of National Unity (GNU), this book focuses upon those who have had to pay a high price for Zimbabwe's economic decline since the year 2000. Very early in the crisis period, the government began to blame all economic problems on sanctions imposed by the West.[33] This has meant, in policy and practice, that the (pre-GNU) government of Zimbabwe accorded itself no responsibility for having precipitated such vast out-migration. In addition, obtaining travel documents and passports continues to be both expensive and practically very difficult, thus adding to the numbers of undocumented migrants.

There is a broad debate around the relationship between migration and development, and it centres on whether migration promotes or hinders social and economic development and the degree to which it should be limited and controlled (Mohapatra, et al., 2010; Crush and Tevera, 2010; Potts, 2010). Here we focus on a more limited consideration of what can be termed South-South migration within the southern Africa region. This phenomenon is often under-valued and under-appreciated, although migration continues to produce highly negative reactions from national and local governments and their populations. Crush and Frayne, however, note that South–South migrants contribute:

> both to countries of origin and countries of destination. Their role is undervalued and denigrated and their lives are often blighted by exploitation, abuse and ill-treatment by employers and state officials. Yet they remain highly energetic and enterprising people whose activities and contributions need to be highlighted as a positive contribution to poverty reduction and genuine development. (2010: 20)

In this book we strive to maintain an analytical balance between the exploitation and suffering of those forced to leave Zimbabwe on the one hand, and their abilities to meet their objectives of employment and contributing to the livelihoods of those remaining at home, on the other. From the perspective of migrants, being able to leave Zimbabwe has prevented the even greater hardships of hunger and survival. Tevera, Crush and Chikanda (2010) sampled 700 migrant Zimbabwean households outside the country, whose remittances are crucial to household survival in Zimbabwe. In general, the most widespread use of remittances was to buy food, followed by clothing and school fees (2010: 316). On the Zimbabwean side of the border with South Africa, Maphosa (2007: 126) found that among 150 households surveyed, 68.7 per cent had at least one member who had migrated to South Africa. In earlier work, Hobane (cited in Maphosa, 2010: 126) had found that in the same community 62 per cent of the working population was in South Africa or Botswana. Most researchers studying this wave of migration have found that the primary motivation for migration was economic, and more than half of Maphosa's sample cited unemployment as the key reason (2007: 127). Our findings basically confirm this picture, though in 2008 the extreme violence around the elections in Zimbabwe was, for many, the decisive 'push' factor.

Academics and migration specialists have debated whether and in what ways migration has affected social and economic development in Zimbabwe and the region. At the same time, in contrast, regional governments have mostly opposed the movement of people seeking jobs and better working and living conditions. As Crush and Frayne (2007) comment, migration and development are seen as independent policy spheres; thus while education is central to South Africa's development strategies and there is a critical shortage of teachers in rural South Africa, it has been almost impossible for skilled Zimbabwean teachers forced out of schools for political activities, or just unable to make a reasonable living, to take up teaching jobs in South Africa.[34] In Mozambique, on the other hand, Zimbabweans found a niche as English teachers, since competence in English is increasingly in demand in addition to the official language, Portuguese.

At a more general level, the exodus of Zimbabweans reveals marked differences in, and new challenges to, the surrounding countries. Each country – Botswana,[35] Mozambique, South Africa and Zambia – has interpreted the crisis in Zimbabwe differently; each has formulated its own policies in terms of what to do with the Zimbabweans now in their country, which in turn relate to the specific historical, political and geopolitical relationships within the region. South Africa is by far the major receiving country but even here there is no real dialogue on what this in-migration has meant (positively or negatively) for South Africa's economy. Still, the affects are regarded as negative. Moreover, internal and external migrations are kept separate in terms of policy and analysis in government. The vast movement of rural South Africans to the cities, the growth of vast shantytowns in and around urban areas, and difficulties of employment creation, housing and service delivery are processes underway (Misago, 2009 and Reitzes, 2009, among many others). These processes have pitted the interests of the new urban migrants against those of Zimbabweans who are now in the country, and still arriving. However, Zimbabweans and other immigrants also create businesses, create jobs, fill niches that South Africans do not, and in general, make important and substantial economic contributions (Landau, 2010; Makina, 2010; Mohapatra, Ratha and Scheja, 2010). Without detailed empirical investigations it is not possible to provide an answer to the more general question about the connections between displacement, migration and development; however, we hope that this volume contributes to debates around the role of Zimbabweans in the region and also to the barriers that they face in emigrating.

National Responses to the Crises in Zimbabwe

The three receiving countries in this study, although located in the same region, possess important differences. Mozambique, having enjoyed peace for almost two decades, is still emerging from the effects of its brutal civil war following independence in 1975. The liberation movement and ruling party, the Front for the Liberation of Mozambique (FRELIMO), was violently opposed from

1977 by the Rhodesian-funded, and later South African-funded, Mozambique Resistance Movement (RENAMO). Fighting came to an end in 1992, and as part of the peace agreement the country's first free elections were held in 1994, with FRELIMO staying in power. During the early years of Mozambican independence, and continuing earlier labour migration trends, Mozambicans sought work not only in South Africa but also in Zimbabwe (known as Rhodesia at that time). Along the borders with Zimbabwe, large numbers of people of Mozambican descent worked on commercial farms. However, after 2000, these trends were reversed, and Zimbabweans migrated to Mozambique seeking work and hard currency. The welcoming of Zimbabwe's white commercial farmers in Manica Province was initially seen as an important social and economic experiment in the Mozambican context. However, for a range of reasons (discussed in Chapter 4), the Mozambican state withdrew some of its initial support, and farming 'the Zimbabwean way' in Mozambique proved more difficult than expected.

In South Africa, the African National Congress (ANC), celebrated for ending apartheid and establishing a progressive human rights based constitution, has nonetheless been faced with challenges in its international policies, its migration policies, and the problem of dealing with violence against immigrants in its cities. The details of South Africa's immigration dilemma are analyzed in Chapter 6, but here we just note the strong continuities between laws and frameworks of the apartheid state and those of the current one.[36] While there has been a long tradition of Zimbabweans (as well as Mozambicans, Malawians and Zambians) seeking work in the mines and cities of South Africa, this tended to be a circular migration, with workers returning home either because they attained their goals or due to the apartheid policy of not permitting black permanent settlement in South Africa. The ANC-led government, established after the first democratic elections in 1994, has faced rising expectations and unemployment among its own populations, and has tried to reduce this dependence on international migrant labour.[37] Reflecting on a growing aversion to 'foreigners' and their perceived threat to already overstretched and unevenly distributed domestic resources, Allister Sparks, one of South Africa's most influential journalists, wrote:

> The point is that the more Africa declines and the more we succeed, the more of them will come until they swamp our success with their numbers. They will exacerbate our unemployment and housing problems, overstretch our limited

social service resources and ignite strife as our unemployed and homeless react against their presence. (Quoted in Murray, 2003: 443-4)

With South Africa as the major destination for Zimbabweans, this kind of anti-immigrant view has intensified tensions within South Africa and raised major issues for undocumented migrants and citizenship (discussed in Chapters 6, 7 and 8).

Zambia, in contrast, has enjoyed peace since its independence in 1964. It is also a comparatively land-abundant country, although fertile farmland along main transportation routes is scarce. Despite this peace, however, and despite possessing Africa's most lucrative mining industry outside South Africa at the time of independence, Zambia remains one of the poorest countries in the world, ranking 164th out of 187 nations in the 2011 World Bank's Human Development Index (three places higher in HDI than in 2006). Prior to the Zimbabwean land reform, Zambia possessed around 1,000 commercial farms, most located in the Southern and Central Provinces. Throughout the 1990s, the government engaged heavily in promotion of commercial farming, and made available new lands for these purposes along the Tanzania–Zambia Railways (Tazara) corridor, as a result of which Zambian exports of commercial crops have been on the rise since the mid-1990s. As in Mozambique, a number of Zimbabwe's white commercial farmers sought land in Zambia. Many relocated to and remain in the Mkushi Block, approximately 200 kilometres north-east of Lusaka. Unlike most land in Zambia, this was designated in 1947 as an area for private ownership, and became the last major area of European agricultural settlement in what was then Northern Rhodesia.

Further south, along the border between South Africa and Zimbabwe, there has been a dramatic expansion of cross-border trading. Informal economic activity has spiralled, and involves large numbers of traders (discussed in detail in Chapter 12). Unregistered, and usually operating on a small scale, the Zimbabweans had previously been formally employed but now had to supplement their incomes or find alternatives. The growth of the informal sector has further been fuelled by a thriving black market, buoyed by the differential in foreign currency rates between the Zimbabwe dollar (before dollarization in 2009) and the Zambian kwacha which was linked to international hard currencies.

In this book, we place the experiences of Zimbabwean migrants in the different national contexts since 2000. The South African government stands out for three reasons: First, its long-standing 'quiet diplomacy' policy towards Zimbabwe; second, the fact that the largest number of undocumented Zimbabwean migrants are found in South Africa, which challenges South Africa's reputation as a supporter of human rights; third, Zimbabwe has been an important issue in national public political debates. In contrast, Zimbabwe has not been a major internal political issue in either Mozambique or Zambia, where there has been limited news and discussion on the local effects of the crisis. On the other hand, both Mozambique and Zambia have been involved in SADC discussions and policies. They participated in sending an election observer team to the presidential elections in 2002. The conclusion of that Mission was that: 'The climate of insecurity obtaining in Zimbabwe since the 2000 parliamentary elections was such that the electoral process could not be said to comply adequately with the norms and standards for elections in the SADC region' (SADC, 2002: 49).[38] Nonetheless, this did not lead to regional changes in the approach towards Zimbabwe. Rather Mozambique and Zambia accepted South Africa's choice of 'quiet diplomacy', which was to avoid public criticism of Zimbabwe's government while seeking solutions to its growing crises.[39] However, the crises in Zimbabwe did not diminish but rather accelerated, culminating in the MDC's victory over ZANU-PF in the March 2008 parliamentary elections. The disputed 'victory' of Robert Mugabe in the presidential run-off precipitated a constitutional and political crisis that the region could no longer avoid addressing. South African President Thabo Mbeki, and subsequently his successor Jacob Zuma, were tasked by SADC to mediate in finding a political solution. This led to the signing of the GPA in September 2008 and the forming of a GNU in early 2009.[40]

Zimbabwe became and remains an important domestic political issue within South Africa. Debates centre on land reform, but also include the control of the media, access to information, the potential dangers of one-party rule, and the issue of being white in southern Africa, particularly related to notions of citizenship and security. In addition, it has exposed significant political differences among the partners in South Africa's ruling tripartite alliance of the Congress of South African Trade Unions (COSATU), the South African Communist Party (SACP) and the ANC, with only the latter supporting ZANU-PF.[41]

As in Mozambique, aspects of the political situation in Zimbabwe have been connected in Zambia to – and interpreted on the basis of – internal political contests. In the Mozambican case, it is clearly the role of Robert Mugabe in the struggle for independence that conditions current perspectives on the political crisis in Zimbabwe. The role – and fate – of the MDC in Zimbabwean elections has, in turn, also been used to question the space for internal political opposition in Mozambique. In Zambia, Zimbabwe has had salience especially at election times. How each country has responded to Zimbabwe's crises politically and through the media will be addressed in more detail in Chapter 2.

While this book emphasizes the processes affecting black Zimbabweans there are two chapters devoted to white farmers who have joined the migration trend in the region. Our research sheds further light on the processes by which a historically privileged ethnic minority adapts to, and in turn affects, societies that are struggling with histories of racial discrimination, economic exclusion, civil war, poverty, and tensions over access to land and natural resources. In particular, questions arise with respect to whether and how migrants are able effectively to transfer farming skills to new natural and social environments, to contribute beneficially to agricultural production and rural labour markets, and to avoid or reduce the tension over access to land that often attends migration. A further issue associated with the migration of the commercial farmers is whether they have benefited from special privileges in recipient societies, and the potential impact of their work and enterprises on political, social, and economic relations in rural areas.

The Selection of Research Sites

In South Africa we selected the most rural province, Limpopo, which is also closest to Zimbabwe. We wanted to find out if and how the farms and their owners altered their management strategies and practices to avoid what has occurred in Zimbabwe. Limpopo Province is also the site of a great number of land restitution claims – some settled but many outstanding – with many consequences for Zimbabwean workers since land claimants tend to enjoy priority access to jobs (Hellum and Derman, 2009). We focused on Zimbabweans who are now employed as farm workers, their conditions of work, their lives in farm compounds, and their aspirations. Based on farm stays, interviews on different kinds of farms, and documents, we explore conditions of work, relations between Zimbabweans and other farm workers, gender relations, and how and if Zimbabweans are able to attain their objectives in the restricted environments of commercial farms. An in-depth ethnographic account of one farm describes the interactions among Zimbabweans and local residents and between men and women.

In Mozambique, we chose to concentrate our research in Manica Province, in central Mozambique, which borders Manicaland on the Zimbabwean side and over time has experienced considerable movement of people – in both directions. While, officially, Mozambique is a Portuguese-speaking country, the local Ndau, Manyika and Tewe languages in Manica can all be considered 'dialects' of Zimbabwean Shona, and this mitigates the language barrier of the official border. Thus a considerable portion of the Zimbabweans who have migrated to Mozambique have headed for and often ended up in Manica Province. Here, our fieldwork has covered both rural and urban spaces. The main rural field site (described in Chapter 5) is Pandagoma, which is located very close to the Zimbabwean border in the north of Manica Province. Fieldwork was also carried out in a rural border area called Penhalonga, close to the small town of Vila de Manica. In addition, a series of interviews with Zimbabweans were carried out in the provincial capital of Chimoio, as well as in Vila de Manica, which, especially around 2008, saw a large influx of Zimbabweans. Lastly, fieldwork was conducted at various times over several years in relation to white Zimbabwean farmers and other 'investors' located in and around Chimoio. This included attention to the expectations of and reactions to these farmers by a range of Mozambicans, both in Manica Province and in Maputo.

In Zambia, we concentrated our fieldwork on the border, in Southern Province in the area of Livingstone, a town very close to the Victoria Falls, as well as in Central Province. Sustained interviews were carried out among white Zimbabwean farmers in the Mkushi block, with cross-border traders, and with a range of government officials.

The Chapters of this Book

In Chapter 2, Kaarhus, Derman and Sjaastad describe and differentiate the national responses of Mozambique, South Africa and Zambia to the crisis in Zimbabwe. In SADC as a whole, governments have, over the last decade, shared an apparent reluctance to deal actively with the situation. At the same time, internal responses in neighbouring states have been highly variable in terms of both discourses and policies. So has the media coverage, not only with regard to the situation in Zimbabwe, but also concerning the influx of Zimbabweans across national borders. This chapter deals with the ways in which the crisis has been reflected in neighbouring countries' media discourses and government policies, seeking to show how these responses provide us with elements for a better understanding of key dimensions in regional post-independence – and post-apartheid – politics, as well as political contests and challenges at national levels in South Africa, Mozambique and Zambia.

Part II concentrates on Zimbabweans in Mozambique. Chapter 3 explores the fate of different groups of people, and focuses on the cross-border movement of Zimbabweans into Manica Province. We find that 2008 was only the peak in a more continuous flow of people seeking alternative livelihood opportunities and shelter. The post-2000 influx of Zimbabweans presented the FRELIMO Government with a challenge they apparently preferred to deal with as a non-topic, and it was basically left to lower-level public servants and local people to receive and support – or exploit – the immigrants. None of the Zimbabweans were ever formally recognized as refugees, and we will never know how many entered the country or how many are now resident in Mozambique. In a border province such as Manica, Zimbabweans are 'everywhere', but they are also, in a certain sense, invisible.

Chapter 3 explores the question of what happened to a number of the individuals in the most recent influx of black Zimbabweans into Mozambican borderlands. The account questions common assumptions about a smooth and easy integration when describing the migrants' experiences of livelihood challenges and 'culture shock'. Through their perceptions and experiences, we get an insight into contemporary realities on both sides of the border.

In Chapter 4, Amanda Hammar reviews the experiences of a small number of commercial farmers who moved across the border into Manica Province. Many were encouraged by multinational companies to come and grow high-value crops such as tobacco and paprika. Land was available, climatic and soil conditions appeared familiar, and suitable enough, and the Mozambique government was initially welcoming. The idea of reproducing Zimbabwe's commercial farming successes was not entirely unreasonable; however, despite the proximity of the two countries conditions were vastly different in historical, political, economic and cultural terms. In combination with external and internal limitations on production, commercial farming as practiced for decades in Zimbabwe was far from viable in Manica. The majority of those who had hoped to recover some of what they had lost in Zimbabwe were faced instead with further losses and many left farming altogether. That there have been some modest successes, raises interesting, if difficult, questions about what this means for local economic growth and an appropriate agricultural policy. Hammar explores the assumptions and expectations on the one hand, and the layered realities on the other, that informed the uneven trajectories of commercial farmers and farming in Manica Province during the 2000s.

In the last chapter on Mozambique, Alex Bolding reports on research work in central Mozambique along the mountainous border zone with Zimbabwe. In Pandagoma in the remote Báruè district, there has been a huge expansion in the cultivated area under furrow irrigation. The activities have resulted in real gains in the wealth and livelihood security of resident smallholders. In the case of Pandagoma (Báruè District), returning Mozambican – and to a lesser extent Malawian and Zimbabwean – labour migrants with experience on white farms and tea and coffee estates in Zimbabwe have been at the forefront of the accelerated development of irrigation furrows and commercial production of tea, coffee, tobacco and paprika. In other rural localities, such as the more centrally located Penhalonga, an increasing number of returning relatives and destitute Zimbabweans has created further pressure on the already intensively used natural resource base of the area (land, water, forest, gold). Thus, the Pandagoma case represents an environment offering real opportunities for newcomers to settle, take out an irrigation furrow, open up new rain-fed land and engage in cattle ranching. In more densely populated areas of Manica Province, however, newcomers, particularly those of Zimbabwean origin without resident families in Mozambique, have been forced to engage in manual labour (tending to irrigated crops or digging for gold) for poor remuneration or else engage in different forms of hawking and petty trading.

In Part III we turn to Zimbabweans in South Africa. Chapter 6 considers how the border between South Africa and Zimbabwe has been governed on the South African side. We describe how it has been used to permit black labour to cross into South Africa but to prohibit long-term or permanent residency. During the apartheid years the border became highly militarized and those coming from the north were viewed as threats. Internally, South Africans tended to see themselves as very different from the rest of Africa, a pattern which continues to the present. And, with strong continuities to the past, the immigration legislation enacted in 2002[42] continues the emphasis upon control and exclusion rather than viewing immigration as a management and development opportunity. Since 2000, the increasing numbers of Zimbabweans have posed new and complex problems for South African law, immigration policy and human rights. South Africa attempted to use political asylum procedures to cope with the post-2008 surge in undocumented immigration and has adopted the Zimbabwe Documentation Programme to regularize the status of migrants. However, the country's interpretation of Zimbabwe's political and economic crisis is reflected in its refusal to grant asylum to over 99 per cent of those who have applied.

In Chapter 7, Ruth Hall uses the narratives of Zimbabwean migrants living (and in some cases working) on South African farms in Limpopo province to develop a schematic way of distinguishing between different types of migrancy and migrants. The narratives reveal both strong commonalities and significant differences. Hall proposes five provisional types, and further offers three perspectives on what is already known and documented about this pattern of migration. First, it builds on historical precedents: observable on these farms is a mix of continuity in and new types of migration and migration networks. Social networks are key to understanding this mobility. Many of the stories of crossing the border and arriving at a destination related how people knew where to go and who to look for – not through direct contact, but indirect networks. Second, it draws attention to the specificities of the ways in which South African 'farm life' is governed through control and coercion, as well as being a place of community and, sometimes, reciprocity – and the often illicit informal economy in which migrants will provide cheap labour to other farm workers rather than to the owner. Third, it focuses attention on the role of transactional sex as a survival strategy, and more generally emphasizes the socially differentiated and gendered ways in which migrants experience their new, often temporary, homes, and how their choices, hopes and fears reflect this differentiation.

In Chapter 8, Derman, Hellum and Shirinda look at the increasing numbers of Zimbabweans in the communal areas of northern Limpopo Province, near the town of Makhado/Louis Trichardt, 100 kilometres from the Zimbabwean border. Communal areas are those which, under apartheid rule, were part of the former 'homelands' or Bantustans; they differ from other areas in that they remain in part under customary authorities (chiefs and headmen) and land cannot be bought and sold – although houses and residential stands are in practice informally transacted for cash. Zimbabwean migrants settling in these areas generate livelihoods by offering various services including construction, fence-building, house-sitting, domestic service and other forms of mainly unskilled labor. They are willing to work at wages far below the minimum earned by farm workers on commercial farms. Many are relatively satisfied with the government of South Africa, despite the difficulties of border crossings, but less so with their employers. Nonetheless, they are under constant threat because of the uncertainties caused by national immigration policies and local people's hostility.

In Chapter 9, Lincoln Addison provides a detailed account of a labour regime on one South African farm and how it promotes individualistic survival strategies among Zimbabwean migrant workers. In this setting, labour relations are guided not so much by paternalism as by a kind of authoritarian neo-liberalism that eschews welfare and espouses 'self-responsibility'. Workers are sharply divided along ethnic, linguistic, occupational, gender and political lines among other markers of difference. The labour regime also grants a small clique of black managers' vast powers over the rest of the work force. Survival strategies, such as transactional sex and high-interest money lending, are responses not only to these oppressive working conditions, but are also related to the way workers privilege aspirations for their Zimbabwean homesteads over improving material conditions on the farm. Addison suggests that building a rural homestead and supporting family ties in rural Zimbabwe are the central aspirations for most workers at the farm. Under the pressure of social expectation from home, and divided by the labour regime at work, most Zimbabweans feel compelled to pursue individualistic livelihood strategies. These practices increase income for some workers, but they also deepen existing divisions. In the case of transactional sex, many women receive cash or groceries, but risk exposing themselves to HIV/AIDS. Moreover, transactional sex fosters male resentment towards women in part due to the income men spend in such relationships. Money lenders increase their personal income, but to the detriment of other Zimbabwean workers, encouraging animosity between lenders and borrowers.

In Chapter 10, Poul Wisborg uses the framework of the Italian philosopher Giorgio Agamben to explore the conditions of 'bare life' on South Africa's farms, which have become ambiguous places where migrants may obtain protection and relief but may also be exploited and humiliated as workers. This is particularly important in a context where policy makers have sought to avoid the potential embarrassment of establishing refugee camps on the border. The chapter is framed within a recollection of how J.M. Coetzee's (1985) fictional character Michael K sought to avoid all camps, and Giorgio Agamben's (1998) analysis of 'bare life' below the thresholds of dignity and rights. For displaced Zimbabweans on four commercial farms, the farms, their houses and secondary economies offer precarious survival options and play a role in upholding an appearance of normal social conditions and state-to-state relations. Yet the farms are poorly equipped to provide relief, governed as they are by private commercial interests. The relief function of the 'camp' is governed not according to the human rights of migrant children, women and men but rather to a bio-politics of human bodies evolved during colonialism and apartheid. While farms contribute to maintaining the invisibility of disaster and its human consequences, displaced and desperate bodies bear witness to the scale and severity of the crisis in Zimbabwe.

In Part IV, we turn to Zimbabweans in Zambia. Chapter 11 examines the Zimbabwean farmers on the Mkushi Farm Block. In the wake of the Zimbabwean farm occupations, some 250 white Zimbabwean families crossed the border to Zambia. Thirty-one of these ended up on the Mkushi Farm Block. Some arrived with substantial capital, others with only their personal possessions. They found land and land use patterns similar to those they left behind. Their relations with farm workers, local government, and agribusiness were, however, very different from what they had experienced in Zimbabwe. The Mkushi Farm Block also has a rich, almost 60-year-old history of waves of settlement by commercial farmers from a variety of regions and ethnic backgrounds. This chapter analyses the difficulties the Zimbabweans faced when settling, their relations to the social groupings already present, and how conflicts were resolved. We also attempt to relate this most recent Zimbabwean wave of settlement to the broader history of the Farm Block, and to currents in Zambian politics towards expatriates.

In the last chapter we examine how the crisis has affected informal trade at the border between Zambia and Zimbabwe. Informal economic activity has spiralled due to factors such as high unemployment, high inflation, high levels of poverty and food insecurity. The informal sector provides people with a source of income. The major thrust of the study was to capture the many narratives about the way Zimbabwean traders go about their cross-border trade activities. Some of them have had to switch from formal employment to selling merchandise such as duvets, blankets, curtains and assorted liquors. A number of female Zimbabwean traders have entered into prostitution to survive and to raise capital for their business whilst they are in Zambia. The study also found that some significant bonds, associations or affiliations seem to have been forged with friends or relatives living in Zambia. Some of these activated kin and non-kin networks in Zambia facilitate the cross-border trade.

With this introduction we, as editors, invite you to read the rest of this book. We hope that our work over the last five years can provide some new and important insights into the complex and volatile dynamics of the Zimbabwean exodus in Mozambique, South Africa.

Notes

1   As editors of this book we would like to thank the Research Council of Norway for its generous support for the research which made the book possible through its Poverty and Peace Programme. We would also like to acknowledge the excellent service provided to the researchers by the administrative staff at the Department of International Environment and Development Studies at the Norwegian University of the Life Sciences. In addition we want to thank our research partners at the Institute for Land and Agrarian Studies at the University of Western Cape, the University of Zambia and the Catholic University of Mozambique. Lastly, we extend our gratitude to our external reviewers for their valuable inputs and critiques.

2   There is a rapidly emerging literature exploring what has been termed *Zimbabwe's New Diaspora* by JoAnn McGregor and Ranka Primorac (2010) and *Zimbabwe's Exodus* by Jonathan Crush and Daniel Tevera (2010). The topic has also been dealt with in a special issue of the *Journal of Southern African Studies*, 2010, Vol. 26 (2).

3   The name given to the expropriation of most of the white- or corporate-owned commercial farm land in Zimbabwe.

4   Two parties fought the war for liberation against the Rhodesian government from 1965–1989. These were the Zimbabwe National African Union (ZANU) and the Zimbabwe African People's Union (ZAPU). They merged in 1987 to form Zimbabwe African National Union Patriotic Front (ZANU-PF).

5   The government says that Fast Track Land Reform and resolving the land question is its Third Chimurenga; the first was against the British South Africa Company in 1896-97, and the second against the Rhodesians from 1965 to 1979.

6   They are almost identical to the A1 villagized resettlements in the current land reform framework, and they continue to parallel land use planning stemming from the Native Land Husbandry Act schemes.

7   'First refusal' means that the government has the 'first' right to acquire land properties available for sale – or indicate formally its lack of interest.

8   Dashwood (2000) and many others.

9   http://news.bbc.co.uk/2/hi/africa/611898.stm (accessed August 10, 2012).

10 A significant civil-service strike was led by the Public Service Association in 1996.

11 The many accounts of the referendum and the subsequent parliamentary election include Hammar, Raftopoulos and Jensen (2003), Raftopoulos (2009) and Blair (2002).

12 He was a physician trained in Poland, and spent most of his time during the Liberation War in Poland. Upon his return he was placed in charge of certifying the war injuries suffered by veterans. As a highly divisive figure, he stated shortly before his death in 2001 that, 'Like in any revolution, the path is always bloody, and that is to be expected, and hence no one should raise eyebrows over the deaths of four white farmers.... God told us to grab the farms: from them we shall get something to eat' (quoted in Bond and Manyanya, 2003: 82).

13 Mercedes Sayaguez provided a flavour of those times in the *Mail & Guardian* on 12 January 2001: 'Bikita is in Masvingo province, a former Zanu-PF stronghold now racked by internal party dissidence. The by-election has turned Bikita into a battleground. Feared war vet leaders Joseph Chinotimba, Francis Zimuto, aka "Black Jesus", and Hunzvi moved in. Their men set up bases at the future polling stations of Bengura and Mutikizizi schools. They include war veterans and the new youth brigades created by the sinister Border Gezi, Minister of Gender, Youth and Employment. As governor of Mashonaland Central province, he left a trail of blood during the parliamentary elections last June. These Zanu-PF militia have been beating up people, forcing them to attend all-night rallies, stealing their property and confiscating identity documents needed to vote. Mission hospitals have treated dozens of wounded residents. Many have fled to the mountains, among them MDC candidate Bonnie Pakai after moving his wife and two children out of the district. He remains mostly in hiding. His house shelters about 80 supporters displaced by violence. At the rally, Pakai, wearing an old black suit with a Mao collar, too hot for January, looks haggard and tired.'

14 Several human rights organizations have documented acts of murder, beatings, abductions, torture, and rape. In addition are the detailed studies of the consequences of the suppression of the media and the use of law to suppress opposition political activity. The Zimbabwe Human Rights NGO Forum is the largest grouping of human rights NGOs. Its mission is to reduce organized violence and torture, and cruel, inhuman and degrading treatment; to challenge impunity and to foster a culture of accountability and the building of institutions of non-violence, tolerance and respect for human rights. The NGOs include: Amnesty International (Zimbabwe), Media Institute of Southern Africa, Media Monitoring Project of Zimbabwe, Research and Advocacy Unit, Women of Zimbabwe Arise, Zimbabwe Association for Crime Prevention and Rehabilitation of the Offender , Zimbabwe Association of Doctors for Human Rights, Zimbabwe Civic Education Trust, Zimbabwe Human Rights Association, Zimbabwe Lawyers for Human Rights, Zimbabwe Peace Project, Zimbabwe Women's Lawyers Association. Their website is: http://www.hrforumzim.org/ (accessed on 10 August 2012).

15 New debates about the scale of success or failure of Fast Track Land Reform have been sparked by Ian Scoones et al. (2011).

16 For an overview see e.g. Hammar, McGregor and Landau (2010).

17 Tibaijuka was the UN Special Envoy on Human Settlement Issues in Zimbabwe based on her position as Executive Director of the United Nations Human Settlements Programme. See Potts 2005 and 2010 for her comprehensive work on displacement, livelihoods and migration.

18 The MDC was now divided into two parties, the larger one led by Morgan Tsvangirai (MDC-T) and the smaller by Arthur Mutambara (MDC-M) who has subsequently been replaced by Welshman Ncube (MDC-N).

19 There were two other candidates: Simba Makoni, a former finance minister, and Langton Towungana, a teacher and small businessman who ran on a religious platform. Makoni received 8.3 per cent , and Towungana 0.6 per cent.

20 http://www.hrw.org/reports/2008/zimbabwe0808/.

21 The text of the GPA can be found at http://www.copac.org.zw/home/government-of-national-unity.html.

22 There are many accounts, amongst the best being Muzondidya (2009).

23 Typical reporting was that in TIME Magazine of 26 March 2009: 'The decision to "dollarize" Zimbabwe's economy, one of the first acts of the new unity government (including erstwhile enemies President Robert Mugabe and Prime Minister Morgan Tsvangirai), has brought a small amount of stability to the economically ruined country. All civil servants now earn a monthly salary of U.S. $100, while shops and banks accept dollars and rands.' Read more: http://www.time.com/time/world/article/0,8599,1887809,00.html#ixzz1TV3tc3b9.

24 Zimbabwe did send its army to support Kabila in the Democratic Republic of Congo. Its government also says that Fast Track Land Reform and resolving the land question is its Third Chimurenga meaning armed struggle against a foreign invader or occupier. In this case white farmers and associated British supporters were the objects of armed attack in the Third Chimurenga.

25 Although tobacco production has been increasing since 2009, production is now only half of 2000 levels. http://www.voazimbabwe.com/content/zimbabwe-tobacco-production-rebounds-99571649/1464847.html and http://www.nytimes.com/2012/07/21/world/africa/in-zimbabwe-land-takeover-a-golden-lining.html?pagewanted=all.

26 There are many interpretations of this initial period, focusing on whether the occupations were 'spontaneous' or organized. Sam Moyo has argued the former in numerous publications while many others the latter. Compagnon (2011), for example, provides a detailed counter narrative. Scoones et al. (2010: 23) claim that it is impossible to say whether it was a groundswell from the bottom or created and orchestrated by ZANU-PF. Hellum and Derman (2004) argue that had land reform been the genuine goal it would have been carried out very differently and with attention to the poor and women, and less violently. The Justice in Agriculture Group (2008) has attempted to document how agriculture has been heavily damaged through the use of political power.

27 We add, however, that Addison, Bolding, Derman, Hammar, Hellum and Zamchiya have carried out field and empirical research in Zimbabwe and recognize the changed terrain that characterizes contemporary Zimbabwe. In this book we focus on those processes since 2000 which have led to the Zimbabwean diaspora rather than focus further on the social, political, economic and cultural processes that characterize contemporary Zimbabwe.

28 There is a growing number of farmers' own accounts of how they were forced off

their farms, in addition to the descriptions provided in *The Farmer*, the former publication of the Commercial Farmers Union. The best known is Ben Freeth's *Mugabe and The White African*, but the classic remains Catherine Buckle's *African Tears: The Zimbabwe Land Invasions*. Two other noteworthy books are *Jambanja*, by Eric Harrison, and *The Unbearable Whiteness of Being: Farmers' Voices from Zimbabwe*, by Rory Pilossof. For a more general consideration of the consequences on individual Zimbabweans of the ongoing crisis, see *Hope Deferred: Narratives of Zimbabwean Lives*, edited by Peter Orner and Annie Holmes. Ian Scoones et al. (2011) also relies heavily on the narratives of those who received land in Masvingo Province.

29 Farm workers were originally recruited from Zambia, Malawi, and Mozambique. Those born in Zimbabwe were supposed to automatically become Zimbabweans if their births were registered.

30 There are several estimates of farm workers numbers. Justice for Agricultural Trust estimates that there were 300-350,000 workers living with their families on the farms. In addition, there were 250-270,000 seasonal workers, an unknown number of whom lived on the farms. The African Institute for Agrarian Studies has a lower number of 350,000 full and part-time workers.

31 According to Farm Workers' Trust and G. Magaramombe. http://www.mokoro. co.uk/files/13/file/lria/rural_poverty_commercial_farmworkers_zimbabwe.pdf (accessed 12 August 2012). Cf. also Mabvurira et al., 2012.

32 They tended to be foremen or supervisors who came with their employers. However, few white Zimbabwean farmers were able to establish new farms in South Africa because of the large amount of capital required.

33 The EU, the U.S. and other countries have claimed that they have not adopted economic sanctions. The EU, for example, states that:

1. 'the measures adopted by the EU, as a result of the breakdown of the rule of law and human rights abuses, are the freezing of personal assets of senior members of government and other high-ranking officials, the prevention of the same to travel to EU Member States and the embargo on the sale of arms. None of these measures could affect or cause any hardship to the Zimbabwean population;

2. the suspension or re-orientation of certain financial and development cooperation programmes with the Government of Zimbabwe is mainly due to the fact that it has not complied with the provisions of the pertinent bilateral agreements and to the political and economic environment which is not conducive to development cooperation with government structures;' http://www.delzwe. See ec.europa.eu/en/ eu_and_country/EU per cent20SANCTION per cent20POSITION.pdf.

34 One explanation is, of course, that proving qualifications with appropriate documentation, providing references etc. is difficult for many of these migrants.

35 While we did not conduct fieldwork in Botswana we noted that the influx of Zimbabweans to Botswana has strained government services. As early as 2004 the BBC was reporting that 'On an average day, the Botswanan immigration authorities load about 100 Zimbabweans onto trucks, and drive them back to the border.' The report

continued: 'It's an expensive and probably futile exercise. Because all of the Zimbabweans I spoke to said that they would try and come straight back to Botswana' (http://news.bbc.co.uk/2/hi/africa/3582459.stm). Estimates of the number of Zimbabweans in Botswana range from 200,000 to 300,000.

36 According to Sally Peberdy, 'Since 1994 immigration policy has been mostly exclusionary, based on a strong national, protectionist and territorial vision' (2010: 147).

37 How to increase the South African economy to absorb labour has been a central theme since 1994 and is part of a set of debates around how to improve the productivity of South African labour while not decreasing wages. These debates are picked up in Chapter 6.

38 Zimbabwe 2002 Observation Report - SADC Zimbabwe. In contrast to the SADC delegation, the South African electoral observers found the election to be free and fair. http://aceproject.org/ero-en/regions/africa/ZW/zimbabwe-parliamentary- election-observation-report.

39 In Chapter 2 we will consider the critiques of 'quiet diplomacy', which viewed it as support for the ruling party and disfavouring the opposition party. The best account of the connections and conflicts over time between ZANU-PF and the ANC, and the relationship between former President Mbeki and Mugabe, can be found in Gevisser (2007).

40 The GNU is a model based upon the solution to Kenya's post-selection crisis which was solved by placing the two major parties in a coalition government during 2008.

41 In October 2004 a COSATU delegation was thrown out of Zimbabwe for meeting with organizations the government disapproved of. In February 2005 a 20-person COSATU delegation was denied entry into Zimbabwe. The South African government refused to criticize its neighbour for these actions, at least publically.

42 Immigration Act, 13 of 2002 (as amended in 2004) and amended again in 2011

2

Reflections on National Dynamics, Responses and Discourses in a Regional Context

Randi Kaarhus, Bill Derman and Espen Sjaastad

Introduction

Neighbouring governments' policies and responses to the developing crisis[1] in Zimbabwe have since 2000 attempted to reduce violence and strengthen democracy in the country while supporting to varying degrees the government and its leader, Robert Mugabe. The Southern African Development Community (SADC) made efforts to end violence during the parliamentary elections in 2000. However, these efforts over the last decade have not been consistent, nor has SADC remained united in its views of the crisis. The governments led by former liberation movements (Angola, Mozambique, Namibia, and South Africa) have tended to be more favourably inclined toward Mugabe and ZANU-PF than those others which did not engage in armed struggle, that is, Botswana, Malawi, Tanzania and Zambia. Tanzania and Zambia were highly supportive of the liberation movements. As the Zimbabwe crisis has unfolded it has produced varied responses not just from governments but also from opposition parties. The exodus of Zimbabweans throughout the region has pressured existing regional immigration policies, government policies toward Zimbabwe, and internal political debates and conflicts about how to deal with it. Reactions to these displacements will be considered in this chapter, as will the media coverage of Zimbabwe. In particular we are interested in the varied understandings, responses and policies produced by the Zimbabwe crisis and displacements.

The South African government has taken the lead both within and beyond SADC.[2] In particular, former president Thabo Mbeki played the central role in negotiations with the government of Zimbabwe to reduce the use of force and violence. Mbeki's role has now been assumed by South Africa's current president, Jacob Zuma. In general he is viewed as less sympathetic to Mugabe

Map 1: SADC countries, with Zimbabwean border crossing points covered in this book

and ZANU-PF but this may have more to do with the general swing of SADC away from supporting Mugabe and his party.[3]

This chapter is organized as follows. After briefly examining how SADC, but also the Commonwealth,[4] among others, attempted to respond to some of the watershed moments in the Zimbabwean conflict, we then turn to more specific and detailed considerations of how South Africa, Mozambique and Zambia responded to events.

Zimbabwe and SADC after 2000

Changes in how the region viewed Zimbabwe were due first to the defeat of the ZANU-PF constitution in the 2000 referendum and the subsequent violent parliamentary elections, which almost produced an MDC victory despite the violence. Mugabe embarked on a campaign of sustained violation of human rights, the abandonment of the rule of law, and the occupation of most white-owned farms.[5] It is important to note that there were strong internal efforts to find solutions to what was thought to be the heart of the crisis, namely land. The Joint Resettlement Initiative (ZJRI) was established, with the purpose of making one million hectares of uncontested land across all provinces and agro-ecological zones available for resettlement. On 5 September 2001, in what was described as a 'historic step' by the Commercial Farmers Union,[6] a proposed 531 farms totaling 976,452 hectares were accepted by the Acting President Joseph Msika on behalf of the government.[7] The agreement was terminated upon the return of the President, who refused to accept the farmers' offer.

Two external efforts were undertaken in order to find solutions to the crises. The first was by the Commonwealth[7] and the second by SADC.[8] The Commonwealth held an emergency meeting in Abuja, Nigeria in September 2001 in an attempt to prevent Zimbabwe from being expelled from the Commonwealth, by assisting Mugabe to implement his agrarian reform programme in an orderly and sustainable manner. The outcome of the meeting was an agreement that acknowledged that the situation in Zimbabwe was extremely serious, posing 'a threat to the socio-economic stability of the entire sub-region and the continent at large'. The parties agreed that 'land is at the core of the crisis in Zimbabwe and cannot be separated from other issues of concern to the Commonwealth such as the rule of law, respect for human rights, democracy and the economy'. It was resolved that Zimbabwe would put an end to all illegal occupations of white-owned farmland and return the country to the rule of law.

Countries such as Britain would provide financial assistance, and a programme of land reform would be implemented 'in a fair, just and sustainable manner, in the interest of all the people of the country, within the law and the constitution of Zimbabwe'.[9] This agreement continues to be known as the Abuja Agreement. It was never implemented since it was opposed by President Mugabe.[10] This was to be one of several agreements that were concluded but then ignored by the Government of Zimbabwe.

Also in 2001, a meeting between the Zimbabwe government and a SADC task team comprising the leaders of South Africa, Namibia, Botswana, Tanzania, Mozambique and Malawi was held in Blantyre to pressure the government to restore the rule of law in Zimbabwe. The SADC chairperson, Malawian President Bakili Muluzi said that state sponsored land invasions and violence, rather than land reform itself, were responsible for the overall crisis in the country. He assured reporters at the conclusion of the meeting that 'things are going to change because the government of Zimbabwe is committed to the issues which we have discussed'.[11] The Abuja and Harare meetings reflected a willingness by the international community to confront the government's concerns about land and land reform.

At the SADC meeting in Blantyre in 2001, President Mugabe assured his fellow SADC heads of state that the upcoming presidential election would be free and fair. According to a communiqué issued at the end of the day-long extraordinary SADC summit, Mugabe promised that international observers would be allowed to monitor the poll, and that he would allow international journalists to cover the elections. Despite these efforts, and agreements outlined above, the March 2002 presidential elections continued the pattern of widespread state-sponsored electoral violence, coercion, intimidation and manipulation.[12] In particular, these two elections incorporated the war veterans and youth militia, whose use of violence and intimidation undermined the legitimacy of the government in the region (Sims et al. 2010: 4). At the same time, the prospect of a political and economic crisis developing into a total collapse led regional and international political actors, including the presidents of Botswana and Zambia, to call upon SADC to take a leading role in designing and negotiating a political solution in Zimbabwe. The process was led by the South African President, Thabo Mbeki, and his approach came to be referred to as 'quiet diplomacy'. In general, Mbeki opposed public criticism of Zimbabwe's government and argued for 'African solutions to African problems'.[13] As condit-ions in Zimbabwe remained unchanged, quiet diplomacy came under detailed scrutiny[14] and became a political issue within South Africa.[15] While Mbeki was urging an African renaissance and peer review of African nations, he was, in practise, blocking it for Zimbabwe.

The Commonwealth and SADC were not done in trying to find a solution following the violent and contested presidential election of 2002. Thus in May 2003 three African presidents, Thabo Mbeki of South Africa, Olusegun Obasanjo of Nigeria[16], and Bakili Muluzi (President of Malawi from 1994 to 2004) went to Harare to facilitate discussions between President Mugabe and the main opposition leader, Morgan Tsvangirai. This effort was unsuccessful although rumours of a break-through circulated.[17] The talks apparently foundered on the demand by President Mugabe that he would only talk to the opposition leader if the latter recognised him as a duly elected head of state, while Tsvangirai rejected Mugabe's legitimacy as president and ruled out preconditions for talks. The opposition party challenged the election results (and those of 2000).[18]

The 2005 parliamentary elections were less violent even if still unfair and subject to the same kind of manipulation as documented in 1995 (Makumbe and Compagnon, 2000). The MDC contested all seats and remained a significant opposition. They were able to field candidates in all of Zimbabwe's districts winning seats in almost all urban areas while denied access to many rural ones.

The Tide Turns against ZANU-PF

2008 marked a significant turning point in the governing of Zimbabwe. Since the combined presidential and parliamentary elections of that year, there has been a Government of National Unity, the creation of which can be looked at as a success of SADC finally bring the parties together.

Despite widespread violence, intimidation and other violations of the SADC electoral code, the legitimacy of the outcome of the 2008 run-off re-election of President Mugabe was officially recognized by South Africa and SADC. This shifted the burden back to South Africa to find a path to form a new government while continuing to favor ZANU-PF and its president.[19] Only Botswana and Zambia refused to formally recognize Mugabe as the democratically elected president of Zimbabwe until after the GNU was formed in 2009. We turn now to a consideration of the national and media responses to events in Zimbabwe. For a range of reasons, including the role of the opposition parties in South Africa, the independence of its trade union movement, its larger and free press, and the historically close connections, South Africa has influenced, and been influenced by, Zimbabwe more than Mozambique or Zambia. Thus we turn first to South Africa.

South Africa

South African responses to Zimbabwe have been shaped by a long history of complicated connections between ZANU-PF and the ANC. These include Mbeki's stay in Harare in the 1980s, the eclipse of Robert Mugabe by Nelson Mandela upon his release from prison in 1990, the political economic power of South Africa in the region, and the difficulties of regulating Zimbabwean migration (legal and undocumented) into South Africa. There were also dividing factors including the Soviet Union's preference for the ANC and China's for ZANU which carried over into the 1980s and '90s. Moreover, events and processes in Zimbabwe were and remain important political issues in South Africa, partly due to the links between COSATU and the ZCTU, a key ally of the MDC. In addition, the South African official opposition party, the Democratic Alliance (DA), has opposed the use of violence to nationalize white-owned farms in Zimbabwe and has seen in ZANU's policies the future of the ANC's in South Africa. Thabo Mbeki also opposed the use of force and violence to accomplish land reform.[20] Unlike Zambia and Mozambique, the government of South Africa has been at the heart of negotiations and discussions with SADC and Zimbabwe on steps to resolve the enduring crisis; South Africa is also the recipient of most Zimbabwean migrants and refugees.[21]

At the centre of controversy over South Africa's responses to Zimbabwe has been its former president, Thabo Mbeki. In response to the elections of 2000, Mbeki seemed to accept how President Mugabe and his ruling party defined the major issues as being about the legacies of imperialism rather than an internal struggle for power. He repeated Mugabe's claims that the British and imperialists in general were attempting to undermine Zimbabwean sovereignty and were opposing the radical redistribution of land. In this view, the MDC represented western colonial interests and were not an authentic African movement. Ending the political symbolism of the deep racial inequality of land ownership resonated with the leadership of the ANC as well as in popular circles in South Africa. Mbeki did not condemn the unfair elections of 2002 despite his advice that free and fair elections were essential for ZANU-PF to regain its legitimacy.[22] At the same time, Mbeki was promoting neo-liberalism and good governance through a peer review process and his New Partnership for African Development (NEPAD) (Freeman, 2005).[23] In December 2003, on the ANC website, Mbeki wrote that:

> Those who fought for a democratic Zimbabwe, with thousands paying the supreme price during the struggle, and forgave their oppressors and torturers in a spirit of national reconciliation, have been turned into repugnant enemies of democracy. Those who, in the interests of their 'kith and kin', did what they could to deny the people of Zimbabwe their liberty, for as long as they could, have become the eminent defenders of the democratic rights of the people of Zimbabwe. (Mbeki, 2003)

Democracy and human rights in Mbeki's view became the enemy of anti-colonial struggles and, in this interpretation, part of the West's continued domination of Africa. The issue of land reform framed in this way generated broad support and a continuous downplaying (until recently) 'of any consideration of the nature of the ruling regime or the political significance and timing of its actions' (Freeman, 2005: 152). It took some years before the political strategy of ZANU-PF to use land reform to stay in power was accepted as an alternative explanation in South Africa and elsewhere on the African continent.[24] Even though it was known that the elections were controlled and manipulated by ZANU-PF and did not follow SADC and AU guidelines, land reform was seen as legitimate. In addition, the ANC and Mbeki tended to ignore the growing economic and food crises in Zimbabwe along with the violence directed against the MDC and its supporters.[25]

South African debates about South Africa's Zimbabwe policy

The internal politics of South Africa have partly shaped the government's responses to Zimbabwe. The deep racial tensions in South Africa are exemplified by Mbeki's analysis that the only reason that Zimbabwe has become a global issue is because white people died (Sparks, 2003: 327). He argued that the West had been extremely hypocritical in the attention given to Zimbabwe, rather than to the wars in the DRC and earlier conflicts in Angola, Rwanda and Sudan. Mbeki contended that Mugabe was being punished because he was black and there were double standards for Africans. He defended Mugabe by accusing the 'white world of a stubborn and arrogant mind-set that at all times must lead'. He continued, 'its demands must determine what everybody else does'. But he ended his 'Letter on Zimbabwe' with an appeal to those north of the Limpopo River to affirm their commitment to democracy.[26]

Issues of sovereignty and the limits of South African influence and power were also cited by Mbeki and the ANC as reasons why Zimbabweans had to sort out their own problems with limited South African engagement. In the 1970s, the Government of South Africa pressured Rhodesia to come to the negotiating table with the liberation movements. The economic linkages between the two countries remain strong, and biased toward the more powerful South Africa. Thabo Mbeki and the ANC are seen as supporting ZANU-PF and Mugabe, and regarding the MDC more as a threat than as a legitimate political party; for several years Mbeki did not meet with Tsvangirai and other MDC leaders. Ironically, Mbeki and the ANC viewed the MDC as too close to the West even as they were pursuing Western investment and NEPAD (Phimister and Raftopoulos, 2004).

In South Africa, Zimbabwe has long been a domestic political issue. One argument, for example, launched by the then leader of the Democratic Alliance of South Africa Tony Leon was that the ANC was not interested in reform in Zimbabwe or in human rights. Rather, the strategy of the ANC was to have South Africa become a one-party state like Zimbabwe. This argument did not gain much traction among black South Africans (at the time). A second argument (Gevisser, 2007; Gumede, 2005; Sparks, 2003) was to examine the historical connections between Mugabe and Mbeki. Mbeki was hosted by Mugabe in the early 1980s when he was in exile, and unlike other ANC leaders he was more supportive of ZANU during the 1970s. Another line of argument suggests that critics of Mbeki have misunderstood his policies. The South African political scientist Adelmann (2004) contends that Mbeki sought in good faith an end to violence and land occupations in 2000 but misunderstood Mugabe's determination to stay in power. And as recounted by Adelmann, SADC did clearly state a demand for democracy to be retained in Zimbabwe during and following the 2000 parliamentary elections. This demand was fully supported by South Africa. And according to Adelmann, the bilateral and multilateral diplomatic efforts failed not because of South Africa and Zimbabwe, but because Mugabe did not live up to his promise to end violence in Zimbabwe. However, despite its failures, quiet diplomacy was continued by Mbeki in the hope that open communication might lead to democratic reform after the election. This did not happen.[27] The Zimbabwe government was able to keep support from liberation movements now in power in Angola, Mozambique and Namibia, and to frame the MDC as a 'Trojan horse' for the West's political and economic interests in the region. By using the term 'imperialist sanctions' and blaming them for Zimbabwe's economic crises, Mugabe deflected criticisms of his policies (Ndlovu-Gatsheni, 2011). This worked to reduce an internationally co-ordinated effort to maintain pressure upon the Zimbabwe government to change policies. And, when that wasn't enough, South Africa blocked further efforts.[28]

Land reform: A window into South Africa's failures?

Fast Track Land Reform in Zimbabwe underlined how slow the land reform process had become in South Africa. And, unlike in Mozambique and Zambia, which are without the vast racial disparities in land ownership, the implications of Fast Track are a source of debate and division in South Africa. Events in Zimbabwe have prompted greater land activism in South Africa. One particular group, the Landless Peoples Movement, pushed land occupations and support of ZANU-PF as an important strategy while critiquing what they claimed was the non-radical and white leadership of other South African land NGOs.[29] The land reform researcher and activist Edward Lahiff wrote (2000: 58) that the forcible seizure of land by the Zimbabwean government poses a 'fundamental challenge to how land reform is perceived, both in Zimbabwe and throughout southern Africa'. There was an expectation, which was partly realized, that land issues would become politically more significant and there would be increasing militancy. Freeman (2005: 155) suggested that there was a high potential for the 'Zimbabwe crisis to serve as a rallying point for mass discontent and radical mass politics', but the South African government argued for staying the course of its own land reform programmes.[30] It did so by saying, repeatedly from 2005, that it would review the 'willing buyer, willing seller' approach to land acquisition, even while continuing to rely on this market-based approach, right through to the ANC's policy conference in 2012. In interviews that Derman carried out with white Zimbabwean former farmers now working as farm managers in South Africa, they contended that had the Zimbabwean land reform post-2000 been carried out in a manner similar to the South African reform, the crisis in Zimbabwe would have been avoided.[31] They were also criticizing the earlier intransigence of the CFU.

To South Africans more generally, the allure of Zimbabwe's Fast Track has faded because of the flight of Zimbabweans into South Africa and the social consequences of this migration. Nonetheless, Julius Malema, the former head of the ANC Youth League (ANCYL), spoke in favour of Zimbabwe's land reform as a good model for South Africa. In April 2010 he praised Zimbabwe's programme for taking over thousands of white-owned farms, and said that his country will follow suit. His comments were made at a rally organized by President Robert Mugabe's ZANU-PF party in Zimbabwe. He claimed that the ANC would follow Zimbabwe's lead, and soon take over white farms in South Africa.[32]

In a fiery speech at a netball complex in Harare's Mbare township, Malema told a cheering 2,000-strong crowd of ZANU-PF youths that after his visit to Zimbabwe he was going to intensify his campaign for the confiscation of farms and mines in South Africa:

> 'In SA we are just starting. Here in Zimbabwe you are already very far. The land question has been addressed. We are very happy that today you can account for more than 300,000 new farmers against the 4,000 who used to dominate agriculture. We hear you are now going straight to the mines. That's what we are going to be doing in South Africa,' Malema said amid cheers.[33]

Surprisingly, ANC's partners in Government – COSATU and the SACP – were and are far more sympathetic to the union-based leadership in the MDC. The SACP has been particularly unsympathetic to ZANU-PF. On its website *Umsebenzi Online* it charged that ZANU-PF is no longer a liberation movement but more and more a repressive machine focused narrowly on holding on to power (3 November 2004). When a delegation from COSATU was blocked from entering Zimbabwe the government said nothing, but the SACP stated:

> The South African Communist Party (SACP) strongly condemns the decision of the Zimbabwean government to block and stop a delegation of COSATU from entering & visiting Zimbabwe on the basis of its invitation to Zimbabwe by the Zimbabwean Congress of Trade Unions (ZCTU). Through this act, the Zimbabwean government and ZANU-PF demonstrate that they are increasingly incapable of engaging honestly with progressive forces and other role-players in the SADC. Instead, they seem engulfed by a siege mentality which sees conspiracies everywhere and thus blocking any opportunity for a confident progressive force rising to the challenge of leading Zimbabwe out of its crisis and putting the Zimbabwean national democratic project back on track. A COSATU delegation in Zimbabwe meeting with trade unions, civil society and even the Zimbabwean government was one such opportunity. (Wednesday, 2 February 2005, *Umsebenzi Online*[34])

And following the elections of 2008 they wrote:

> The SACP remains convinced that the principal cause of the deteriorating situa-

tion in Zimbabwe is that of a degenerating national liberation movement, which once fought a heroic struggle, but now paying the price of being trapped in state power that is not buttressed by the people's will.

The intransigence of not releasing the results, and the deployment of police and the army within communities, represents the growing alienation of sections of the Zimbabwean elites from control and monopoly of bureaucratic state power.

Failure to release the election results is tantamount to stealing the elections from the people and risks whatever little credibility that ZEC still had. [35]

However, the ANC Youth League continued to support ZANU-PF. Whether it will continue to do so after the ANC forced Julius Malema out of the party remains to be seen. In any event the ANCYL is consumed with leadership issues for the moment. The opposition Democratic Alliance has long held that the government's support for ZANU-PF and Mugabe hurts South Africa and reflects a tendency of the ANC to promote a one-party state in South Africa. In this view, Mbeki's dismissal of criticism of Mugabe as racist meant that similar events could take place in South Africa. In short, when migration and unemployment issues are raised in South Africa, they are invariably linked to what has happened and is occurring in Zimbabwe.

There are several civil society organizations that focus on Zimbabwe. One which deserves note is the Crisis in Zimbabwe Coalition, registered in Johannesburg in 2004. There was an effort to establish branches throughout SADC but the most important office is in South Africa. There is a regional co-ordinator supported by a Board of Directors. The mission of the regional chapter is to coordinate civil society efforts to find a lasting solution to the multi-layered crisis in Zimbabwe and build a new democratic social, economic and political order.

A brief comment on the South African media's consideration of Zimbabwe
There are a large numbers of daily and weekly newspapers in South Africa, as well as specialized monthlies for economic and financial affairs, farming, investigations into corruption, and culture. There are numerous radio stations, broadcasting in all the official languages, and several TV channels, governmental and private. And this is not to mention the web-based media. Like anything that touches Zimbabwe, there is profound controversy over how the media covered the fast-track land reform and subsequent economic decline. There have long been suspicions that the government-owned South African Broadcasting Corporation (SABC) was overly sympathetic to Mugabe and ZANU-PF. This

now seems to have been confirmed by a High Court ruling in Johannesburg on 24 January 2011 that the SABC was guilty of manipulating the news in 2005 and 2006. Judge Neels Claassen of the South Gauteng High Court concluded that there had been widespread manipulation of news under the SABC's former head of news, Snuki Zikalala, and that he had 'dishonestly tried to cover up this manipulation'. The judgment accused Zikalala of 'unlawfully manipulating' news items on Zimbabwe's 2005 elections, and blacklisting certain commentators to silence critical voices.[36]

On the other hand, the print media, often said to be dominated by white business interests, has been far more critical of ZANU-PF.[37] It has run innumerable stories on the violence, on the victims of violence, the extent of hunger in the rural areas, the massive inflation that lasted until the dollarization of the economy, and the failures of land reform. And, like most other reporting globally as well as in southern Africa, it pays little attention to the lives of the poor. There is a clear urban bias in the South Africa media not only toward Zimbabwe but also towards South Africa itself. The major urban dailies in Cape Town, Durban, Johannesburg and Pretoria provide a heavy dose of crime and celebrity, like their counterparts across the globe. It is the weekly *Mail and Guardian* that stands out for its more thoughtful and careful coverage of Zimbabwe. It has been highly critical of Zimbabwean government policies but has been more balanced in its coverage; it also hosts the cartoonist Zapiro who has been highly critical of Mugabe.

The owner of the *Mail and Guardian* is Trevor Ncube, a Zimbabwean and an opponent of Mugabe who was forced out of Zimbabwe in 2005. Ncube created Alpha Media Holdings, a company that played a critical role in filling the void created by the closing of the *Daily News*, the only independent daily newspaper in Zimbabwe, and in ensuring that Zimbabweans have access to critical information and alternative views through two weekly newspapers, the *Zimbabwe Independent* and *The Standard*. His company now also publishes a daily newspaper, *NewsDay*.[38] Ncube exemplifies the interconnections between South Africa and Zimbabwe. In the face of a powerful independent media, the ANC has launched its own newspaper, *New Age*, to provide a more balanced view of ANC and South Africa.[39]

No longer a hero?

Times have changed for President Mugabe in South Africa. Following the initiation of the Fast Track Land Reform he was cheered at the World Social and

Economic Forum in Johannesburg in 2002 and also at the ANC meeting preceding the forum. But Mugabe no longer makes public appearances in South Africa. As the Zimbabwean immigrant communities have grown and because of COSATU and the SACP, he would be greeted with widespread protests by both South Africans and resident Zimbabweans. McKinley (2004) and Phimister and Raftopoulos (2004) argued that South Africa's deep economic interests (especially mining interests) in Zimbabwe combined with ongoing support for former liberation movements explain the South African government's long-standing denial of the depth of Zimbabwe's problems, while viewing them as racial and part of the enduring anti-colonial struggle. As hundreds of thousands of Zimbabweans entered South Africa illegally it became harder and harder to hide what was happening. This is discussed in detail in Chapters 6 and 8. However, one might recall the words of Doris Lessing, the Rhodesia-born Nobel Prize-winning novelist, who wrote in 2002 that the West also had to take some responsibility for Zimbabwe's plight: 'Initially, the only stories that were reported were about the white farmers. But the black population of Zimbabwe had things a thousand times worse.'[40] She caught early on the bias toward reporting on 'the whites' in Europe and North America. This real and longstanding bias was used effectively by Mbeki and other international supporters of ZANU-PF to accuse the generic 'west' of double standards and racism.[41]

Mozambican Perspectives and Responses

When we turn to Mozambique, there are contrasts as well as parallels to South Africa in the way the government has responded to the recent crises in Zimbabwe. If we go further back in history, the dynamics of the relationship between the Zimbabwe and Mozambique have also differed from the historical relationship between South Africa and Zimbabwe. During the 'scramble for Africa' in the 1880s, Portugal – as the established colonial power along the coast of present-day Mozambique – became subject to increasing pressure both from the British Empire and Cecil Rhodes' expansionist ventures into present-day Zimbabwe. When Portugal and the British eventually signed a treaty on borders in 1891, it confirmed the establishment of Rhodesia as a landlocked settler colony. While the 'economic hinterland', with its wealth of mining and agricultural land resources, fell into British hands, 'Rhodes... was cut off the sea' (Newitt, 1981: 31). Still, the treaty contained provisions for building a railway connection from Southern Rhodesia to the Indian Ocean (Ibid.: 34), along what later became known as the 'Beira corridor', and which has been a central element in Zimbabwe-Mozambique relations for more than a century.

Back in 1891, in their efforts to 'assert effective occupation' in the area (Newitt 1995: 369), the Portuguese granted a private company – *Companhia de Moçambique* – the right to levy taxes, to issue currency, and to give out land and mineral concessions in central Mozambique. The company prioritised the building of the railway from the Rhodesian highlands to the fairly close – but muddy – port at the River Pungue estuary. This railway line opened in 1898, the year that Southern Rhodesia was formally recognised as a British Protectorate managed by the British South Africa Company. After 1909, the Mozambican company was taken over by British and South African capital. The company was operative in the area until 1941 (Ibid.: 396-97). Meanwhile, Beira became in practice 'the port of Rhodesia', and was almost a British town, 'with an English-language press, a sterling currency, and property and commercial development carried out by British capital' (Newitt, 1981: 34).

Turning to more recent history, Mozambique was among the last European colonies in Africa to gain its independence – in 1975. The Mozambican Liberation Front (FRELIMO) had been established in exile, in Tanzania in 1962. In 1969, its first leader, Eduardo Mondlane, was killed by a bomb in the FRELIMO headquarters in Dar es Salaam and was succeeded by a triumvirate, including Samora Machel who led the guerrilla attacks on the Portuguese military forces in northern Mozambique. At this time, Robert Mugabe was a political prisoner in the unilaterally declared republic of Rhodesia. After the Portuguese military forces, determined to end Portugal's colonial wars in Africa, led a revolt and brought about the Portuguese revolution in April 1974, they also brought FRELIMO to the table of negotiations (Newitt, 1995: 539). By September 1974, the so-called Lusaka Accord was signed, providing for the transfer of power in Mozambique to FRELIMO after a short period of transitional government. And in 1975, Mozambique became an independent state with Samora Machel as its first president. Robert Mugabe, who had by then been released from prison, left Rhodesia to join the Zimbabwe War of Liberation (also called the Second Chimurenga) from bases in Mozambique located in the area of the Beira corridor. The FRELIMO government in Mozambique at the time also gave support – and shelter – to ANC leaders and activists.

Rhodesia, followed by apartheid South Africa, responded to the establishment of an independent socialist government in Mozambique, as well as its position in regional politics, by funding and supporting an emerging Mozambican National Resistance (RENAMO). This support contributed to turning local discontent into an armed and brutal conflict, also playing out the global Cold War in a regional African context. RENAMO's leaders largely originated from Shona-speaking groups (for example, Ndau) in central Mozambique, and the rebel movement also had its main strongholds in the Beira corridor area (Ibid.: 569). A common estimate is that one million people died and five million were displaced as a result of the civil war in Mozambique. Starting in 1977, just two years after the end of the liberation war, it ended with a Peace Accord in 1992. The civil war is still an important reference on all sides of the political debate.

In 1980 Zimbabwe had gained independence with majority rule, and in 1982 the new government intervened directly – but now on the Government's side – in the Mozambican civil war. The Zimbabwean military intervention gave support to the Mozambican military forces and to FRELIMO and as an 'old ally' in the struggle for liberation, but also had another motive – to keep the Beria corridor open. South Africa, meanwhile, continued to support RENAMO. In 1983, South African air forces even crossed the border to bomb Maputo – also targeting the ANC presence there. The following year, both Tanzania and Zimbabwe sent troops to support FRELIMO. When President Samora Machel was killed in 1986, in an air crash just inside South African territory, in Mozambique this accident was – and still is – believed to be politically motivated, with apartheid South Africa playing an active role. Machel had been flying home from a meeting in Malawi where he, Mugabe, and Kaunda had tried to persuade President Banda to end the Malawian government's clandestine support for RENAMO-related activities (Ibid.: 568-69). In 1992, when the war finally ended, significant external factors were the end of the Cold War and, in a regional context, the dismantling of the apartheid regime in neighbouring South Africa.

Given these intertwined histories, especially in their most dramatic moments, it may seem surprising that Mozambican media have not given any broad coverage to the developing crises in Zimbabwe over the last decade. Neither have the political challenges presented to the Mozambican government as a result of the crises in the neighbouring country, or its responses more generally, been subject to debates or polemics. One exception is the independent weekly, *SAVANA*, which has covered the 'Zimbabwe issue' through the lens of a critical-journalism perspective.[42] To the extent that there have been debates in response to the violent land invasions and the land reform in Zimbabwe, a prevailing view seems to have been that 'Now it is their turn.' As seen from Mozambique, Zimbabwe under President Mugabe was known to prosper and develop, while Mozambique was being demolished through a devastating war. After the 1992 Peace Accord in Mozambique everything had to be reconstructed almost from scratch, while laws and policies had to be revised in order to respond to the challenges of a new era. This revision, importantly, included the legal framework for land relations.

In Mozambique, land rights remained a central issue of political debate and negotiation for several years after 1992. With a new Land Policy approved in 1995 and a new Land Law enacted in 1997, the basic principles for the current land regime in Mozambique were laid down. There still seems to be broad support for these basic principles – to the extent that land policy and legislation is actually known among the population. The policy and law maintained the post-independence, one-party-state principle of the State as the owner of all land. At the same time, they guaranteed access to and use of land for the population, as well as for investors. These rights included the recognition of customary rights of access, use and management of land for the resident rural population, as well as 'occupation in good faith' for ten years – a provision made to accommodate people who had been displaced or had migrated during the civil war (Ikdahl et al., 2005: 47). So, while people and political leaders in South Africa would see parallels, potential domestic threats, or even model opportunities in the Zimbabwe land reform, from a Mozambican perspective, 'We have had our turn.'

More generally, in what may be perceived as a general lack of engagement with the evolving crises from 2000 onwards, we can identify a marked – though temporary – shift in Mozambique in 2008, especially in connection with the combined parliamentary and presidential elections in Zimbabwe that year. The media's attention was all of a sudden directed towards the political contest across the border, and towards the responses of the regional political forums in SADC. The media, including a number of different newspapers,[43] closely followed the post-election process, providing their audience with sharp and evocative, but fairly diverse, interpretations of the situation as it developed.

In April 2008, with media and public still waiting for the results of the presidential elections, an extraordinary summit of SADC was called in Lusaka, exclusively to discuss the situation in Zimbabwe. *SAVANA*[44] reported from the event on 18 April 2008 that Mugabe did not accept 'the way he was informed about the meeting in Lusaka', and had refused to attend. The four ministers whom Mugabe had sent to represent him at the meeting 'repeated to their counterparts over and over again that they were informed about the initiative... through BBC, Sky News and CNN'.[45] That is, they claimed they had been informed through channels representing what in the dominant political discourse in Zimbabwe would be referred to as western interests. The reader of *SAVANA* would, however, from the context in which the Zimbabwean ministers' statements appeared, also understand that Mugabe's reluctance to participate in the meeting was due to the fact that his opponent Tsvangirai had also been invited. And Tsvangirai came to Lusaka. At the meeting, 'he told the presidents in the region that he had won the elections with 50.3 per cent of the votes'.[46] After long hours of negotiations in Lusaka, however, the participants of the summit left, according to *SAVANA*, with 'their hands full of nothing'.[47] The *SAVANA* columnist Machado da Graça pointed to the 'total lack of respect by Mugabe for the SADC meeting'.[48]

The day before, in its edition of 17 April 2008, the editorial of *Zambeze*[49] was even more explicit in its criticism of Mugabe, when it referred more generally to the elections and 'what is happening here next door in our neighbouring Zimbabwe'. According to *Zambeze*, what was happening was not only 'a flagrant case of abuse of power and an undisguised violation of justice and the fundamental democratic rights of the people of that country, but also a signal of warning that something very serious is happening in our region'[50]. *Zambeze* followed up by drawing a comparison to the Mozambican elections in 1999, alleging parallel cases of election-rigging in the two countries:

> If in this Zimbabwean electoral process of 2008, the manoeuvre used has been the recounting of votes, some nine years earlier, in Mozambique, the counting of votes was interrupted in order to make possible the cooking of results that it was convenient to announce.[51]

With reference to the Lusaka summit, *Zambeze* describes the outcome of the meeting as a 'bucket of cold water for those who had hoped to hear the voice of reason from statesmen'. But it finds an explanation in SADC having turned into a 'virtual Masonic lodge':

> where nepotism rules and social exclusion is the official political line... besides the unbecoming holding-of-hands with those who provoke series of social, economic and political crises, with consequences that are easy to foresee, with

neighbouring countries that may very soon be subject to unexpected population flows [across the borders].[52]

The following week, on 23 April 2008, Morgan Tsvangirai landed at Maputo Airport during a tour of regional capitals. He was still waiting for the release of the results of the presidential elections of 29 March. On this occasion, *Zambeze* emphasized the role of RENAMO's leader Afonso Dhlakama as the host, facilitator and mediator during Tsvangirai's visit.[53] *Zambeze* refers to Tsvangirai as Dhlakama's 'former counterpart' as leader of the opposition in the Zimbabwean 'brother country', and thus indirectly to Tsvangirai as the newly elected president of Zimbabwe. In this capacity, Tsvangirai is solemnly received by the leader of the Mozambican opposition in his office.[54] Dhlakama himself had the following message concerning the political situation in Zimbabwe: 'Let MDC govern, as they won. That is the popular will. Only in that way can we avoid what happened in Kenya.'[55]

After seeing Dhlakama in his office, Tsvangirai also met briefly with the former Mozambican president Joaquim Chissano in his capacity as leader of the forum of former African presidents. Chissano, however, was very cautious about giving any explicit interpretation of the situation in Zimbabwe. After the meeting, he said to *SAVANA*: 'We will follow the situation and will be in contact when possible, but for the time being we can do nothing more.'[56] Finally, Tsvangirai had a brief meeting with the Mozambican President Armando Guebuza, whose office, according to both *Zambeze* and *SAVANA*, had been very reluctant to organize such a meeting, with Tsvangirai being received 'through the back door'. After the meeting, Tsvangirai told the press that the purpose of his visit to Mozambique:

> was to convince president Guebuza about the need for African leaders to intervene as mediators in the crisis which Zimbabwe is going through today. And more specifically inform him... about the urgent need to find mechanisms to put an end to the violence in his country.[57]

On 25 April 2008, *O País*[58] reported from a public meeting in Maputo that gave room for diverging views on the situation in Zimbabwe, as well as on the role of SADC and President Mbeki's 'silent diplomacy'. Several of the panellists at the meeting stressed that the line of silent diplomacy should continue until 'all peaceful means have been exhausted'.[59] Others thought that in this process, SADC had been discredited. A common concern was, however, the need to avoid an escalation of violence, evoking what had recently happened in

Kenya after the presidential elections in December 2007. At the meeting, 'all agreed that it is necessary to avoid a war in Zimbabwe'.[60] More generally, it was observed that:

> Africa is at the moment going through a 'phase of transition in leadership' in the sense that those who have governed since independence are or at least should now be 'giving room for leaders from the new generation'.[61]

On 26 April 2008, the Beira-based newspaper *Diário de Moçambique*[62] also gave a summary of different positions voiced at the meeting in Maputo. In *Diário* it is pointed out that Maputo is now – finally – recognizing that there is a crisis in the neighbouring country. The fact that Morgan Tsvangirai was eventually received by the President is taken as a signal that 'Mozambique recognises the existence of a real crisis in this African country.'[63] But the *Diário* also indicates that a 'shift in dealing with the Zimbabwean regime' from the Mozambican side should have come a long time ago.[64]

Another and very general perspective voiced at this public debate and on numerous other occasions was that Mozambique has a special importance for Zimbabwe. Quoting a journalist in the meeting panel, the *Diário* asserts:

> We must not forget that Mugabe started out from Mozambique, he had his troops here during the time of Samora Machel – the first President of independent Mozambique (1975–1986), and one of the principal mediators leading to the agreements on the independence of Zimbabwe in 1980.[65]

It is interesting to note that this commonly held view concerning the close links between Zimbabwe and Mozambique does not translate into a broader discussion about the present, and how Mozambique should handle the special relationship with a neighbour in crisis. One might ask if this relationship is relevant only at the level of political leaders and governments. If that is not the case, there is a remarkable lack of discussion about how it extends to the people of Zimbabwe, and what its implications are. The question of what the Mozambican authorities think about and do in relation to the economic and humanitarian crisis in the 'brother country' is rarely discussed – at least in the media or on the public scene.[66] In *SAVANA*, on 2 May 2008, however, the columnist Machado da Graça under the heading 'Shall we continue in silence?' directly criticizes the lack of responses by Mozambican civil society to the crisis in the neighbouring state:

> it remains regrettable, this lack of response on the part of our Civil Society when confronted with what is happening. As far as I know, it is only the [Mozam-

47

bican] Human Rights League that has spoken out loudly. It is time that more voices join in ... to say publicly that what is happening in Zimbabwe is completely unacceptable and should stop immediately.[67]

Meanwhile, in Zimbabwe, the votes were counted and recounted, finally producing a result to be presented to the public – with none of the presidential candidates getting more than 50 per cent, a result which required a second round of presidential elections. The date was set for 27 June 2008, and on that day the front page of *SAVANA* had a drawing of Mugabe tearing a map of Zimbabwe into two pieces, under the heading 'Once there was a country'. [68] On the next page, Tsvangirai's decision to withdraw from the second round due to excessive electoral violence and intimidations was discussed, and explained.[69] On the same day, *O País* reported on the attempts made by SADC representatives to call for a postponement of presidential elections that had Mugabe as the sole candidate.[70]

The following week, the elections were still the theme of the week in *SAVANA*. The paper even (this is not so common in the Maputo press) sent a journalist to the Province of Manica to interview Zimbabweans crossing the border into Mozambique. Under the heading 'We were forced to vote', *O País* asserted that:

> The second round of presidential elections in Zimbabwe were marked by the intimidation practices of the Government's security forces, who obliged the voters to go to the polling stations to cast their votes, according to people witnessing the events in the field who were contacted by *SAVANA* at Machipanda, the principal border crossing point between Mozambique and Zimbabwe.[71]

With only one candidate, it could not come as a great surprise that Robert Mugabe won the election. What raised a debate in Mozambican media was, however, the reaction of the Mozambican government to the election results. An opinion piece in *SAVANA* described the contradictions and dilemmas:

> Never ever had I expected that the Frelimo party would publicly condemn the gross abuses that their allies in Zanu-PF have been committing to the people of Zimbabwe over the last decade. But honestly, I must admit that I never expected the collective morals of the party in power to fall to the level of seeing themselves obliged to congratulate Zanu-PF with the results in the farce that passed as presidential elections on the 27 of June.... If *Frelimo* does not see the need to openly disapprove of what their allies in Zanu-PF are doing to the people of Zimbabwe... when making it known to anybody who wants to know that they

support those barbaric acts and undermining of democratic processes, it sends a clear signal that *they themselves will never hesitate to use the same tactics as Mugabe to remain in power...* [But] I wish I were wrong.[72]

Will the party in power in Mozambique use 'the same tactics' to remain in power? This appears as the crucial question in the critical media in Mozambique. The editorial of the *Zambeze* the following week seemed to be in line with the opinion published in *SAVANA* when criticizing the Government's felicitations to 'ZANU-FP for what it regarded as Mugabe's "victory" in the second round of the so-called presidential "elections" in Zimbabwe.'[73] But *Zambeze* also took a stance on internal party politics in Mozambique: 'the Maputo regime led by Armando Guebuza applauds fraudulent elections that are considered as a farce by the [AU] African Parliament and by SADC itself'. The editorial concluded: 'Those who congratulate a party led by a despot can only be seen as somebody with tendencies to himself become a tyrant.'

Here, however, *Zambeze* took a more controversial next step, pointing not only to the civil war in Mozambique, but also to the role of armed forces in making politics in independent modern states:

> The civil war in Mozambique was a struggle for Democracy. It ended because possibilities were opened up for the citizens to freely elect those they want into government. This, however, presupposes that the arms are moved far away in order that the elections can be considered free.... While in Zimbabwe it is now clear that some of the military are dictating the rules of the game and refuse to adapt to a universal modernity.[74]

The *Zambeze* followed up this reasoning in its editorial the following week, 'Necessary to prevent "Mugabization" in Mozambique' in which it urged every citizen above 18 years of age to get duly registered for the upcoming local elections in Mozambique.[75] The argument here is that if people want change, they have to get registered and cast their votes in clean and democratic elections. At the same time, the paper saw a disturbing trend in voter turnout in Mozambique, and linked that to perceptions of irregularities in national elections. It cast doubt on the government that did not 'dare' to criticize Mugabe, and found it necessary to call upon citizens to counteract the tendency of 'giving up going to vote because they no longer believe in the elections'.[76]

Meanwhile, in Zimbabwe, Thabo Mbeki was seeking to establish conditions for negotiations between the two parties in the past elections, negotiations that finally ended with the agreement on the Government of National Unity ten months later. In Mozambique, the media also reported on the negotiations between Mugabe and Tsvangirai. SADC's role in relation to the crisis in Zimbabwe, the diverse responses of regional presidents to Mugabe's 'victory', and the question of why the Mozambican government had actually sent their felicitations after the official results were known, remained as the major issues in the press.

In his analysis of the influence of the media in Mozambique, Helge Rønning (2009: 254) holds that newspapers voice different views and conflicts 'between different subgroups and factions of the politico-economic elite'. As such, they are also mostly read by the elite. What is striking in this context, however, is the virtual absence of the 'Zimbabwe issue' in the official daily newspaper in Mozambique, *Notícias*, an absence which is also reflected in the lack of quotes from *Notícias* here. This daily is generally seen as the Government's 'spokes-paper'.

When two young *SAVANA* journalists sought to explore further this silence, and find out more about how it is related to the special relations between Zimbabwe and Mozambique – or Mugabe and FRELIMO – their approach was an extensive interview with one of the party's founding fathers. The chosen – or, maybe, available – informant is one of the 'old' supporters of Samora Machel's political line and Minister of Culture and Communication in the first FRELIMO government, Jorge Rebelo.[77] When interviewed in July 2008 by the young *SAVANA* journalists about the government's 'total silence' surrounding Zimbabwe, he responded:

> Personally I have, like most of the Mozambicans who were connected to the liberation struggle in Mozambique, a sympathy for Mugabe, since he was our comrade in the struggle. He actually fought for the liberation of his country, and for many years Zimbabwe experienced growth... and development.

This statement is probably fairly representative both concerning the 'special relationship' with Mugabe and the perception of Zimbabwe itself as prosperous and developed. When asked about SADC and the attempts to negotiate with Mugabe, Rebelo's response pointed to linkage that also has been explored earlier in this chapter:

> I believe some of these countries are faced with a situation which is not very different from that of Zimbabwe, before Mugabe took back the land. In South Africa and in other countries here in southern Africa, the land is not yet in the hands of the people.[78]

Again we see that attention is directed towards unresolved land issues. From a Mozambican vantage point, land has not been a burning issue for years. The Land Law of 1997 was, and to a great extent still is, considered to serve its purpose of both providing for poor people's rights to land and opening up for – necessary – commercial investments. During the past few years, however, the entry of new commercial interests and new public-private partnerships to develop larger-scale investment, seems to be bringing land back as a political issue in Mozambique (Åkesson, Calengo and Tanner, 2009; Kaarhus et al., 2010; Hanlon, 2011; Kaarhus, with Martins, 2012). In 2012, the small-scale farmers' union UNAC has made clear pronouncements against the Government's plans for promoting large-scale commercial agriculture as a vehicle of development. After the civil war in Mozambique, there is widespread reluctance to open political conflict. At the same time, there is awareness – and concern – that land also in Mozambique can turn into a highly conflictive issue.

Zambian Perspectives and Responses

When farm invasions began in Zimbabwe in 2000, Frederick Chiluba of the Movement for Multiparty Democracy (MMD) was president of Zambia. Chiluba followed the majority of leaders from the region in refusing to criticise Mugabe and his policies. Chiluba would later, from the position of an ex-president accused of plundering the resources of his country,[79] become a vocal supporter and defender of Mugabe.

In 2002, Chiluba was succeeded by Levy Mwanawasa. Although Chiluba had purportedly handpicked Mwanawasa to be his successor, intolerance towards corruption quickly became one of Mwanawasa's major political platforms,[80] and his anti-corruption policy included a high-profile legal campaign against the former president (van Donge, 2009; Dugger, 2009).

Mwanawasa initially welcomed Mugabe's re-election as president in 2002; he spoke up in defence of Zimbabwe's sovereignty and opposed the move to suspend Zimbabwe from the Commonwealth (Chifuwe, 2003a, b). With time, however, Mwanawasa would become one of the few African leaders to criticise Mugabe. In March 2007, he compared the Zimbabwean economy to 'a sinking Titanic' (BBC, 2007). Mugabe is reported to have shouted at Mwanawasa and subsequently stormed out of a SADC meeting in August 2007, after Mwanawasa suggested that the situation in Zimbabwe needed to be discussed by African leaders (Gava, 2007). Shortly before his terminal illness, Mwanawasa described the political situation in Zimbabwe as an embarrassment to SADC (of which he was chairman at the time) and to Africa, stating at a press conference in Lusaka that SADC could no longer afford to remain silent about the problems in Zimbabwe (*Times of Zambia*, 2008). As noted above, he also invited Zimbabwean opposition leader Morgan Tsvangirai to a summit for African leaders in Lusaka after the first round of Zimbabwe's presidential elections in 2008, urged a postponement of the upcoming second round from which the opposition MDC had withdrawn, and later branded Mugabe's winning result as illegitimate (SouthAfrica.info, 2008; *The Telegraph*, 2008). He is also reported to have branded Mbeki's quiet diplomacy ineffective and called Mbeki's approach counterproductive and insincere (*Insider*, 2011).

Mwanawasa further annoyed Mugabe by welcoming white commercial farmers who fled from Zimbabwe (*The Telegraph*, 2008). His open-arms policy included visits to areas of Zambia where they had settled, and also, reputedly, government involvement in financing of loans to Zimbabwean farmers in Zambia's Southern Province.

Mwanawasa's death came as a blow to what appeared to be a gathering momentum towards the possible end of SADC's quiet diplomacy and indifference to the plight of ordinary Zimbabweans. However, it also marked the beginning of the end of Zambia's open criticism of the Government of Zimbabwe. The new President, Rupiah Banda, who was born in Zimbabwe, was never openly critical of Mugabe. Indeed, he attended the power-sharing agreement signing ceremony. Mugabe reciprocated by attending Banda's inauguration as Zambia's President. However, the absence of Banda at the Extraordinary SADC Summit meeting in South Africa on 9 November 2008 was arguably a tactic to avoid 'looking Robert Mugabe straight in the eyes' and making an honest contribution to the post-election Zimbabwe crisis. In September 2011, Zambia held its fourth presidential elections in ten years. Michael Sata ran for a third time as the candidate for the Patriotic Front and this time he defeated Rupiah Banda and the MMD.

The Zambian press's reactions to Mwanawasa's stance on Zimbabwe were in part predictable. Two major newspapers – *The Times of Zambia* and the *Daily Mail* – are generally regarded as government mouthpieces, as is the national broadcaster, ZNBC. In these media, Mwanawasa was generally hailed as courageous and forthright on an issue that most other regional leaders avoided. The attitude of the popular and influential independent newspaper, *The Post*, was, however, far more complex.

During the reign of Chiluba, *The Post* had been a constant thorn in the side of the MMD government, which in turn made several attempts to close it down and silence its editors. In consequence, when Mwanawasa attempted to have Chiluba convicted of corruption, *The Post* and its editors became government allies of sorts. However, the newspaper also maintained its support of Mugabe. So when Mwanawasa turned against Mugabe, the paper found itself with a problematic and somewhat divided loyalty. The support of Mugabe has continued, also following efforts by Rupiah Banda to mend relationships with Mugabe; this despite the fact that the paper seems to have renewed its hostilities with the Zambian government after Banda succeeded Mwanawasa. The paper has described Mugabe as a 'fearless leader', has questioned the motives of Morgan Tsvangirai, but has also at times expressed concern over developments in Zimbabwe. A 2010 editorial sums up the position on Mugabe (Post Online, 2010b):

> But there can be no denying that President Mugabe is an outstanding leader, revered and respected by not only his subjects but also by his colleagues in Africa and beyond. He is even respected by his enemies. There can be no denying that Zimbabwe still needs his position in the driving seat in order to attain the vision that the country aspires for.

This vehement leader has successfully steered the party through turbulent times, especially through the crisis of the last decade, in these times when most liberation parties are either struggling to survive or have gone down. He literally had no opposition in the first 20 years of his reign, until he embarked on land reforms that threw the country into chaos.

During his first 20 years in power, he won several accolades for his outstanding leadership, including being awarded several honorary degrees, some of which have been stripped from him since he fell out with the West.His reason for staying on is that his vision of an economically independent Zimbabwe has not yet been achieved. To him, political independence of a country is just half the phase of total independence. Having led the country to political independence almost 30 years ago, the Zimbabwean leader has now vowed to lead the country once again to economic independence, where the country's economy that was in the hands of the white minority – who made up only 15-20 per cent of the population – has to be shared with the 80 per cent natives, who have always been loitering on the fringes.

To President Mugabe, the economy is not yet securely in the hands of the blacks as his vision dictates. The first phase (of land reforms) is complete and the second phase (of having natives control all major foreign-owned companies) has just been embarked on. This programme is scheduled to be completed in the next five years. When that happens, that's probably when we will hear of him thinking of stepping down.

In an earlier editorial, *The Post* had this to say about sanctions and the MDC (The Post Online, 2010a):

> All along, the MDC has been untruthful and insincere about their role in the sanctions against Zimbabwe by the US and the EU. They have maintained that they have no role in the removal of sanctions…

The question is, if the MDC has had no role in the sanctions, why would the British government wait on its advice to remove them?

This only plays into what President Mugabe and ZANU-PF have always believed and have said consistently since 2000, that the sanctions came about following a lobby by the MDC and can only be removed following a similar lobby by the same party. This also plays into what President Mugabe has been saying all along, that actually sanctions were never about conditions in Zimbabwe but about an imperialistic agenda.

At the same time, the managing editor of *The Post* would write a laudatory, official biography of Mwanawasa, published after his death (Malupenga, 2009). The stance taken by *The Post* is, perhaps, a better reflection of Zambian opinion towards Zimbabwe than that adopted by government-sponsored media; yet it must also be seen in light of political developments and campaigns within Zambia, as discussed below.

Because of the Zimbabwean crisis, Zambia has benefited from a diversion of tourists from Zimbabwe, particularly to Livingstone (*The Telegraph*, 2008), as well as increased production in commercial agriculture through the influx of Zimbabwean farmers. Mwanawasa's concern over the Zimbabwe situation, however, was partly caused by the growing number of Zimbabwean refugees that spilled into neighbouring countries, South Africa and Zambia in particular. The border between Zambia and Zimbabwe has traditionally been permeable, with day-passes issued as a matter of course at the three main border crossings and illegal migration never a major concern. Yet with the growing crisis in Zimbabwe, more and more Zimbabweans were crossing into Zambia. At the Kariba border post, for example, official statistics show that average monthly entries into Zambia rose from 4,653 in 2003 to 13,676 in 2008, while net entries rose from a negative 433 to a positive 941.[81] Part of this increase can be attributed to the 'xenophobic attacks' on Zimbabwean immigrants in South Africa in May 2008, after which many Zimbabweans fled north across two borders (IRIN News, 2008):

> recent attacks by South Africans against foreign nationals, which [have] killed over 60 people and displaced tens of thousands, has seen an influx of about 25,000 Zimbabweans from South Africa to Zambia according to the Red Cross, more than double the number already thought to be in the country.

Occasional round-ups of Zimbabwean immigrants in Lusaka were a largely ineffective response, and there was increasing concern that the South African attacks could be replicated in Zambia.

Woven into this patchwork of issues and concerns was, undoubtedly, the domestic political scene in Zambia itself. In the 2006 presidential elections, Michael Sata of the Patriotic Front (PF) had run second to Mwanawasa, and his campaign had included fierce attacks on the influence of foreigners in Zambian politics and economic life and included, reportedly, threats to deport them (BBC, 2006). Moreover, Sata has always been a loyal supporter of Robert Mugabe, defending his land reform policies, the associated treatment of white farmers, and his entrenched position towards Western influence in the region. Thus, although Sata's comments on 'foreigners' were mainly direct-ed towards Chinese economic interests in Zambia and the large population of Zambian traders of Indian lineage, Zimbabweans (both black and white) in Zambia found the prospect of Sata as president a source of apprehension; and the MMD government undoubtedly felt that growing numbers of 'illegal' Zimbabwean immigrants could become a source of serious public disaffection and play into the hands of the PF. This became a particular concern in 2008; just as the number of immigrants rose dramatically, President Mwanawasa was taken ill and died (in August), and a new election was scheduled for October that year. Sata would lose that election by a narrow margin, and would accuse the MMD of electoral fraud. The PF became a very powerful presence in Par-liament, however, and became particularly powerful in the major urban areas of Zambia.

Since Sata won the 2011 presidential elections, he and Mugabe have met on several occasions, among other things signing collaborative memorandums of understanding on youth development and tourism. None of these meetings has been short of generous and friendly statements; Sata, on one occasion, supported Fast Track and described Western sanctions as illegal (Zambian Watchdog, 2012) while Mugabe recently described Zambia and Zimbabwe as 'Siamese twins' (Kawadza and Maodza, 2012). Sata's chanting of ZANU-PF slogans at an international trade fair in Bulawayo angered MDC officials, while similar chants at a SADC meeting reportedly embarrassed even Zimbabwean officials and led to protests among Zimbabwean residents during a visit by Sata to the Commonwealth Economic Forum in London (Bulawayo 24, 2012).

There is some disagreement as to the precise nature and strength of the Zimbabwe crisis's influence on Zambian politics and elections. While Sata's admiration for Mugabe seems genuine, most commentators see Sata primarily as a populist and opportunist. Thus, when President Mwanawasa took to criticising Mugabe, it presented an opportunity for Sata to further distance himself from MMD policy and rhetoric and cash in on popular anti-colonial feelings and apprehension for how the influx of Zimbabweans might affect the job market in Lusaka in particular – feelings from which many considered the MMD to be too aloof (Gould, 2007; Larmer and Fraser, 2007). Zambian politics is often fiercely bipolar, with the major parties lining up on each side of specific issues rather than along well-defined ideological paths. In this sense, the rhetoric of the PF presidential campaigns with respect to foreigners, Mugabe, Zimbabwe, and colonial influence may to a greater degree reflect a need to define and mark out a given political territory as the opportunity arose rather than any long-term shift within, or 'ethnicization' of, Zambian politics (Gould, 2007). Since his election as president, Sata has gone out of his way to assure potential investors and multilateral donors that privatization will continue and that there is no reason to fear the perceived nationalization rhetoric of his presidential campaigns (*Times of Zambia*, 2012). There is little evidence to date to suggest that Sata's ascendancy should be a cause of apprehension for Zimbabwean farmers in Zambia. Meanwhile, *The Post*, after having suffered through three presidents with whom it either disagreed in general or disagreed on the issue of Mugabe, finally received a president with whom it could largely agree on all counts. The coverage of Zimbabwean matters has been reflective of this.

Besides its influence on Zambia's own elections in the ten years after the Zimbabwe conflict commenced, the press coverage of the crisis in the three major Zambian newspapers was extensive but unremarkable, largely consisting of reports of statements made by the key protagonists. All papers would occasionally include reports from special correspondents on various aspects of Zimbabwe's economic collapse as it unfolded – the inflation, the migration, the collapse of tourism, the joblessness and local famines – but the coverage now seems strangely unreflective on the implications for Zambia's own economy and for the economy of the region as a whole.

Regional Responses: Common Themes and Diverse Contexts

The responses of the Mozambican, South African and Zambian governments to the twists and turns of events in Zimbabwe have not been the same. Each has had a different history of relationships to the Zimbabwean government, and each varies in terms of its political economy. The liberation history of Mozambique and, above all, its more recent civil war condition Mozambican responses. In South Africa, the connections between ZANU-PF and the ANC have remained strong since 1994 but more so under Mbeki than under Mandela. And the early support of Zambia for the Zimbabwe African People's Union (ZAPU) and its leader Joshua Nkomo by Zambia's first president Kenneth Kaunda created a distance that arguably has never been overcome. In the same way, press coverage from the three countries has also varied due to media differences.

While migration to all three countries has been high, the preferred destination for Zimbabweans has been South Africa. The borders have remained relatively open to Mozambique (see Chapter 3) and Zambia, which has meant easy access for Zimbabweans. The South African border is discussed in depth in Chapter 6, but suffice it to say it is more heavily regulated, and South Africa – with the exception of the years 2008-10 – has followed a policy of formally deporting undocumented Zimbabweans in large numbers. Unlike Zambia and Mozambique, there has in South Africa been a long-standing public and governmental debate on what to do with foreigners. These debates have centred on the harm rather than the positives that immigrants bring to South Africa and on the changes in laws and policies required to keep them out – except those who are highly valued in terms of skills.

Politically, Mozambique, South Africa and Zambia are all active members of SADC, where they have sought co-operation with Zimbabwe rather than confrontation. While we have described SADC and other efforts to limit the conflict in Zimbabwe, the Zimbabwe government's interpretation of the nature of the crisis has, until the elections of 2008, seen it in terms of being colonial in nature, as a conflict between the Zimbabwean and British governments rather than an internal crisis of governance. The welcoming of white farmers in Mozambique and Zambia did not seem to influence those country's more general policies toward the Zimbabwe government. And in turn the South African government did not defend the property rights and interests of South African citizens who owned farms in Zimbabwe. Neither Mozambique nor Zambia has the high levels of race-based land inequality as South Africa. Thus when debating land issues in Zambia and Mozambique the reference point is not Zimbabwe. This is different in South Africa where, as we have noted, Zimbabwe's land reform looms over most discussions of land-ownership and policy.

Lastly, the South African national leadership has been tasked by SADC to lead the negotiations to implement the GPA from 2009. The three-nation group of South Africa, Mozambique and Zambia has been unable to forge an agreement between the three political parties in the Zimbabwe government. Whether or not Zambia will change its position to accord with the policies of President Sata is unclear. Mozambique remains closely tied to President Mugabe, but has still been pursuing the broader SADC agenda.

The Media

The press coverage of the Zimbabwe crisis in the three of its neighbours covered in this book contains several common themes: the migration of commercial farmers and farm workers; the image of Mugabe as a freedom fighter who never gives in, and the associated reference to the imperialistic influence of the West and racial narratives; and the fear, especially in South Africa, of Zimbabwean turmoil spilling across the border and generating similar events at home. These themes emerge in quite different ways in each of the countries, depending on the specific manifestations of spillover effects, the political and economic context into which these effects were inserted, and the specific history that each country shares with Zimbabwe.

Thus, while the migration of commercial farmers from Zimbabwe was largely ignored in South Africa, the migration of large numbers of other migrants would receive vast attention among the media and eventually result in xenophobic attacks on the migrants. In Zambia, in contrast, the migration of farm workers (and other jobless Zimbabweans) would receive comparatively little attention, while the influx of white commercial farmers became a hot issue for both domestic and international reasons. In Mozambique, the migration of a relatively limited number of white farmers to Manica Province did receive a lot of attention as a 'project' of commercial agriculture development (see Chapter

4), but was not considered an issue of regional politics. This difference is not due simply to corresponding differences in the numbers received of each group of migrants, but rather to context. In South Africa, the national political contest during the first ten years of the millennium took place within the ranks of the dominant party – the ANC – but including its COSATU and Communist Party partners who opposed ANC policies. Opposition parties, particularly the Democratic Alliance, also continuously criticized what they saw as President Mbeki's direct and indirect support for Mugabe. The print media remained highly critical of the Zimbabwe government, if less so of its own. And the government-owned SABC reportedly favoured the Mugabe government and tried to suppress criticisms in its TV and radio programming.

On the other hand, there was also rising discontent with the South African economic trajectory, particularly with respect to the low number of jobs being created and the prospects for people to escape poverty. In Zambia, on the other hand, the last decade saw four fiercely contested presidential elections, and the issue of the Zimbabwe crisis, Mugabe's role in it, and the associated migration of white commercial farmers became issues to exploit in the respective political campaigns. The influx of other Zimbabweans (including former farm workers), however, barely raised an eyebrow, except for the occasional mass deportation of those who had overstayed their welcome. The union in which the two countries at one time had found themselves, the close relations between people on either side of the border, and the traditional permeability of the border itself undoubtedly played an important part. In Mozambique, meanwhile, the migration of Zimbabweans into the country would remain largely a non-issue on the national stage. Like Zambia, the border between Zimbabwe and Mozambique has been relatively open. The same ethnic groups are inhabitants on both sides of the border, and Shona 'dialects' are spoken, especially in Manica Province in central Mozambique. The life histories presented in Chapter 5 further demonstrate how interlinked the eastern border of Zimbabwe was and is with Mozambique.

In terms of the potential spread of Zimbabwean turmoil, South Africa already possessed a large population of white commercial farmers, and farm occupations were a familiar phenomenon. Many would also argue that it possessed a land reform programme that could hardly be said to be more successful than the Zimbabwean efforts that preceded the 'Fast Track' version, having emerged from a comparable white-minority regime just 14 years after Zimbabwe. While the prospect of 'Fast Track' emerging in South Africa was not seriously considered, there remain intense debates about how to speed up national land reform and make it work better. Judging by *Farmers Weekly* and *Landbouw* – the two weekly agriculture publications – they became far more open to 'new farmers', to land reform, and the contributions of agriculture to the national economy after 2000 than they had been before. That is not to say that they haven't emphasized what they regard as the horrors of Zimbabwe's land occupations and violence.

Zambia has remained poor but peaceful since independence in 1964, and farm invasions (rather than robberies) were virtually unknown. The fear of Zimbabwe-like conditions emerging in Zambia, although perhaps more of a populist spectre evoked by Sata, still received serious attention in the press and among the commercial farmers themselves. This was almost certainly accentuated by a popular and growing disaffection with Chinese influence in the country, and a perception that urban markets were being swamped by cheap imports (French, 2010). Again, however, political statements around this issue and the coverage in the media were largely restricted to the presidential campaigns. While in Mozambique, the developing crises in Zimbabwe have, at a political level, to a large extent been viewed through the prism of the country's own conflictive and violent recent history.

The presence of Zimbabwe and Zimbabweans in the life of Mozambique, South Africa and Zambia has, in general, been much larger since 2000 than before. The remaining chapters of this book will further contribute to document this assertion with an emphasis upon Zimbabweans themselves. In the subsequent chapters we will focus on more detailed accounts, including ethnographic studies, of how Zimbabweans – black and white – have altered life while seeking survival and at least temporary livelihoods in Mozambique, South Africa and Zambia.

Notes

1 As noted in the introduction, the Zimbabwe 'crisis' includes economic decline, decline in life expectancy, political violence, an exodus of Zimbabweans out of the country, decline in agricultural production, and reliance on food importation.

2 SADC was tasked by the African Union to handle the Zimbabwe crisis.

3 Julius Malema, the former leader of the ANC Youth League went so far as to claim that Zuma hates Mugabe. This is one more example of how Zimbabwe fits into South African national politics. http://www.swradioafrica.com/2012/06/25/malema-wades-into-zuma-over-zimbabwe/. In addition, ZANU-PF expressed unhappiness

with Zuma's mediation timetable. http://www.voanews.com/zimbabwe/news/Zuma-Says-No-Change-in-Zimbabwe-Mediation-Team-122672449.html.

4 The Commonwealth of Nations, usually referred to as the Commonwealth (and formerly known as the British Commonwealth), is currently composed of 54 nations. All except Mozambique and Rwanda were part of the British Empire. Zimbabwe was suspended in 2001 and withdrew in 2003 in protest at Zimbabwe's continued suspension. Thabo Mbeki was the sole defender of the government of Robert Mugabe during those years.

5 There is a general consensus that there were between 3,800 and 4,500 white commercial farmers and 300-500,000 fully employed farm workers. Selby (2006) estimates that there were 4,200. Because of the dispersal of workers and farm owners it is not possible to furnish precise numbers.

6 This was the name of what had been the powerful organization of commercial farmers (almost entirely white) which had opposed almost all efforts at land reform.

7 In the absence of President Robert Mugabe, who was out of the country at the time, Acting President Joseph Msika described the ZJRI as 'a home-grown solution, which amply shows that Zimbabweans are capable of solving their own problems'. *Sunday Independent*, 12 August 2001.

8 South Africa's role in both the Commonwealth and SADC is relatively clear, as discussed below. However, Mozambique and Zambia's roles remain less clear, if not hidden.

9 Partial text of the Abuja Agreement on Zimbabwe Land Reform, 6 September 2001. (Source: BBC/Africaonline.com, 7 September 2001) Its significance lies in how the Zimbabwe government appeared to sign agreements, only to ignore them. The meeting recognized that as a result of historical injustices, the current land ownership and distribution needed to be rectified in a transparent and equitable manner. It also agreed on the following: Land is at the core of the crisis in Zimbabwe and cannot be separated from other issues of concern to the Commonwealth such as the rule of law, respect for human rights, democracy and the economy. A programme of land reform is, therefore, crucial to the resolution of the problem. Such a programme must be implemented in a fair, just and sustainable manner, in the interest of all the people of Zimbabwe, within the law and constitution of Zimbabwe. ... the meeting welcomed assurances given by the Zimbabwe delegation as follows: Commitment to the Harare Commonwealth Declaration and the Millbrook Commonwealth Action Programme on the Harare Declaration. There will be no further occupation of farmlands. To speed up the process by which farms that do not meet set criteria are de-listed. For farms that are not designated, occupiers would be moved to legally acquired lands. Acceleration of discussions with the UNDP [United Nations Development Programme] with a view to reaching agreement as quickly as possible. Commitment to restore the rule of law to the process of land reform. Invitation by the foreign minister to the committee to visit Zimbabwe.

10 It remains unclear why the government signed it except as a delaying tactic to prevent further sanctions and to appear co-operative to the Commonwealth.

11 *Financial Gazette* (Harare), 'Muluzi Blasts Continued Violence', *4 October 2001.* 'Malawi's President Bakili Muluzi, the chairman of the 14-nation Southern Africa Development Community (SADC), has once again blasted the continued violence in Zimbabwe caused by the government's controversial fast-track land reform programme. Responding to questions from the *Financial Gazette*, Muluzi yesterday said President Robert Mugabe had assured African leaders at meetings both in Abuja and Harare that his government was committed to the restoration of law and order.'

12 Compagnon, 2011; Vollan, 2002; Solidarity Peace Trust, 2003.

13 Thabo Mbeki has formed the Thabo Mbeki Institute to promote the African Renaissance and to promote African solutions to the profound problems now existing in the continent. http://www.thabombekifoundation.org.za/SitePages/Home_New.aspx.

14 For example, at the G8 meetings in July 2008 Mbeki was challenged to show how 'quiet diplomacy' was working. http://www.guardian.co.uk/world/2008/jul/07/zimbabwe.southafrica1.

15 For example, the South African political scientist Tom Lodge analyzed how Zimbabwe became a significant political issue within, and outside, the African National Congress. Kgalema Motlanthe, the ANC's political secretary, warned that if Tony Blair, the former British Prime Minister, could decide that only if the MDC won the 2002 elections, would they be 'free and fair', then the British could do the same in South Africa (Lodge, 2004: 4).

16 He headed the Nigerian government as the outcome of a military coup and then left to be replaced by a democratic government. In turn Sani Abacha overthrew that government and Obasanjo was imprisoned. After the death of Abacha new elections were held; Obasanjo won them and served as president from 1999–2007.

17 http://www.sadocc.at/news/2003-137.shtml.

18 There appeared to be some initial hope as Mugabe and Tsvangirai agreed on the urgent need for dialogue to rescue the country from a spiraling decline. This, however, did not occur. MDC viewed Mbeki, Obasanjo and Muluzi as too close to the president. http://www.sadocc.at/news/2003-137.shtml.

19 There was no need for South Africa to have recognized the outcome of the 2008 presidential run-off so quickly, especially since the ballots had disappeared for six weeks and there was no independent electoral commission to count them. The sensitivity of South Africa's role in Zimbabwe continues. The *Mail and Guardian* tried for several years to obtain a report produced by two South African judges on the 2002 election.

20 In an interview with Mathatha Tsedu and Ranjeni Munsamy of the Sunday Times in 2002 Mbeki stated, 'In 1998 I spoke to President Mugabe and to the British Prime Minister, Tony Blair, and said to both of them: This land question in Zimbabwe is going to explode unless you people handle it properly. You have got to handle

it in such a way that, indeed, the Zimbabwe government is able to address this land question, because it must be addressed. You can't allow a continuation of this colonial legacy, but it has to be addressed in a manner that doesn't create other problems. And we did, indeed, agree with the British Prime Minister that that must happen. We agreed with President Mugabe that that was going to happen. As a consequence they then held an international conference in Zimbabwe in 1998 to address the land question and everybody was there and they reached an agreement. That was because of an intervention we made in '98, concerned that the matter had to be handled in the correct way.'

21 The Zimbabwe Solidarity Forum is a network of progressive South African civil society organizations, including youth, women, labour, faith-based, human rights and student formations. The forum started in the late 1990s and was consolidated in 2004. This is another example of the links between South Africa and Zimbabwe.

22 For example, the official Norwegian delegation report known as the Vollan Report diverges markedly from the ANC assessment.

23 Linda Freeman. 2005. 'South Africa's Zimbabwe Policy: Unraveling the Contradictions', *Journal of Contemporary African Studies*, 23, 2, May, pp. 147-72.

24 Compagnon (2011: 166) writes, 'The technical/developmental approach of resettlement... does not address the core issue: the politicization of the land question from the outset and its harnessing, in the current crisis, to serve the political survival of Mugabe's regime.'

25 There is considerable documentation by Zimbabwean and international human rights organizations of the violence and other pressures directed against the MDC. They are all catalogued on the Zimbabwe Human Rights Forum website. The Zimbabwe Human Rights NGO Forum (the Forum) is a coalition of nineteen human rights NGOs in Zimbabwe which, while having their own objectives, are concerned with the level and nature of organized violence and torture in the country perpetuated mainly, though not exclusively, by state agents and their ancillaries. It came into existence at the time of the Food Riots in 1998. Another source of documentation can be found at the Kubatana website, which stores the documentation from numerous human rights NGOs. http://www.kubatana.net.

26 Thabo Mbeki, Letter From the President, 'Zimbabwe: Two blacks and one white', *ANC Today*, Vol. 2, No. 10 (8-14 March 2002).

27 A rather unique and unsupported explanation is provided by David Monyae (2006), who writes from a pro-South African government position, pointing toward what he viewed as the broader South African international interests: 'The failure to limit the abuse of power by President Robert Mugabe has been largely due to the fact that South Africa initially avoided becoming involved in a crisis that it had perceived to be one between Harare and London. President Mbeki also wanted President Mugabe's support in his African initiatives, Nepad, transformation of the then OAU to AU, South Africa's successful bid for the World Cup 2010, and lastly, a possible

seat in the restructured United Nations Security Council (UNSC). In all these diplomatic initiatives South Africa needed to avoid to be seen as a regional bully and promoting Western countries' interest in Africa. South Africa has managed to win over trust and legitimacy in Africa with minimal image bruises by its Zimbabwean policy. South Africa has applied a pragmatic policy thus allowing President Mugabe to exhaust all his diplomatic cards. Lastly, South Africa ought to learn how to effectively communicate its Africa policy. South Africa's Africa policy shows the level of commitment that South Africa has on promoting constitutionalism and democratization of the region and indeed the continent.'

28 On 29 April 2008, when the Security Council held a special session on the situation in Zimbabwe, some EU and Latin American members wanted to send out a special envoy, but this was successfully vetoed by South Africa which chaired the session. They further vetoed any draft resolution on Zimbabwe in the period before the 27 June 2008 run-off election, and subsequently argued that the UN risked complicating the situation in Zimbabwe that at the time had not reached the levels of Kenya's December 2007 post-election violence. Furthermore, when the Security Council met on 12 July 2008 to agree on a US- and UK-sponsored draft resolution that sought to impose sanctions on Zimbabwe, South Africa together with Russia, China and Vietnam voted against it. Partly as a result of South Africa's actions and inactions (alongside those of China and Russia), the Security Council has not been able to pass a resolution on Zimbabwe. Thus, South Africa has consistently shielded Mugabe from potentially devastating US- and UK-sponsored international action.

29 See Derman, Hellum and Shirinda (2010) for an account of the land NGO in Limpopo Province.

30 Of course there are significant differences between South Africa and Zimbabwe. Goebel (2005) provides a careful assessment of how the two nations differ despite a history of race-based colonial land dispossession.

31 Interviews conducted in August 2008 at South African Farm Management (SAFM) farms. Name withheld. SAFM has since gone bankrupt.

32 His statements were quickly condemned by the ANC and President Zuma especially since they are supposed to be neutral as the SADC mediators.

33 http://www.timeslive.co.za/sundaytimes/article385668.ece/Malema-lauds-Bob-says-SA-will-copy-Zims-land-seizures.

34 http://www.sacp.org.za/main.php?include=docs/pr/2005/pr0202.html.

35 http://www.sacp.org.za/main.php?include=pubs/umsebenzi/2008/vol7-06.html.

36 http://www.mediainzimbabwe.com/?p=3114.

37 Many newspapers share the same ownership, and reprint each other's articles.

38 In 2002, The British *Guardian* newspaper reduced its shareholding in the *Mail and Guardian* to 10 per cent, selling a majority share in the newspaper of 87.5 per cent to Newtrust Company Botswana Limited, owned by Zimbabwean publisher and entrepreneur Trevor Ncube. Having relocated to South Africa, Ncube also took over

as CEO of the company.

39 It is also available on the web at http://www.thenewage.co.za.

40 http://www.guardian.co.uk/uk/2002/aug/20/arts.zimbabwe.

41 Willems (2005) contends that the British media (specifically the *Guardian* and the *Daily Telegraph*) simplified and racialized the conflict which permitted the Mugabe government to use events in Zimbabwe as a struggle against imperialism.

42 Thanks to Professor Helge Rønning for pointing out that SAVANA's editor Fernando Gonçalves previously worked in Zimbabwe for many years.

43 This account is based on a systematic reading of Mozambican newspapers, mostly weekly papers – for sale in the streets of Maputo, Beira and Chimoio (Manica Province) in the period 2008-2009. In the following text, newspaper quotes have been translated from Portuguese by Randi Kaarhus.

44 *SAVANA* is an independent weekly paper with news and commentary, owned and published by *Mediacoop jornalistas associados* Ltd in Maputo.

45 'Flashes da Cimeira de Lusaka', *SAVANA* 18 April 2008.

46 Ibid.

47 Neither can any information be found on SADC's informative website concerning the Lusaka summit in 2008.

48 Machado da Graça 'Zimbabwe: A situação agrava-se', *SAVANA*, 18 April 2008.

49 *Zambeze* is a newspaper owned by *NOVOmedia* Ltd, published in Maputo. It is often critical of the Mozambican government, presenting the views of the opposition.

50 'Democratização sempre adiada: África Austral precisa urgentemente de novas mentalidades', Editorial, *Zambeze*, 17 April 2008.

51 Ibid. The official result of the 1999 elections in Mozambique was that the governing FRELIMO got 48.55 per cent of the votes in the Parliamentary elections, while the opposition's RENAMO-UE got 38.7 per cent. In the presidential elections, FRELIMO's Joaquim Chissano got 52.3 per cent and RENAMO's Afonso Dhlakama 47.7 per cent. As many as 9.37 per cent of the votes were categorised as 'invalid'.

52 'Democratização sempre adiada: África Austral precisa urgentemente de novas mentalidades', Editorial, *Zambeze*, 17 April 2008.

53 In Mozambique, RENAMO has been the main party in opposition to the governing FRELIMO party since the 1992 Peace Accord ended the civil war. With the Peace Accord the Mozambican National Resistance (RENAMO) turned into a political party.

54 'Eleições no Zimbabwe continuam a mexer: Morgan Tsvangirai não aceitará nenhuma 2ª volta nas presidencias', *Zambeze*. 24 April 2008.

55 Ibid. The post-election violence associated with the elections in Kenya in December 2007 had made a great impact in the region. This violence, in brief referred to as "Kenya", having taken place only a few months before, also became a point of reference in discussions about possible scenarios of protest in connection with the Zimbabwean elections.

56 'Guebuza recebe Tsangirai pela porta dos fundos: Gaffe diplomática', *SAVANA*, 25 April 2008.
57 Ibid., *SAVANA*, 25 April 2008.
58 *O País* is a relatively new paper, owned and published by *Sociedade Independiente de Comunicação* in Maputo. Starting out as a weekly, it went daily later in 2008.
59 'SADC é cúmplice?', *O País*, 25 April 2008.
60 Ibid.
61 Ibid.
62 *Diário de Moçambique* is owned by *Sociedade Comercial Notícias de Beira* Ltd, and published in Beira.
63 'Maputo reconhece "crise real" no Zimbabwe', *Diário de Moçambique*, 26 April 2008.
64 Ibid., *Diário de Moçambique* 26 April 2008.
65 Ibid.
66 The apparent 'invisibility' of Zimbabwean migrants in Mozambique today is further explored in Chapter 3.
67 Machada da Graça: 'Continuamos em silêncio?' *SAVANA*, 02 May 2008.
68 *SAVANA*, 27 June 2008. Drawing by Zapiro, cf. South Africa section above.
69 'Tsvangirai explica desistência', *SAVANA*, 27 June 2008
70 'Que futuro Zimbabwe', *O País*, 27 June 2008.
71 'Fomos forçados a votar – Em Machipanda aumentam entradas de zimbabweanos', *SAVANA*, 04 July 2008.
72 Fernando Gonçalves, 'Felicitar a Zanu-PF foi um grave erro estratégico', *SAVANA*, 04 July 2008. Our emphasis.
73 'Prevalece a esperança na SADC', Editorial, *Zambeze*, 10 July 2008.
74 Ibid.
75 'E preciso impedir-se a "Mugabização" de Moçambique', Editorial, *Zambeze*, 17 July 2008.
76 Ibid. If we look at presidential elections in Mozambique, the turnout fell from 79.59 per cent in 1994, to 69.54 per cent in 1999, and to 36.42 per cent in 2004. In 2009, it increased to 44.63 per cent. However, the percentage of invalid/spoilt votes was 9.99 per cent in 2009, while in 1994 it was only 2.93 per cent. http://www.eisa.org.za/WEP/mozelectarchive.htm.
77 Rebelo is regarded very much as part of the old Samoristas in FRELIMO, and is also seen as an ideologist of the left of the Party.
78 'Jorge Rebelo: As falas da velha raposa', *SAVANA*, 04 July 2008
79 Chiluba was in fact convicted in an English civil court in 2007, but acquitted in Zambia in 2010. He died in June 2011.
80 Although Mwanawasa himself was also accused of election rigging and nepotism (see Gould, 2007).
81 Based on data we collected at the border. The 2008 statistics are based on figures through September of that year.

3

Poverty, Shelter and Opportunities
Zimbabweans' Experiences in Mozambique

Randi Kaarhus[1]

Introduction

It was during the year 2008 – the year of the most dramatic and most contested elections in Zimbabwe to date – that unprecedented numbers of Zimbabweans crossed the border to seek refuge in Mozambique. While the majority of those who left the country during the decade from 2000 went to South Africa (UNHCR, 2010), thousands also crossed into Mozambican territory. A significant number of them ended up in the border province of Manica. In 2008, during the tense, violent period between the first round of elections on 29 March and the second round on 27 June, the UN Refugee Agency (UNHCR) made operational plans for the reception of Zimbabwean refugees in neighbouring countries. By June 2008, it had plans for five refugee camps sites in Mozambique; two of them were to be located in Manica Province, with a capacity to receive around 70,000 people (UNHCR, 2008). These plans were, however, never put into practice. This chapter seeks to describe the Zimbabwean presence in Manica Province against a backdrop of their virtual absence from both the public scene and public debate in Mozambique. It also provides an interpretation of why no refugee camps were ever established to receive the overwhelming influx of people into the border zones in 2008.[2]

With hindsight, we can see that the cross-border movement of Zimbabweans into Manica Province in 2008 only represented a peak in a more continuous flow of people seeking alternative livelihood opportunities and shelter from the economic and political crisis in Zimbabwe. This movement should, in turn, be placed in a historical context of more than a century of cross-border migration. A range of historical and more recent analyses describes the local and regional dynamics of migration ever since the present-day border-line, after considerable controversy, was agreed upon through the treaty signed by Britain and Portugal in 1891 (e.g. Newitt, 1995: 355; Hughes, 1999; Allina-Pisano, 2003; Tornimbeni, 2007).[3] The influx of Zimbabweans into Mozambique during the last decade has, by contrast, not been extensively documented and analyzed. Duri (2010: 128) even refers to contemporary cross-border dynamics in the area as 'conspicuously underrepresented in scholarly works'.

Data sources and fieldwork

This chapter draws on a diversity of published and unpublished written sources in combination with on-site fieldwork. A review of academic literature on Mozambique in general, and studies concerned with the border region Mozambique/Zimbabwe and the Province of Manica in particular, was supplemented with reports on refugees and migrants in the region and reports on the human-rights situation in Zimbabwe, as well as in Mozambique. Fieldwork was carried out in Manica Province during five stays in the period between October 2007 and April 2010, totalling approximately eighteen weeks. Through informal visits and participant observation in various locations in the province, as a researcher I was able to meet with civil society organizations and NGOs working in Manica, and also had the opportunity to carry out ten formal interviews with people representing different locally based organizations. I further conducted 40 in-depth interviews with Zimbabweans living in Manica, in addition to having a large number of informal conversations with both Mozambicans and Zimbabweans.[4] Here the identities of the Zimbabweans interviewed are concealed in order to protect their privacy and security, as most of them have had to resort to some form of extra-legal procedures in order to survive and make a living in Mozambique. Finally, I had a limited number of informal interviews with people on the Zimbabwean side during brief visits across the border. The analysis presented in this chapter is, furthermore, based on the author spending a total of more than three years in Mozambique during the period 1999–2011.

Background and context

In early 2000, when a majority of Zimbabweans did not support President Mugabe's ZANU-PF in the constitutional referendum called that year, it was commonly seen as the first serious challenge to the party-in-power since Zimbabwean Independence in 1980. Soon after the referendum, the land invasions on commercial farms, induced by the President and officially legitimized through the new and radical Fast Track Land Reform programme, resulted in increasing numbers of evictions both of white farm owners and black farm workers on large commercial farms. By February 2003, the Commercial Farmers Union in Zimbabwe estimated that 2,300 of their members were no longer engaged in farming (IDMC, 2008: 31). A small group had by then, with the acceptance of the Mozambican president, Chissano, left Zimbabwe to establish themselves as commercial farmers in Manica Province. The hopes and failures associated with this so-called 'Manica miracle' have been much discussed in Mozambique (AIM, 2006). The farmers' experiences have also been described and analyzed, in particular in Hammar's work (Hanlon and Smart, 2008: 71-88; Hammar, 2010).[5]

As concerns the fate of the former farm workers on the 'white' commercial farms, the information is rather scarce (Human Rights Watch, 2005: 9; IDMC, 2008: 4; cf. Scoones et al., 2010). We know that during the colonial period, white Rhodesian farmers relied heavily on recruiting farm workers from the neighbouring countries, including the areas under Portuguese control (Rutherford, 2007: 108). Over time, some of these workers remained on the farms, raising families. Still, as farm workers on the commercial farms, even immigrants' descendants were commonly seen as 'foreigners' rather than as 'real citizens' both in colonial times and after Zimbabwean independence (Rutherford, 2007). Some of the farm workers crossed back and forth, being able to make use of opportunities on one side of the border, while seeking to escape hardship or conflict on the other side.[6]

Within the diverse sample of people who agreed to serve as 'key informants' in the in-depth interviews reported in this chapter, there were no former farm workers from commercial farms in Zimbabwe. Most of my informants were interviewed in an urban setting, either in the provincial capital Chimoio, or in Vila de Manica, closer to the Zimbabwean border. With diverse backgrounds and mostly between 20 and 40 years of age, these informants had left Zimbabwe for a complex set of reasons, very often a mix of political, economic and personal factors. They were not direct victims of farm evictions, but most of them would say that it 'all started' on the white farms. The Zimbabwean migrants have been referred to as 'humanitarian migrants' or 'livelihood-seeking migrants', and their crossing the border characterized as 'forced migration' especially in the periods of severe humanitarian need (Kiwanuka and Monson, 2009: 17). But officially they have not been categorized as 'refugees' (Hammar and Rodgers, 2008: 361). I will here argue that the lack of official categoriza-

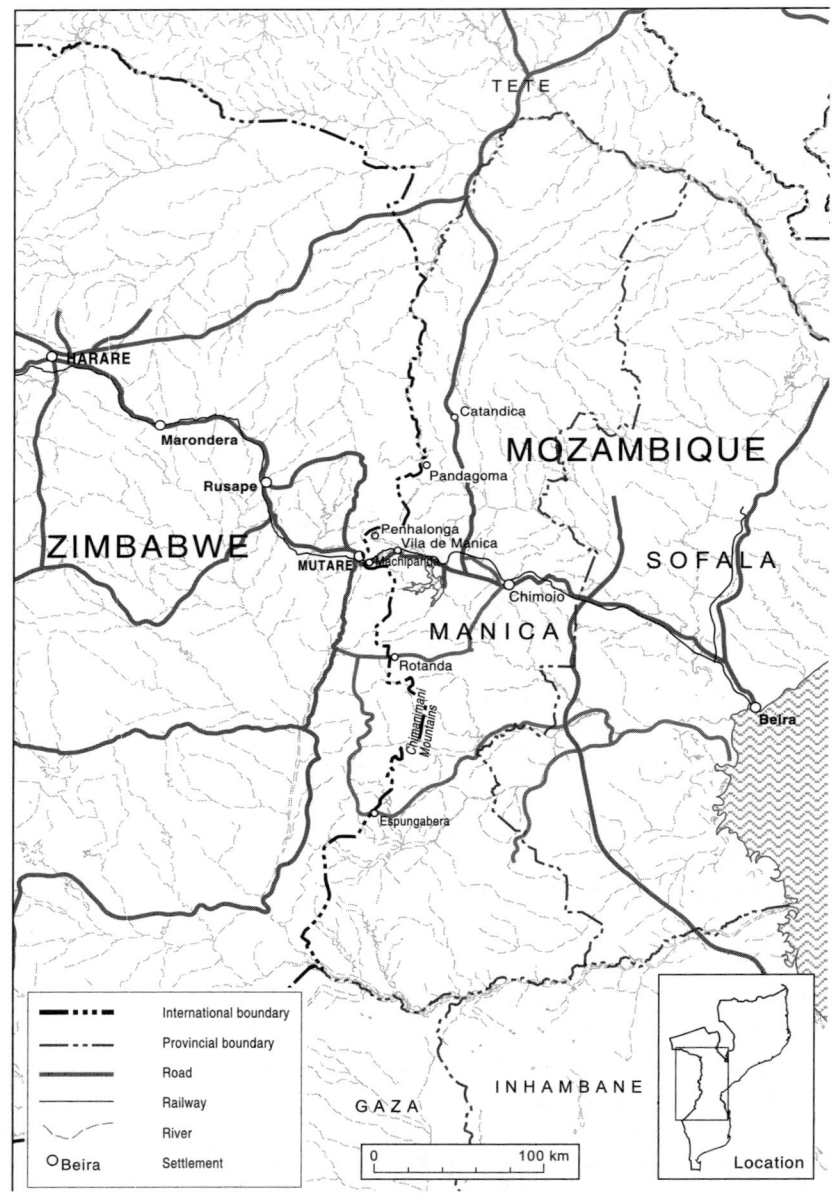

Map 2: Manica Province in Mozambique and Beira corridor

tion and registration in Mozambique is part of their *invisibility*, which is both a political and social construction.[7]

At the level of statistical overviews, there is very little information available on Zimbabweans in Mozambique. And available statistics say nothing about the extent to which former farm workers of Mozambican origin have 'returned home' after 2000 as a consequence of the invasions on commercial farms and the Fast Track land reform in Zimbabwe. According to official statistics in Mozambique, none of the Zimbabweans who have crossed the border into the country are 'refugees'. Neither have they been classified as refugees – or as 'other groups or persons of concern' – by the UNHCR. The information given on Zimbabweans in Mozambique on the UNHCR website was for several years restricted to the following statement of intention: 'Situations of statelessness will be addressed for some farm workers from Zimbabwe with historical links to Mozambique' (UNHCR, 2010: 2).

With this relative lack of statistics and written information as a starting-point, I sought to find out more about the thousands of black Zimbabweans who have crossed the border into Mozambique. If they have not returned to Zimbabwe, where are they now? And *who* are they? According to a report from the Forced Migration Studies Programme (Kiwanuka and Monson 2009: 31),[8] Zimbabweans in Mozambique are mainly found in Manica Province, but also in Tete and Gaza – that is, the provinces which border Zimbabwe. In addition, considerable numbers are found in the major cities of Maputo and Beira; while small numbers can be encountered 'everywhere'. My study has concentrated on Manica Province. There are no official numbers of Zimbabwean migrants in Manica, but estimates have ranged from 4,000 to 40,000 plus. The number is no doubt higher than 4,000, but any exact figure would be impossible to verify.[9] Numbers have also varied over time, as have the estimates I have obtained from (knowledgeable) informants in Manica during the period 2007 to 2010. The fact of the 'missing numbers' is in part due to the way in which the Mozambican government has related to and dealt with the crisis in Zimbabwe and the resulting migration into the country; that is, as basically a non-topic.[10] In public, as well as private discourses the missing numbers also create some real uncertainty about the scale of the problem – to the extent that it has actually been considered a problem.[11]

In 2008, however, among the events that did create concern in Mozambique were the waves of xenophobic violence that started in poor townships in the Johannesburg area and spread to other parts of South Africa. Many

71

residents fled, or were relocated in tents provided by UNHCR.[12] The violence was reported as targeting Zimbabwean, as well as Malawian and Mozambican immigrants in South Africa. In Mozambique a main question that arose was: Why did it happen? But it also brought up another question: Can it also happen here? (Serra, 2010: 20).

If we search for historical roots and precedents of such xenophobic violence, a commonly held view is that the colonial regime in South Africa to a larger extent than the colonial power in Mozambique left a legacy of dividing people by race, language and identity (Hanlon, 2010: i).[13] In contrast to the British, Portuguese 'indirect rule' in south-eastern Africa did not use the concept of 'tribe' as a key element in the administration of colonized territories. This may be one of the factors behind the fact that in Mozambique today, 'tribal' or ethnic differences are not so easily mobilized in conflict situations. In Maputo, street revolts erupted in February 2008, when young and unemployed people attacked 'state power' and cars, which are often seen as signs of wealth and privilege. In South Africa the violence and attacks starting in May were directed at 'foreigners' in particular (Ibid., vi). There was concern that this wave of violence could also spread to Mozambique. At this point there also seemed to be a need for more research-based knowledge about the attitudes to immigrants among the Mozambican population.

As a result, in 2009 a sociological study was carried out by a group of Mozambican researchers associated with the University Eduardo Mondlane in Maputo (Serra (ed.), 2010). A total of 400 questionnaires were distributed to Mozambican respondents in four cities: Maputo, Beira, Nampula and Pemba. Responses were obtained from 73 per cent of the sample. Of the respondents, as much as 86.5 per cent agreed to the statement: 'We ought to receive foreigners and treat them well'. A total of 72.2 per cent agreed to the statement: 'Foreigners are welcome' (Huo, 2010: 182).[14] There were no significant differences in these responses according to respondents' gender or level of education. The respondents were further asked about perceptions of racism. As much as 68.2 per cent agreed to the statement 'Foreigners have racist practices'.[15] But when questions distinguished between different categories of foreigners, the answers revealed a more differentiated picture. While almost 70 per cent agreed that 'Whites have racist practices', about 33 per cent agreed that 'Blacks have racist practices', and only 22 per cent agreed that 'Zimbabweans have racist practices' (Huo, 2010: 191). The analyses presented in Serra (2010) thus indicate that Mozambicans' frustration with high levels of poverty, lack of development, increasing economic differences, and a growing privileged elite have not, so far, been channelled towards foreigners and immigrants, or Zimbabweans, in particular. Instead, according to Hanlon, there is frustration with an 'inoperative, distant' State (Hanlon, 2010: vi).

Why Leave Zimbabwe for Mozambique?

This is actually a question that most of the Zimbabweans I met in Manica have asked themselves repeatedly. In my account here, I will begin with *David* – not his real name. David was born in Harare, but left Zimbabwe in 2003. He was young and left because of 'the difficult situation, problems of employment – to seek for greener pastures', and came to Manica. As he did not speak Portuguese it was difficult for him to find a job, but he managed to get employment with one of the white Zimbabweans who had come to Mozambique as a result of the Fast-Track land occupations. From Zimbabwe, David had some experience working in a hotel, and with these qualifications he was able to get a job 'in the white man's house'. His employer was involved in logging timber in Manica, and his house was 'in the bush'. David stayed there, but with his urban background he said he 'couldn't sustain it' for more than a year. After that he was able to get employment with another white Zimbabwean farmer, who had started a paprika project closer to Chimoio town. As one of the Zimbabwean migrants who arrived in Manica between 2001 and 2003, David was able to get employment with the white farmers who established themselves with expanding enterprises in that period. He is still in Manica, and now has Mozambican identity papers.

In May 2005, an unprecedented Zimbabwean-government initiative resulted in large-scale evictions and displacement of people throughout the country; this time through demolitions of informal housing and business structures in high-density, low-income urban areas. Under the name Operation Murambatsvina,[16] it began in Harare but spread to other urban centres. The operation was officially presented as aiming to clean up and restore order in urban slums. My informants in Manica all call it the 'Tsunami',[17] which may reflect more accurately how this military-style operation was perceived among the residents targeted by waves of (man-made) demolition (Sachikonye, 2006). According to the Special Envoy appointed by the UN Secretary General, it resulted in an estimated 700,000 men, women and children 'losing their homes, their source of livelihood or both' (ICG, 2005: 2). At the time it was also noted that a fairly large number of Mozambican migrants and their descendents existed among the residents in the affected low-income suburbs of Harare. These were mainly people who had sought refuge in Zimbabwe during the devastating Civil War in Mozambique, which only ended in 1992 with the signing of a General Peace Agreement (Mazula et al., 2004). Mozambique came out of sixteen years of post-independence war as one of the poorest countries in sub-Saharan Africa, with a large part of its population displaced. But most of the Mozambicans who had sought refuge in Zimbabwe, Malawi or South Africa during the war were 'repatriated' during the 1990s.[18] By the end of the decade, post-conflict reconstruction and the return of both refugees and internally displaced people led to new economic growth, as well as increasing food production in Mozambique (World Bank, 2006: xiii). By the end of the 1990s, Zimbabwe, by contrast, already showed the first signs of an economic crisis, which only escalated from the year 2000 onwards.

World Bank (2010) indicators tell that Gross Domestic Product (GDP) per capita in Zimbabwe in the year 2000 was 594 US$. In 2000, it was in Mozambique calculated to 234 US$ per capita – less than half of the national domestic product in Zimbabwe.[19] In 2001 the annual growth rate per capita was 9 per cent in Mozambique, while the figure for Zimbabwe was -3 per cent. In 2003, the annual growth rate was in Mozambique 3 per cent and in Zimbabwe -10 per cent. In 2005, the last year for which this database provides comparable statistics on Zimbabwe, the growth in GDP per capita was -0.5 per cent in Zimbabwe and 6 per cent in Mozambique. By 2005, the calculated GDP per capita in Zimbabwe had fallen to 274 UDS. In Mozambique it had increased to 320 US$, and thus actually passed the GDP in Zimbabwe. If we look at UNDP's Human Development Index (HDI), Zimbabwe in 2010 was ranked as number 169, with a HDI value of 0.140. This is down from a HDI value of 0.232 in 2000, and placed the country at the bottom of the HDI ranking list.[20] Mozambique was in 2010 ranked as number 165. With a HDI value of 0.284 in 2010, the index thus indicated a gradual rise from a HDI value of 0.224 in 2000.[21]

According to estimates, between 2000 and 2005 formal employment in Zimbabwe shrank by twenty per cent (Sachikonye, 2006: 13). At the same time, there was a marked expansion in the informal economy – ranging from flea-markets and individual travellers buying and selling basic goods from neighbouring countries, to black-market foreign currency transactions and illegal mineral extraction.[22] But while illegal diamond trading took place at the high-status parties of the relatively affluent political class in Harare,[23] the informal market transactions were mostly associated with the low-income suburbs that were targeted for demolishing during the Zimbabwean tsunami. Several of the 2005 tsunami victims were among my key informants in Manica. One of them was of Mozambican descent, and I will call her *Laura*. Laura was born in Manica, but while she was still an infant her parents moved to Harare. This was in 1981 during the civil war in Mozambique. Laura grew up and went to school in Harare, she learnt to speak Shona and English – but not Portuguese. She married a Zimbabwean, a teacher, who died in 2000 and left her with two small children. After that 'life became hard', and she started selling tomatoes in the streets. As she managed to save some money, it also became possible for her to engage in the expanding cross-border trading, which grew out of the escalating economic crisis in Zimbabwe. While the scarcity of basic commodities, including groceries, was a serious problem for most people in Zimbabwe, it also represented opportunities for informal trading (Duri, 2010: 142-3). Since part of Laura's family still lived in Manica, she started travelling there to buy rice and cooking oil, later sandals and shoes, to sell in Harare, where she had a market stall in a flea-market area.

In May 2005 she had been travelling. When she returned to Harare her stall had been destroyed and all the goods taken. Then, at short notice, the house where she lived with her two children was also destroyed. This was her tsunami: 'They said it was a clean-up [Murambatsvina]!' It left her not knowing what to do. But when her Mozambican family found out what had happened they sent her enough money to travel with her children by bus to Mozambique, to look for work and new livelihood opportunities. Still, she had lost all her 'capital' and 'came with nothing'. With time, she was able to get several temporary jobs. But in spite of her skills and energy, as a Zimbabwean, it was in practice impossible for her to get permanent employment. A potential employer said to me: 'It is difficult to employ a Zimbabwean when there are so many unemployed Mozambicans!'

Nelson was another Zimbabwean who had to deal at many levels with the aftermaths of Murabatsvina. Nelson had lived with his family in one of the suburbs of Harare that was destroyed during this period. After that his family split up, his mother left for Botswana, his sister got involved in sex work, trying to raise money to go to South Africa. His was a 'broken family'. But a friend who had decided to leave the country for good helped him with 'start capital' for cross-border trading. Travelling first to Botswana to buy cosmetics, then to Mozambique for groceries, Nelson established his base in the small shop he had taken over from his friend in Harare, and was in this way able to make a living. In 2007, however, trade became more difficult, and it became illegal to 'walk with *forex*'.[24] Young people were also under surveillance by the police who wanted to make sure they supported ZANU-PF. Nelson said:

> They came to my place and asked: 'What was the last rally that you attended?' Then they took all the groceries in the shop and said: 'Our children are also starving...'.

In 2007, the police took Nelson's passport: 'They said: "You have travelled a lot; you are the ones who are spreading the wrong message about our country".' Using so-called 'travel documents', Nelson in 2008 crossed over to Mozambique to buy groceries. But on his return to Harare he was arrested and beaten up by the police. After that they let him go. The next morning he learnt that a friend he knew from travelling together to Botswana had been killed: 'I thought, I am the next one'. This was in February 2008, just before the elections. He left immediately, crossing the border back to Mozambique, carrying only the clothes he wore and his cell phone – 'to avoid suspicion'. At the border crossing he said he had left something behind during his last visit, and was just coming to pick it up. But this time he came to Manica to stay; 'It was escaping death, it was the only way'.

Nelson had no family in Mozambique, but he had a Mozambican friend in Harare who had come to Zimbabwe during the Civil War in Mozambique. This friend's brother had spent the years of war in Malawi, but was now back in Manica. Here he made a living as a traditional healer, a *curandeiro*.[25] In his modest shelter the *curandeiro* also made a space for Nelson – giving him a place to sleep on the ground, sharing a blanket with five persons.

Crossing the Border

As a result of the steadily aggravating political and economic crisis in Zimbabwe from 2005 onwards, increasing numbers of people were crossing the border back and forth between Zimbabwe and Mozambique. Many of them came to buy basic commodities to bring back to Zimbabwe, where the shelves in the grocery shops were usually empty. Some would, like Nelson and Laura, enter Mozambique at the major formal border crossing at Forbes/Machipanda, between Mutare in Zimbabwe and Vila de Manica on the Mozambican side. This is the main border post in the Beira corridor, on the road linking Mutare and Harare in Zimbabwe with the port of Beira on the Indian Ocean. In this period of economic and political crisis in Zimbabwe, the formal visa requirements for passing the border between Zimbabwe and Mozambique were relaxed. According to the SADC Protocol on the Facilitation of Movement of Persons approved at a SADC summit in 2005, citizens from SADC member states were granted a maximum of 90 days' visitors' permits at the border, with the objective of 'enabling the movement of people in the region'.[26] From November 2007, an agreement between the governments in Zimbabwe and Mozambique allowed citizens' a 30-day stay in either country upon presenting a passport or valid 'travel documents' at the border post (Duri, 2010: 146). One-day border passes for citizens without passports were also introduced (Kiwanuka and Monson, 2009). But people living on both sides of the border would still cross the border ('informally') on foot, following narrow paths as they had always done, crossing the forests, hills or mountain passes of the Chimanimani and Vumba mountains and the forested border areas ('bush') further north.

The author, in October 2008, after 'informally' crossing the border from Manica into Zimbabwe on one of the footpaths in the Chimanimani mountains, interviewed a young couple working in the field. They said that they would go to Mozambique to get basic commodities – soap, cooking oil and sugar. In their case, the closest market was the small town of Rotanda in the district of Sussundenga. They had been there 'last week'. Their small farm on the Zimbabwean side had earlier been part of a larger commercial farm. Now they cultivated mostly wheat, and through a variant of a share-crop arrangement with a government-employed extension agent, they got access to seed and fertilizer. Back in Mozambique in the late afternoon, on the dusty roads of Sussundenga District, we met scores of minibuses – so-called *chapas* – heading towards the Zimbabwean border, overloaded with people and bags of commodities to be sold or consumed on the other side.

In April 2009, after a 'formal' border crossing at Machipanda/Forbes, in a small house in a suburb of Mutare in Zimbabwe I interviewed an elder couple. Originally from Maputo, they had left Mozambique in 1974, during the last days of the struggle for independence, to live in Rhodesia. The husband now worked as a furniture upholsterer, and was busy repairing both furniture and worn-out car seats on the veranda of their small rented house. During the peak of the economic crisis, in 2007-08, the wife had been travelling once a week to

Mozambique to buy goods and groceries. Often she had gone as far as Beira. In this way both earned a living and provided a network of family members on the Zimbabwean side with basic commodities. With the new Government of National Unity's introduction of US$ as the only valid currency in Zimbabwe, 'the shops had filled up'. Thus the business of reselling goods from Mozambique had dwindled. In 2009, the wife only went to Mozambique to buy groceries for consumption in the family. But they had managed to buy a plot where, after 35 years in Zimbabwe, they were finally planning to build their own house.

2008: Responses at the Peak of Political Crisis

On 2 May 2008, the Electoral Commission in Zimbabwe announced that in the presidential elections Mugabe had received 43.2 per cent and Tsvangirai 47.9 per cent of the votes. With these results a second round of presidential elections were announced to take place on 27 June (ICG, 2008: 5). The response of the party still-in-power to Mugabe losing the first round of the presidential elections was to launch a systematic campaign of violence, seeking to dismantle MDC structures and intimidate opposition activists and voters (Ibid.: 6; Human Rights Watch, 2009). As a result, 163 MDC supporters were reported to have been killed. Tsvangirai withdrew from the second round of elections; Mugabe, as the only remaining candidate, was re-elected in June. At the same time, an unprecedented surge in cross-border migration was observed in Manica Province, as new waves of tormented and frightened people sought refuge in Mozambique. One of them was *Tarusenga* – one of my key informants in Manica:

> When the results were announced, we were supposed to undergo another round of elections. The government announced the run-off…. I came here just before the second round of elections. There was this general tendency of stigmatizing teachers. I was in charge of a school… we were trying to develop the community, and it so happened that I got victimized. They actually brought to my attention that one day they would come after me, that was during the March elections. After that I was informed by some Party insiders just to be alert; they were planning to come and attack me…. Sometimes I would sleep in my house, sometimes I would sleep in the forest; I was not very sure when they would come. They were going around doing all these attacks, so we would hear news: 'they have attacked so-and-so; they have attacked so-and-so….'. Then one sympathizer came and told me, you have to leave now. Fortunately, by then I had

organized everything, it was just myself, a few clothes.... I got a lift to Harare, and then proceeded to Mozambique. My younger brother had a friend, who used to work in Zimbabwe before, so they knew each other. He gave me the phone number, and when I got here, I had to call him and managed to locate his place. So I lived there, with his family, till I got a job.

For Tarusenga is was not the first time he crossed the border to Mozambique. He had come to Manica in 2002 seeking alternative livelihood opportunities, and had worked for one of the white Zimbabwean farmers who had tried to develop a large-scale tobacco farming industry in Manica Province. On his own family's – especially his mother's – request he had in 2004 returned to Zimbabwe, and after that he tried to survive as a teacher in a difficult economic situation:

> I remember the salary we got was just enough to go to town, buy two litres of cooking oil, and come back. We had to do some farming, some buying and selling to survive with the family. I had a passport, and I could go to South Africa to buy and sell a few things. Of course, we didn't have groceries. There were no groceries in the shops. So I would go to South Africa, buy soap, cooking oil... these basic commodities. I would buy groceries for my family, and the rest I could sell. For me and a lot of other civil servants that was how we survived. That was in 2006, 2007...

In 2008, it was the political situation and the fear of getting killed that made Tarusenga leave Zimbabwe and go back to Mozambique, seeking refuge, and a job and livelihood. Meanwhile one of my key informants representing Mozambican civil society (*A*) observed with growing concern the influx of Zimbabweans during the year 2008:

> A lot of people came over the border, from March onwards. They came fleeing... beaten, burnt.... But then, we believed the problem would be solved with the second round of elections.... There were whole families who came crossing over. Early in the morning, we could see people walking in the forest, Zimbabweans, carrying something to sell to get food. They may not have been allowed to cross the border. But the forest has many paths.... After the second election day... there were thousands coming, thousands! Desperate! Many, most of them, seeking food.[27]

A also mentions another, contrasting cross-border phenomenon: Buses of Mugabe-supporters – people wearing T-shirts stating 'I am with Mugabe' – crossing at Forbes/Machipanda border post during the period of elections.

People 'with money in their hands' heading for the Shoprite supermarket in the Province capital of Chimoio. *A* continues:

> Shoprite is big... and they emptied the place, everything, [and were] contented.... And in that way they showed people on this side that they were happy with Robert Mugabe!

Among the Zimbabweans who were seeking 'refuge from Mugabe', at this point about 5,000 were registered only in Vila de Manica, according to *A*. Of these, 280 wanted to seek protection as political refugees.[28] In this group there was also 'people with money', according to *A*, people who were able to rent houses, and even start building houses in the town. As expressed during our interview in April 2009, *A*'s general view on the Mozambican response to the crisis in Zimbabwe was the following:

> The Government of Mozambique would not accept that there were refugees here. They said these were people who just came to do business, to buy things to sell over there. And people also came for that purpose, there were different types.... There were people fleeing persecution, people persecuted for some suspicion or other.... And artists.... And those who came searching for food, to work to get something to eat.

The problem, *A* said, was that the government did not want to recognize the situation. FRELIMO (Frente de Libertação de Moçambique) is 'still bound by the gratitude' resulting from Mugabe's support during the civil war.

Policies and Displacement
Gendered aspects

In 2008, in the border town of Vila de Manica the streets were lined with young men, equipped with portable stalls to sell sugar, soap, cigarettes, condensed milk, jam, peanut butter, or sweets; but ready to fold up their stalls and run if the police appeared. By April 2009, most of these young men had either returned to Zimbabwe or travelled further into Mozambique. A group of women had, however, stayed on in Vila de Manica, and around 80, some of them with children, were living in the remnants of the waiting hall of the Old Manica railway station. There they were sleeping on pieces of cardboard on the cement floor, each occupying a few square meters where they had put a bundle of clothes or a couple of plastic bags. They were trying to make some money by cooking 'sadza' to make snacks to sell for ten *meticais* (MZN) at the local market.[29] In 2008, there had been about 200 women at the Old Station. Many had come to Mozambique 'through the bush', and not through a formal border crossing. 'You know there is no electric wire between Zimbabwe and Mozambique', said a local Mozambican NGO representative. During the first quarter of 2009, most of the women at the Old Station had been deported back to Zimbabwe, being escorted by police to Mutare just across the border. The official reason was that they did not have valid passports or identity papers.

In April 2009, *Joyce* was among the women who were still at the Old Station. She had come to Manica in late 2007. Growing up in a small town on the road between Harare and Bulawayo, she had been to college, where she studied interior decoration. But 'there was no food', and in 2007, with the salary of a normal job 'you could not buy anything'. Joyce started as an informal trader to Botswana. When she went to Mozambique, it was because some people had said that it was 'easy to cross the border', and 'very cheap in Mozambique'. While in Manica, the situation in Zimbabwe got more difficult, and she decided to stay on. She managed to survive, but did not earn enough money to return home. Staying in Mozambique was also a mixed experience:

> The Mozambicans... most of them are so friendly, just the police, they come at night and say they want money.... If you walk at night, they will take your money. They ask you *50 mil*.[30] Only if you have got a passport, they won't. You keep on working [selling sadza at *10 mil*]. They ask you *50 mil* every time. They are too rough, the policemen; and especially those *guarda-fronteiras* [border police] – you know them? I think they harass us because we have got poverty in Zimbabwe. That is why they harass us. If South Africans come here to stay, they don't do that. Because South Africans, they have got everything... I'm struggling. Mozambique is too tough.

The women at the Old Station describe a situation of contradictions, and in part desperation. According to Kiwanuka and Monson, it is a 'widespread belief that the majority of women migrants are sex workers' (2009: 44). Therefore, they say, women are 'often targeted for police harassment, arrest and deportation'. Among male Zimbabwean migrants in Manica, there also seem to be sympathy for the women who are engaged in sex work. The men recognize that it is more difficult for the women to get a decent job in Mozambique, women are paid less, they may be more vulnerable to harassment, and probably 'they have no choice'. My key informant, *C*, who works with a local civil society organization in Manica, says that among the women sex workers, the majority actually have children and family in Zimbabwe. Their families depend on the food or money they as livelihood-seeking migrants are able to send – or bring – back home. Their families in Zimbabwe may not know what 'trade' they are actually involved in across the border. Still, she holds that only a limited number of Zimbabwean women are actually involved in sex work, and they most likely represent only a minority of the female migrants. Her estimates were about 30 women in Chimoio and 20 in Vila de Manica. Nevertheless all the Zimbabwean women I interviewed in Manica had, in some way or other, to deal with the reputation of Zimbabwean women as being associated with prostitution.

The policy of a non-topic

The gendered actions of the Mozambican police, aimed at targeting assumed or real Zimbabwean sex workers can, however, also be seen in a larger political context. In Mozambican media, the migration of livelihood-seeking Zimbabweans into Mozambique has at times been represented as an influx of women engaged in prostitution. This particular focus constitutes an element in a more general misrepresentation of the 'Zimbabwean issue' as a whole. When 'scandalous' elements are reported in the media, they don't challenge predominant perceptions of the Zimbabwean migration into Mozambique as a rather peripheral phenomenon involving rather peripheral individuals. When for instance the weekly *SAVANA* on 2 November 2007 reported on the economic situation in Zimbabwe, it told its readership that:

> The Zimbabwean economy is at present one of the most devastated in the world.... Since 2000 the country has been in a deep crisis, in addition to hyper-inflation there is a high rate of unemployment, poverty, and a chronic lack of fuel, food and foreign currency.[31]

This information was, however, given under the heading: 'Zimbabwean prostitutes assault Manica and Sofala', and the story of the article was highlighting a street quarrel between a Zimbabwean and a Mozambican woman involved in sex work in Beira:

> Angry and shouting, the Mozambican woman accused the Zimbabwean of having grabbed her client and of charging low rates. 'It is disloyal competition. These Zimbabweans are destroying our business', claimed the Mozambican woman.[32]

The misrepresentation of the problem is, however, not only made in terms of gender. One of my key informants among civil society workers in Manica, *B*, gives another example of how 'the problem' is socially constructed in the public sphere: 'One day, say 20 Zimbabweans may be captured as "illegal migrants" at the border; or the police may arrest 40 for deportation or repatriation.' These actions may be met with acclaim by their superiors in the police hierarchy, but what they also do is to contribute to the misrepresentation of the real scale and complexity of the problem. The deportation of 20 or 40 Zimbabweans masks the fact that large numbers of Zimbabweans have crossed the border because of a real crisis in their country, and are seeking means of survival and livelihood in Mozambique. However, *B* said that 'in the government's official discourse this is not an issue'.[33]

In the process of collecting data for the FMSP report, the authors had considerable problems when seeking to obtain information from officials. The research team also found that there was no 'statistical evidence to back up claims about the nature and scale of migration over time' (Kiwanuka and Monson, 2009: 32). When they managed to get interview appointments, 'officials tended to be dismissive or evasive when asked to provide information about Zimbabwean migration into Mozambique' (Ibid.: 23). At a more general political level, the 2009 FMSP report makes the following observation, which basically confirms my own findings:

> In Mozambique, which has a strong historical relationship with the Zanu FP leadership in Zimbabwe, there seemed to be widespread political pressure to underplay the levels of and motives for Zimbabwean migration in order to resist acknowledging the complexity of the crisis. (Ibid.)

During the most critical time of the elections in Zimbabwe in 2008, UNHCR sent a representative to the Province of Manica. But this representative 'couldn't do anything', according to my civil-society informant *B*. The Government did not recognize the situation; that is, a situation of Zimbabwean citizens seeking refuge in Mozambique as the result of a real crisis in their home country. On 31 March 2009, the UNHCR representative packed up and left the Province, as the critical situation that required monitoring – of the 'non-refugees' – at the central offices was apparently defined as over. *B* commented: 'You need courage to oppose the official discourse'.

What has been the *policy* of the Mozambican government with regard to the thousands of Zimbabweans whom they must know have formally crossed

– or informally 'jumped' – the border into Mozambique? According to *B*: 'The government alleges that the local society, the local community, can manage to absorb this population'. The idea seems to have been that black Zimbabweans will 'naturally' integrate, and through merging with the local population, they will become politically 'invisible'.

Language and policy

As amply documented in research-based literature, in the Manica border region over time there have been close connections across the border between present-day Mozambique and Zimbabwe (for example, Hughes, 1999; Allina-Pisano, 2003; Tornimbeni, 2007). This relationship has been linked to, and facilitated by, the use of the same or mutually comprehensible local languages. In Zimbabwe, in addition to English, Shona is a national language, together with Ndebele. Most Zimbabweans speak or at least understand 'modern Shona' – the Zimbabwean standard representing a continuum of closely related varieties or 'dialects', including Ndau and Manyika on the Mozambican side. In Mozambique, however, only Portuguese plays the role of national language. In the Province of Manica, a majority of the population speaks several local languages, which from a Zimbabwean perspective can be classified as Shona dialects: *Ndau/Cindau* (29 per cent of the population in Manica), *Manyika/Cimanyika* (15 per cent) and *Tewe/Citewe* (21 per cent) according to Mwitu (1999: 14).[34] This adds up to 65 per cent of the population speaking a mutually comprehensive language for Shona-speakers.

Thus, the border has been permeable due to the lack of local-language barriers, and this characterizes the relationship between, in particular, Zimbabwe and the Province of Manica. One of my Zimbabwean informants in Chimoio said: 'It is easier in Manica Province, one speaks Shona, one speaks in Cimanyika, and they can understand each other easily'. In informal settings, at the market, making contacts and communicating with local people, Zimbabweans easily get along with Shona. However, my Zimbabwean informants perceive some important differences and barriers in other settings. In Zimbabwe, they say, you can speak Shona 'even in the offices'. In Mozambique, 'when you go into somebody's office, you have to speak in Portuguese', which is the language used in any public or official context. 'The paperwork here, it is all in Portuguese….' None of the Zimbabwean migrants knew any Portuguese before they came, and most share the experience of helplessness when not being able to understand or communicate in the official language in Mozambique.[35]

Livelihood challenges

Several of my Zimbabwean informants actually experienced a 'cultural shock' when they arrived in Mozambique, and not only discovered but also had to share the livelihood conditions of people in the least well-off suburbs of Chimoio and Vila de Manica. Nelson said: 'I did not know what to expect. But what can you do?' An artist I interviewed said:

> When I got here I was very surprised, the buildings, constructions… so different! Things are disordered…. No hygiene. Zimbabwe is really organized.

A technician told me:

> At first I got a big problem. Here it was too dirty…. Maybe it's a cultural thing. Now, it is going bit by bit, but it was difficult in the beginning…. In Mozambique you have to be patient.

Still, there was food in Mozambique, and the economy was growing. Zimbabweans in Mozambique also felt fairly safe. For many, or most, leaving Zimbabwe to stay in Mozambique was mainly a question of survival. They sought livelihood opportunities; if possible a job where they could earn enough money to buy new shoes when the old ones were worn out and, furthermore, be able to support their family back home with some food and money. But formal jobs are not easy to find.

Rosalind is 23 years old and comes from Rusape in Manicaland, a town situated on the road from Harare to Mutare. She came to Chimoio in 2005 to work as a housemaid. Later, her sister *Lily* followed her, coming to Chimoio in January 2008. Out of seven brothers and sisters in the family, five have left Zimbabwe, while their parents have stayed back home. Their father used to work in Harare, but has retired. He is just doing 'a little agriculture' on land inherited from their grandfather, growing maize, groundnuts and sweet potatoes: 'But there is a shortage of fertilizer, so we cannot grow enough.' While working in Chimoio, Rosalind went to visit them, bringing some money, some forex. 'If I can't go, I just buy some goods, especially food, and send them', she told me in 2009. Most Zimbabweans were, like her, sending groceries to their families back home with fellow Zimbabweans who were travelling to their home town. Rosalind said, 'instead of suffering there together with my mother, it is better that I come here'.

Her sister Lily had worked as a maid in Rusape, but when the economic situation in Zimbabwe became so difficult that with the monthly salary '[she] could not even buy one pair of shoes', she also decided to come to Chimoio. Her sister assisted her in getting a place to stay – three people sharing a room – and a job as a housemaid. 'Washing and cooking for three different people', Lily was receiving 1,200 MZN per month.[36] 'But now they said I must buy my own food!... I must pay where I am staying, every month I go to the border to have my passport stamped, and our parents they are waiting.... It is difficult.' But the sisters recognized that other housemaids, and many Mozambicans, earned less than Lily. Rosalind mentioned one of her fellow 'sisters' in the Church they both attend in Chimoio:

> I knew her in the church here. She worked for 500 [MZN], doing a lot of job, cooking in the market and selling food [for somebody with a food stall]. She had to get up early in the morning to go and prepare breakfast for the customers – lunch – supper – whatever, but she only received 500. So she decided to go there... at the Madrinha....[37] She had some friends who told her, 'It is better to come and work with us here at Madrinha'... Almost every day she's there... I used to pass by that road, and she told me 'With that little money I could not support my parents there in Zimbabwe, even for myself I cannot buy anything with 500'... I believe her parents think she's still going to church, but... we can see, now she doesn't go to the church any more.

Francis is one of the Zimbabweans who have managed to rent a small place for his business in a permanent market in Chimoio. He is 29 years old and was born in Harare, but has his origin in Rusape, Manicaland. In 1999 he had finished education up to A-level, with special courses in business, but failed to find a job. So in 2000 he 'bought his passport' and started travelling to South Africa and to Tete, in Mozambique, to buy goods and to re-sell in Harare. With the rising inflation, this business collapsed already in 2001. Then he became a part-time teacher, working with the government until 2006. But he also did video filming at weddings during weekends. – I asked: 'How were you able to buy the video camera?' He explains:

> It was just that my father, he was working, and before this he was, just, in the middle class... so he had some money. He could manage to give me the money... so I could buy the video camera and do that filming, and save some money.... That was how I was making ends meet. I was one of those people who didn't want to go out of Zimbabwe.... Some of my friends, most of my friends, they had gone to South Africa, and Botswana. They were even calling me: 'What are

you still doing there?'... Or maybe they could say, 'There is no food there, the conditions are going down every day!' But I did not want to go out of Zimbabwe... I regarded Zimbabwe as one of those beautiful countries that had everything. African standards, Zimbabwe was one of the best!

Francis had been to Mozambique back in 2001, and found it was not 'one of those countries I could think of coming to stay'. When the economic situation was getting worse in Zimbabwe, he was made aware of an emerging market for video filming in Chimoio. In early 2008, he brought his equipment from Harare and started a joint business with a Mozambican partner. Francis put his equipment and technical knowledge into the business, while his Mozambican partner contributed with knowledge of the language, the environment, and networks to local clients. They agreed on a 50/50 sharing of profits. But this joint business lasted for less than a year. According to Francis, after only a month he discovered that his share of the profits was less than 50 per cent and 'that guy actually started exploiting me'. But there was not much he could do about it until he started a new 'informal' business on his own. That was after discovering a new economic niche for people like himself, this time in electronic equipment maintenance. While he still goes to the border every month to get his passport stamped, in order that it is always 'valid', he cannot operate his new business legally. Trying to avoid being rounded up by the police, he also avoids going 'into town' – that is, into Chimoio city centre:

> If you walk into town, you may meet policemen.... Then you pay then, to get out of it. Even if you know I'm right... sometimes you end up paying them, so that you can get out quickly. If not, you can spend a day or so within the cells.... If you go into town, maybe you can get caught every day.

Paying the police to 'get out' means that a significant part of what he can earn will be spent on 'corruption' – a concern he shares with the women at the Old Station in Vila de Manica. But in contrast to them, Francis has private 'shelters' and more opportunities to make himself invisible to state officials, and can operate by 'drawing lines, where to go and where not to go'.

The Construction of Invisibility

The Zimbabweans I met in Mozambique generally believe it is a country with 'a long way to go' in terms of development. In 1992, when the General Peace Agreement was signed and Mozambique started a process of reconstruction after sixteen years of civil war, the country was generally ranked close to the bottom of all poverty indexes.[38] Since the 1990s, the reconstruction of state and society in Mozambique has, in practice, been closely linked to the building of a national political and economic elite. During this period, Mozambique has like most post-independence states in Africa been under the pressure of neo-liberal principles imposed from the outside (Eriksen, 2000: 34). As a result, according to Dorman et al. (2007: 20), political leaders in Africa have sought to deal with the challenge of managing the 'unstable and fragmented states' with which they entered the 21st century by claiming control over the definition of *citizenship* and nationhood. Dorman et al. (Ibid.) further hold that one way of maintaining such control is to 'cast a negative other against which to rally their nation' (Ibid.) This is a perspective that may be used to explain certain political processes in Zimbabwe over the last decade. But as an analytic perspective it clearly contrasts with the perspective indicated in Serra ((ed.), 2010) for Mozambique, where one result of the national political elite implementing neo-liberal economic policies is that popular discontent turns against the State.

My account here reveals, I believe, that the official Mozambican policy has *not* been to cast the Zimbabweans as 'negative others' (Dorman et al., 2007: 8). On the other hand, the Mozambican central authorities' non-recognition of the Zimbabwean crisis, and the political construction of the Zimbabwean migrants as officially invisible, has had other implications. As suggested by Polzer and Hammond, these are implications which can be identified both at the theoretical and empirical level:

> [A] Foucauldian understanding of the structural and elite politics of invisibility and visibility must... be matched with a perspective famously described by Scott (1985) as the 'weapons of the weak': the ways in which the vulnerable work to stay invisible to the 'powers that be' by hiding and obscuring identities and activities. (2008: 418)

It must be recognized that for a researcher to reveal and describe more concretely how 'invisibility' is used as a survival resource by 'the weak' raises some ethical questions. One question is to what extent a description of migrants' creative livelihood strategies and flexible identities can alert those 'who have the power to see or choose not to see' (Ibid.: 421). Can it result in measures that further 'reduce the space for life-saving creativity and flexibility'? (Ibid.: 418). This is a dilemma I have encountered at several points when writing this chapter.

Still, I believe my account is not complete if I leave out the issue of 'identities'. In fact, a large number of the Zimbabweans I met in Manica have, sooner or later, acquired Mozambican identity papers; most of them 'illegally'. That is, they have paid local officials to get new identity papers, which document that *X* was born in Mozambique of Mozambican parents. For those who have learnt to speak Portuguese, there has even been a discount. Most of the 'new Mozambicans' see these papers as a necessity in order to survive and sustain a livelihood in Mozambique. Those who neither have such papers, nor valid Zimbabwean passports, like the women at the Old Station in Vila de Manica, may become extremely vulnerable. For them, Mozambique easily becomes 'too tough'. As they can hardly sustain themselves, it also becomes increasingly difficult both to support their families back in Zimbabwe, and to return home.

What we end up with is a mixed picture. Even the practices of local corrupt officials who exploit – or help – the Zimbabwean migrants have mixed outcomes. The Mozambican identity papers officially make the immigrants invisible *as Zimbabweans*, but provide them with civil rights as Mozambican citizens. While local people will know they are 'really Zimbabwean', their new identities officially make them part of the local population in Manica Province. This also means they cannot, any more, be registered or counted as Zimbabwean immigrants, even if Mozambican central authorities should want to redefine their policy of 'invisibility', and in the future should wish to make the Zimbabweans into a *visible* political issue.

Notes

1   As author of this chapter, I express my sincere gratitude to all my informants in Manica Province, Mozambique. I was impressed by your trust when giving personal and sensitive information. In particular I must thank a few people who in many ways facilitated my research without ever asking for any compensation. For reasons more thoroughly explained in the text, their identities are not revealed here.

2   On debates about the 'Zimbabwe issue' in the Mozambican press in 2008, see Chapter 2.

3   Allina-Pisano (2003: 61) describes cross-border movements already in the first decade of the 21st century as generally reflecting 'strategic decision-making on the part of Africans who faced a choice between British and Portuguese administrations' and their respective demands on African labour when analyzing movements from British territory into Manica in the period 1904-08. Hughes (2003) analyzes how people seeking refuge from civil war and droughts in Mozambique in the 1980s

sought to negotiate access to land for cultivation across the border in Zimbabwe. Tornimbeni (2007) provides an interesting interpretation of the interplay of national policies and the local control exercised by traditional leaders on both sides of the Mozambique/Zimbabwe border.

4 Funding for this fieldwork war provided by the Research Council of Norway, through the programme 'Poverty and Peace'.

5 Hammar's analyses are further developed in Chapter 4 of this volume.

6 In Chapter 5, Bolding gives a detailed account of various individual experiences, focusing on people now settled very close to the border on the Mozambican side.

7 Polzer and Hammond (2008: 421) has a definition of the concept of *invisibility* which in this context refers to 'a relationship between those who have the power to see or to choose not to see, and… those who lack the power to demand to be seen'.

8 Forced Migration Studies Programme (FMSP), Wits University, South Africa.

9 In September 2009, ZIMOSA – an organization for Zimbabweans in Mozambique – carried out a study seeking to indentify Zimbabwean migrants in all ten provinces of Mozambique. The total number identified in the course of two weeks was around 3,600, of which a majority (55 per cent) was encountered in Manica Province (ZIMOSA, 2009).

10 See also Chapter 2, this volume.

11 A striking contrast emerges from the material presented in Chapters 6 to 8 of this volume concerning the situation of Zimbabweans crossing the border into South Africa.

12 See also Chapter 6.

13 For a different perspective focusing on the historical legacy of violence as punishment in southern Africa, see Alexander and Kynoch (2011).

14 Author's translation from Portuguese.

15 In the Portuguese original: *Os estrangeiros praticam racismo.*

16 In the Shona term *murambatsvina*, the noun element *tsvina* means 'dirt', 'filth' or 'trash'. The name of this government operation has been translated as 'Clear the filth' (Human Rights Watch, 2005) or 'Clean up the filth' (Hammar et al., 2010), while the (official) translation used by the UN was 'Restore Order' (ICG, 2005: 1).

17 The distrastrous (natural) tsunami that affected the coasts of the Indian Ocean during Christmas 2004 also lent its name to the Zimbabwean government's 'sweeping' operation.

18 In the 1990s, the Mozambican repatriation programme administered by UNHCR promoted the return of an estimated 5.6 million internally displaced people and cross-border refugees (Hammar and Rodgers, 2008: 359).

19 These statistics are taken from the World Bank website: *WDI Online – World Development Indicators*. http://ddp-ext.worldbank.org/ext/DDPQQ (accessed 15 March 2010).

20 http://hdr.undp.org/en/statistics (accessed 25 November 2010). It is worth noting that 'Human security', one of the indicators in the HDI, only counts altogether

16,800 refugees from Zimbabwe. For number 168 on the HDI ranking list, the Democratic Republic of Congo, the indicator counts 368,000 refugees. Lack of data means that Somalia and the Democratic Republic of Korea, for example, are not ranked.

21 Zambia was ranked number 150 and South Africa as number 110 on the HDI list for 2010.

22 Duri (2010) and Pophiwa (2010) both describe the informal trading and transport of goods across the border, referring to it as 'smuggling'.

23 Source: Informant interview in Manica.

24 Cross-border traders would try to get US$, South African Rands (ZAR), or Mozambican Meticais (MZN) in order to avoid the escalating inflation rates of ZWD (Duri, 2010: 146).

25 Many of the traditional healers in the border provinces of Mozambique were refugees in Malawi or Zimbabwe during the war. While staying abroad they became possessed by 'foreign' or Christianised spirits, who are believed to assist *curandeiros* in the diagnosis of illnesses (Kaarhus and Rebelo, 2003: 12).

26 http: //www.sadc.int/archives/read/news/537 (accessed 28 February 2010).

27 Interview, 7 April 2009.

28 However, according to Kiwanuka and Monson (2009), and confirmed by UNHCR (2010), no Zimbabweans were officially recognized as *refugees* in Mozambique.

29 Sadza made from maize meal and cooked in oil was sold at 10 MZN i.e. at the time 0.30 US$.

30 At the time 50 MZN equalled approximately 1.5 US$ (with an exchange rate of 0.03). Ordinary rates known to be charged by Zimbabwean sex workers ranged from 30 to 50 MZN.

31 'Crise economica na terra de Mugabe: Prostitutas zimbabweanas assaltam Manica e Sofala', *SAVANA*, 2 November 2007.

32 Ibid.

33 Interview, 17 April 2009.

34 These percentages are based on the 1997 General Census in Mozambique.

35 ZIMOSA's study lists language as the 'biggest challenge which the migrants face in Mozambique' (2009: 29).

36 Based on an exchange rate of approximately 0.03 US$ to 1 MZN, Lily's monthly salary of 1,200 MZN equalled about 36 US$.

37 Madrinha is a main location associated with prostitution in Chimoio. It is a relatively new hotel, located at the ring road with ample space for parking, and surrounded by smaller shops and bars. The ring road steers the heavy traffic along the Beira Corridor, outside the city centre of Chimoio. From here, the road continues westward to Machipanda and Zimbabwe, with a branch heading northwards to the Province of Tete, and from there to Malawi.

38 In 1997, Mozambique was still in bottom position among the fourteen SADC countries (UNDP, 1999: 15).

4

Settling for Less?
Zimbabwean Farmers and Commercial Farming in Mozambique

Amanda Hammar

Introduction[1]

With the start of large-scale evictions on commercial farms in Zimbabwe from 2000 onwards, and a much wider series of political and economic crises, Mozambique's Manica Province (hereafter referred to as Manica[2]) along the central-west border with Zimbabwe became a preferred site of relocation for a relatively small yet not insignificant group of displaced white commercial farmers and other 'investors' searching for a secure future.[3] Even if it represented a somewhat circumscribed migratory 'wave' with mixed results, this uneven mix of displacees both faced and precipitated several changes and challenges in the various environments they came to occupy across the border from Zimbabwe. Their experiences of displacement, settlement and adaptation, and the responses of their differently positioned Mozambican hosts, have been documented in some detail elsewhere (Hammar, 2010). The present chapter revisits these issues, providing some updates as well as paying specific attention to the effects on the productivity of the farming community in Manica of the shifting policy environment in Mozambique.

The chapter draws on a combination of primary and secondary data sources. The empirical material that informs the arguments outlined here is grounded in numerous fieldwork encounters in Mozambique during the 2000s. To begin with, between 2003 and 2005 I was engaged in monitoring and further developing a programme of Swedish support for transboundary water resources management in the Pungwe River Basin, which stretches from Zimbabwe's eastern border to Mozambique's coastal city of Beira. This required intermittent visits to the area and numerous interviews with, among others, Mozambican officials at national, provincial and district levels in agencies related to water, agriculture, mining, environment and so on; international development agencies; private companies; and a range of local Mozambican stakeholders including commercial farmers, traditional leaders, and rural and urban traders, as well as the newly arrived Zimbabwean commercial farmers. Given their ambitions to expand commercial agriculture in the region, the Zimbabweans were explicitly concerned with the availability, access and affordability of future water supplies.

Even in those early days, they were making a visible mark in Manica. Their physical presence was evident not least in the increased number of farmers' pick-up trucks on the roads, and the growth in bars, restaurants and accommodation in Chimoio established by or frequented by these Zimbabweans, but also in the raised demand for goods and services that was positively affecting local businesses. My contact with the farmers and the changes observed in the area more generally during the initial period of their arrival began to generate a set of questions that were not part of my formal terms of reference at the time and therefore could not be explored during those visits. However, between 2006 and 2009 I was able to conduct several periods of fieldwork in Manica (and some shorter ones in Zimbabwe) as the basis of an independent research project that focused explicitly on the context, experience and effects of displacement of these same white Zimbabwean commercial farmers in Mozambique.[4] Although this research was initiated and located at the Nordic Africa Institute in Uppsala as part of a larger programme I co-ordinated on Political Economies of Displacement, it dovetailed neatly with the aims of the 'In the Shadow of a Conflict' research programme that was being developed at Noragric. Thereafter it became integrated into and partly supported by that programme.

The research included looking at the various ways in which these farmers reinvented themselves and developed new modes of living and livelihoods in Mozambique in a dramatically different social, cultural, political and economic environment from that which they had known previously. I was also interested in how their presence affected those amongst whom they had come to live, but equally how the terms set by Mozambican officialdom affected their possibilities for productive and settled lives. The present chapter is divided into two main sections that focus respectively on two phases of the Zimbabweans' move to Manica: the initial period of exploration of the options they found there, in which new routes to an alternative future – or just a liveable present – were being tested; and a later period in which the weight of the challenges they had to confront – especially production challenges and business failures – would eventually lead many, though not all, of the migrant farmers to leave.

Zimbabwean Commercial Farmers in Manica

This section explores why the Zimbabwean farmers moved to Manica in Mozambique in the early 2000s, and some of the conditions they were faced with in trying to establish themselves there.

Moving to Manica

In the face of the violence, loss and uncertainty that the majority of white farmers in Zimbabwe were experiencing during the land invasions and Fast Track Land Reform programme that began in the early 2000s, the initial and ultimately futile hope amongst many was that eventually the 'madness' of *jambanja*[5] would subside, farms could be recovered, and 'order' – that is, the familiar order of the previous legal and administrative frameworks – would be resumed. Many of the evicted farmers (eventually numbering close to 4,200 out of approximately 4,500 prior to the start of the invasions) preferred to remain in Zimbabwe, or did not have the means to relocate elsewhere.[6] Among those that stayed, some tried fighting it out on the farms themselves (Hughes, 2010), others in the courts.[7] Some tried to find ways to remain connected to farming by other means. This included: leasing land from new black farmers to continue producing crops; acting as managers or advisors to new farmers, or in some cases even becoming silent partners in commercial farming enterprises; and leasing out the farm equipment that they had managed to salvage from their farms during eviction (not always the case) to new individual or collective farming enterprises.[8] Others sought alternative ways of making a living in town by setting up transport or engineering businesses, establishing agricultural or even financial advisory services of various kinds, or trading in whatever it was possible to trade in during the country's ever worsening economic crisis.[9] Others opened shops or tea gardens or galleries.

But especially in the early 2000s, with the farm invasions and evictions so fresh, widespread political violence on the increase, and the sense of loss and uncertainty so strong, some saw their only chance of sustaining themselves and their families as being to move elsewhere in the southern Africa region or in some cases even further afield.[10] This was certainly the strategy of millions of impoverished and/or politically persecuted black Zimbabweans who saw no option but to cross Zimbabwe's borders in order to survive, as well as of a much smaller group of better educated and better resourced professionals, many of whom have managed to find relatively good positions in the region.[11] Specifically with regard to the evicted white farmers, as well as some whites whose businesses had depended on a viable commercial agricultural sector such as those involved in agricultural supplies, they were in desperate need of finding land, livelihoods and personal security that was no longer available to them in Zimbabwe.

Mozambique was far from the preferred destination at the time.[12] Language was a concern (few spoke Portuguese, although the common indigenous use of Shona on both sides of the border helped). They also had to contend with cultural barriers, an unfamiliar and convoluted legal and administrative system, and an alien social and political environment. In addition many Zimbabweans, both white and black, held stereotyped notions of Mozambique's comparative lack of development and its 'disorder' relative to Zimbabwe.[13] A certain sense of disjuncture marked the early experiences of many of the new migrants, both the white farmers, and various black Zimbabwean migrants as Kaarhus has noted (Chapter 3, this volume). Specifically among the white farmers, my interviews and observations revealed a constant grappling with the mismatch between the order they claim to have known – and now missed – in Zimbabwe, and the disorder they experienced, perceived and projected onto multiple domains of life and work in Mozambique.[14] Nonetheless, Mozambique represented one of the few viable options to pursue.

An exact or stable number of those farmers who settled in Manica was never easy to confirm as there were a variety of often spontaneous and often untraceable ways over time in which people arrived, stayed, commuted, reorganized and/or eventually left the area. Some came as individuals, some as families, and many as part of business syndicates. Some came permanently or were there full-time for a period; others were only ever there temporarily or part-time. Some came without any of their own resources. Some invested what little they had salvaged from Zimbabwe either as deposits within larger enterprises or as capital in their own new businesses, while others were there as resident employees or on various contracts with multinational companies. In all, an estimated eighty or so 'entities' (single or collective) would attempt to settle in some way in the area during the first half of the 2000s.[15]

Despite reservations about such a move, one of Manica's key attractions was its proximity to Zimbabwe, which allowed relatively easy movement back and forth across the border. In a number of cases, husbands came to work in Mozambique either on their own or as part of the above-mentioned syndicates or through other kinds of business partnerships, while their wives and children stayed in Zimbabwe. Some of the farmers were working plots far into the bush where they struggled with poor access roads, very rudimentary living conditions and often quite basic incomes for months if not years, and felt it unsuitable to bring their families with them. One person working on contract as an agronomist to another farmer trying to start a market garden operation that ultimately failed, described living in a tent for over a year while his wife remained just across the border in Zimbabwe, living a rather precarious existence herself. Another I interviewed who was part of a syndicate trying to grow tobacco, spoke of how the group lived in caravans and a makeshift campsite for over eight months as they cleared and planted the lands. Eventually he decided to leave and move to England where his wife was able to find a teaching job while he retrained in computer technology.

Either way, the relatively well-maintained main national road between Manica's provincial capital, Chimoio, and Zimbabwe's border town, Mutare, 80 kms away, was an important life-line that facilitated a necessary straddling strategy between the two countries. In the face of the perceived financial and legal-political precariousness for the farmers in Mozambique, one key reason to maintain a base in Zimbabwe was the partial insurance provided by wives working or sustaining businesses where this was feasible in the increasingly collapsing economy. In addition, schooling remained better in Zimbabwe, although by the mid-2000s, a private English-speaking school (Njerenje) was established by Zimbabweans just outside Chimoio. This provided local options for 'Zimbabwe-style' education for those who could afford it.[16]

Another key factor initially drawing people to Manica Province was the proclaimed availability of agricultural land.[17] Significantly, this was land located in seemingly similar topographical and climatic conditions, although subtle differences about which there was insufficient knowledge both amongst farmers and investors, would subsequently impact negatively on production. (See Sjaastad et al., in Chapter 12 regarding this latter issue of environmental familiarity as an important draw also for those moving to Mkushi Block in Zambia). At the time, Manica was viewed officially as land abundant, and the Mozambique government was willing to offer plots to the Zimbabwean farmers (for *lease* only, according to Mozambique's Land Law) although not exceeding 1,000 ha.[18] Actual occupation and use of such plots was furthermore conditional on following legally prescribed consultation processes with local communities.

All the farmers I met with, as well as provincial agricultural staff, confirmed that some kind of related procedure was followed. An average of two if not more consultation meetings were said to have taken place per plot, and various forms of 'compensation' paid, although it was hard to establish precisely to whom this was paid and who actually benefitted. In at least one case a farmer noted that there had been a meeting only with a chief and his assistants, with no larger community in sight. On a more general level, prescribed 'community consultations' always need to be viewed sceptically in terms of situated political economies. At the very least, one needs to take into account the unevenness of resource control and political voice amongst local leaders and elites on the one hand and more vulnerable community members on the other, and of clearly differentiated social environments, as well as the pressures exerted by both national and local bureaucrats asserting various institutional interests.[19] But while a relevant topic for deeper investigation, this was not a primary area of my research. Suffice it to say that while some small tensions and disputes did arise, no *major* contestations erupted over local land allocations to the white farmers I engaged with in Manica during my research.

Perhaps this was due to the fact that few, if any of them, ever worked areas much larger than 30 to 50 ha (in some cases it was close to 100 ha) given their limited finances and capacity. By contrast, various land conflicts arose in relation to larger-scale land-based enterprises in Manica such as the IFLOMA forestry plantation and timber company (Durang and Tanner, 2004). Scale is a key, if not solitary, factor in such contexts. This has become evident with the intensification of the land- and 'green-grabbing' debates since the late 2000s, linked to the emergence of the global energy and food crises. Mozambique features in these debates in terms of an increasing number of large-scale land concessions being given and considered for biofuel and agrifoods production.[20]

Besides the circumscribed allocation of plots to the Zimbabwe farmers, the Mozambique government also placed clear limits on the potential concentration of the foreigners in any single area. (This could be compared with the emerging patterns of informal settling of black Zimbabweans – or 'returnee' Mozambicans – in the border regions that Bolding discusses in Chapter 11.) Alongside the memory of Portuguese colonial agrarian settlement in Mozambique, and the long history of racialized land relations in neighbouring Zimbabwe, a more recent negative experience in Mozambique's Niassa Province in the 1990s with a cluster of white Afrikaner farmers from South Africa, made the Mozambicans understandably wary of exclusive white/foreign enclaves.[21]

The idea for a large settlement programme for white Zimbabwean farmers in Manica was in fact proposed in the very early 2000s by a Zimbabwe-based company called Southern Technical Services (STS). STS was among the first companies to recognize the opportunity that Manica offered in the face of the Zimbabwe crisis. It envisaged a 'win-win' situation in which the displacement of white commercial farmers in Zimbabwe and their losses as well as the general decline, especially in tobacco production, on the one side of the border could become gains for a range of actors on the other side of the border. It estimated that these same farmers' expertise and circumstantial, displacement-generated availability could be combined with Mozambique's apparent land availability and under-development, to initiate productive investment in Mozambique that would be to everyone's benefit. At least this was the spin that STS put on its promotion to Zimbabwean farmers, who were actively recruited and encouraged by the company to commit themselves to a stake in the grand vision that STS was attempting to create in Manica.

STS had developed an ambitious, multifaceted strategic plan for a large-scale settlement of Zimbabwe farmers in the Catandica area of Barué District, located along the main route between the provincial capitals of Manica and Tete Provinces, (see Map 2, Chapter 3). With very detailed delineation of plots and other aspects of production, processing, and storage on well-drawn technical diagrams and maps, it reflected a rather old-style form of modernization. The anticipated motor of change was to be the assumed capacities and other resources of the displaced Zimbabwean farmers, undergirded by substantial external funding being sought from the World Bank and other international funding sources. All this would be harnessed to establish not only extensive commercial agriculture (with job creation and other technical and economic off-shoots), but also schools and health facilities and even an agriculture-oriented university. What such a scheme represented and what may well have contributed to so many farmers being convinced to sign up with the company was not only the prospect of future livelihoods in Mozambique after losing their farms and incomes in Zimbabwe. There is a sense that in the face of their displaced and increasingly disordered lifeworlds, it seemed to represent the possibility of ordered and legible systems and spaces of production that could be 'read' according to once-familiar and more predictable codes.

STS claimed to have made numerous attempts to raise international capital for the project, and while doing so solicited deposits of up to several thousand US dollars from a number of the Zimbabwe farmers who expressed interest. Among those I interviewed both in Mozambique and in Zimbabwe, at least one third had in fact been persuaded to make such an investment in the hope of establishing themselves anew. Most had travelled to Mozambique with an STS representative and been shown potential lands. But in the end it all came to nothing. Not only were the international loans not forthcoming, but the Mozambique government clearly rejected this type of 'colonizing' enterprise, while not being averse to farmers migrating to Mozambique as individual investors. For those farmers taken in by the STS vision, all their deposits were forfeited and yet another loss incurred with much resentment generated.[22] Yet indirectly, the initiative had the effect of prompting a keen interest amongst some farmers, enough to get them to cross the border to investigate the prospects and implications of moving to Manica.

Initial optimism

Leaving aside the failures of STS, its vision was not in itself entirely misjudged. In fact there were other companies in the early 2000s that were reading the opportunities similarly, and the Mozambique government itself was exhibiting a clear if cautious welcome to the Zimbabwe farmers. With STS itself out of the picture and most individuals having very little if any of their own resources left to invest, many of the farmers found themselves being wooed by Mozambique Leaf Tobacco (MLT), the Mozambican satellite of a large transnational merchant tobacco company.[23] MLT had seen commercial production of high-end, good quality Virginia tobacco fall dramatically in Zimbabwe as the crisis there intensified, and it was hoping to recover production levels by supporting migrant Zimbabwean farmers in Manica. The company was already well established in Mozambique, mainly in Tete Province further to the north, producing lower-value Burley tobacco through a vast out-grower scheme[24] (this had approximately 35,000 growers by the late 2000s), and was starting something similar in Manica. But it wanted to establish a commercial front for production both of higher-grade and larger yields of the crop. The assumption was that the commercial growing expertise of the Zimbabwean farmers, under seemingly comparable climatic and soil conditions in Manica, would produce the same, or similar, world-class tobacco.

The company's expectations were rather high, yet little time or investment went into research and development for what was in reality a rather different environment, ranging from basic natural growing conditions, to levels of critical infrastructure, to various production input costs, to the status of policy and political support. In addition, MLT's financing framework, while seemingly generous to begin with, had an unrealistically short-term perspective, contrasting with the long-term (independent) agricultural financing common in Zimbabwe. Eventually, the blind spots and very real constraints would emerge, and disappointment on both sides would erupt into serious conflicts, but these issues were not anticipated when the contracts were signed. For the farmers, the MLT opportunity appeared to be a lifeline that would not only enable them to access resources and begin earning a living, but would allow them to get back to farming, a profoundly personal desire in itself that many emphasized. As an example, although subsequent events changed his mind, one of MLT's initial contract farmers whom I interviewed in Chimoio – a man with decades of farming experience who had lost his farm as had his brothers and sons – spoke about how at first the company gave him and his family 'a second chance'.[25]

> I must admit, you know MLT helped us a lot. For us it was a second chance. To start from nothing again, from nothing. And me and my two sons, we really worked, seven days a week from six until six. And we were very successful with that. Very, very successful. Even we were so thankful that we gave MLT a thank-you card, for giving us a second chance.[26]

Key to the uptake of contracts with MLT was the problem of finance in Mozambique, primarily the *lack* of it. Unlike Zimbabwe, Mozambique had no history of commercial agricultural banks. So that even if land was being made available (conditioned by the provisions of the Land Law) to the incoming Zimbabweans to lease, there were no affordable loans available with which to develop it. This situation had long retarded the expansion of medium- to large-scale commercial agriculture in Mozambique, even in suitable land abundant areas like Manica.[27] For the migrant Zimbabwean farmers evicted from their farms, having lost the collateral that had previously been the basis for agricultural financing in Zimbabwe, there were now simply no private or public financing options to speak of.[28] MLT's offer therefore provided many with their only chance to begin anew in Mozambique. Consequently, the Zimbabweans were more than willing to take up this opportunity despite the contracts having uncomfortably restrictive binding conditions and unrealistic short-term production expectations. Again, this was in sharp contrast to the kinds of long-term loans from agricultural banks in Zimbabwe, grounded in an understanding of the inevitable fluctuations and need for an extended time perspective in farming. At the same time, there was a clear conflict of interest inherent in having a tobacco merchant company (MLT) lending to farmers on the one hand, while controlling grading levels and crop prices on the other.[29]

Yet not all the Zimbabwean farmers were bound into dependent contracts with MLT. A few did have some limited resources of their own to invest, or they managed to raise sufficient external loans to start small, independent farming businesses or become part of larger partnerships, while others established related agro-enterprises in or close to the provincial capital, Chimoio. Some of the more significant yet still fairly modest farming enterprises involving Zimbabweans alone or in partnerships with various forms of external investors (whose fate shall be discussed briefly later), included a paprika trading company that contracted several of the migrant commercial farmers as well as thousands of peasant contractors on small family plots;[30] several specialised flower growing companies (one growing roses, and another proteas); a company that focused on horticultural crops – that again included peasant out-growers in this case organized in group schemes – which also established a local packing factory; and a dairy farm with a cheese-making factory, the first of its kind in Mozambique. The inclusion of export-oriented agro-processing in several of these enterprises meant added jobs as well as added value.

Others were far less well-resourced but still wanted to be independent of MLT, and this often meant trying out numerous farming options before either giving up and leaving or finding one that worked well enough to allow them to stay and build a future. One young couple, for example, tried growing tobacco then cabbages then potatoes, none of which succeeded. Eventually they tried pig farming, and after a few initially tough years where they were barely able to pay themselves any salary at all, they managed to build up a very successful enterprise.

Indeed, despite start-up difficulties on all fronts – bureaucratic, technical, physical, financial, social – at least up until 2005, there was an optimism about new opportunities that made the inevitably hard work seem worth it. The signs of an emerging space of enterprise and productivity in Manica in general were very positive. In addition to the indicators of growth mentioned earlier in the urban settings, in the countryside land was being cleared, crops were being planted, jobs were being created, and in some areas out-grower schemes were being established. Linked specifically to the expansion in agriculture, new seed and other agro-supply companies were being established and building companies and various engineering services were also emerging.

At the same time, the Zimbabweans established their own association which they called Associação Comercio, Industria e Agricultura Investidores de Manica (ACIAIM). This provided a platform for practical information, mutual support and government lobbying especially but not only for farmers, as well as a space for socializing and general networking. This was much in the mode of the local branches of Zimbabwe's national Commercial Farmers Union (CFU). However, by 2007 this had to be disbanded due to political pressure. The argument was that it was excluding Mozambicans (by default, since all meetings were held in English) and that its continuity reinforced the lack of integration of the white Zimbabwean community into local Mozambican society. But for the first few years, it was an important site of cohesion and belonging for the rather fragmented white Zimbabwean community in Manica,[31] and many felt its absence when it shut down. Only a few of the Zimbabwean farmers subsequently joined the more general Manica business association, which held its meetings only in Portuguese, while others preferred to become members of the neighbouring Sofala Province business association that operated a bilingual service.

While few of the farmers themselves were accumulating much in the way of wealth especially in the early years, money was circulating in general and both agricultural and urban jobs were being created. The mushrooming of new producers, markets and services in Manica both stimulated and challenged local Mozambican commercial farmers in the area[32] who had been operating at generally lower and less predictable levels for some time, albeit with some exceptions. All in all, these developments led some observers to think in terms of a 'boom' in the area (Hanlon and Smart, 2008). On the other hand, according to one cynical Zimbabwean in Manica reflecting back on this period, it was a 'false boom' at best: 'A boom means someone makes a profit. But no-one was making any money.'[33]

It is important to emphasize here, however, that what was crucial in the early stages of the Zimbabwean farmers' arrival was the welcome offered by the Mozambique government, an irony difficult to ignore at the time. While white commercial farmers in Zimbabwe were being displaced in the name of ZANU-PF's project of radical land redistribution, in Mozambique – even if only tentatively – these same farmers were being recognized as a resource for helping to kick-start commercial agriculture and contribute to economic growth in an era of increasing liberalization in Mozambique, or so it seemed. By all accounts, the Provincial Governor of Manica in office during the early 2000s was particularly positive and supportive, often visiting the farmers and trying to address the numerous problems they confronted. Even if there was a notable lack of policy coherence or support from the national level, farmers uniformly spoke very highly of the ways in which the Governor would take their concerns seriously and try to find workable local solutions to a range of practical and political barriers to progress. This might include trying to speed up disruptively long bureaucratic delays in processing permits, or curtailing the imposition of exaggerated – and unaffordable – fines by various local officials for minor by-law infractions.

Perhaps more than practically helpful, these gestures of assistance were symbolically significant for the farmers whose experiences of political and economic displacement in Zimbabwe, and continuing levels of uncertainty in Mozambique, left them feeling vulnerable. However, the subsequent marked shift away from this positive (perhaps mostly personal) support from the Governor following the 2004 change in FRELIMO national leadership – that translated into related changes in the provincial level leadership – would noticeably alter conditions for the farmers for the worse, a point to which I shall return in more detail later. This would reinforce several other factors that by the mid-2000s would undermine the anticipated trajectory of agricultural development in Manica. Some of the key factors are discussed in the following section.

Challenges of Production

A combination of internal and external dynamics contributed to a reversal in the trajectory of modest yet significant local growth originally witnessed with the arrival of the Zimbabwean farmers in Manica. This section explores some of the challenges they encountered, particularly with respect to production and sustainability.

Companies, contracts and conflicts

As already hinted at, the relationship between MLT and the majority of farmers they signed up proved far more complicated and messy than either party had anticipated, leading to bitter legal and personal wrangles. Most critical were disagreements over the crop prices paid by MLT to the farmers. A number of those interviewed, including the grateful farmer quoted earlier, could recount from memory the specific figures they had been guaranteed for each season, and the much lower figures that they were actually paid by MLT, in some cases due to what the farmers considered questionable and unfair adjustments to leaf-grading criteria. According to MLT – who remained difficult to interview formally about this matter – at least some of the farmers they had contracted were viewed as either 'incompetent' or 'charlatans'. They were represented as failing to fulfil their side of the agreements, and allegations were made of loans being used for 'personal luxuries' rather than for farming operations.

Ultimately, even after several seasons of successful crop output, most of the farmers were unable to cover even their basic input and labour costs, let alone repay capital and equipment loans to MLT. Those that had used their own fragile savings to supplement company loans – as the once-hopeful 'second chance' farmer quoted earlier had done – not only went into additional debt and had the continuous threat of long-delayed court cases hanging over their heads, but they also suffered deep psychological strain. As we sat in a noisy café in Chimoio, the farmer in question described being forced to let the entire 90 acres of 'a beautiful crop' rot in the ground because of the dispute with MLT. In an emotional recounting of the story, this sun-burnished, robust man of 60 had to stop to regain his composure. Then he continued:

> The hardest part for me was to see the crop growing out and then everyday to see it all getting destroyed. It was... it was just.... I just want to survive. I don't know what these guys intended with what they put in the contract to pay me. And why do they have to punish me, and for my people that works for me. Why the punishment? I told them they gonna destroy me and they did.[34]

As with many others who shared their stories in interviews, these narratives revealed multiple layers of lives undone. On the other hand, depending on how recent or severe the latest economic or emotional knock had been, most demonstrated some level of optimism or at least resolve to keep going.

By 2006, the scale of misunderstandings and incompatibilities between MLT and their contracted farmers had resulted in an almost complete cessation of the company's larger-scale commercial farming venture in Manica.[35] Yet problems also surfaced with many of the other enterprises. Counter-accusations of crime and betrayal were expressed by the various interested parties in many of the ventures mentioned previously. There is no space here to detail the fate of each. To summarize, the paprika company (Hyveld Limitada Paprika) faced similar contractual conflicts and legal battles with commercial farmers, as did MLT, which together with falling global paprika prices in the mid-2000s led to its demise in Manica. Similarly, the rose exporting company (Vilmar Investmentos Lda) eventually closed down, embroiled in various cross-allegations among partners, employees and investors regarding poor management, technical incompetence and fraudulent financing practices.[36] By contrast, the horticultural company started by Zimbabweans (Companhia De Vanduzi) has flourished. However, the original Zimbabwean owners were (forcibly, according to them) bought out by British-based investors, although the company is now owned by a South African-based multinational company, Mozfoods S.A. It has since invested in an expansion that has boosted exports of fresh produce to South Africa and Europe and increased the employment of local labour.[37]

In addition to the legal battles mentioned above between farmers and companies, a number of other 'external' factors had combined by 2006 to undermine the viability of many of the Zimbabwe-run farms and other enterprises and to force a significant proportion of the original white migrants to give up and leave Manica. These factors included slumps in global commodity prices for key crops (especially tobacco and paprika) and negative shifts in international exchange rates, which combined with the lack and/or high cost of loan finance in general. In addition, worsening political and economic conditions in Zimbabwe especially by the mid-2000s affected costs and availability of farm inputs needed in Manica. Besides this, one cannot discount the reality that not all those who came to farm were in fact skilled farmers and that there were some who were chancing their luck in the face of devastating losses in Zimbabwe. In other words, a degree of failure needs to be attributed to the lack of capacity among some of those who came, and the fact that the kinds of safety nets that may have cushioned them in a different era in Zimbabwe had entirely vanished.

Yet even as the initial optimism faded and the so-called boom in Manica disintegrated, not all left Mozambique. My rough estimate is that between a quarter and a third remained. Of those who stayed, some who had originally started off with MLT as well as the more financially independent farmers, explored several alternative directions with greater or lesser success. What is critical to reiterate at this stage, is that besides the factors mentioned above, there were also serious production constraints reinforced if not produced by the increasingly unsupportive policy and political environment.[38] It is this aspect of the situation of migrant Zimbabwean commercial farmers in Manica to which the discussion now turns.

Official constraints to production

Similar kinds of production challenges as discussed here face agricultural producers everywhere, including elsewhere in Mozambique (Kaarhus and Woodhouse, 2012). However, under more stable conditions, and with relevant political and policy support, more affordable loan finance, and more predictable costs of production, some of these challenges may have been weathered more effectively. But the reality for the Zimbabwean farmers in Manica – particularly after the change in FRELIMO leadership in 2004 – was quite pointedly an *un*supportive government position, and this exacerbated other more immediate and ongoing production constraints. These more generic constraints – affecting all commercial farmers in the country, not just the new arrivals – were repeatedly identified by the Zimbabwean farmers and reinforced by comments from local Mozambicans, as including: the excessively high costs of fuel and of transport in general (given Manica's underdeveloped road infrastructure); the unaffordable costs of connecting to the electricity grid, the high price of inputs such as seeds and fertilizer, and the high cost of labour (higher in Mozambique than elsewhere in the region).

In addition, the Zimbabwean farmers complained about the high taxes and excessive local bureaucratic fines and harassment they were constantly confronted with, that also entailed endless hours attending to associated bureaucratic processes or legal proceedings. It seemed clear from the lack of intervention by the authorities especially after 2004 that the central state was reluctant to interrupt or curtail such rent-seeking opportunities and practices at local levels. These were seen by some local observers as constituting an approved form of salary subsidy by the centre, and a way to ensure party loyalty to FRELIMO in the provinces and districts. Such rent-seeking and stalling practices at both local and national levels are widely recognized as posing a serious constraint to doing business in Mozambique in general. Citing an International Finance Corporation (1996) study of administrative barriers to investment in Mozambique, Cramer (2001:84) notes that a 'great deal of regulation in a country like Mozambique does constrain the individual and 'red tape' is a genuine bane of entrepreneurial activity'.

Returning to the problem of high input and production costs, these are commonly faced by farmers operating in marginal regions elsewhere, with governments paying more or less attention to these concerns. In the Manica context of the mid-2000s, one might argue that many of these problems could have been partially resolved or their detrimental effects reduced with positive and creative intervention by the Mozambique government, at least to the extent of providing some temporary relief and creating more conducive conditions for greater viability. Thus for example, certain phased tax exemptions and targeted subsidies, say for electricity, might well have been considered in the start-up period when the Zimbabwean farmers began to arrive (and simultaneously provided to interested Mozambican farmers), much as they were in the Nigerian state of Kwara, which directly supported Zimbabwean farmers who migrated there in the mid-2000s (Mustapha, 2011).[39] This kind of support could have been eased out later as farmers became more established. Interestingly, this may have actually begun to happen to some extent. In a recent initiative to stimulate agricultural development in the larger Beira Corridor region,[40] an internal notice was circulated in late 2011 to members of the interim Beira Corridor Fruit and Nut Producers Group advising them that 'agricultural producers are entitled to apply to EDM [the Mozambique electricity supply parastatal] for a discount'.[41]

The lack of government support contrasted with the experience across the border where both the Rhodesian and post-colonial Zimbabwean state preferentially supported white commercial farmers for decades. While highly problematic in terms of having sustained a dualistic land system defined by crudely skewed race, class and gender patterns of exclusion – that underpinned both the national liberation war in the 1960s and 70s and the post-2000 land invasions – one effect was the creation of a sophisticated, export-oriented commercial agricultural sector that was key to the national economy. (This is not to forget that the peasant sector in Zimbabwe was key to domestic food security especially with respect to maize production, and in addition was always central to national cotton production.) Clearly there is no suggestion here to reproduce a similarly distorted regime in Manica. Rather it is to flag how the absence of meaningful support contributed to otherwise potentially avoidable failures in agricultural development, with consequences not only for the migrant farmers themselves but for many others in the area. In particular, this reversed notable growth in the agricultural sector that was invigorating the local rural as well as urban economies in various ways.

Especially critical in the early period was job creation.[42] One farmer noted how when they began clearing the lands in the bush, even without advertising for labour at least ten new people per day would appear, often walking for hours to seek work. As several scholars have pointed out, rural wage labour in areas like Manica is highly significant for poverty reduction, especially for women (Sender et al., 2006; Cramer et al., 2008). Surplus labour supply of this kind in

Manica, however, did not mean that the farmers could circumvent strict labour laws which included adhering to minimum wage levels. This was enforced through periodic visits by bureaucrats, and as already noted, was one of the factors that the Zimbabwean farmers 'complained' about and that contributed to the high (and for most, unaffordable) production costs.

It was in the face of the dramatic reversal in the trajectory of these initially promising developments in Manica from late 2004 onwards that urgent appeals were made by representatives of the Zimbabwean farmers to the Mozambican government. A public presentation made to officials in Maputo in May 2006 spelled out very clearly what progress the farmers had initiated in Manica, and the major constraints that they saw as largely responsible for reversing this trajectory, which, if left unaddressed, would lead to further drops in production and further farm closures with continued job losses. To illustrate their argument, and to reinforce the idea of the farmers' indispensability, figures of the decline in production of key crops since the peak in 2004 – linked to the problems listed earlier in this section – were provided by Brendon Evans, then chairman of the subsequently abandoned ACIAIM in Manica Province:

- Hectares (ha) of tobacco grown commercially dropped from a peak of 1,650 ha down to 280 ha in 2005 (first having risen from 202 ha in 2001)
- Hectares of paprika dropped from 340 ha in 2005 to 30 ha in 2006
- Hectares of maize dropped from 900 ha in 2004 to 70 ha by 2006
- Farm employment dropped from a peak of 4,385 in 2004 to 2,245 in 2005 and then as low as 600 by 2006 (having risen from 885 in 2001).

Even if the total hectareage under commercial cultivation by the Zimbabwean farmers at the peak in 2004 was relatively low compared to commercial farming levels in pre-2000 Zimbabwe, it was a meaningful increase for this part of Mozambique and had, until then, looked likely to expand in the future. Yet despite the losses both to the farmers themselves and to local labour and market growth, the appeal was ignored.

Reflections on a Glaring Refusal

In making the appeal at the time, there was an implicit assumption made by the Zimbabweans that the decline in production and employment, and the detrimental effects on development in the area in general, would be of concern to the Mozambican government. According to the logic of many of the Zimbabwean farmers I interviewed, they had assumed that the government would be interested in optimising rather than wasting the opportunity for enhancing local development that the expansion of medium-scale agriculture in Manica could create. This had been their general experience from Zimbabwe prior to 2000. On one level such an assumption was reasonably well founded in principle. Mozambican government rhetoric by the mid-2000s – partly underpinned by aspects of the 1997 Land Law (de Wit, 2000; Marini, 2001), partly by the shift to privatization and market-based reforms since the 1990s (Pitcher, 2002; Cramer, 2001; Hanlon and Mosse, 2010; Sumich, 2010) – claimed that the country was gearing up towards a 'green revolution' that would contribute to poverty reduction in large part through expanding commercial agriculture. This envisaged positive spill-over effects on the *sector familiar*/family sector or peasant farming through commercialization at this level.

Various commentators have pointed to the striking mismatch between this emerging discourse and the very limited results in rural development and poverty reduction in practice (Hanlon, 2011). Among other explanations, some have connected this to historically over-simplified and somewhat contemptuous views of 'the peasantry' by the largely urban-biased FRELIMO elite (Cramer, 2006; Wuyts, 2001). This speaks to a much wider debate beyond the scope of this chapter. However, even more striking is the limited view or 'diagnostic' that the emphasis on the family sector represents. To date, agricultural policy as a whole has demonstrated little coherent analysis of the broader rural economic environment in terms of its connectivities and potentials in relation to a wider range of agricultural opportunities and options. As Phil Woodhouse (pers. comm.) helpfully points out:

> The most recent PARP (2012) and the strategic plan for agriculture (PEDSA) emphasise support to small-scale agriculture but omit any reference to medium or large-scale investment. The policy thus treats small-scale agriculture as disconnected from the contemporary processes of large-scale commercial investment. It is arguable that the small-scale focus is designed to bring Mozambique into line with the NEPAD policy on agriculture (CAADP) and thus gain credit with external funders. There is little in the policy that shows a clear understanding or commitment to supporting small-scale agriculture to exploit opportunities or overcome adverse trading conditions in 'actually-existing' agricultural markets in Mozambique.[43]

This is clearly part of the explanation of why the Mozambican government at the time so glaringly refused to consider the Zimbabwean farmers' concerns, despite clear evidence of their actual and potential contributions to growth in Manica that was much in line with emerging official policy on agricultural development. One dimension of this reluctance that needs to be considered, though by no means the only one, is related to the question of race. The historical memory of Portuguese settler colonialism in Mozambique, including in Manica itself cannot be discounted, nor can the various forms of dispossession created by colonial farming and brutal labour practices. To some extent this informed the government's categorical rejection of the STS proposal for a concentrated pioneer-type settlement of Zimbabweans in Catandica, as already noted.

At the same time, even if there was a general welcome of the Zimbabwean farmers in the early 2000s, one cannot ignore the long-standing (if partially declining) political alliances between FRELIMO and ZANU-PF, whereby the rhetoric of the latter during the 2000s was overtly anti-white farmer. In fact, according to one skeptical Mozambican entrepreneur in Chimoio who had a somewhat jaded view of FRELIMO based on his own experiences, the initial acceptance of the farmers by the Mozambican government was purely instrumental and predictably short-lived:

> When the Zimbabwean farmers first came in, the government [and here he tapped his shoulders, metaphorically signalling the 'chefs' with their imaginary epaulettes, AH] was interested in having them. They wanted their knowledge, their experience, their wealth. But after two or three years they wanted to get rid of them. Most of them don't like whites.... And in any case the chefs aren't interested in long-term development. They want what they can get now. [44]

Interestingly though, there has been what some might consider to be an inconsistency between the lack of support to the mostly individual white farmers on rather modest-sized farms, and the government's positive relationship with large foreign-owned agri-business companies (often staffed by white Zimbabweans) such as MLT. This has two interrelated analytical dimensions to it, linked on the one hand to FRELIMO's broad party interests, and on the other, to questions of party-connected elite accumulation.

In relation to the first dimension, there has been a clear intensification of 'Frelimo-ization' across the country since Guebuza assumed the presidency in 2004 (Sumich 2010). Connected to this, the FRELIMO party-state has demonstrated a reluctance to allow the development and accumulation of *independent* local capital (meaning, not tied to the party in some way) especially in a place like Manica.[45] Manica had previously been a stronghold of the opposition army then turned political party, RENAMO. In more recent years, with RENAMO's increasingly poor performance in elections since 1999, there have been hints at the emergence of more independent parties. In this context, independent domestic wealth accumulation by those without any particular loyalty to FRELIMO, which might have the potential to be directed towards supporting the political opposition, is certainly not welcome. As such, the party-state seems disinclined to cultivate the growth of smaller, independent entrepreneurs like the Zimbabwe farmers, whose loyalties and local alliances they could not entirely control or be sure of. But according to several local residents interviewed in Chimoio, this wariness and in some cases deliberate sabotage has applied even more so to independent Mozambican entrepreneurs than to outsiders.

The Zimbabweans themselves had no interest or intention to involve themselves in supporting alternative political parties in Mozambique (especially not after the backlash in Zimbabwe from supporting the opposition there). But neither were they keen to engage directly with FRELIMO itself. Several spoke of trying to 'stay out of politics altogether', much of which they equated with a tendency towards corruption. Nonetheless, there were often guarded comments made about 'being pragmatic', and in other ways having to accept 'becoming Mozambicanized' (Hammar, forthcoming) in order to survive in Mozambique. But as far as I could tell, few, if any, had succumbed directly to the pressures to 'buy' FRELIMO protection or support, and in their relative autonomy have still been able to survive and grow. This suggests that FRELIMO control is not absolute, nor is party-state backing necessarily a make-or-break condition for operating as a business, even though the challenges are perpetual. In fact, over time, one could even sense a grudging respect from the Mozambicans in general towards those who had stayed and seen things through, and who had not only managed (like other ordinary Mozambicans) largely on their own, but at the same time contributed to local development in a number of ways.

With regard to the second analytical dimension concerning party-related elite accumulation, a number of commentators have linked this process to direct shareholding or directorship deals between the FRELIMO elite and various foreign companies (Hanlon, 2011; Sumich, 2010). It is widely 'known', for example, that a member of President Guebuza's family has a share in MLT, which, to its credit, has substantially expanded out-grower tobacco production primarily in Tete Province and established a local processing plant there. Most of the Zimbabwean-run farms or businesses, however, are at a much smaller scale and perhaps less significant in this regard. And it seems scale does matter. In general, at least from the mid- to late 2000s, there has been a clear strategy in Mozambique of welcoming deals with large multinational companies investing in various biofuel and agro-foods megaprojects (Theting and Brekke, 2010; Kaarhus et al., 2010).

Notwithstanding the complex questions raised in the 'land grabbing' debate about large-scale concessions of this kind – but which seems to ignore the opportunities and challenges of middle-range farming operations as represented by the Zimbabweans in Manica – this could be read as part of FRELIMO's dual project of party-state control over key economic and environmental resources, and sustaining its hegemony. However, in addition, the presence and promise of such companies has contributed to private accumulation by the FRELIMO-allied elite. This fits with a broader picture that has been emerging over the past few decades of a partisan concentration of capital accumulation in very few hands in Mozambique (mostly allied to the 'FRELIMO family'), and the positive indicators of GDP growth in recent years in fact only benefitting the richest twenty per cent (Thaler, 2010).

What this appears to point to is growth without (much) poverty reduction, and accumulation without (much) redistribution. This reflects what Ferguson (2006) suggests is a global shift away from national development projects that benefit ordinary citizens, to projects that facilitate bureaucratic and party-controlled elite accumulation. This is clearly part of the unfolding Mozambican story and even the Manica story, partly explaining the overt lack of government support to the Zimbabwean farmers whose enterprises had in fact begun to stimulate local growth. But it does not constitute the whole story. Some of these trends may not be quite as total/izing in their form or effects as Ferguson's scenario implies. Several scholars, for example, have begun to read these practices somewhat differently, challenging more standard or simplistic critiques of corruption or (neo-)patrimonialism through conceptualizing and applying such terms as 'developmental patrimonialism' (Kelsall and Booth et al, 2010) or 'elite developmental capitalism' (Hanlon and Mosse, 2010). In the Mozambican setting, Hanlon and Mosse (2010) positively stress the strong national orientation and domestic investment focus of the Guebuza/FRELIMO accumulation strategy rather than the externalization of wealth that marks other regimes.

Either way, this general picture has had implications for the Zimbabweans who moved to Manica, and especially for those who were struggling to keep going in the mid-2000s. Yet as indicated below, the picture is not static. For those who managed to stay, things have begun to look a little brighter, albeit within limits.

Persisting against the odds

As already discussed, a relatively small number of Zimbabwean farmers continued to farm in Manica well after the so-called boom subsided and the exodus trickled to a halt, persisting against the odds. Most farmers that were contracted to MLT left. Of those independent farming enterprises mentioned earlier, only the dairy farm and cheese factory just outside Chimoio remains in the hands of the original Zimbabwean owners. With the help of Dutch public-private sector financing they are expanding into milk production (the first enterprise of its kind in Mozambique).

Several other ventures have since grown at a more modest and organic pace, such as the pig farm located in Sussundenga Distict, which has systematically increased production levels over the past five years. The young Zimbabwean couple running this have contracted smallholder soya producers in the vicinity and set up a soya processing plant for pig feed, and established a busy butchery in Chimoio together with older family members who moved to Manica in the mid-2000s after losing their farm in southern Zimbabwe. Another Zimbabwean has invested in a long-term tropical-fruit-growing project. At the same time he provides consultancy services to local initiatives in the commercial agricultural sector such as emerging specialist producer/commodity associations[46] and the regional Beira Agricultural Growth Corridor (BAGC),[47] as well as to various (mostly donor-funded) agricultural development programmes.

These latter kinds of activities in fact reflect a recent notable shift in policy orientation and actual political commitment by the party-state not only to the family sector but also to more middle-range commercial agriculture of the kind the Zimbabweans have been engaged in since they arrived (as compared with the large land concessions).[48] Not by chance, this has accompanied a related shift in direct donor support to the commercial agricultural sector which has been remarkably long in coming. During the early period of my research in Mozambique, I was struck by how little interest was expressed among key donors about the potential role of this kind of medium-scale commercial farming – whether undertaken by Zimbabweans or Mozambicans – in spite of evidence of its local growth and wider linkage effects being demonstrated in Manica (at least until 2006). There now seems to be much more attention to the potential of such a sector. There are several bilateral agencies beginning to actively support the

BAGC initiative, for example.

In this more open policy and funding environment, several new Zimbabwean-driven ventures have surfaced. Among these, one Zimbabwean ex-manager from MLT who had helped to develop its successful out-grower schemes but resigned from the company a long time back, has been adapting his extensive experience with contract tobacco production to develop an intensive out-grower programme. This has a combined commercial and developmentalist orientation and is fully consistent with Mozambique's new agricultural policy direction as well as initiatives supported by international organizations such as the Alliance for a Green Revolution in Africa (AGRA).[49] The company is hoping to raise both grant and loan capital from new funding scenarios arising in the area. The programme, outlined in a very detailed (and modernization-inflected) business plan, is aimed at 'smallholder household food security, with additional production of high value crops such as soya, cow peas, sesame and sugar beans which will serve as cash crops to increase household incomes'.[50]

While struggling against both serious personal health challenges and recurring loan set-backs and forms of corruption that continue to affect business in Mozambique, the particular migrant Zimbabwean behind this venture has retained an ongoing commitment to and productive investment in Manica since first arriving in 2001. Even though he and his wife retain social connections to friends and family in Zimbabwe – and in fact their home on the outskirts of Chimoio is a lively stop-over for friends travelling between Zimbabwe and the Mozambican coast for holidays – their lives and futures are clearly bound up with the future of Mozambique. As with the others mentioned above, and as with migrants or exiles anywhere, they are increasingly learning to adapt to local conditions. And even while they all continue to identify culturally and emotionally as 'Zimbabweans' and mostly hold Zimbabwean passports, the everyday context of their lives is slowly changing the meaning of this identity into something else: perhaps a form of hybrid white southern African.

Conclusion

Thinking about the particular Zimbabweans who stayed in Manica after things declined around 2005/6, raises broader questions about why and how some are able to stay and why others leave such places under such challenging conditions. There is no simple conclusion. The evidence suggests that multiple factors are at play both in general and in relation to individual cases of displacees who try and settle in new places.

Clearly, levels of economic and social vulnerability are key in terms of whether a particular individual, couple or larger family have any kind of financial resources to fall back on or social safety net that allows them to weather subsequent major losses after their original displacement and loss (as happened with many of the farmers in Manica whose relationships with MLT in particular fell apart, after having previously lost their farms in Zimbabwe). Yet this does not translate into any simplistic reproduction of the pattern of prior class differences amongst migrants.[51] Even though differentiation always exists to some extent within social groups, this can deepen or change under conditions of displacement and movement to new places. In the Manica situation, for example, differential levels of wealth or more basic financial security among the farmers depended partly on how or if farming profits in Zimbabwe (if there were any) had been invested or saved. If this had all been ploughed back into the farm itself, as it had for many, most of this was entirely lost following their evictions. If not, as in some cases, it meant there was some capital of their own to draw on and therefore some margin for manouevre in their new situations.

Another important factor is skill level and its appropriateness and adaptability to a new context. In Manica, this was not just about the obvious technical farming or business skills required, but the kinds of skills needed to deal with the legal complications and bureaucratic frustrations the migrants were constantly confronted with. Some were better equipped in this regard than others. In addition, age plays a critical role in terms of the level of risk that people are willing or able to take. In Manica, younger single men or women or couples who moved there, especially those who hadn't yet had children or who were just starting families, appeared to be more adaptable over longer periods to the very real hardships and uncertainties of the early arrivals. Many of those who stayed were in their thirties or early forties at most. They could envisage these trials as being limited in time, eventually giving way to a workable, perhaps even profitable future in Mozambique that they could no longer envisage for themselves or their families in Zimbabwe. In other words, they had the time to find out. It was more difficult for those from older generations, although a number of them stayed too, especially if they had invested their last savings in new ventures in Mozambique and couldn't afford to leave.

But undeniably there are also personal histories and personality traits that shape the ways in which different people deal with their individual and collective circumstances and the wider conditions of possibility they are faced with when displaced and forced to seek futures elsewhere. Having conducted detailed interviews with well over 40 migrants who stayed in Mozambique as well as almost a dozen who had left at various times, it was not possible to discount this dimension of human experience and expression alongside other structural, political and social factors that affected 'stay-ability'. Characteristics such as fortitude, determination, adaptability, optimism, openness to difference and change, humour – and their opposites – may not be easily measurable in social-scientific terms, but they are nonetheless part of what explains the variations in how people adapt to displacement and how they create settled lives in unforeseen places.

Notes

1   I would like to express my sincere appreciation here to Bill Derman and Randi Kaarhus in particular for inviting me into the programme and providing valuable support including, together with Espen Sjaastad and Phil Woodhouse, helpful critical comments on an earlier version of this paper.

2   Not to be confused with the town of the same name (Vila de Manica) which lies close to the Zimbabwe border.

3   At the same time, and increasingly through the 2000s, black Zimbabweans from both rural and urban areas began moving into Manica for similar reasons. Both Bolding and Kaarhus (this volume) address aspects of these parallel migrations. See also Duri (2009).

4   The research did not explore the position of farm workers or other employees of the farmers and other Zimbabwean 'investors'.

5   This is a chiShona word referring to chaos, but it gained common use in different settings to describe either what for some were anarchic invasions and their disruptive effects, and for others the bold radicalism of reclaiming the 'lost lands' for Zimbabwe's black majority.

6   On the fate and strategies of farm workers, hundreds of thousands of whom lost jobs, homes and broader security while others reshaped their lives on the former farms, see for example Magaramombe 2010. An estimated 7 to 8 per cent were allocated land in the Fast Track Land Reform programme (see Scoones et al, 2010). The conditions for Zimbabweans who became farm workers in South Africa, especially in Limpopo Province, close to the Zimbabwe border, are discussed in this volume by Zamchiya and Derman, as well as by Bolt (2010), Rutherford (2008), and Addison (2007).

7   The most prominent of these cases involved Ben Freeth and his father-in-law, who took their case to the SADC Tribunal. Freeth became a popular figure in the Western media, and was awarded an MBE (Member of the British Empire) in 2010 'for

services to the farming community in Zimbabwe'. See BBC interview with Freeth at http://www.youtube.com/watch?v=fRoXXEExqtc.

8　This is drawn from a range of scholarly and media sources over many years, but also from personal communication with former commercial farmers, both in Mozambique and Zimbabwe.

9　The Classifieds section of the Justice for Agriculture (JAG) electronic newsletter during the 2000s revealed a fascinating range of activities that (ex)farmers were engaged in to generate livelihoods.

10　Concerning the Zimbabwean farmers in Mukushi Block in Zambia, see Sjaastad, this volume. For a useful analysis of Zimbabwean farmers who moved to Nigeria, see Mustapha (2011).

11　For a sense of some of these movements in the region over the past decade, see contributions to the special issue of *Journal of Southern African Studies* (Vol. 36, No. 2, 2010) on 'The Zimbabwe Crisis Through the Lens of Displacement'. See also Crush and Tevera (2010); Kiwanuka and Monson (2009); Duri (2009), as well as chapters in this volume.

12　By contrast, Sjaastad et al. (this volume) note that Zambia was 'an obvious destination' for the Zimbabwean commercial farmers who moved to Mkushi Block due to a long history of farmer migration and similar climatic and environmental conditions. I would add to this other administrative as well as language commonalities inherent in Zambia's and Zimbabwe's shared British colonial histories, also including being part of the central African Federation of Northern and Southern Rhodesia and Nyasaland.

13　I have explored this notion of constructed distinctions between 'order' and 'disorder' in Zimbabwe and Mozambique respectively in Hammar (forthcoming), 'Becoming Mozambicanized'. See also Kaarhus, 'Poverty and Dignity', this volume.

14　Sjaastad et al. (this volume) note something similar – if limited – in Zambia with regard to the Zimbabwean farmers' surprise at the lack of organized water allocation systems that were a crucial element of catchment management and regulation systems in Zimbabwe's large-scale commercial farming areas.

15　A report produced by the Beira Agricultural Growth Corridor (BAGC) gives a figure of 112 farmers, 'mainly from Zimbabwe', having started farming in Manica from 2000. As already noted, this would not necessarily have translated into 112 actual enterprises as a number were established as syndicates or partnerships. The figure also seems to include an unspecified number of non-Zimbabweans. See: http://www.beiracorridor.com/documents/IBlow.pdf.

16　The school is still running despite the threat of closure when many of the Zimbabweans left in 2006/7.

17　36 million hectares of land in Mozambique (approximately 45 per cent) are considered suitable for agriculture, of which only 10 to 12 per cent is currently estimated to be under direct cultivation (Nhantumbo and Salomão, 2010: 14). Percentages and forms and concentrations of land occupation and use inevitably vary by province. Manica Province is broadly understood to be land abundant. Together with Sofala and Tete Provinces, it falls within the Beira Agriculture Growth Corridor (BAGC), and of the 230,000 square kilometres that make up this region there is an estimated 10 million ha of arable land. Of this, just under 23,000 ha are currently estimated to be under commercial cultivation of which around 22,000 belong to two large sugar plantations. Additionally, it has been noted that of total land under cultivation in Mozambique, 'agribusiness covers only three percent' (Borras Jr, Fig and Suárez, 2011: 215). The figure might be higher if considering land concessions allocated or mega-projects under application but not yet realized, as well as other enterprises possibly operational but not formally registered (see Kaarhus et al., 2010).

18 This contrasts strikingly with the scale of concessions that have been awarded to foreign companies for biofuel development in Mozambique in recent years (Borras Jr, Fig and Suárez, 2011), or even to companies like Mozambique Leaf Tobacco (MLT) for tobacco-growing, especially in Tete Province.

19 See Durang and Tanner (2004) for a useful discussion of the principles and realities of the community consultation and delimitation aspects of Mozambique's progressive 1997 Land Law. They evaluate a number of diverse cases (and varied outcomes) of such processes specifically in Manica Province itself, although none linked to the kinds of individual farm allocations of the farmers I was investigating.

20 On the land-grabbing debate in general, see for example Borras Jr., Hall, Scoones, White and Wolford (2011); de Schutter (2011); Vermeulen and Cotula (2010); Li (2011). Specifically on Mozambique, see Hanlon (2011); Borras Jr., Fig and Suárez (2011); Nhantumbo and Salomão (2010); Theting and Brekke (2010); and Kaarhus et al. (2010).

21 For a discussion of the Niassa experiment, which was a scheme agreed upon between the Mozambican and South African Governments, see Juergensen and Krugman (1997).

22 Numerous attempts to trace and contact STS throughout my research period were unsuccessful. My information was based only on the available documentation – which was primarily the STS project proposal and blueprint maps – and on statements concerning the affair from farmers interviewed in Mozambique and Zimbabwe.

23 There were other tobacco companies on the scene at that time, but MLT managed to muscle them out and retain a form of monopoly in the area. Unprovable yet widely circulating rumours suggested that this was possible due to vested interests of the President and FRELIMO elite in MLT.

24 See Little and Watts (1994) for a discussion of the pros and cons of contract farming in sub-Saharan Africa.

25 This interview and other material related to it in this section are drawn from Hammar (2010).

26 Interview, Chimoio, 18 May 2009.

27 See Kaarhus and Woodhouse (2012: 43-50), for a comprehensive discussion of the historical and evolving context of agricultural financing in Mozambique.

28 Only recently have some commercial agricultural financing options in Mozambique begun opening up (although all with high interest rates), alongside a few limited donor-funded, development-oriented grant and loan facilities mostly managed by non-governmental organizations.

29 In Zimbabwe, these aspects of the tobacco business were kept completely – and appropriately – separate.

30 Hanlon and Smart (2008: 27) put the figure at 3,000.

31 For more detail, see Hammar (2010).

32 Hanlon and Smart (2008: 32-3) have estimated there to be around 100 Mozambican 'small commercial farmers' in Manica, but make no distinction between them in terms of size of plots or scale of operation. Some they mention are only working two hectares, yet one would expect significant variations. There are also a number of larger-scale Mozambican commercial farmers (growing maize, potatoes, and other vegetable and fruit crops, as well as a large producer of fresh chicken) who are not discussed.

33 Interview, Chimoio, 20 May 2009.

34 Interview, Chimoio, 18 May 2009. On a subsequent visit to Chimoio in August 2010, I learned that this same man had passed away.

35 Only one of their original Zimbabwean commercial contractors continued to farm tobacco for them. However, they continued with the development of a smallholder, out-grower tobacco scheme for some years, similar to their operation in Tete, but eventually this too was closed down in the late 2000s.

36 A very personal account of events at Vilmar, including the loss of both salaries for themselves and for workers, and of the promise of a future (also told to me in an interview in Harare), was written as an open letter in 2006 by Zimbabwean farm manager Bryan Saunders and his wife Kathryn. This can be found at: http://www.google.dk/url?sa=t&rct=j&q=&esrc=s&source=web&cd=1&ved=0CFAQFjAA&url=http per cent3A per cent2F per cent2Fwww.open.ac.uk per cent2Ftechnology per cent2Fmozambique per cent2Fpics per cent2Fd70314.doc&ei=Ro_QT5-BJsf0-gbeuNCNDA&usg=AFQjCNECN6lEBx0WaXhYieKT4lSYnomWQg&sig2=nC4qoDu_NLlszx3rlW9kag.

37 In 2009 there were changes in management at Vanduzi, and at one point there were threats to close down, primarily because of the impossibly high costs of electricity. However, the company appears to have survived this and is still in operation.

38 This is not to say there was no support to any agricultural sector. See Buur (2011) for a detailed assessment of the range of political and bureaucratic measures of support to the sugar, cashew, fishery and poultry sectors, all, however, having a semi-industrial dimension. By contrast, Bolding (this volume) provides evidence of the self-generating, local agricultural 'revolution' amongst peasants at the edges of Manica

Province, on the border with Zimbabwe, which has emerged despite the complete absence of state support.

39 For decades both the Rhodesian and post-colonial Zimbabwean state preferentially supported white commercial farmers in Zimbabwe, stimulating an advanced – and highly advantaged and exclusive – commercial agricultural sector. The point here is not to suggest any similar preferential support – certainly not to Zimbabwean farmers specifically – but rather to flag how the absence of any meaningful support altogether resulted in avoidable failures, and to underscore the waste of an opportunity to stimulate more widely the development of medium-scale agriculture in an area that was/is clearly well suited for such purposes.

40 This has the current designation of Beira Agricultural Growth Corridor (BAGC).

41 Email correspondence from Monty Hunter, a Zimbabwean consultant to BAGC and a local fruit-grower himself, to members of the group, dated 11 November 2011. My thanks to Randi Kaarhus for sharing this.

42 See, for example, 'Zim farmers make work in Moz', News24 (SA), 13 January 2004; 'Resettled Zim farmers create 4000 jobs', *Business Day* (SA), 15 January 2004.

43 PARP stands for Plano de Accão para Reducão da Probeza. PEDSA stands for Plano Estratégico Para o Desenvolvimento do Sector Agrário (the Strategic Development Plan for the Agricultural Sector). The problems of policy incoherence in the agricultural sector are well outlined by Woodhouse in a forthcoming chapter entitled 'Agriculture, Poverty and the PARP Prescription' for *Desafios para Mocambique 2012*.

44 Interview, Chimoio, 3 October 2006.

45 My thanks to Lars Buur for this insight.

46 These are distinct from the national producer organizations of smaller-scale commercial growers, which, even if envisaged to link eventually with the larger-scale sector, are not part of the scope of this chapter. For a discussion of the small-scale sector and its organizations see Kaarhus and Woodhouse (2012).

47 See an outline of the initiative at: http://www.beiracorridor.com/documents/IBlow.pdf.

48 The most recent national agricultural policy – PEDSA 2011–2020 – underscores this direction. For a discussion of its main parameters see Kaarhus and Woodhouse (2012: 2-5). A Portuguese version of the policy document is available at: http://www.open.ac.uk/technology/mozambique/.

49 For AGRA's programmes in Mozambique see: http://www.agra-alliance.org/where-we-work/mozambique/.

50 This is part of the Mission Statement of a Zimbabwean-run company called Empresa de Comercialização Agricola, Lda (ECA), self-defined as a 'market-based extension company'. See 'Commercialization of Small Scale Agriculture', ECA Business Plan, August 2011.

51 See Selby (2006) with respect to historical differentiation amongst Zimbabwe's large-scale commercial farmers.

5

Reversing the Flows of People, Skills and Goods
Rural livelihood changes in central Mozambique

Alex Bolding, with Rodriguez Lino Piloto[1]

Introduction

The Manica miracle is over! The dreams of a commercial agriculture boom in Manica driven by foreign investment and foreign farmers have proved to be a mirage.[2]

Mozambique's much talked-about 'green revolution' cannot be simply providing a few inputs or even a range of new technologies. It requires radical changes to the entire agricultural value chain, new ways of thinking about rural development, a hugely increased role for the state, and large amounts of money.[3]

These quotes highlight some hidden aspects of the impact of the Zimbabwe crisis on central Mozambique. While many white farmers from Zimbabwe faced bankruptcy in 2006 (the end of the 'Manica miracle', see Chapter 4), the Mozambican government launched a 'Green Revolution' strategy for small-holder farmers, which was in turn criticised for its ineffectiveness and paucity. Simultaneously an invisible but widespread 'green revolution' was taking place in the mountainous border zone with Zimbabwe, riding on the back of an influx of cheap labour and skilled smallholder irrigators from Zimbabwean commercial farms. This chapter highlights what may prove to be one the few 'success stories' about the Zimbabwe crisis in the first decade of the 21st century; though also in this case, the relative success is mixed with conflict. The chapter examines increased agricultural production and creation of rural wealth by independent smallholder farmers without access to government subsidies or other forms of government support in the border zone of central Mozambique.

The mountainous, central Mozambican border zone with Zimbabwe has always been characterized by its fluidity, exceptional agricultural status, and intense social and cultural cross-border exchange. It is a border zone with a shared cultural and political heritage dating well before colonial borders were established (Allina-Pisano, 2003; Bannerman 1998; Bhila, 1982; Hughes, 2006; Pophiwa, 2010; Tornimbeni 2004). Despite this history of exchange, the impact of the current Zimbabwe crisis on the region has differed in intensity, as well as in the scale of human movement and its impact on the Mozambican side.

When the intensified commercial farm invasions in Zimbabwe, associated with the Third Chimurenga, began in earnest in 2000, they drove increasing numbers of destitute farm workers of Mozambican and Malawian origin into Mozambique. These people had been confronted with targeted violence, mass expulsion from their farm homes, and the loss of their livelihoods. Finally, the accelerated economic meltdown and hyperinflation in the years before the dollarization of the Zimbabwe economy (2006–2009) created yet another type of displacement affecting many sections of Zimbabwean society. It gave rise to intensified cross-border hawking and trading in basic commodities (soap, cooking oil, sugar) along the main road arteries. Little is known, however, about migration into rural zones along the border.

This chapter attempts to situate the recent crisis-driven immigration into the rural border district of Báruè within the historical dynamic of population flux and exchange in the mountainous area of Zimbabwe and the central Mozambique border zone. It focuses on what is particular about the movement of people, skills and goods to and from Zimbabwe since the beginning of its political and economic crisis. The newcomers transferred part of their social fabric and 'ways of doing things' to Mozambique, affecting, and in the process transforming, local forms of governance, land allocation, and ways of mobilizing external resources. Equally, avenues that had been left unexplored before the massive influx of cheap and skilled labour from Zimbabwe provided new pathways to the generation of rural wealth.

The empirical material informing this chapter has been collected by a variety of Mozambican and Dutch researchers over a long span of time, roughly from 2006 to 2009. Intensive fieldwork in Pandagoma (also spelled as Mpandagoma or Phandagoma) in Báruè District on emerging furrow irrigators[4] was undertaken by the main author in 2006-07 (see Bolding, 2007) and two *licenciatura* thesis students from the Catholic University of Mozambique (Quingstone, 2006; Silota, 2007). Fieldwork consisted mainly of in-depth interviews, a limited number of life histories, one survey questionnaire amongst all irrigating households in Pandagoma, and group discussions and meetings as well as extensive GPS measurements to facilitate the making of maps of the area. A one-day follow-up visit was made in 2009 by Bolding and a team of international researchers (see Van der Zaag, 2010).

The chapter displays some limitations: Firstly, it doesn't provide in-depth narratives of displacement. Rather the chapter focuses on the livelihood strategies pursued by smallholders and displaced farm and estate workers previously employed in Zimbabwe. Secondly, the underlying bias of the empirical material presented in this chapter is on irrigation and water-related activities and livelihood practices. This bias reflects the main author's original professional interest as an irrigation engineer (Bolding, 2007),[5] as well as an interest later transformed into a longitudinal study on hydraulic property creation in several case study areas along the mountainous border besides Pandagoma (Bolding et al., 2010).[6]

In the remainder of this chapter, first of all the historical context and exchange of people, skills and goods along the border zone are highlighted. Next, an in-depth case study on the emerging 'green revolution' in the remote border zone of Pandagoma, Báruè district is provided by delving into the settlement histories of Mozambican labour migrants from Zimbabwe and the rise and demise of the irrigated Farming Association they set up. Finally, the conclusions identify the short- and long-term strategies applied by immigrants, the opportunities offered and effects produced in terms of livelihood practices and political conflicts at the Mozambican end. The Pandagoma case study area findings are contrasted with findings from a less remote, more densely populated case study in Manica District reported on elsewhere (Ibid.).

Historical Contexts and Exchange Flows in the Case Study Area

Pandagoma is situated on the eastern side of the mountain ridge called Serra Nhamahôno, which runs parallel to the border with Zimbabwe in a north-south direction. In terms of local government structures, it is located in Báruè District, with Catandica as district capital.[7] In the fairly remote Pandagoma, the recent influx from Zimbabwe mostly concerns returning Mozambican[8] labour migrants with previous experiences in irrigated agriculture and the production of commercial crops (tea, coffee, tobacco) at invaded white commercial farms and tea plantations in Zimbabwe. Thus, their knowledge of agricultural production technologies differed from the traditional rain-fed agriculture practiced by a majority of the rural population in the area. Amongst these former farm labourers are people of other nationalities as well (Malawian, Zimba-

Map 3: Border area Manicaland, Zimbabwe – Manica Province, Mozambique

Table 1: Dominant population fluxes and their drivers

Period	Direction	Motive
1890-1900	Moz → Zim	Education, marketing, work opportunities (general trend)
1900-10	Moz → Zim	1902 Conquest of Báruè and 1917 aftermath of Báruè rebellion
1920-30	Zim → Moz	Entrepreneurial African farmers who want to expand
1940-60	Zim → Moz	Conservationist Rhodesian policies drive wealthy smallholders across the border with their cattle
1950s	Moz → Zim	Young men fleeing harsh forced labour (*chibalo*) regime
1970s	Zim → Moz	War (*chimurenga*); many young men join ZANLA
1980s	Moz → Zim	War refugees (civil war in Mozambique)
2000s	Zim → Moz	Economic meltdown and land invasions in Zimbabwe

Sources: Bolding, 2004; Newitt, 1995; Tornimbeni, 2004.

bwean). In addition to these new settlers who open up new irrigation furrows and dry land (often on steep mountain sides, investing in bench terraces like in Penhalonga in Manica District), there was an increasing flood of destitute Zimbabweans jumping the border on a daily basis, as Zimbabwe's economic and political crisis deepened between 2006 and 2009. The latter phenomenon was more pronounced in well-connected areas (like Penhalonga) than in the remote Pandagoma.

Historically, the proximity of the border to Pandagoma has played an important role in power relations and land distribution, marketing opportunities as well as in education and training. The local population is Barwe, and part of the larger Shona group which forms the majority of Zimbabwe's population. The links with these Shona in Zimbabwe have been maintained through kinship relations, cross-border chieftaincies, and labour migration (for Manyika, see Bannerman, 1993; Bhila, 1982). In addition, many Mozambicans from the border area were educated in Zimbabwe and went there to secure agricultural inputs and training. The seesaw effect of population movements and their drivers is presented in Table 1.

This back and forth movement of families and relatives facilitated by a porous border can be illustrated through a family's three generational perspective (Den Ouden, 1989). The brief life histories of two senior inhabitants of Pandagoma manifest these processes.

Sekuru Isaac Dick Matsikira claims to be the founder of the first irrigation furrow in Pandagoma.[9] To open the furrow he paid two goats to job seekers to assist him. Isaac Dick originally comes from Pandagoma, where he was born in 1937. He worked for many years in hotels in Bulawayo and subsequently in Harare. He later managed to own a shop and a butchery in Zindi. He was wealthy then, owning a big herd of *mombe* (cattle). As a wealthy individual in the Mapostori church (Apostolic Faith), a church that fosters polygamy, he took many wives. The prime reason for his return to his native Pandagoma was the implementation of the Native Land Husbandry Act (1951) in Zimbabwe, threatening to reduce his wealth by culling his 'excess' cattle.[10] After he started irrigating in Pandagoma he managed to marry some ten more wives, giving him a total of fifteen, of whom five had died by the time we met. With his fifteen wives he had had a total of 105 children of which 50 had passed away. Many of the surviving children have married and left Pandagoma, settling mostly in Mozambique. Only three married sons have stayed on and have become irrigating smallholder farmers.

In contrast to Isaac Matsikira, Sekuru Kahute Chimhungwe's father came from a village north of Pandagoma.[11] Kahute's father, Mangaira, witnessed the war between Chief Makombe and the Portuguese, in 1902. Mangaira fled to present-day Zimbabwe to escape the vagaries of that war and the threat of being recruited for forced labour under the Portuguese. Kahute's father went to Penhalonga, on the Zimbabwean side of the border, where he married and worked. Kahute was born as the couple's second son in 1918, in Penhalonga (Zimbabwe). His elder brother married at the Katiyo tea estate in Zimbabwe, where he died in 1965. When Kahute's parents had both died, he returned to Báruè to marry, after which he returned to Zimbabwe and settled, initially in Zindi, Nyanga. He worked as a cook in Harare in 1940, leaving his wife in Zindi. Finally, in 1953, he left Harare, taking his wife and then three children with him back to Pandagoma, where they had 'good fields':

> The granaries were always full. But we were always running, we were not settled, because of the *mutarato* [forced labour]. We were captured to go and work for nothing. This made me to cross the borders now and again. When it is quiet I come and when they start taking people, I used to return to Zimbabwe.[12]

Kahute also claims he was the first to dig a canal in Pandagoma, taking his inspiration from the Katiyo estate. Like Isaac Matsikira, Kahute is with the Mapostori church, having married five wives who gave birth to twenty children, all of whom have left Pandagoma ('gone to town'). During the War of Independence in Mozambique, Kahute assisted the FRELIMO freedom fighters who sought refuge in Pandagoma, preparing food for them. Later on he became *secretario do bairro* (local party functionary) for FRELIMO. In that capacity he also became entangled in the Zimbabwean chimurenga:

> You know, I am older than Mugabe. I saw him when he came here in Mozambique. He came with Chief Rekayi Tangwena. They used a path that crosses Pandagoma mountain. We helped them find the way.[13]

During the Civil War, Kahute and his family fled to Zimbabwe, only to return after the Peace Accord of 1992.

These two generational life histories demonstrate the extent of mobility displayed by inhabitants of the central Mozambican border zone. A mix of marriage, livelihood opportunities and political processes informed their movements.

Extra-legal trading of goods and resources also has a long history in the region. The mountainous terrain combined with the proximity to the Harare-Beira corridor enabled the area to be at once remote and connected. It provided trading opportunities which the national authorities could not monitor (Schippers, 2008: 12) and other possibilities for formal trade, while (irrigation) technology and farming inputs have been more easily accessible here than elsewhere in Mozambique (cf. Bannerman, 1998). Chingono (2001) places this phenomenon of informal and extra-legal exchange of goods and services in the context of the intensifying Civil War (1982–92), which caused massive displacement in Manica Province and a loss of state control over the economic and legal spheres of governance, particularly in the border districts:

> In Mozambique, the years of war released latent entrepreneurial potential that catalyzed economic change, especially through the grass-roots economy. Given the virtual collapse of the formal sector, the centrality of this alternative economy to the livelihoods of many displaced people cannot be overemphasized. (Chingono, 2001: 90)

The war facilitated the emergence of a grassroots economy, driven by displaced peasants who became 'barefoot entrepreneurs' in peri-urban zones around Chimoio, Manica and Catandica. These informal markets thrived on commodities supplied by corrupt Mozambican bureaucrats, NGO employees and Zimbabwean soldiers manning the Beira Corridor. The latter groups capitalized on their (extra) legal access to scarce commodities making use of their official function (officials), their potential to import duty-free goods from Zimbabwe (soldiers), or their involvement in the distribution of so-called *calamidades* (NGO-supplied emergency goods, like clothes). In the border areas beyond the Beira Corridor such as Pandagoma, a very different dynamic took hold: those who had not fled across the border into Zimbabwe (mainly into Chipinge and Nyanga in two separate waves in 1987 and 1991-92) were often subjected to extreme forms of exploitation and violence (Chingono 2001: 100; Pophiwa 2010: 295).

During the present crisis in Zimbabwe, the impact of the influx of highly skilled ex-farm workers in Pandagoma has been radically different from what is described in several chapters of this book dealing with South Africa. Rather than providing a cheap source of labour for resident smallholders, the abundance of available land and water offered the newly arriving immigrants an opportunity to establish themselves as independent smallholder farmers. They were able to engage in furrow irrigation, cultivating a rapidly expanding area with cash and food crops. There has, however, been a shift in marketing: while the tea, coffee, paprika, green mealies and beans previously produced in Pandagoma were sent to Zimbabwe for sale, they now produce for the Mozambican market. The collapse of the Zimbabwe dollar forced the smallholder irrigators to reorient themselves, initiating a process of 'Mozambicanization'.

A Remote Frontier Zone Experiencing a Green Revolution

Pandagoma is situated in the south-western corner of Báruè district, to the south-west of Catandica, the district capital. The area has been scarcely populated until recently. The first detailed map, which the Portuguese produced on the basis of aerial photographs taken between 1958 and 1960, does not show any concentration of people and only few cultivated fields in the area now known as Pandagoma. The first two irrigation furrows were constructed in 1969 by Isaac Dick Matsikira, (see above), and Kahute Chimhungwe, a Zimbabwean of Mozambican parentage (see above). The next canal was established in 1974, after the fall of the Caetano regime in Lisbon, but just before Independence. In the early 1980s, when the Civil War intensified, residents fled the area for Zimbabwe. It was only two years after the Peace Accord of 1992 that some migrants began to return. Gradually more people came to the area, invited by either former labour migrant friends or relatives, or simply seeking new opportunities. This triggered the first boom of irrigation furrow construction – an impetus possibly fuelled by the terrible drought of 1992. This second wave of furrow construction lasted from 1994 to 1998, and was mainly undertaken by Mozambican labour migrants who had waited for peace in Mozambique in order to return home from Zimbabwe. The third boom in furrow expansion and the exploration of new land began around 2002 and has continued since. This last wave was facilitated by both the success of the newly established Chakwaedzera Association in attracting assistance from foreign funding agencies, and by the deepening economic crisis in Zimbabwe, which resulted in many Mozambican labour migrants losing their jobs.

Most of the irrigators originating from Mozambique are former labour migrants who lived and worked in Zimbabwe before settling in Pandagoma. Less than half of all furrow irrigators originally came from Báruè District, the majority hailing from other districts in Mozambique or from Zimbabwe or Malawi. The reasons why these new irrigators came to select Pandagoma as their destination are various. A number of settlement patterns can be discerned that draw on different types of social networks. One pattern involves family members or people who originally hailed from Pandagoma or neighbouring villages returning to Pandagoma, whereby kin networks provide a first port of call. Another pattern involves the active pursuit and mobilization of labour migrant networks, whereby farm workers or tea-estate workers from the same farm/estate invited each other to settle in Pandagoma or Phanze, because it was a good place to farm and become established as independent smallholders. Below we elaborate two examples of the latter type of settlement history.

Simango's irrigation furrow: a multi-national venture of former tea-estate workers

Thomas Simango originally comes from Chibabava, a dry district in Sofala Province.[14] He left there in 1961 to work at Southdown Down tea estate in the Chipinge district of Zimbabwe, then Rhodesia. In 1970, he moved to the Eastern Highlands tea estate in Honde Valley, which is right on the border with present-day Mozambique. As soon as the Portuguese coup was announced and the Lusaka Accord signed on 7 September 1974, opening the way for a FRELIMO takeover, he went back to Mozambique. But he didn't return to Chibabava. Instead, he went to Pandagoma and joined an irrigation canal that had been constructed by a Zimbabwean tobacco grower, called Boore.[15] Simango extended the canal to his present dwellings. However, when RENAMO stepped up its war effort in 1979, Simango left once more for Zimbabwe and joined the Aberfoyle Tea Estate as a worker. He returned only in 1992, during the terrible drought.

Simango is married to three wives and has a total of 22 children. His first two Zimbabwean wives refused to join him in Mozambique, so he is left with one wife, who bore him nine children. Simango is a member of the Zion church. He speaks fluent *Chewa*, which he learnt from the Malawian workers at the tea estate. He has a lot of friends among them and invited some of them to come and settle in Pandagoma when the estate started to lay off workers due to the economic meltdown in Zimbabwe. One of them joined his irrigation canal, while another (Master Jim) constructed his own canal in Pandagoma.

The last irrigator to join the canal at its tail-end only arrived in 2002. Michael Magado was born in Phanze, about 10km from Pandagoma. He went to Phanze school, yet he speaks fluent English. Father and son moved to Harare (Salisbury) in 1963 and the former found employment at the Cecil Hotel. Magado returned to Mozambique in December 1973 and joined FRELIMO as a freedom fighter (*camarada*). He stayed in the army until 1980. In 1982 he returned to Harare to work in the administration department of a transport company. In 2002, foreseeing trouble, he returned to Mozambique to start farming, and joined Simango's canal, by extending it to his present land. His irrigated area is larger than 5 hectares. One of his sons remained in Harare working for the transport company.

Michael was married to two sisters, Joana and Susan, in 1978. His first wife had six children, one daughter and five sons; his second wife had four sons. The daughter, who was living on the farm when we visited it in June 2006, holds an M.Sc. degree from the University of Zimbabwe. Michael claims that his wives are the secret of his success; they work the land. Another major factor in the success of his farming enterprise is his affiliation with FRELIMO as *antigo combatente* (war veteran). His farm was visited in early 2006 by the Deputy Minister for Fisheries, who came to have a look at his (huge) fish-pond. They arrived by car on the road that Michael constructed himself. The deputy minister was brought to Michael's farm by the director of the District Agricultural office for Báruè, a FRELIMO party official who had enticed him to settle in Pandagoma.

*Ndaiona irrigation furrow: entrepreneurial farm workers
from a Marondera tobacco farm*

The genesis of the Ndaiona irrigation scheme in Phanze involves prior common employment.[16] Four of the five men involved in the construction of the furrow are former farm labourers at an irrigated tobacco farm in Marondera, Zimbabwe. Three men, Manuel Jornal, Paulo Ketane and Lucio Bechane, were employed by a white commercial farmer known to them as Mr Bygone. In 1995, Lucio Bechane decided to return to Mozambique. He ended up in Phanze, in Báruè district, because 'they have good and plenty land here'. When the tobacco farm in Marondera was invaded in 2005, Lucio was joined in Phanze by his former fellow workers Paulo Ketane, Manuel Jornal, and the latter's married son, Moises Manuel Jornal. Once they had reunited they decided to construct an irrigation furrow to water their new fields. Moises has been building houses all his life, and he has been their main man in devising the ingenious structures that take water around a rock as well as the intake structure. The other members of the furrow are the wives of these four and another couple who has settled in the same area.

The experience of constructing the furrow has been a strengthening and unifying one. They originally started at a much lower point than the present river intake, but soon found they could not make the water rise to the altitude they needed to irrigate their lands. This is when they were forced to move upstream and met their first real obstacle: a rock of some 4 meters in diameter. Here Moises constructed his first aquaduct, made of stones and soil, which is reinforced and held in check by a bamboo structure. They then discovered that they had to dig deeper still, and hit another rock. This time, they decided to dig around it. They were now some 4.5 metres under the ground. Without dynamite, and without money for an irrigation pipe, they resolved the issue with their bare hands, picks and *badzas* (hoes). Once they had managed to bring the water through this section of some 100 metres with a deep trajectory, they knew they would succeed, and after some two months of hard work, they progressed until everyone had water. From Zimbabwe they brought the knowledge of how to grow tobacco and each of them acquired a seedbed from which they nurtured between 0.2 to 0.5ha of tobacco, a money-spinner. Moreover they all irrigate green mealies, allowing them to sell fresh maize at the height of the 'hunger season' in February-March.

The Rise and Demise of the Chakwaedzera Association

The story of the Chakwaedzera Association, an umbrella organisation super-seding eleven smallholder farmer associations operating in Pandagoma and its environs, was begun by Samuel Magassosso, who won the UNDP Poverty Eradication Award in 2004. Galvanized by his prize money and a grant from an American bank, the association expanded its activities despite failing market outlets in Zimbabwe and failed attempts[17] to enter contract-farming arrangements in Mozambique. After a promising beginning, leadership conflicts emerged which ultimately resulted in a split of the association into a District Association for an elite group of wealthy smallholder irrigators, and a local association for peasants. In our narrative, we seek to show how 'Zimbabwean-ness' became a factor both in the rise and in the ultimate socio-economic differentiation and split of the association.[18]

Samuel Magassosso was born in 1968 in Espungabera in the south of Manica Province. In 1978, when the Civil War began, Samuel and his parents fled to Zimbabwe, where he went to school, completing Grade 4 at a school on a tea estate. He continued his education at Rattleshoek tea estate, specialising in metalwork. In 1988 the tea estate became the object of attacks by RENAMO fighters (*matsangas*), so Samuel moved to Chipinge, and later Mutare, where he earned a living repairing bicycles and doing odd jobs as a mechanic at a garage. He married a Zimbabwean who gave birth to a daughter. In 1996, four years after the peace agreement, Samuel went home. He left for Machaze district. His Zimbabwean wife and daughter only visited him once, as they did not want to live in Mozambique. Samuel decided to marry a Mozambican wife, but when she failed to give birth to another child he married again. His second Mozambican wife gave birth to a son in 2003. By 1997/98, Samuel and his family had settled in Pandagoma after he took up a new job as an Environmental Health Officer at the clinic in nearby Phanze. Once in Pandagoma, Samuel became a founding member of the Chakwaedzera irrigation association, thus beginning his career as a green-fingered farmer.[19]

In 1999, Samuel and nine others (six women, four men) started a collective tea field irrigated by Isaac Dick Matsikira's furrow (see above). Samuel acted as the leader of this group of tea growers, but from the word 'go' his leadership was contested, particularly by the wife of a traditional leader (*sabhuku*), Mai Dupwa. Local people accused Samuel of being a 'foreigner', and unfit for lead-

132

ership. For example, in the aftermath of the terrible floods of 2000 (Cyclone Elaine), his authority to act on behalf of the community was contested after he had called for help for the local clinic, where there were not enough nurses to cope with the injured. A rescue team were proceeding on foot towards Phanze when they got in touch with the traditional leader. He denied knowledge of any problems and told the rescue team they had acted on misinformation. So the rescue team turned round, reporting that they had been sent out in vain. A couple of months later, Samuel was called to Catandica, and upon arrival in the district capital found himself jailed for over a month for suspected sabotage.

But the floods also provided new opportunities. In 2001, as part of the national reconstruction effort, the co-operative group of tea growers managed to secure MZN10,000 (US$400) from a UNDP-funded social support programme. Samuel was instrumental in securing the funds. To receive and manage them, the tea producers established the Chakwaedzera Farmers Association and invited others to become members.[20] The funds were used to buy seeds, 2,000 tea plants, fertilizers, hoes, seven cows, ploughs, and carts (UNDP, 2004). In no time, many more members joined and started growing tea, coffee and beans, irrigated in their own fields by an expanding number of furrows. The success didn't remain unnoticed. In 2003 Samuel was elected chairperson of the Báruè Association of the Provincial Farmers Union (UCAMA). During an agricultural show in Chimoio, organized by UCAMA, Samuel's processed tea won first prize; one given, it should be noted, by President Joachim Chissano.

On 30 April 2004, the association, now 70 members strong, organized a field day for a delegation of district and provincial officials from the Department of Agriculture. It was accompanied by three American UNDP officials, who were looking for a suitable Mozambican candidate for the UNDP Poverty Eradication Award. The delegation was impressed by the irrigated produce. They must also have been impressed by Samuel Magassosso's life history as a former war refugee and his command of the English language, because soon after the field day Samuel was informed that he was to fly to New York as Mozambican competitor for the Award. In October 2004, he spent a week in New York, receiving US$10,000 in prize money on behalf of the Chakwaedzera Association 'for his leadership towards achieving the Millennium Development Goals'. An auspicious visit to the City Bank Group yielded another US$23,100 in the form of a grant.

The Association spent the prize-money on farming and irrigation equipment, a grinding mill (and a shed to house it), and the construction of an office and a toilet block. Some funds were forwarded for officially registering the Association in Catandica. The remaining US$160 was donated to an HIV/AIDS charity in Pandagoma which cared for orphans.

By this time the pace of new arrivals from crisis-hit Zimbabwe had grown from a trickle to a stream. Everywhere along the tributaries of the Messambize river, trees were felled, land cleared and new irrigation furrows made. By 2006, some eleven producer groups had established themselves under the umbrella of the Chakwaedzera Association, totalling 114 members. Each group ran a shared tea nursery, though not all groups operated a joint irrigation furrow. Members paid a membership fee of MZN5 per month in two annual instalments, amounting to an operating capital of MZN70,000 per annum. A school was established by the Association in Pandagoma and a teacher was assigned by the government. Twenty irrigation furrows, with from two to twenty-two members, were used to grow a variety of commercial crops including tea, coffee, green mealies, beans, paprika and tobacco, a suite of vegetables and rain-fed maize for home consumption. The crudely processed tea and unprocessed coffee beans were sold across the border in Zimbabwe at neighbouring tea estates and the Honde Valley Coffee Association respectively.

Magassosso actively promoted the settlement of new arrivals from Zimbabwe, giving advice and pointing out good locations on which to construct new irrigation furrows. Samuel himself became the most productive and successful farmer in Pandagoma, operating an irrigated farm of ten hectares, a string of fish-ponds and always trying out new crops. Pandagoma itself began to resemble a 'little Zimbabwe', with crops being planted in straight lines, a combination of furrows and clicking sprinklers irrigating the lush fields, children going to school in the morning, and English and Shona being the prevailing languages.

However, the deepening of the Zimbabwe crisis combined with hyperinflation of the Zimbabwe dollar rendered this market virtually worthless. In addition, a series of leadership wrangles ultimately forced the Pandagoma irrigators to reorient themselves towards the Mozambican market outlets. A process of socio-economic differentiation amongst members ultimately led to a split of the Association into a newly established commercial farming organization run by the emerging farming elite, whilst the residue crumbled under the weight of its peasant membership and a multitude of increasingly vicious leadership conflicts.

For Magassosso the bubble burst less than half a year after the pinnacle of his success at the UNDP headquarters in New York. Magado, the war veteran from Phanze went to see Chief Njanji and accused Magassosso of acting like a *sabhuku* (village head), dishing out land to new immigrants without the knowledge of the chief. The latter, who was himself a relatively recent arrival in Pandagoma, and had not yet been recognised as the *Autoridade Comunitária* by the government, was not happy with what seemed to be a powerful contender for the post. Magado and the chief thus teamed up and stage-managed the removal of Magassosso as president of the Báruè Farmers Association in April 2005. Moreover, as Magassosso could no longer act as chairman of the Chakwaedzera Association, he was succeeded by Mai Dupwa, the wife of one of Chief Njanji's *sabhukus*. Nonetheless, in recognition of his pivotal role as intermediary with outside donors, he was asked to stay on in the newly created post of co-ordinator.[21]

In March 2006, however, Magassosso resigned his job amidst mounting accusations that he was defrauding the Association of the American prize money. At the same time, more and more destitute immigrants from Zimbabwe flocked to the Association asking for a place to settle and wanting to enjoy the fruits of its labour. The leadership had been replaced through new elections, but was still embroiled in increasingly frequent and vicious conflicts. Both the leadership and membership were split between a large group of relatively senior members of the Mapostori church (who jointly celebrated Páscoa-Easter celebrations in Zimbabwe)[22] and an elite group of young, entrepreneurial farmers who followed the example set by Magassosso[23]. A third faction, consisting of the chief and his *sabhukus*, seemed initially ill-disposed to both groups, but ultimately aligned with the Mapostori group of polygamous farmers who maintained close links with Zimbabwe where traditional authority had not been as contested as in Mozambique. Notably, a fourth faction comprising the *secretario do bairro* (FRELIMO party secretary) and other Portuguese-speaking native Mozambicans was co-opted by Magassosso and his gang of young farmers in their attempt to secure new product markets in Mozambique.

In April 2006, a conflict broke out between Isaac Dick Matsikira (see above) and the Association over the maintenance of Matsikira's furrow, which supplied water all the way to the offices and grinding mill. Since the Association drew water from his irrigation furrow to make bricks and allow for the construction of the office block, Isaac claimed that the Association should also assist in cleaning the canal. When this was not forthcoming, Isaac closed the furrow, forcing construction activities to stop. The leadership then decided to report the case to the People's Tribunal in Honde rather than settle the matter amicably. However, the case was never settled, primarily because neither the claimants nor the accused could ever convene at the same time.[24]

Whilst this conflict was simmering, in October 2006, another conflict with Matsikira boiled over during a special meeting of the Association. This time it was Chief Njanji who took issue with the former's practice of inviting immigrants from Zimbabwe to settle in Pandagoma without sending them to the 'proper authority' (i.e. Chief Njanji himself). The conflict soon became a shouting match, whereby Matsikira claimed that he was a more senior resident in Pandagoma than the chief: 'Where were you when I came here in 1969? I never saw you then! So what makes you think you can settle people here?'[25] The conflict clearly revealed that competing factions were coalescing around different patrons, each creating their own group of followers or clients, and remained unresolved. While Matsikira drew on his authority as the most senior settler in Pandagoma and mobilized his followers through the Mapostori church, the Chief and his *sabukhus* were desperately trying to make mileage out of their (revived) authority as traditional leaders.

The conflict between the young leadership and the old Mapostori became a recurring feature during Association meetings. John Marengera, another old Mapostori settler in Pandagoma, soon came to rue his decision to build the 'Blair toilet' and grinding mill shed for the Association. As chairman of the animal husbandry sub-committee, he was promised by his fellow leaders that he would be paid as soon as the work had been completed. When this did not happen, he reported the matter to a general meeting and asked to be paid his expenses. He was then accused of trying to make money out the Association and of abusing his position as an office bearer. Marengera was asked to leave the Association's leadership, and so he did: 'As I pray, I am Apostolic Faith. I thought to be quiet is better. So I am just staying at home.'[26]

A similar, but even more expensive, fate befell the Mapostori treasurer of the Association, Nyapimbi, who was forced to resign in early 2007. Basically, the young chairman of the Association, Trymore Parato, discovered a shortfall on the anticipated income from the grinding mill to be used to pay off builders of the association offices. Magassosso was made to settle the arrears from his own pocket. In turn, Magassosso then asked for reimbursement of the funds with interest. The Association, suspecting foul play by Nyapimbi, decided that Nyapimbi was to pay the interest while the original debt was to be settled through profits made from the mill.

Nyapimbi collected the money at the end of each day from the man operating the grinding mill. But the shortfalls continued and ultimately internal auditors were called in, and the case was reported to the Police. After that Nyapimbi resigned as treasurer. Follow-up interviews with the man operating the grinding mill revealed that it was common practice amongst the leadership of the Association to borrow small amounts of cash from the grinding mill operator. This privilege was part of being an Association leader. The cash borrowed was noted on small papers, which ultimately got lost. Hence the shortfall.[27]

The final conflict concerned a brawl between Matsikira and chairman Parato. When the former publicly accused the young chairman of taking money from the Association's grinding mill to pay for the construction of his own shop and grinding mill in Phanze, Parato exploded with anger:

> Can you sit down! You people who have no fields and who produce nothing! You make a lot of noise but when we go to your fields there is nothing there. And now you want to know more about the money in the Association?[28]

In response, an agitated Matsikira stood in front of Parato and forced him to sit down, tearing his shirt in the process. Parato then reported the case to the Police in Catandica as a case of public assault and Matsikira was arrested and found guilty. The court convicted and sentenced him to a fine of MZN4,500 or four months imprisonment. Since he didn't carry any money on him, his beard was shaved and he spent two weeks in prison before his family had sold enough cattle to raise the money to pay the fine. When Matsikira came home many people felt sorry for him: his long beard, the trademark of his Mapostori church, had disappeared. From then onwards a split in the Association seemed inevitable.

In 2008 the split was effected. Magassosso and his young followers decided to register a new association at the provincial level, reflecting the scope of their ambitions. It responded to the much-advertised 'Green Revolution' initiative of the Mozambican government that was directed at commercially oriented smallholder farmers. The association was named the *Associação dos Agricultores de Báruè*. To become a member one needed to cultivate at least ten hectares of land. Magassosso himself commented that the new association was for 'farmeiros' and that they had seventeen members. Those who had remained within the Chakwaedzera Association were in his view mere 'camponeses' (peasants). The new leadership in Pandagoma consisted of a mix of Mapostori church members and a local traditional leader (*sabhuku*).[29]

What we have observed is how the 'Green Revolution' was actually taking place in Pandagoma. By 2008, most of the densely forested hills of Pandagoma had been opened up for irrigated and rain-fed production of a variety of crops. However, as with such initiatives in Asia during the 1970s, this process of agricultural intensification also precipitated a process of increased socio-economic differentiation. This was not only based on available resource wealth, household labour, farming skills or entrepreneurial inclinations, which differed notably amongst early settlers and the more destitute latecomers. The astounding success of the Chakwaedzera Association in attracting outside funding only precipitated an increasingly vicious leadership struggle amongst patrons vying for influence by appealing to different idioms of leadership. The major divisions were: types of church membership, 'traditional' authority, entrepreneurial farmers, and ruling-party affiliation. Each leader brought his own constituents (of settled immigrants) and associated claims regarding proper management, organization and future directions of the Chakwaedzera Association. Morever, the deepening economic crisis in Zimbabwe forced the commercially oriented smallholders in Pandagoma to look for ways to tap into Mozambican markets, to link up with key FRELIMO party networks at provincial level, and to break away from the mother association and form a new one. The majority of local Mapostori residents remained in the Chakwaedzera Association, forging an uneasy alliance with the local Chief and his *sabhukus,* and producing mainly for subsistence.

Conclusion

This chapter highlights some of the less studied aspects of Zimbabwe's crisis-driven immigration in one specific case study area in central Mozambique. It identifies the short- and long-term strategies applied by immigrants, the opportunities offered and effects produced in terms of livelihood practices, but also political conflict, at the Mozambican end. Below we summarize our findings as brief answers to three key questions. In our response to these questions we try to contrast the findings of the Pandagoma case with those from another case study performed in the well connected, densely populated Penhalonga area in Manica District.

(1) What is special about the immigration produced by the Zimbabwe crisis into rural border districts in central Mozambique?

Our first response is its massive nature, as well as the levels of destitution of many of the immigrants, particularly in the wake of Operation Murambatsvina in 2005 (see Chapter 1) and in subsequent years the almost worthlessness of the Zimbabwe dollar. As the crisis deepened, the levels of poverty of border cross-ers increased. This astonished their rural Mozambican hosts who wondered how a well organized, proud country like Zimbabwe could become so impov-erished. The mass immigration had all the trappings of a country at war, with refugees begging rural residents for food and a place to stay. This phenomenon triggered a mixed reaction on the part of the hosts, with some expressing soli-darity based on their own previous experience of war and destitution and the shared cultural heritage with the new arrivals. Others could not deny a sense of retribution, thinking of previous occasions when they had taken refuge in Zimbabwe and had been treated like second-class citizens and blamed for local cholera outbreaks and increases in crime.

What is borne out clearly by the Pandagoma narrative of successful small-holder irrigators setting up shop in rural remote Mozambique and creating the conditions for a silent Green Revolution, is the reversal of the flow of people, skills and goods that their case represents. Hence, the Zimbabwe crisis facili-tated a break in the overarching, twentieth-century trend of a steady flow of the same towards Zimbabwe for an earlier Green Revolution there (see Rukuni and Eicher, 1994).

(2) What kind of employment, livelihood options and short- or long-term strategies for gaining a livelihood did the various immigrants pursue?

We found two types of displacement. The first involved those who looked for long-term settlement in Mozambique because of the loss of livelihood (e.g. evicted farm workers or former urban residents who had their homes destroyed in Murambatsvina); or those who had long cherished plans to return to their motherland. The second were border crossers who engaged in cross-border trading to maintain a certain standard of, or an absolute basic, living in the face of hyperinflation. The latter type of displacement was much more prevalent in a densely populated and accessible place like Penhalonga than in remote Pandagoma. In addition there were those who could tap into previously exist-ing family, clan, labour or church networks often on account of a Mozambican ancestry, and finally those Zimbabweans and Malawians who had no previous ties with rural Mozambique and had to forge their own links.

For those who could not tap into previously established social networks or previous links with Mozambique, the livelihood options were limited in a place like Penhalonga, where land could not be had. Some immigrants offered their labour in exchange for food and shelter or else in exchange for hard currency (Mozambican *meticais*), often at unfavourable exchange rates. Others engaged in the cross-border trade, illegally traversing the mountainous border on a daily basis to exchange opaque beer ('scuds'), or whatever product was still easily obtainable in Zimbabwe, for bars of soap or cooking oil. Still others drifted to town to engage in money changing, mobile trading of basic commodities or 'sex work' (see Chapter 3). The numbers of people involved in this kind of cross-border trade increased steadily from 2006 to 2009 as the Zimbabwe currency plunged. After the dollarization of the Zimbabwe economy the numerous day traders, money changers and prostitutes plying Mozambique's roads and public spaces more or less disappeared overnight. In contrast, the presence of hawkers and other types of daily border crossers was never as numerous in a remote zone like Pandagoma.

Those who could tap into a previously established network could to some extent plan their arrival and pre-identify possibilities for making a livelihood in their new homes. Such mechanisms were at play in the transnational networks of former tea estate workers and former farm workers who mediated the arrival of newcomers in Pandagoma. Irrespective of the network that one mobilized to arrive in rural Mozambique the opportunities for sustaining a longer term presence depended not only on the strength of one's social network but equally, if not decisively, on the livelihood opportunities on offer. And it is in this latter sense that the Pandagoma case contrasts sharply with densely populated areas like Penhalonga close to the Beira Corridor.

(3) What opportunities were available and effects produced upon livelihood pursuits and changes in rural governance?

The Pandagoma area offered very real and tangible possibilities to set oneself up as an independent, irrigating, smallholder farmer. And the skills and commercial orientation of some of the new arrivals proved instrumental in turning Pandagoma into a very productive irrigation hub engaging in commercial production of tea, coffee, green mealies, beans and tobacco in a relatively remote zone of Mozambique. When the marketing outlets in Zimbabwe started to collapse, the highly successful irrigators united in the Chakwaedzera Association were forced to look for alternative market outlets in Mozambique, and entered an arduous and conflict-ridden process of linking up with existing Mozambican road, agro-business and political networks.

In contrast, the densely populated and heavily irrigated Penhalonga area, near Manica town, displayed a different response to the influx of immigrants from Zimbabwe. There, the availability of cheap mass labour resources and riverine gold deposits resulted in a boom in artisanal gold mining, whereby cheap immigrant labour was used to facilitate both the arduous dry season job of gold panning and intensified commercial irrigated production under the patronage of local Mozambican smallholders (Bolding et al., 2010).

The smallholder irrigation 'boom' is not limited to the two areas under study. A study undertaken in seven Districts in central Mozambique (five in Manica and two in Sofala Province) in 2010 (Beekman, 2011: 22) has demonstrated that the area of smallholder irrigation has expanded from some 786 hectares in 2003 to a staggering 9,492 hectares in 2010. Some of this increase can be attributed to underestimations in the 2003 study, but no doubt some of it is due to the influx of highly skilled former tea estate and farm workers setting up shop, and other immigrants from Zimbabwe providing a source of cheap labour. Whilst Mozambican policy makers and donor agencies cracked their heads over appropriate strategies to facilitate a Green Revolution in rural Mozambique, a silent and smaller-scale 'green revolution' was unfolding on the back of a wave of Zimbabwean immigrants.

At the same time, the politics of land and settlement have also been influenced by Zimbabwean ways of doing things, as Zimbabwean settlers have become the clients of fledgling patrons of Chiefly lineage by approaching local *sabhukus* as well as unofficial Chiefs for a place to settle. In the Pandagoma study location, relatively recently returned Chiefly claimants have made active use of this trend to create a political support base and revive previously outlawed practices – such as rain-making ceremonies – and claiming a say over land and water management practices. The same processes can be observed in more 'centrally' located areas such as Penhalonga – which is close to both Manica town and the main transport corridor between Harare and Beira on the Indian Ocean. However, aspiring Chiefs have not been the only participants in this authority gaining practice.

In Pandagoma we see that various patrons sought to create their own following and have a corresponding say over natural resource governance through the mobilization of different leadership idioms (church, farming entrepreneurs, ruling party, traditional). Some of these idioms can be explicitly linked to Zimbabwe, like the Mapostori Johane Marange church network (cf. Alexander, 1997). The Chakwaedzera Association was, in the beginning, very successful in sustaining the irrigation boom by mobilizing funds and other forms of support from outside the locality, leading to a 'little Zimbabwean island' being developed right on the border.

However, the competing sources of authority gave rise to internal dissent, which became more pronounced as the market outlets in Zimbabwe collapsed and the Association had to find ways to link up with Mozambican market outlets and support networks. Members of the farming elite responded by developing links with the ruling FRELIMO party, whereby they aligned to form a new association. In short, the Zimbabwe 'phase' may have been short-lived, while alignment with Provincial party barons and government agents may make for longer-term commercial success. It remains to be seen how many migrants eventually return to Zimbabwe if and when the economy recovers, as well as how dependent the 'green revolution' economy of Pandagoma will be upon the continued supply of Zimbabwean labour resources and farming skills.

Notes

1 The authors gratefully acknowledge the useful additions and comments made by James Bannerman, Bjorn Bertelsen and Stefaan Dondeyne on an earlier version of this chapter. The editors' patient and diligent way of handling the main author's stubbornness is also highly appreciated.

2 'O milagre de Manica acabou', article by Joseph Hanlon and Teresa Smart on the Zimbabwean commercial farmers in Manica Province, Mozambique (see Chapter 4). The article was published on 12 May 2006 in a Mozambican newspaper, *O País*.

3 Quote from a news summary by Joseph Hanlon, 17 September 2008, 'Mozambican experts say: Green revolution must be more than a techno-fix', http://www.open.ac.uk/technology/mozambique/, accessed 19 November 2008. The quote summarizes the critical observations of two Mozambican experts: Professor Firmino Mucavele, former Chief Executive with NEPAD, and then professor at the Agronomy Faculty of the Eduardo Mondlane University in Maputo, and Professor Carlos Nuno Castel-Branco, director of the Instituto de Estudos Sociais e Económicos in Maputo, see: http://www.iese.ac.mz/lib/publication/dp_2008/Discussion_Paper2_Revolucao_Verde.pdf

4 The irrigation ventures reported on in this chapter consist of hand-dug, unlined furrows abstracting water from open streams and rivers by means of simple stone weir intakes, using gravity irrigation to produce a variety of crops in the dry season (predominantly green beans, tomatoes, wheat, green maize and a variety of commercial niche crops such as tea, coffee, tobacco, paprika, chillies, peas, and baby corn as well as horticultural crops like bananas, mangoes, lettuce, rape, and cabbage). The

size of the land irrigated by these furrows varies from 0.1 to 25 hectares, involving 1 to 50 irrigating members. In Pandagoma more than 30 irrigation furrows were established over time from 7 different streams that form part of the Messambize river catchment.

5   This post-doc research was entitled 'Ideal or Real? Cultural divergence in accountability and legitimacy in multi-stakeholder governance of water resources shared by Mozambique and Zimbabwe', funded by the Netherlands Research Council (NWO), 2004-07.

6   This research was undertaken in 2008-09 under the auspices of the Challenge Programme 66 entitled 'Water rights in informal economies in the Limpopo and Volta rivers'.

7   The Catandica area was where the first plan for a large settlement for white Zimbabwean farmers was proposed in the early 2000s, see Chapter 4 and Map 3.

8   Throughout this chapter reference is made to nationality. In most instances the nationality refers to the place of birth of either the person him/herself or that of his/her parents. Hence Mozambican labour migrants may refer to migrants who were either born in Mozambique, but spent their labour careers in Zimbabwe, or who were born in Zimbabwe, but whose parents originally hailed from Mozambique.

9   Interview by the main author with Sekuru Isaac Dick Madzikiri at Pandagoma, 9 May 2006.

10 The NLHA was implemented over a period of 20 years with a brief suspension in 1961 of one year. In the area where Matsikira came from in Zimbabwe, implementation only took place by the late 1960s when he was 30-33 years of age. See Bolding (2004) for an explanation of the staggered implementation of NLHA.

11 Interview by Rodriguez Lino Piloto with Sekuru Kahute Chimhungwe at his home in Pandagoma, 5 July 2007.

12 Interview by Rodriguez Lino Piloto with Sekuru Kahute Chimhungwe at his home in Pandagoma, 5 July 2007.

13 Interview by Rodriguez Lino Piloto with Sekuru Kahute Chimhungwe at his home in Pandagoma, 5 July 2007. The story refers to Robert Mugabe and Edgar Tekere's famous escape from Rhodesia, guided by Chief Tangwena in April 1975 (see Tekere, 2007). In a romanticized version of the 'long march into Mozambique', with explicit reference to Mao's long march in China during the 1930s, the Mugabe escape party passed a couple of lions: 'the male lion raised its mane and rose up as if preparing to spring on them. But it seemed to realize that it was Mugabe marching for freedom' (Moyana 1987: 43). The party got away unharmed and spent a month working in the fields at a small village near present-day Pandagoma, before they were taken into a FRELIMO camp at Phanze.

14 Interview by Rodriguez Lino Piloto with Thomas Simango at his Pandagoma home, 5 July 2007.

15 It is usual for farm workers not to know the real or full name of the farm owner.

16 Field visit to Ndaiona irrigation furrow by author and Rodriguez Lino Piloto on 10 October 2006.

17 Attempts to grow paprika and tobacco under contract for two Mozambican companies resulted in failure due to the companies' repeated refusal to collect the produce from a remote and difficult to reach place like Pandagoma.

18 What would stand out as 'Zimbabweanness' or 'Zimbabweanization' in this context was reflected and manifested in several ways, such as: Making straight planting lines in the field; fighting as a community for a school to be established as soon as they got donor funds in; the fact that they organized themselves in an Association at their own initiative, in contrast to what has been common in Mozambique in the post-civil war period, when associations have been formed in response to donor-funded initiatives; the fact that English (and Shona) were the dominant languages and not Portuguese; and the fact that virtually all commercially marketed produce was originally sent to Zimbabwe for processing and sale.

19 Interview by author and Rodriguez Lino Piloto with Samuel Magassosso at his Pandagoma home, 10 October 2006.

20 *Chakwaedzera* means 'a new day, a new start', in Shona.

21 Interview by Rodriguez Lino Piloto with Samuel Magassosso at his Pandagoma home, 4 July 2007.

22 The ceremony can be said to strengthen their identity and capacity to act as a group. It also strengthens the argument that Pandagoma can partly be viewed as a little Zimbabwe. The Mapastoris' ties with Zimbabwe are spiritual as well as originating from personal experience as smallholders, students and refugees from Zimbabwe.

23 The difference in farming style between these two groups resembles the difference that Cheater (1981, 1984) observed in the Msengezi African Purchase area in Zimbabwe. The traditionalist idiom as pursued by members of the African independent Mapostori church took its inspiration from indigenous African practices of polygynous marriages combined with *nhimbe* work parties thus producing an abundance of predominantly female (family) labour for undertaking extensive under-capitalized agricultural production ventures. In contrast, the modern idiom was practised by mission-educated families engaged in monogamous marriages, relying on hired labour and practising capital-intensive modern agriculture. In Msengezi, Mapostoris proved in general to be more successful in achieving agriculturally based wealth than the 'modern' capital-intensive smallholders (Bolding, 2004: 80). In Pandagoma, the Mapostori group was initially successful, until Magassosso and his group of young entrepreneurial followers managed to link up to capital funds provided by various donors.

24 Interview by author and Rodriguez Lino Piloto with Isaac Dick Matsikira along his Pandagoma furrow, 9 May 2006.

25 Chakwaedzera Association Meeting attended by the author and Rodriguez Lino Piloto at Pandagoma sede, 10 October 2006.

26 Interview by Rodriguez Lino Piloto with John Marengera at his Pandagoma home, 4 July 2007.
27 Interview by Rodriguez Lino Piloto with the grinding mill operator at Pandagoma *sede*, 3 July 2007
28 Interview by Rodriguez Lino Piloto with Isaac Dick Matsikira at his Pandagoma home, 4 July 2007.
29 Interviews with Samuel Magassosso and Isaac Dick Matsikira during a field visit to Pandagoma by the CP66 challenge programme research team, 16 September 2008.,,

6

Governing the South African/Zimbabwean Border

Immigration, Criminalization and Human Rights

Bill Derman

Introduction

Borders in the contemporary world mark independent nation-states that attempt to control movements of people and goods across them. In southern Africa these national boundaries have a profound historical importance due to the efforts by the colonial governments of what are now Zimbabwe, Namibia, Mozambique and especially South Africa to mark the division between colonial and independent Africa. The term 'Border War' or *Grensoorlog*[1] in Afrikaans given to the conflicts in Angola/Namibia was ubiquitous in white South African public discourse during the 1970s and 1980s. Border war also came to include the border with Zimbabwe which was viewed as harbouring dangerous communists and African nationalists. More generally, an ideology of fortress South Africa was erected in order to protect its white citizens from the combined threat of communism and black nationalism from the north. And as Angola, Mozambique, Zimbabwe (Rhodesia) and Namibia (South West Africa) gained their independence through armed struggle there were real threats and armed incursions while the apartheid government emphasized the *swartgevaar* (black peril). In addition, South African supported (and many argue created) *Resistência Nacional Moçambicana* (RENAMO) in Mozambique which undermined *Frente de Libertação de Moçambique* (FRELIMO) and its newly gained independence for Mozambique. On the Zimbabwean border a 'no man's land' was established between the two countries consisting of two lines of barbed wire fences with a clear track between them for army patrols. During the 1980s sisal was planted in between the fences and west of Musina the fence was electrified. The African National Congress (ANC) armed wing, *Umkhonto we Sizwe* (or MK) (translated 'Spear of the Nation'), placed landmines on white border farms, labeling such places as legitimate military targets. In sum, pre-

1994 the borders of South Africa were highly militarized and governed to keep out other Africans.

In this chapter we focus on the new and profound challenges to South Africa stemming from the movement of Zimbabweans across its border from Beitbridge in Zimbabwe to Musina in South Africa. There is a bridge across the Limpopo for legal border crossers while others ford the Limpopo either east or west of the bridge. It details why and how efforts to keep Zimbabweans out of South Africa have failed. The border according to the South African and Zimbabwean governments should mark national territories and be subject to clear laws, rules and practices. However, it has become subject to a range of policies and practices that deviate from the intentions of each government, the conflicting interests of police, army and immigration personnel along with international humanitarian and human rights organizations, gangs and syndicates, tourists, business people and those seeking to enter South Africa or those seeking to leave. In Chapters 1 and 2 we focused on how the economics and politics of Zimbabwe have produced large numbers of displacements, while in Chapters 3, 4 and 5 we examined how these complex displacements have taken place in selected areas in Mozambique. In this chapter we examine how, at the border between Zimbabwe and South Africa, the various contradictory state and public interests have produced a series of temporary and unsatisfactory policies. The border has a long history which helps shape contemporary events. However, the ending of apartheid created new conditions in South Africa which have produced a series of new challenges to the foundations and legitimacy of the post-apartheid South African state.[2] In a similar manner, the outbreak of xenophobic violence which saw 64 foreigners killed and thousands rendered homeless (Kupe and Worby, 2009) delegimatized the South African state internationally. It also rendered visible contesting visions of who the state should be for within South Africa. In a parallel fashion, how the border is governed renders problematic South Africa's claims to be based upon human rights. By focusing on the border and how it is governed we hope to illuminate the central contradictions within the broad South African polity produced by the Zimbabwe crisis.

The chapter is organized as follows: we begin a short account of the scale of issues involved in Zimbabwean contemporary immigration into South Africa. This is followed by a short history of migration from the region to South Africa followed by an account of the shifting policies employed to control the border. In the next section we explore the dilemmas facing the government of South

Africa and Zimbabwean migrants in South Africa. Xenophobia and its influence upon efforts to find solutions to the large numbers of foreign nationals in South Africa form the basis of the penultimate section before our conclusions. In Chapters 7 and 8 we focus upon Zimbabweans living on the commercial farms and communal areas in Limpopo Province.

A New Border?

With the end of apartheid and the end of white domination of South Africa, new policies slowly emerged but with many continuities from the past. Surprisingly, the barbed wire fences, the military bases and military tracks remained.[3] The militarized border remained as did the special exemptions for temporary migrant farm workers. Zimbabweans seeking work on farms north of the Soutpansberg Mountains continued to be welcomed. Under Section 41 of the Aliens Control Act the government continued to have the power to grant temporary residence and work permits to otherwise prohibited persons. This was done in order to allow certain employers to register their undocumented workers and legitimize their use of such labour. Despite this exemption for farm employment, many employers did not and do not use this path due to expensive fees and just inconvenience.

The government of South Africa has strived to ensure that those entering South Africa are funneled through the legal border posts with the appropriate immigration personnel and procedures for entering. Following the end of apartheid, immigration has dramatically increased, despite the decreasing numbers of foreigners hired for the gold, platinum, coal and other mines. As high as these numbers were, they have dramatically increased with the growing economic difficulties and political conflicts in Zimbabwe. With this sustained crisis, the South African government has struggled to find ways to cope with the large numbers of Zimbabweans who have sought work, safety and political asylum in South Africa.

Despite its militarization, although less so than prior to 1994, the border is literally porous. It is porous physically because of gaps in the fence and sandy soils which are easy to dig under and it is porous due to corruption and crime. To reach the border on foot, Zimbabweans walk approximately fifteen kilometres through the bush from Beitbridge (the border town in Zimbabwe) to the area near Musina. There has been a more recent formation of syndicates, including immigration officers that let Zimbabweans bribe their way across the border.[4] At the height of the violence in Zimbabwe during the presidential runoff Rutherford wrote:

> the continuing catastrophic unraveling of livelihoods, social services, and personal security for the majority of Zimbabweans in their own country as ZANU (PF) has unleashed terror in a vain attempt to hang onto power as the national economy implodes. (Rutherford, 2008: 36)[5]

Despite the political origins of much suffering and displacement, the South African government[6] has insisted that Zimbabweans leave Zimbabwe as voluntary economic migrants and not political refugees. In short, there are strong links between the South African 'quiet diplomacy' approach to Zimbabwe (discussed in Chapter 2) and the internal immigration (and asylum) crisis. The South African government has been unwilling to entertain the idea that it has been the deliberate economic policies promoted and implemented by the ruling party supported by systemic violence that has produced hundreds of thousands of immigrants, many of whom have sought relief in South Africa. Indeed, the African National Congress in December of 2011 pledged continued support to ZANU-PF. Gwede Mantashe, the ANC's Secretary General, stated at the ZANU-PF Congress that:

> We should continue engaging to take our relationship to a higher level. It is important that Zanu-PF continue regaining lost grounds and represent the interests and the aspirations of the vast majority of the people of Zimbabwe. This message of solidarity is an acknowledgement of the fact that we belong together. Our relationship has been historically sealed by blood since we fought the same white colonialists.[7]

While such a statement can be seen as an obligatory reaffirmation of a long-standing relationship it can also be understood as a bias toward ZANU-PF by the ANC, thereby undermining South Africa's claims to be a neutral arbiter.

South Africans have long seen themselves as different from the rest of Africa. The contemporary South African state according to Peberdy 'has drawn the line between citizen and non-citizen more clearly than before' (2009: 166). How the state constructs national identity will influence if not determine the shape and practice of immigration policies. Migration into the nation is seen as a problem and this has intensified because of the large numbers of African migrants who have come to South Africa since 1994. The election of Nelson Mandela and the African National Congress increased the desire of black Africans to seek better lives[8] while South Africa was attempting to control and limit immigration to the skills and qualifications of potential immigrants. Despite South Africa's human rights emphases it has not protected people from discrimination by the state on the grounds of nationality (Peberdy, 2009: 166).[9]

The recent outbreak of what has been termed 'xenophobic' violence in 2008 reflects those hostile feelings toward immigrants who are blamed for taking jobs, for keeping South Africans out of business and for increasing crime.[10] It is part of a long history of hostility and violence toward immigrants. For example, in one case among many there was a 1995 pogrom called *Buyelekhaya* or 'go back home'. According to a 1998 Human Rights Watch report, immigrants from Malawi, Zimbabwe and Mozambique living in Alexandra township, Johannesburg, were marched by armed gangs to the police station in an attempt to 'clean' the township of foreigners. While xenophobia is less relevant for the rural studies in this book, it is important to keep it in mind as South Africa shifts policies again to resume deportations for undocumented or illegal foreign nationals. These long-standing patterns of violence produce insecurity if not fear among most undocumented immigrants who constitute the majority of Zimbabweans in South Africa.[11] The porous condition of South Africa's borders took high priority in 1997 with the recognition that new trends were at work after the end of apartheid. Efforts, however, to unify and systematize border control management failed and remain highly problematic primarily due to the difficulties of interdepartmental co-ordination among Customs, Home Affairs, intelligence services, Health, Agriculture, Transport, Police and Defense Forces, to name the most important.[12] From the perspective of Zimbabwean undocumented migrants, they are primarily affected by the police and Home Affairs (immigration). Both citizens and immigrants tend to blame the police and Home Affairs for poor policies, poor enforcement and corruption.[13]

Earlier History of Migrations

At its height in 1972 the South African mining industry employed over 600,000 black migrants from Malawi (33 per cent), Mozambique (26 per cent), Lesotho (25 per cent), Botswana (7 per cent), Zambia (5 per cent) and Swaziland (4 per cent).[14] What is quite surprising is that Zimbabweans do not figure in this listing despite the long common border. They were to be found, despite earlier employment in the mines,[15] more as farm workers, construction workers, hotel employees and as domestic servants. The South African government attempted to see that migrants' contracts ensured that they would not stay in South Africa but return to their countries of origin.[16] These patterns changed with the civil war in Mozambique (1977-92) but especially after 1990, when approximately 200,000 Mozambicans entered South Africa with many staying on after the war ended. With the 1994 elections in South Africa and Nelson Mandela's overwhelming victory, official apartheid came to an end. As if acknowledging the end of the apartheid era, the flow of immigrants from Africa to South Africa dramatically increased. This can partly be accounted for by the declining economic and political situation in neighboring countries and to expectations of employment in a changed South Africa. However, despite the dramatic increase in immigration to South Africa from the region, the number of 'legal immigrants' entering the country with permanent residence and work permits declined. The total number of permanent residence permits issued between 1990 and 1996 was 62,257, of which only 5,407 were issued in 1996 (International Labour Organization (ILO), 1998: 12).[17] These legal migrants were overwhelmingly professional, managerial, clerical and sales workers and, surprisingly, continued to be whites from Europe.

The underlying reasons why immigrants come to South Africa vary spatially and temporally. Large numbers came in from Mozambique during the civil war. In Lesotho, land pressure, weak returns from agriculture and urban unemployment meant that, in 1995, 60 per cent of Lesotho's GNP was attributable to wage remittances from South Africa. These immigrants tended to have come without permission, or they came on temporary visas and then didn't leave. According to the South African government, based on the computerized National Movement System of the Department of Home Affairs (DHA), during the 1990s the numbers of immigrants who overstayed their visas rose sharply. In March 1997, 883,000 people were identified as overstayers (Ibid.: 16). The Department of Home Affairs estimated that there were 2.4 to 5 million total migrants in South Africa as of 1998. However, while these figures are contested there is no way of knowing now what the actual numbers were. What they do indicate is the scale of people involved and the pull of South Africa throughout the continent. These high numbers existed, even though estimates for South Africa's unemployment level were around 40 per cent in the mid-nineties. Still, people from the region were coming for work. The question is why? The ILO suggests four interconnected reasons:

1. The actual unemployment level in South Africa was much lower than surrounding countries especially with opportunities in the informal sector or in

contract labour.

2. South Africa's size and economic diversity presents many more opportunities.

3. Pay levels for comparable work are much higher in South Africa than in surrounding nations.

4. The South African economy can absorb far more migrant labour and its neighbour's populations than other countries.

What is harder to document in our view is employers' and industries' preference for migrant or foreign workers. They are easier to discipline and harder to unionize and were not part of the immediate anti-apartheid struggles. In addition, for professional and semi-professional jobs black South Africans have been relatively poorly educated in comparison to Zimbabwean and other African nationals.

Migration and South African Agriculture

As many historians have noted,[18] South African agriculture was heavily subsidized by the national and provincial governments during the apartheid years. This took varied forms depending upon the time and context, including: providing land for purchase at extremely low interest rates, making lands available for returning veterans from World War II and building infrastructure such as dams for struggling white farmers. In addition, the government had assisted farmers in obtaining black labour, as farm work was invariably less attractive because it offered lower wages than the mining sector. Much black South African labour was obtained through various forms of sharecropping. According to Dan O'Meara (1983), profits from agriculture soared during World War II and continued to expand afterwards. After the war, and with the growing strength of the Nationalist Party, new labour patterns were set in motion in the farms of what is now Limpopo Province (part of the former Transvaal).[19] The trend of white farm owners' right after World War II was to increase the number of days tenant farmers had to work for them; they rose from 90 to 180 days per anum. Many black South Africans chose to move to the Bantustans rather than to live in such tough conditions on the farms. The farmers responded by substituting migrant labour for South African labour. And as apartheid came into effect during the 1950s and 1960s farmers were now able to force squatters off their land with government-backed force to send them to the homelands or reserves. Labour tenancy continued but gradually diminished.[20] Labour conditions on the farms themselves were by most reports themselves awful. The workers were poorly paid, housing was sub-standard and often they were locked on the farms to prevent their leaving. And, as was often the case, if the workers were not in South Africa legally they could only disobey the owners and managers with great difficulty.[21] White South African farmers in Mpumalanga and the Northern (now Limpopo) provinces were permitted to register their undocumented resident farm workers in order to avoid prosecution from the 1960s onwards. They did this by applying for a corporate permit.[22] However, the farmers did have to pay for the corporate permits, which led many to not bother.[23]

During the 1990s, South African workers and their labour unions contended that immigrants were driving down wages and taking South African jobs. In general, South African unions have a minimal foreign worker membership and try to maintain high wage levels in the face of labour over-supply for the unskilled and semi-skilled sectors. However, the current hostility toward immigrants has deeper roots. In general, migrants are afforded few, if any, social protections. The ILO report (op. cit) concluded that there was a lack of full protection for immigrants who stayed in South Africa after the end of apartheid. A general amnesty from deportation was offered to SADC citizens if they had been living and working in South Africa before the election of 1994. Those who applied for and were granted amnesty became eligible for unemployment insurance fund benefits, while coverage for state old age and disability pensions was restricted to South African citizens. In short, migrant workers were treated differently than other South African workers even after they had been granted amnesty to stay legally in South Africa.[24] The issues of job security, social services access and occupational health and safety for migrants were left unaddressed in South Africa and more generally in the region as a whole. In addition, it is well known that the mining industry is dangerous, with its high risk of illnesses and accidents, which has led to longer-term issues for former miners who had to leave work and have difficulties upon returning home. Forestry and agriculture are also fairly dangerous professions and has even fewer provisions for those who are injured and subsequently disabled.

By the end of the 1990s, a new white paper and a new immigration act were proposed and enacted in South Africa in 2002.[25] The policy and Act continue to place the emphasis upon control and exclusion rather than a management and development opportunity (Crush, 2008: 2).[26] For example, in Section 19 of the Immigration Act it is specified without exemption that no learning institution shall knowingly provide training or instruction to an illegal foreigner, along with other clauses to prohibit those without explicit study visas. While it is possible that an unaccompanied child would not be considered an illegal foreigner, the text nonetheless appears to foster exclusion.

Exclusion, however, is not the only policy. In Limpopo Province, the older policy of allowing employers to employ non-South Africans from Mozambique and Zimbabwe in seasonal farm work continues. This policy issued B-17 permits to undocumented workers to temporarily live and work in South Africa, but only north of the Soutpansberg mountains. With such permits workers could not legally move off their farms of employment since they were issued to the employer for specific employees and specific places. Many, however, used the permits to move in search of employment further south. Lastly, we need to mention the long-standing hostility that has existed towards Zimbabwean farm workers, especially in more recent years. In one of the better-known strikes at Maswiri farm in the area of Tshipise, Zimbabwean farm workers were brought in to replace striking South African workers in 1999. More recently, the influx of large numbers of Zimbabweans has greatly enlarged the labour pool for farm owners, to the disadvantage of South African workers.[27]

Having briefly placed labour migration in a historical frame we turn now to the post-2000 border realities between South Africa and Zimbabwe.

The Porous Border

Distinct and well-marked borders with official crossing points arise with nation-states. Whereas the border served in apartheid South Africa to keep out potential enemies it was also used as the path to import temporary foreign labour. In a reversal it now marks an effort to keep foreign labour out. While there has been a dramatic decline in the number of foreigners or migrant labour to the South African gold mines, there remains heavy pressure as documented and undocumented Africans seek work. In response, the border is being re-militarized. It seems that despite globalization, increasing flows of capital, and an ideology of African unity the South African government views migrants as a threat to their economy and well-being. As South Africa seeks to increase the power of the South African state it draws important distinctions from all other Africans. South Africa, like many other states, is caught between an increasingly global economy and the need to defend its sovereignty due to the large numbers of people seeking opportunities within its borders. Like other post 9/11 states, South Africa is increasingly reliant on fingerprints, passports, identification documents and other surveillance measures to distinguish between citizens and others.

As discussed earlier, there are no accurate figures for the number of Zimbabweans in Limpopo province much less in South Africa as a whole. Indeed, according to Landau and Segatti (2009: 5) no one knows how many international-al migrants are in South Africa, how long they have been there, how long they stay, or what they do while they are in the country. This is due to the lack of clear and consistent data-collection mechanisms over time. Nonetheless, Landau and Segatti contend that the numbers are less than generally assumed. According to them, and about which there is no disagreement, the largest number of migrants since 2000 have been Zimbabweans. To assess this number, one indicator of the scale of emigration prior to the large number of asylum seekers is the number of deportations from South Africa to Zimbabwe. The recent past marks a break from pre-2000, when most Zimbabweans did not intend to remain permanently in South Africa (Crush and McDonald, 2001: 7). Some numbers which provide a clear indication of the flood of Zimbabwean migrants since 2000[28] include Zimbabwe's former principal immigration officer at the Beitbridge border post, Dennis Chitsaka, reporting that a total of 294,678 undocumented Zimbabwe-ans were deported between January and December 2008, a sharp increase com-pared to the previous year when 204,827 illegal immigrants were brought back home in 2007. In 2006, 266,000 migrants were deported,[29] most of whom were Zimbabweans. And, many of the deported returned to South Africa though some of the deportees wanted to return home to Zimbabwe and thereby got free transport. In 2011, the numbers coming across the border has dropped. In part this appears due to the resumption of deportation by the South African Minis-try of Home Affairs, an improvement in Zimbabwe's economy and a wait-and-see attitude among prospective immigrants. Whether or not this will remain the case depends upon socioeconomic and political conditions in Zimbabwe as a new election approaches.[30] Nonetheless, the scale and resources required to move so many people has been dramatically under-reported and under-ana-lyzed. They are an enduring testament to the mismatch between South African policies and Zimbabwean realities.

Due to a loophole created by the South African government, Zimbabweans who applied for political asylum were allowed to stay in the country (see below). This led to the situation whereby South Africa had the distinction of holding the largest number of asylum seekers in the world in 2009, 2010, and 2011, mostly Zimbabweans for reasons discussed below.[31]

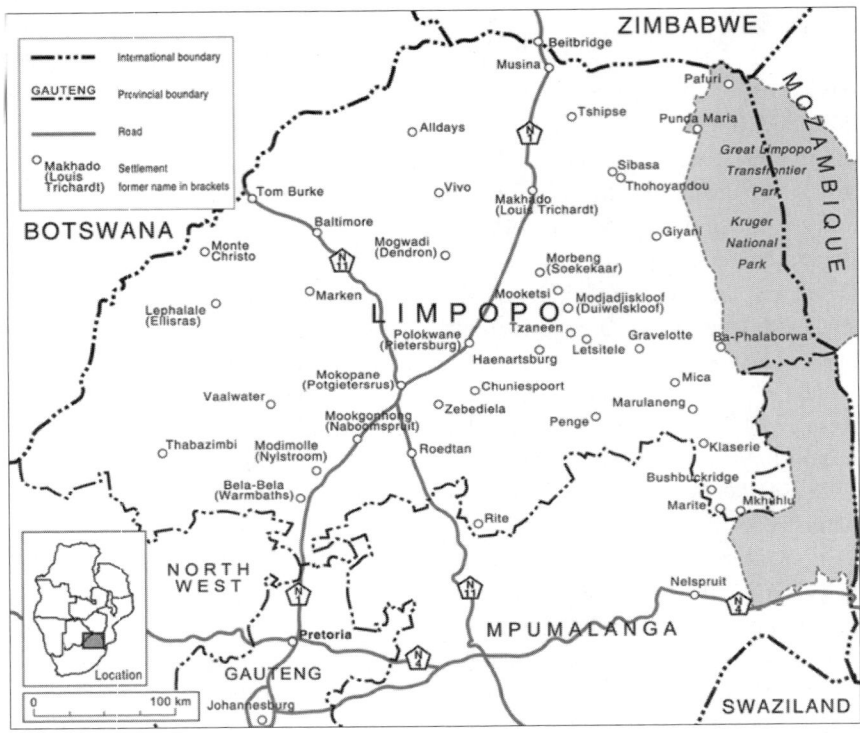

Map 4: Limpopo Province, South Africa

Border Crossings from Beitbridge to Musina

For many Africans, there was the expectation that with the ending of apartheid and a new government, apartheid-era policies toward 'aliens' would be altered.[32] However, this has not been the case. South Africa has nonetheless remained a magnet for those seeking to live in South Africa for employment, to avoid violence, hunger, or terror. In addition, South Africa has also attracted smugglers, drug dealers, arms dealers and the like. For undocumented migrants, the border zone has long been dangerous. The barbed wire and razor-wire fences, the military track in their middle and military control posts continued after the end of apartheid. The militarized fence is interrupted by large, locked gates that enable farm owners to access their irrigation pumps in the Limpopo River. The keys to these gates are often left with key members of the African staff that may or may not be sympathetic to those crossing illegally or to smugglers. This has been one way that Zimbabweans with contacts have been able to enter South Africa.

In addition to traversing the gates, the border fences have deteriorated through cutting and erosion. Undocumented immigrants cut through the fences and they often stay cut for months, if not years. In addition, floods in the seasonal rivers would wash away parts of a fence, providing relatively easy means to slide or dig under the fence. Over the past two years the South African government has been replacing the old fence with a new one and increasing the number of military patrols. The upgraded militarized border has begun to make it more difficult for border-crossers not to use the official crossing points. It seems from interviews with LHR, IOM and UNHCR in 2011 and 2012 that army units were becoming far more active in their patrols and efforts to prevent undocumented border crossers from entering Zimbabwe.

While there is substantial and important undocumented immigration, there is also a large legal traffic across the formal border crossing with Zimbabwe at Beitbridge every day. This includes business people, tourists, truckers, traders, and short-term visitors from the region. For those with passports it is easy to traverse the border for short visits, but it is difficult to legally obtain work. Those without passports who come to the legal border but have the means have been able to pay bribes to some (and it is impossible to know how many) immigration officers. In an interview in July 2012, the South African Lawyer for Human Rights observed the growing influence of 'syndicates' (or gangs) who had organized to lead undocumented immigrants to the immigration officers who took bribes.[33] If a legal crossing was not possible, and for many years Zimbabwean passports were expensive and difficult to obtain, then the option was to cross the Limpopo River. And this remains the path for those who do not have proper documents. The greatest risk in crossing the border is from criminal gangs that are locally known as *maguma-gumas*.[34] They are known for their violent attacks upon border crossers. These include stealing, beating and rape.

During the late apartheid years, racial discrimination was at the heart of South Africa's immigration policy toward Rhodesia. White Zimbabweans were welcomed, many Rhodesians/Zimbabweans attended South African universities, and many South Africans became landowners in Rhodesia/Zimbabwe. In addition, there were many business ties and when Zimbabwe became independent many white Zimbabweans migrated, without difficulty, to apartheid South Africa. These conditions changed with the ending of apartheid. Beginning in 1994 the South African government treated immigrants from Zimbabwe as temporary economic migrants. Claims for political asylum were routinely rejected. Zimbabweans entering South Africa were not permitted by the Department of Home Affairs to apply for asylum from 1994-2002. It wasn't until the Wits Law Clinic[35] tested the legality of South Africa's policy of denying all Zimbabwean claims for refugee status. As a result, the Department of Home Affairs conceded in 2002 that any Zimbabwean had a right to apply for asylum. Even so, very few Zimbabweans have succeeded in having their applications for refugee status accepted. Home Affairs officers and lawyers whom we interviewed in 2008 through 2012 estimated that less than one per cent of applicants succeed. They are, according to several lawyers, routinely denied political asylum.[36] The rejections we saw in 2009-11 were all the same. They all stated that Zimbabwe is not at war and that the Government of National Unity (GNU) was reducing the conflicts that existed.[37] To make matters more difficult for asylum-seekers, the only application location for those entering South Africa seeking refugee status was in Johannesburg until 2008. This meant that people who crossed the border had to travel from the border to Pretoria with no papers and were subject to arrest by the police. It is clear from the deportation numbers cited earlier that this was a frequent occurrence.

The 2008 Zimbabwean elections saw a new inundation of the South African border due to increasing violence, extreme monetary inflation, lack of staples and economic decline. Musina, the first town across the main transit point from Beitbridge in Zimbabwe, was overwhelmed with Zimbabweans trying in a variety of ways to find jobs or trying to obtain transport to Pretoria, Johannesburg and other cities. Responding to pressures by human rights NGOs, research by Human Rights Watch and the Centre for Forced Migration, the South African government set up temporary offices for those seeking asylum to make their applications in Musina.[38] Beginning in 2008 we visited Musina twice yearly through 2012 to document the conditions and circumstances faced by undocumented immigrants.

Musina The frontline in the crisis of Zimbabweans entering South Africa

Musina, a small mining town just south of the Limpopo River and the Zimbabwean border, has been the main entry point for Zimbabweans entering South Africa. It had a population of around 20,000 in 2000, while the larger area known as Musina Municipality had a population of 39,301 in 2001, rising to 57,195 in 2007.[39]

Musina and its environs began making major news in 2004. It did so because five members of the South African National Defense Forces were arrested on multiple charges of rape of and theft from Zimbabweans in the border area (Solidarity Peace Trust, 2004: 58). Unaccompanied minors were not being registered and were being forcibly returned across the border. More generally, the police were deporting around four truck-loads of Zimbabweans a week. And they were holding them in an open fenced area with no toilets or water tap within its perimeter. The authors of the above report visited the official location in Beitbridge where the deportees were deposited. They found that they were spoken to by the Zimbabwean police and then released without any penalties. Many attempted immediately to head back across the border. There are others, of course, who arrived in Beitbridge without resources or money and were given no assistance from the police. It is clear that the South African government and police authorities were not respecting their obligations toward the human rights of migrants. In 2006 when Human Rights Watch visited Musina they commented that the Department of Home Affairs practice at the Musina police station was to assume that all Zimbabweans were economic migrants. This assumption deprived those seeking asylum of declaring their status to a DHA official. In an ironic twist, Malawians at the post were able to seek asylum even though Malawi was not at war at the same time that Zimbabweans were being denied that right on the same basis (Human Rights Watch, 2006: 24).

In 2007, with even more Zimbabweans crossing the border, respected reporters began writing of the events and processes taking place in Musina. In July 2007, Basildon Peta, a well-known Zimbabwean reporter, went to the border because of a new influx and wrote:

> One border official called the situation a 'human tsunami'. The reality of the influx hits home on the drive along the 200-mile perimeter fence along the border. While the three parallel lines of fencing are relatively intact close to the official border crossing, a few miles further on they have been shredded. The night crossings are staged by trafficking gangs known as 'Maguma-guma', or scavengers. It has become a violent trade, with clashes between police and traffickers becoming more common.[40] (*The Independent*, UK, 18 July 2007)

The problems well described in 2004 were ongoing. Eddie Matsangaise of Zimbabwe Exiles' Forum's Programme Manager had this to report after the trip:

> The migrants' situation in Musina is desperate and the numbers are depressing to say the least. We visited 3 camps housing asylum seekers, each with between 150 and 200 inhabitants. There is no shelter except for the fences. They are using blankets donated by Doctors without Borders for shelter from the scorching sun. The local authorities stopped the churches from sheltering migrants, destroying the tents donated by UNHCR and other well-wishers. Food is inadequate and soup kitchens by the churches are provided once a day. The situation for women and children is much worse [than for men].[41]

Andrew Gethi, chief operating officer of the International Organization for Migration (IOM), which opened an office to assist deported Zimbabwean refugees, stated that his organization was handling on average 17,000 deportees every month in 2008, but that figure reflect only those caught and deported by the South African authorities (quoted by Peta, ibid.).

Many immigrants arrive at Musina hungry, tired, without money and increasingly subject to violence and rape by the *maguma-gumas*. Many also come into contact with smugglers known locally as *malaishas*. The local municipal authorities of Musina opted to minimize their expenses and to lower, they thought, the number of people coming through by declining to provide any services, including food, water and toilets, no matter what their experiences or their hunger. In the absence of a government response (at all levels, including national, provincial and local), local churches and individuals began to assist. And as the numbers of people arriving increased after the violent elections in 2008, international organizations stepped into the breach. The UNHCR, the IOM, South African Lawyers for Human Rights (LHR), Doctors without Borders and local NGOs arrived or increased their services. Doctors without Borders, for example, opened a tent to provide health care and referrals as migrants were routinely denied medical attention. LHR attempted to let people know of their rights and to block the police from repatriating unaccompanied minors and those who requested asylum status. They were assisted in this by the IOM, which also assisted immigrants if they were deported back to Zimbabwe.

Lawyers for Human Rights and the Detention Centre in Musina

After years of concern, in February of 2009 the LHR launched an urgent case against the DHA, the Department of Social Development (DSD) and the South African Police in Musina, alleging that the arrest, detention and deportation of Zimbabwean nationals from the Soutpansberg Military Grounds (SMG), located just south of Musina, were unlawful and unconstitutional.[42] LHR asked that the facility be closed because it had not been designated as a detention facility for purposes of deportation under the Immigration Act, and because conditions at the facility did not meet the minimum standards for detention. In May, the North Gauteng High Court ordered SMG's immediate closure. In a strongly worded decision, the court held that: (1) the use of the military grounds near Musina (i.e., SMG) as a detention facility under the Immigration Act was unlawful; (2) the conditions of detention at SMG were unlawful and unconstitutional; and (3) the conditions of detention and treatment of children were unlawful and unconstitutional. Nonetheless, in direct violation of the court ruling, the Musina police continued to detain people at SMG before taking them to a Refugee Reception Office. As South Africa prepares to resume deportations of undocumented immigrants, a new holding camp has been built adjacent to the SMG although it was not in use through August of 2012.[43]

Responding to the Post-Election Crises in Zimbabwe

In 2008, overwhelmed with the numbers of undocumented Zimbabweans inundating Musina and facing pressures from international and national human rights and refugee organizations, the Department of Home Affairs rented the showgrounds[44] in order to effect a dramatic shift in policy. The policy changes were to allow the use of Section 22 of the Immigration Act 2002 for Zimbabweans to remain legally in South Africa. The Section 22 Permit is an 'asylum seeker permit'. It demonstrates that the person has applied for asylum and is legally in the country, but it is only valid for a short time, usually between three months, and automatically renewable.[45] The second policy change was to cease deportations of Zimbabweans, even if undocumented, and when not accused of any criminal offense. Potential asylum-seekers were allowed to apply for asylum in Musina, i.e. they no longer had to travel to Johannesburg, as had been the case until 2008. The permit granted tens of thousands of Zimbabweans the right to live and work in South Africa as well as access to health care and education for an initial period of at least six months (assuming automatic renewal). The mass deportation of undocumented migrants was halted until

October 2011. It was thus almost a decade into the Zimbabwean crisis before South Africa's Department of Home Affairs attempted to regularize the status of thousands of undocumented migrants and put an end to mass deportations as a first step to a long-awaited new policy on a thorny issue. The new policy – the Zimbabwe Document Project – is briefly described at the end of this chapter and it once again allows the deportation of large numbers of Zimbabweans.

However, enabling all Zimbabweans to apply for political asylum led to new and unforeseen consequences that did not necessarily reduce their suffering or sense of insecurity.

The Musina Showgrounds

Showgrounds, including exhibition halls, offices and rooms, in South Africa are usually used for farm and livestock exhibitions, flower shows, large meetings and other community events. A fenced open area in southern Musina, the grounds were preempted by the DHA and converted into a temporary centre for processing applications for political asylum from thousands of Zimbabweans. Two DHA buses were brought inside to serve as temporary offices where part of the processing could take place in addition to other buildings. When the DHA officers arrived in the morning, guards would admit the first 300 applicants in the line, the maximum number that could be processed in one day. No one else would be admitted. The officers refused all responsibility for what happened outside the fence, nor did they establish a system that would stop people from sleeping outside it overnight. They consistently refused to allocate numbers to the people waiting outside, nor did they do anything to let those denied on the first day know when they would be admitted.

Musina municipality provided no shelter, water or toilet facilities for those waiting outside. In order to avoid possible arrest and deportation, sometimes hundreds, and even thousands, of undocumented asylum-seekers would sleep outside the fenced area. If they left the area adjacent to the showgrounds they risked arrest. Applicants could wait for days or even weeks.[46] After the initial opening of the showgrounds to the immigrants, it took months for toilets, drinking water, showers, and medical assistance, etc., to be provided. Another unresolved issue was food. No governmental authority was willing to provide food for immigrants and the vacuum was filled by local churches. These tended to be those in the high-density area of Nancefield, which was about 15 km from the showground. Many Zimbabweans came with money, at least enough for a few days, but those who had been robbed were indeed desperate. Three churches in particular, the Catholic Church, the Anglican Church and Uniting Church of Christ, provided some meals, and the latter two also provided temporary shelter. The Anglican Church ultimately couldn't cope with so many refugees and ceased doing the latter. Their place was taken by another church ('I Believe in Jesus' in Nancefield) that would shelter migrants and provide meals for a couple of days. These places also served as recruiting grounds for commercial farmers working with immigration officials. Delays in processing asylum-seekers occurred adding to the backlog. Computers would fail, or a refugee officer was sick, meetings would be held (or multiple other events) resulting in less than the maximum number of applicants being 'processed', meaning that the person successfully opened a case for political asylum.[47]

More generally, Musina was operating in a crisis mode with a working group formed consisting of all those assisting Zimbabwean immigrants with food, sleeping places, medical assistance, legal assistance, rape counselling and transport. It also included the police and Home Affairs. In August 2012 the group was still meeting, although only twice a month instead of weekly. In addition to the regular meetings, there were long official and unofficial negotiations held with the police to have them cease harassing migrants, at least in Musina municipality. LHR and the IOM sought direct access to migrants before their deportation to inform them of their rights and their options while being held by the police. LHR lawyers also went to the detention/deportation facility to block the deportation of unaccompanied minors, attend in a limited fashion to other human rights violations and increasingly to assist immigrants with applying for asylum. When the Consortium for Refugees and Migrants in South Africa (CoRMSA) visited the Musina detention facility at the SMG in February 2009 they found, on consecutive days, 27 children and 50 children in detention awaiting forcible deportation. The Department of Social Development had not intervened to support such children. Save the Children assisted some by providing for them in Thohoyandou, while most were cared for in shelters run by two Roman Catholic Churches in Nancefield. With, however, only one lawyer for three or four hundred people who spent only a day there, the lawyers were unable to attend to the needs of most deportees.

From the perspective of an undocumented immigrant, he or she was now able to apply for asylum in Musina rather than having to travel to Johannesburg.[48] Officers were tasked with assisting them in claiming that they were seeking asylum. The DHA officer would take down the details of the person, issue them the Section 22 Permit according to the Refugee Act and give them an appointment where they would make their case of staying.[49]

With the permit stating that they had applied for refugee status and an appointment with a DHA officer, they were free to move about the country. Many immigrants did not attend their appointments and then claimed they had lost their paper and were given new appointments. Others did show up, knowing that there would be a long delay before they would be denied refugee status. However, this has changed because the South African government has substantially reduced the time between the application and the interview determining the success or failure of the application.

From interviews with the leading DHA officer at Musina,[50] and from observing their work, it was clear that the new measures provided only a temporary and inadequate solution. The officer firmly believed that the applicants did not qualify for political asylum but only wanted to work. However, he was working under instructions. Moreover, most applications were routinely denied on the grounds that Zimbabwe was not at war and that its Government of National Unity would lead to an improvement in the governance of Zimbabwe.[51] He also commented on the substantial costs that maintaining this temporary system incurred: this included, for example, eight officers staying and eating in the best hotels in Musina, plus other expenses for living away from home.

In our view, the use of the system at the showgrounds failed to guarantee dignity to those who sought services from the DHA. The problems that asylum-seekers faced included shelter, water, sanitation, access to food, access to health, arrests, detention and deportation. Unaccompanied minors were particularly vulnerable; in addition to the above, they were in constant danger of exploitation, theft and rape. Taken together, they indicate the weaknesses of the South African government's responses to Zimbabweans.

More generally, the South African government has resisted its human rights obligations toward asylum-seekers and immigrants. In its immigration policies South Africa has sought to block or to impede the implementation of procedures that would enable Zimbabweans to stay in South Africa. For example, the DHA would refuse to renew Section 22 Permits when they expired, even if an immigrant was unable to make an appointment. It took the intervention of the Cape Town High Court to rule that the process of not renewing Section 22 Permits was unlawful. It ordered the DHA with immediate effect to renew all Section 22 permits across the country.[52] The South African government has also neglected its international legal responsibilities by its lack of ensuring the well-being and care of unaccompanied minor children. It is also obliged to not repatriate them, something which has been all too commonly done. Lastly, the SMG itself was found to be below minimum standards for holding those awaiting deportation. In the three years prior to the issuing of Section 22 Permits, around 15,000 Zimbabwean nationals were deported from the centre each month. The High Court ordered the facility closed – something which was not done for more than a year.

A New Policy: The Zimbabwe Documentation Project

In April 2009, the South African government imposed a moratorium on deportations to Zimbabwe, partly as a result of the use of Section 22. Consequently, South Africa acquired the highest number of asylum-seekers in the world. Refugee Reception Centres were now clogged and the system couldn't cope. Two new temporary initiatives followed. The first was a 90-day free visa for those seeking to come to the country to visit or to do business. Many Zimbabwean day traders benefited. Then, in September 2010, the South African government announced an end to the special dispensation that had enabled Zimbabweans to enter and stay in South Africa with only their Section 22 Permit. To manage the process, the Ministry of Home Affairs created the Zimbabwe Documentation Project that seeks to have all Zimbabweans in South Africa regularize their status by applying for the proper documents. This process has several elements: One dimension has meant that Zimbabweans in South Africa should apply with a Zimbabwean passport for the appropriate visa from the Department of Home Affairs in South Africa. The application had three primary components:

(1) A completed application form, together with fingerprints
(2) A Zimbabwean passport[53]
(3) Documentation confirming one of the following:

    (a) proof of employment (e.g., an affidavit from the employer);
    (b) proof of registration with an educational institution; or
    (c) proof of business (e.g., company registration, registration with the South African Revenue Service).

Second, there are many fraudulent South African documents in circulation, and the Department of Home Affairs wanted them turned in. Third, all those Zimbabweans who did not have the correct documents after 1 August, 2011[54] were subject to deportation. However, the government promised that there would not be mass deportations. Fourth, the government met with the banks and the insurance industries to figure out what to do with people who had fraudulent documents.

According to the government, it has adjudicated 263,141 applications out of a total of 275,762. And, as of 4 July, 2011, 133,331 permits had been issued. There were also amnesty applications: 6,243 people handed in their false identity documents and received amnesty from criminal charges.[55] It has been a huge task, but if estimates are to be believed it leaves at least 1.3 million Zimbabweans without documentation. It also leaves approximately 500,000 Zimbabweans with Section 22 permits without a decision on their asylum applications. It was hoped that the Ministry of Home Affairs would drop or eliminate asylum applications when it changed the procedures.

From the perspective of undocumented Zimbabweans in South Africa, it has been an arduous and time-consuming process. Under pressure from UNHCR and IOM, Zimbabwe reduced the time and expense for obtaining a passport. Nevertheless, as indicated above, substantial and difficult documentation is required to obtain a passport. In addition, it disadvantages those who were forced to leave Zimbabwe due to political violence or hunger. To return to Zimbabwe and join very long queues to collect and present the documents in Zimbabwe without losing one's job in South Africa is indeed difficult and expensive. Having a new passport to obtain the documentation in South Africa and deliver it to a centre located only in a major city has meant an additional expense and burden to rural applicants.[56] Lastly, the conditions at the centres can be awful, including long queues, barren land, lack of sanitary facilities, bribery to gain entry and officious, and sometimes violent, security officers. There was a well-reported stampede at the Marabastad refugee centre that injured fourteen people, with a second one later in July 2011.[57] In sum, the conditions at the refugee centres have been very difficult for asylum-seekers. The numbers of Zimbabweans applying have consistently been higher than the Refugee Reception Offices could handle, thus often leading to inhumane conditions for the waiting applicants. At the same time, emphasis will now be shifted by Home Affairs to deportations. The police are now holding the potential deportees at a police station in Musina with lawyers unable to address many concerns although they are able to check for unaccompanied minors and other vulnerable people. It is not just Zimbabweans, however, who are being deported. In an effort to reduce all undocumented immigrants there are Congolese, Somalis, Nigerians and others being deported as well, although not through Musina. The new holding camp at the SMG base specially designed for deportees has yet to be put into operation.

Zimbabweans in South Africa: Xenophobia and the Stereotyping of Zimbabweans

There are interconnections among the presence of 'illegal' immigrants, the defense of the border, the scale of immigration and the existence of xenophobia. The existence of 'strangers' in a society can be categorized as stateless persons, refugees, asylum-seekers, temporary workers, documented workers and illegal migrants. While these different categories of persons exist in the South African context, they tend to be lumped in entirety as aliens or strangers (*makwerekwere*) and not protected by formal and informal norms and practices.[58] Lacking an appreciation for the distinctions among and between immigrants, asylum-seekers and refugees, they tend to become stereotyped, which makes violence more likely. In addition, the media emphasis is negative in its portrayal of migrants, though less so in 2000-05 than it was 1995–2000.[59] Most recent evidence suggests that the police ignore the warning signs of xenophobic violence and use inappropriate violence in its containment.[60]

The South African government struggling with xenophobia, violence and pressures from below to increase employment, housing and good education, has found itself unable to meet expectations. In the focus upon violence stemming from anti-immigrant demonstrations there is also evidence to suggest that ANC Councillors and other officials have also been involved in, or fanned, violent episodes.[61]

In terms of the latter we provide an example from 2011: At a parliamentary hearing on 16 August, 2011 the Labour Committee Chairman Mamagase Nchabeleng was quoted as saying that 'there was a township at Musina called Nancefield where the language "on the streets" was Shona – the main language of Zimbabwe' (IOL Business News, 17 August 2011). Aside from this provocative, untrue assertion, the purpose of the hearing was to investigate the costs to the South African welfare system of illegal nationals, especially Zimbabweans. Certainly, some have acquired fraudulent documents or illegally obtained social welfare grants, but statements such as Nchabeleng's only serve to reinforce national stereotyping, especially under headlines such as 'Foreign ID fraud bleeding SA fiscus' from a major web-based newspaper.[62] The mass emigration of Zimbabweans to South Africa without legal permission has only reinforced the stereotype of Zimbabweans as criminals (while also exposing the South African government to various accusations of human rights abuse). Indeed, they are now blamed for increasing crime in Musina, in Johannesburg and in the rural areas. Potential for violence is increasing in these areas. Such perceptions, along with multiple changes in policies, and deportations, only result in the continued insecurity of Zimbabweans in South Africa. Based, however, on our and others' research, we find that most Zimbabweans are hoping to find work in South Africa and to escape more generalized suffering. There are, of course, those who engage in criminal activity but given crime levels in South Africa to say Zimbabweans are responsible is simple scapegoating.

Distrust if not overt dislike of 'foreigners' is certainly not unique to South Africa and not linked to particular states. Racial, ethnic and national stereotyping can be found in almost all nation-states with varying degrees of intensity and efforts to restrict the entry of 'foreigners' or non-nationals. The case of South Africa, however, is marked by two additional dimensions: the first is its rights-based constitution and its emphasis upon democracy; the second is the level and scale of violence. In terms of the first dimension, there is, according to the southern African Migration Project (SAMP), and confirmed by later surveys, that South Africans compared to other nationalities are 'the most intolerant and hostile of people towards outsiders' (Crush, 2000: 108). SAMP surveys indicate high levels of societal intolerance towards non-citizens (whether legal or illegal, immigrants or migrants, refugees or asylum-seekers) (Ibid.: 118). These results have been repeated in 2008 in Afrobarometer's Round 4 of public opinion surveys in African democracies. Supporting these views have been media analyses (Fine and Bird, 2001; Danso and McDonald, 2001; McDonald and Jacobs, 2005). It is not possible to know how much media analysis shapes public opinion or follows it. In either case, the outcomes have been the use of African immigrants as scapegoats for South Africa's lack of jobs, enduring levels of poverty, growing inequality and the overall sense of disappointment in post-apartheid South Africa (Mattes, 2011).

In general, public opinion data demonstrate that regardless of racial group, the majority of South Africans are distrustful of foreign nationals. The Afrobarometer survey of 2010 indicates that South Africans are extremely distrustful of foreigners: 60 per cent of respondents say that they don't trust foreigners at all and another 23 per cent say that they trust them 'just a little' (Afrobarometer 2010: 2). There is strong agreement that the government should either prohibit all foreigners or restrict them. In a somewhat contradictory vein, most South Africans think the government should only deport foreigners back to their country of origin for very specific reasons. Only 23 per cent support deportation without cause (Ibid.: 4).[63] These recent views continue a long history of reproducing racial and national stereotypes about migrants from other African countries. This includes depicting, for example, Mozambicans as car thieves and Nigerians as drug smugglers. It is made worse by continuing to use the terms 'illegals' and 'aliens' to describe them (Danso and McDonald, 2000).

The Future of the Zimbabwe/South African Border

As we have demonstrated, immigration in general, and Zimbabwean immigration specifically, has been a long-standing issue for South Africa. The violent attacks upon immigrants collectively referred to as xenophobia[64] are a fierce reminder of how serious migration issues are and how it has distinguished South Africa from many other African states. In the spate of attacks in 2008 by South Africans upon immigrants, more than 60 people were killed and tens of thousands displaced in June of 2008. There has been continuing violence since then. Links between border controls, or rather their lack, and the violence has been made by the South African Institute of Race Relations. They apparently blame the lack of enforcement as a major cause. They write:

> The collapse of proper border control mechanisms saw literally millions of people gaining entry to South Africa illegally. The responsibility for this law enforcement failure rests jointly with the army, police and the government who saw fit to hand many border duties to the police when it should have been obvious that the police were unable to handle the responsibility. The closure of the commandos is instructive in this regard as it suggests a government more interested in ideology than in pragmatism. During a period when South Africa experienced some of the highest levels of violent crime in the world the state saw fit to close down one of the key organs responsible for rural policing.[65]

William Gumede, a South African political analyst, has written:

> The xenophobic sentiment cuts across race and levels of income. White farmers pay black immigrant workers pitiable wages. Black professionals think white companies use them as 'scabs', rather than appointing more local blacks. Africans are regularly accused by the police, media and local politicians of fuelling

the country's high crime rate. Police routinely stop and search foreign Africans, sometimes even mistaking locals for foreigners, and deport them if they don't have their identity documents with them. Corrupt police force members often extract bribes from African foreigners to shield them from arrest or deportation.[66]

In addition, there are many links made between the failure of the government to deliver services to the poor and the assumption that Zimbabweans or other migrants were benefiting from resources that should have been given to South Africans. The worst violence has been in urban centres, although there are some reported attacks in rural areas. However, it cannot be assumed without further enquiry that just because an attacker is a South African and the victim a non-South Africa that it is xenophobia.[67]

While accepting the complicated and varied nature of 'xenophobia' in South Africa, the question of citizenship and the hardening of national identities also need to be emphasized. In a very fine ethnographic portrait of a community known as Winterveld (now in Northwest Province) Reitz and Bam (2000) describe how its residents, who are made up of South African, Zimbabwean and Mozambicans, shared a common racial identity during the apartheid years. After 1990 they were encouraged to be part of the larger community of Winterveld only to find that by 1996 the Mozambicans and Zimbabweans were categorized as immigrants, subject to police raids and their integration threatened. The 'immigrants' position was strongly influenced by the broader national debate that had concluded that they have a negative impact on South African economy and society. And, more generally, that 'immigrants' are responsible for increasing levels of crime. Parallel to our experiences at the border and in rural Limpopo the police are hostile to those labeled as immigrants and treat them differently.

The human rights culture that South Africa has emphasized is not applied to those not legally in South Africa. While the 2002 Immigration Act, which replaces the old Alien Act, is greatly improved, there is little evidence that the opinions, attitudes and actions toward foreigners, especially Zimbabweans, has changed. The exaggeration of the numbers of Zimbabweans, and the focus on the jobs they 'steal', continues to contribute to an atmosphere of hostility. At the same time, attitudes toward 'foreigners' is highly gendered according to the roundtable discussion in Pretoria in 2008.[68] South African men contended that:

With these people (illegals) one person takes on the workload of three people

170

because they don't know about the Labour Relations Act. I won't work for peanuts but that doesn't bother them because they know that they will break into your home and steal your possessions. (2008: 20)

As one woman expressed it at the same roundtable, in distinction to the men:

I think those people (foreign nationals) are hard workers, they will do anything for a job. They will work for minimum wages. We South Africans are trying to chase the fast, glamorous life: foreigners work in low positions; they get noticed by the employer for their hard work when they get promoted. Then South Africans get angry at that? (Ibid.)

These differences are mirrored in the importance placed by men and women toward more effective border controls and keeping foreigners out who don't have passports. Thus the insistence by the South African government upon Zimbabweans (and others) having passports reflects a major concern from its own citizenry.

Conclusions

Zimbabwe immigration to South Africa highlights complex unresolved issues in South Africa's policies toward Zimbabwe as well as the large number of documented and undocumented Zimbabweans in the country. South Africa has downplayed the depth and extent of the crisis in Zimbabwe while not acknowledging the linkages between its economic and political dimensions. It has also tested the South African government's commitment to human rights and to the international agreements on refugees, unaccompanied children and rights to asylum to which it has acceded. The Zimbabwe crisis signifies failed governance, political violence, food insecurity, manipulation of food for political ends, high unemployment and, through 2009, shortages of many consumer items. And, the South African government did not publically explain or analyze why so many Zimbabweans wanted to enter South Africa. In short, the Zimbabwean migrants are products of an economic crisis that is indeed political.

The acceptance of asylum-seekers and immigrants more generally means a statement or conclusion about what is taking place. Or, as Baumann (2010) puts it: 'the problem with giving someone asylum is that you have to make a statement about that country that individual is leaving' (2010: 84). Linked to this political crisis has been South Africa's policy of 'quiet diplomacy' that has left South Africa unwilling and unable to focus on events and processes in its northern neighbor. By using Section 22 (suggesting to all Zimbabweans that they apply for asylum) it has created a doubly false illusion: 1) That the Government of South Africa actually believes there is a huge refugee crisis in Zimbabwe and 2) That it is using the term 'refugee' even though it has every intention of denying asylum status to almost all asylum-seekers from Zimbabwe.

The latest twist in this saga is the closure of refugee reception centres in Cape Town, Pretoria, Johannesburg and Port Elizabeth and keeping them operational only on the major border-crossing areas from Zimbabwe into South Africa.[69] According to LHR, this policy, although as yet unannounced, will pose enormous difficulties for those resident in the cities.[70] It means that those awaiting disposition of their asylum applications will have to travel to either Musina or Alldays for their appointments or hearings. This requires substantial time and money to accomplish. It seems reasonable to assume that because of these difficulties it will lead to more undocumented Zimbabweans in South Africa.

As service delivery protests increase, and while there appears to be little lessening of hostility toward undocumented Zimbabweans (and other Africans), Zimbabweans are inserted into most facets of South African life. Efforts to assert national borders and controls in the current context seem futile, or difficult at best. There remains a big gap between what individual South Africans do, how they do or don't relate to Zimbabweans at their work places, in their socializing and in their home communities and neighborhoods, as will be documented in the following chapters on Zimbabweans in Limpopo and on the farms.

In terms of stereotyping of labeling, the continued use of the term and concept *makwerekwere* applied toward non-South Africans reinforces notions of foreignness that overrides other ways of conceptualizing and categorizing black Africans. Whether or not these categories harden or weaken depends upon numerous factors, including resolution of the crises in Zimbabwe, increased wages and employment in Zimbabwe, increased employment, especially of youth, in South Africa, policies of the South African government toward foreign nationals and what happens with the deadlines for Zimbabweans to formalize and legalize their stay in South Africa. The policies of the current government leads to an exclusionary ideology and one that reinforces the notion that 'foreigners' or 'aliens' are disrupting progress toward a new South Africa.

The Zimbabwe exodus has exposed fractures, disagreements and difficulties for the South African state. It has placed a discomforting light on the links between national identity and immigration policies. The complexities and ambiguities have been and are being performed at the border as multiple government agencies, churches, human rights organizations, the police, the army and humanitarian organizations attempt to cope with the willingness of Zimbabweans (and others) to endure hardships and risks to seek new opportunities. Rather than seeing immigrants as contributing to the economy, they have been stigmatized. In critiquing current South African government policies, Landau (2011) contends that the framing of who should benefit from the post-apartheid order in South Africa has had significant implications for the framing of debates around non-South African citizens. If the South African government continues to emphasize that only those who suffered under apartheid deserve the benefits that come from post-1994 achievements, it excludes those who come from other countries and the contributions they have made, he maintains. In practice it also seems to exclude those who came from the former northern homelands (Gazankulu, Venda, Lebowa and parts of Bophuthatswana). The view of outsiders as threatening South Africa makes little empirical sense given the actual situation of approximately three per cent of the population being foreign and the high levels of unemployment. However, as Landau emphasizes, it is neither facts nor logic that drives the politics around the false threat of foreign workers. Instead it is immigration and related policies that emphasize differences between South Africans and others that will perpetuate those differences. Current policies that emphasize difference and claim that only those who suffered under apartheid should benefit from the new dispensation will have the consequence of undermining South Africa's commitment to human rights. The government, through its border policies, its deportation of Zimbabweans, the corruption in the treatment of those with asylum-seeker permits, the stereotyping of Zimbabweans, the deportation of unaccompanied minors, among other practices, has failed to live up to several human rights conventions.[71] If to govern the border focuses on keeping out those who are conceived to be those seeking to undermine achievements post-1994, then it will be difficult to view migrants as important contributors to development and the building of South Africa. Morever, the continued perspective that Zimbabweans are only economic migrants will reinforce this distinction.

In the next chapters we examine Zimbabweans in different contexts in rural Limpopo Province, on the spaces of large-scale commercial farms and in the communal lands. These chapters underline how much Zimbabweans are willing to risk in order to work under highly exploitative and difficult contexts.

Notes

1 The Bush war lasted from 1966 until 1989, making it one of Africa's longest conflicts. It was fought in Northern Namibia (former South West Africa), and also in Southern Angola – so-called 'Operational Area' or 'Border'.

2 Richard Wilson has analyzed how the Truth and Reconciliation Commission was as much about legitimizing the South African state as it was about justice. *The Politics of Truth and Reconciliation in South Africa: Legitimizing the Post-Apartheid State*, Cambridge University Press: 2001.

3 The regulation of immigration can be found in the Aliens Control Act of 1991, which was amended in 1996 to further tighten up on all immigration.

4 Interview with Lawyers for Human Rights, July 2012.

5 We have detailed in the introduction the ebbs and flows of violence.

6 The relationship between the governments of South Africa and Zimbabwe are discussed in Chapters 1 and 2.

7 http://www.radiovop.com/index.php/national-news/7707-anc-pledges-continued-support-to-zanu-pf.html, accessed on 6 August 2012.

8 The single best account of South Africa's migration history is *Selecting Immigrants: National Identity and South Africa's Immigration Policies 1910–2008* by Sally Peberdy.

9 One could add that the failure of the state to adequately deliver public goods makes it less legitimate and more likely to blame others (Carter 2011).

10 Xenophobia is defined as 'attitudes, prejudices and behaviour that reject, exclude and often vilify persons, based on the perception that they are outsiders or foreigners to the community, society or national identity'. Source: the Declaration on Racism, Discrimination, Xenophobia and Related Intolerance against Migrants and Trafficked Persons. Asia Pacific NGO Meeting for the World Conference Against Racism, Racial Discrimination, Xenophobia and Related Intolerance. Tehran, Iran. 18 February 2001.

11 According to the Department of Home Affairs, more than 275,000 Zimbabwean nationals applied for permits under the Zimbabwe Documentation Programme, whereas there are somewhere between one and three million Zimbabweans currently in South Africa. http://www.pmg.org.za/report/20110920-department-home-affairs-zimbabwean-documentation-project.

12 For a complete assessment of the range of departments involved in border control see J. Steinberg (2005).

13 Human Sciences Research Council, 2008.

14 F. Wilson, Migrant Labour: Report to the South African Council of Churches. The South African Council of Churches, Johannesburg: 1972, p. 109.

15 This is described in van Onselen (1976) and Phimister (1988).

16 Zimbabweans working on Limpopo farms were largely Venda people living in settlements just across the border and may have been accustomed to crossing the river since pre-colonial times. What is significant is that since the late 1990s most of the

Zimbabwean farm workers are Shona speakers from further afield.

17 Labour Migration to South Africa in the 1990s, Policy Paper Series No. 4 (February 1998), International Labour Office, Southern Africa Multidisciplinary Advisory Team, Harare, Zimbabwe.

18 Tim Keegan, Charles van Onselen, Alan Jeeves, Jeremy Krikler, and Jonathan Crush, among others.

19 Transvaal Province became, over time, the Gauteng, Limpopo and Mpumalanga provinces. A large part of Northwest Province and a very small part of KwaZulu-Natal Province were also included. To add complexity to the story, the northern region of the Transvaal was initially named Northern Transvaal. The following year, it was renamed Northern Province, which remained the name until 11 July 2003, when the name of the province was formally changed to Limpopo Province.

20 This forced removal has led to numerous restitution claims.

21 We will not deal here with the competition in recruiting workers between the mining and agricultural industries.

22 A corporate permit may be issued to a corporate applicant to allow him/her to employ a predetermined number of skilled/semi-skilled/unskilled workers.

23 The Immigration Act (No 13 of 2002) deals with immigration and migration. It repeals the Aliens Control Act of 1991 as well as the Aliens Control Amendment Act (No. 76 of 1995) and regulates the admission of people to South Africa and their right to live and work here. The Act uses a licensing fee to manage the process of allowing foreigners to work and live in South Africa. The idea is that if someone is willing to pay more to employ a foreigner than they would to employ a South African, then that foreigner is needed.

24 This issue was not taken up by any major South African union.

25 Immigration Act, 13 of 2002 (as amended in 2004) and amended again in 2011.

26 Section 39. Learning institutions (for example):

(1) No learning institution shall knowingly provide training or instruction to—

  (a) an illegal foreigner;

  (b) a foreigner whose status does not authorize him or her to receive such training or instruction by such person; or

  (c) a foreigner on terms or conditions or in a capacity different from those contemplated in such foreigner's status.

(2) If an illegal foreigner is found on any premises where instruction or training is provided, it shall be presumed that such foreigner was receiving instruction or training from, or allowed to receive instruction or training by, the person who has control over such premises, unless prima facie evidence to the contrary is adduced.

27 Interviews with farm owners and farm managers, 2008–2010. Most expressed the view that Zimbabweans made better workers. However, other views are reported in Human Rights Watch 2006.

28 This is the official number of Zimbabweans found or caught in South Africa. It doesn't count repeat offenders, nor does it count those who return home on their own.

29 This is nothing new. Between 1994 and 2000 over 600,000 people were forcibly removed from the country by the police (Crush and McDonald, 2001: 6)

30 Interview with Mr Mohamed Hussein, International Office of Migration, Musina, October 2011, and Jacob Matakanye, Musina Legal Assistance Office, October 2011, and observations in Musina.

31 The number of asylum applications in South Africa was 207,000 in 2008, 222,000 in 2009 and 180,000 in 2010. For the fourth consecutive year South Africa received the highest number of individual asylum applications lodged in a single country – more than 106,900 in 2011. This data is found in Global Trends: Refugees, Asylum-seekers, Returnees, Internally Displaced and Stateless Persons Country Data Sheets, 15 June 2010; Global Trends: Refugees, Asylum-seekers, Returnees, Internally Displaced and Stateless Persons Country Data Sheets, 2011; UNHCR Global Report, 2011.

32 Foreigners are, by law, not permitted to enter or sojourn in SA with a view to permanent residence unless s/he is in possession of immigration permit issued in terms of Section 25 of the Aliens Control Act. South Africa Citizenship Act, 1995 [South Africa], 6 October 1995, available at http://www.unhcr.org/refworld/docid/3ae6b50514.html [accessed 30 November 2010]

33 Interview in Musina, 26 July 2012. Name withheld.

34 Organized gangs preying on immigrants are also present in cities. For example, the issue of the *maguma-gumas* was important for asylum-seekers waiting outside the Refugee Reception Office in Johannesburg. Consortium for Migrants and Refugees in South Africa (CoRMSA), CoRMSA NEWSLETTER, Edition 5-18th December 2007.

35 Although located on the University of Witwatersrand Campus in Johannesburg, the Wits Law Clinic is an independent NGO. It was very active during the xenophobic violence, pressuring the government to develop policies for the reintegration of immigrants into their communities after they were driven out or had fled for safety.

36 Interviews with Department of Home Affairs officers and South African Lawyers for Human Rights. They are being kept anonymous.

37 In 2004 the Solidarity Peace Trust produced a report entitled No War in Zimbabwe: An Account of a Nation's People. In Part 1 it attempted to demonstrate the political reasons why Zimbabweans were leaving. It attributed a great deal to the breakdown of law and order, torture, political abuse of food, the collapse of the economy and the collapse of social services. The Solidarity Peace Trust is a non-governmental organization registered in South Africa. Its trustees are church leaders in southern Africa who are all committed to human rights, freedom and democracy in their region. See http://www.solidaritypeacetrust.org/.

38 There were two Human Rights Watch reports (2006 and 2008), a series of papers by the Center for Forced Migration, lobbying by the Lawyers for Human Rights among others. There was also the concentration of Zimbabweans at the Home Affairs offices in Pretoria and large numbers living at the Central Methodist Church in Johannesburg.

39 Statistics South Africa. 2008. Community Survey 2007 Basic Results: Municipalities. Pretoria: Government Printers available on line at http://www.statssa.gov.za/publications/p03011/p030112007.pdf.

40 http://www.opensubscriber.com/message/osint@yahoogroups.com/7169920.html.

41 As quoted by Gabriel Shumba. See www.chapter2.org.za/gbOutputFiles.asp?WriteContent=Y&RID=2395.

42 See Lawyers for Human Rights v Minister of Safety and Security & 17 Others (5824/2009), North Gauteng High Court (15 May 2009). Available at http://www.saflii.org/_za/cases/ZAGPPHC/2009/57.pdf. Protecting Non-Citizens in South Africa 2009.

43 Human Rights Watch wrote that the 'Most serious of all are reports that in 2007 many Zimbabweans in the immediate border areas were being taken to a detention facility in Musina, on the South Africa-Zimbabwe border. The facility is located on a military base previously used by the South African National Defense Forces (SANDF), and is being run by the South African Police Services (SAPS). Most Zimbabweans were deported within hours or days by the police without immigration officials verifying their legal status and authorities are bound to comply with basic minimum standards of detention for immigration-related detainees.' (2008: 99-100). It went on to note that those being deported were not being informed of their rights to appeal the decision to deport them, which is a clear breach of the Immigration and Refugee Acts. These practices have reportedly continued in 2008. Numerous civil society organizations have been refused access to the detention facility. UNHCR has also repeatedly been refused access (2008: 100). As we have noted, this situation has improved since 2008.

44 The showgrounds are a municipally owned facility used for agricultural shows and meetings and can be rented for demonstrations.

45 The permit needs to be renewed at any Refugee Reception Office/Asylum Determination Office until the person's refugee status is determined. With a Section 22 Permit a person is entitled to work and study in South Africa.

46 In 2008 and 2009 we interviewed people who had been waiting for more than a month. The refugee officers refused to implement any system to assist those outside the fence surrounding the showgrounds. They also initially refused to accept external intervention in allocating numbers to waiting applicants.

47 The scale of immigration in 2008 took many by surprise. In 2008 115,800 Zimbabweans applied for asylum, including 25,000 to 30,000 in the last half of the year in Musina alone (HRW, 2009: 15). One could guess that most came during the presi-

dential run-off that saw widespread violence throughout Zimbabwe. Even with success in obtaining a permit, asylum-seekers initially waited for months or years before having a status review. Human Rights Watch has reported over 100,000 unresolved asylum cases from 2008 alone on top of a pre-existing backlog of 100,000.

48 The Johannesburg Refugee Reception Centre was closed in October 2011 and a temporary one established in Pretoria. Home Affairs is planning to move Refugee Reception Centres to its borders.

49 The second interview is called the Status Determination hearing and is conducted by a Refugee Status Determination Officer. Following this interview and the submission of supporting materials and affidavits, an overall decision on the application will be made.

50 Interview by Bill Derman, July 2009.

51 Based on interviews with Home Affairs Officers, Lawyers for Human Rights and the Legal Resources Centre of Musina.

52 CoRMSA Newsletter, Edition 11-19th December 2008, p. 4.

53 Obtaining a Zimbabwean passport is no simple matter. It takes the following: All of the following documents and photocopies are required to be produced in person in order to process a passport application:

1. Birth Certificate (long Birth Certificate)
2. National Identity Card (Driver's license not accepted)
3. Marriage certificate/National Identity Card in married name/Divorce order
4. Two passport colour photographs (Size 3.5 x 4.5cm)
5. Citizenship certificate (for citizens by registration)
6. Old passport or Emergency Travel Documents if any
7. Letter on citizenship status from the country you have lived in for five years or more.

Identity cards are only issued in Zimbabwe where registrants have to appear in person in order to get their photos and fingerprints taken. If you happen to be in a situation where you need a new passport but don't have an ID card, the next best thing is to apply for an emergency travel document to get to Zimbabwe and apply for the necessary documents.

54 The date was pushed back for a few months but is now in force.

55 http://www.info.gov.za/speech/DynamicAction?pageid=461&sid=19609&tid=36304. Since the deadline of 1 August 2011 very few new permits were issued through this programme.

56 The cities are Johannesburg, Pretoria, Cape Town, Port Elizabeth, Durban and the border town of Musina.

57 We also observed the use of sjamboks (leather clubs) on asylum-seekers at the Musina showgrounds as people were chased during the arrival of then presidential candidate Jacob Zuma in 2008. There have been multiple other reports provided to CoRMSA and LHR of violence launched against asylum-seekers.

58 The term *makwerekwere* is the label used for all African migrants. The term according to Nyamanjoh, Peberdy and Sichone, among others, refers to undeserving outsiders who are 'babblers' or 'barbarians'. It can be understood as a pejorative term which continues deeper historical patterns of regulating access to the cities and the economy. By contrast, it appears that white migration is not a problem, only black. (Nyamanjoh, 2006: 68.) Labeling people as makwerekwere deprives them of their language and full humanity, increasing the possibility of violent attacks upon them.

59 McDonald and Jacobs, 2005: 305.

60 Von Holdt et al., 2011.

61 Ibid., Anton Harber 2012.

62 http://www.iol.co.za/business/business-news/foreign-id-fraud-bleeding-sa-fiscus-1.1119121.

63 In a disturbing finding, those who access television, radio and print news on a daily basis hold intolerant views of immigrants. For a detailed consideration of the media see Fine and Bird, 2006.

64 http://www.hsrc.ac.za/Document-2807.phtml.

65 Xenophobia: Nine Causes of the Current Crisis by Frans Cronje 20 May 2008. Frans Cronje is the Deputy CEO of the South African Institute of Race Relations. http://www.politicsweb.co.za/politicsweb/view/politicsweb/en/page71619?oid=89859&sn=Detail.

66 http://www.independent.co.uk/opinion/commentators/william-gumede-mbeki-must-face-up-to-south-africas-xenophobia-831476.html.

67 For example, there are attacks upon accused or suspected witches and thieves, usually by young men and only involving South Africans.

68 http://www.hsrc.ac.za/Document-2994.phtml. Violence and Xenophobia in South Africa: Developing Consensus, Moving to Action. Report on a meeting hosted by the Democracy and Governance research programme of the Human Sciences Research Council (HSRC) and the British High Commission.

69 This includes Alldays, which is much smaller than Musina.

70 Derman interview at Musina, 28 July 2012, with South African Lawyers for Human Rights.

71 For example, the United Nations Human Rights Council in March 2012 launched a global campaign to end immigration detention of children. This year the campaign is focusing on seven countries: Australia, Greece, Israel, Malaysia, Mexico, South Africa and the United States. Countries have been chosen for inclusion in the campaign based on the extent to which immigration detention of children is an issue, combined with the commitment of local civil society groups. See http://www.lhr.org.za/news/2012/global-campaign-end-child-detention-focus-south-africa.

7

Hierarchies, Violence, Gender

Narratives from Zimbabwean Migrants on South African Farms

Ruth Hall[1]

As a Zimbabwean I have no right to say anything, only to work
Edmond, Malamula farm, Tshipise, South Africa, 2007

I came as a river jumper but was given a work permit. This shows mercy....
But my mind is in Zimbabwe
Obed, Makwembe farm, Musina, South Africa, 2008

If you follow the law, when you are poor, you die
Patience, Mbhongolo farm, Mopane, South Africa, 2008

Introduction

By 2008, the number of Zimbabweans working on farms on the South African side of the border was conservatively estimated at 20,000. This excluded the growing number of Zimbabweans living on farms without the knowledge or consent of owners. In this period of economic collapse and hyperinflation in Zimbabwe, and the rapid movement of growing numbers of Zimbabweans into South Africa, immigration authorities were kept busy deporting hundreds, and sometimes even thousands, of people every day. Many returned within 24 hours. Many did not manage to get very far into South Africa.

South African commercial farms present a laboratory for a potent mix of dazzling social and economic inequality, national and linguistic identities, forms of governance and control and isolation that make up some of the experiences of Zimbabwean migrants. Within the boundaries of white-owned farms in the border zone close to the Limpopo River – boundaries that are sometimes more forcefully fenced and guarded than the nearby national border – the paradoxes that animate social relations between owners and workers are everywhere evident: the stark *isolation* of owners, managers and workers, both from one another's realities and from the surrounding world, and the *intimacy* of their social relations brought about by their physical proximity and the intrusive forms of control that this permits.

This intimacy takes forms that Rutherford (1997), in his study of farm labour regimes in Zimbabwe, named 'domestic governance': the substantial influence of unilateral decisions by farm owners over many dimensions of the lives of those living there, and the exclusion of these relations from the reach of the public sphere of the state, law and rights. Underpinning this is the fusing, on the farm, of a place of work with a place of residence – and thus the extension of control by farm owners over the private lives of workers, their families, friends and visitors, outside of working hours. While Rutherford rightly draws attention to the hegemonic forms of control exerted by white farm owners over black workers, our study shows how this intersects with another feature of life on farms: the agency of mostly illegal Zimbabwean migrants who are either employed as workers, or stay there with friends or family members, or arrive without prior connections, hoping to create a niche for themselves, or are 'passers-through'. With these varied credentials, Zimbabweans must navigate this new social world of farm villages or compounds, and their complex relations of inequality, reciprocity, dependence, solidarity and violence.

One of the aims of the research on which this book is based was to record and analyze the narratives of migrant farmers and farm workers in order to understand how they view the events that led them to leave Zimbabwe and why they chose their particular destinations. Attention in this chapter falls on the stories and subjectivities of Zimbabweans in the commercial farming districts in the north of South Africa. The discussion considers how they depict their experiences, and how they view themselves in terms of citizenship and levels of identity. The chapter is based on in-depth interviews with migrants, both legal and undocumented, with a focus not only on farm workers but also on other, unemployed, migrants living on white-owned farms. These interviews were conducted over a period of just over two years, from early 2007 to 2009. In these interviews we aimed to trace the life histories of some migrants, focusing on the stories underlying their displacement, migration and arrival on the farms. These interviews were supplemented with interviews with members of recipient communities, such as South African farm workers and farm owners, and other key informants, including policy-makers and government officials, NGOs such as the Legal Advice Office in Musina, Nkuzi Development Association and the International Organization on Migration (IOM). Field observation focused on three farms where Zimbabweans were living and/or working (see Chapter 10 by Poul Wisborg for a more detailed elaboration of the field sites). Understanding of the wider context was also informed by desktop data gathering of available data (media, government documents, published and unpublished reports) on migration and policy responses – though the focus in this chapter falls directly on the voices and experiences of migrants themselves.

How and Why they Crossed

Doing fieldwork from 2007 to 2009, many of those we met and interviewed on the farms had crossed the border in recent weeks, some for the first time, and were still acclimatizing to their new, and precarious, existence as illegal workers. These first-time migrants were encountering the gap between 'idealization' and 'reality', observed in many migration studies (Tannenbaum, 2007). These conditions were shaped in large part by the context of official policy which denied and criminalized the massive movement of people across this border – at least until mid-2008. After years of official denial of the scale of migration across this border, the opening of a refugee reception centre in Musina in July 2008 offered some respite to border-crossers, but it also exposed the deep-seated contradictions underlying South Africa's official response as discussed in Chapter 6. Having applied for asylum, border-crossers were issued with permits temporarily legalizing their residence in the country, pending interviews with authorities. Although processing the asylum applications was slow, and these were routinely denied, this official acknowledgement of the abnormality of the situation proffered to those crossing the chance of three months of suspended illegality, during which they might establish themselves somewhere, including on the farms. The establishment of the asylum centre created geographic and legal ambiguities: those without their papers found between Beitbridge and Musina could claim to be on their way to the showgrounds to register for asylum, while those further south of Musina would be deemed illegal unless they had received the permit and so deported. This had reportedly contributed to the concentration of Zimbabweans on farms in this northern region. Whereas in the past police had been kept busy arresting people in this border zone to detain them ahead of deportation, police were now providing lifts to the asylum centre. As a captain in the South African Police Service in Musina explained to us: 'When we pick people up we have to drop them at the showground. Those who have gone past the showground we arrest' (Ringane, 2008: pers. comm.). Effectively, the police told us, the border had moved south: Zimbabweans were no longer illegal in this new 'no man's land' in Musina or north of it; beyond the showground at the southern outskirts of town was the real 'South Africa'.

Yet this cosy picture is in friction with the narratives of migrants themselves, who had endured hardship, exploitation, danger and often violence in the course of crossing the border, and whose arrival in the country often signaled not an end to their difficulties, but a new set of social relations to navigate.

Stories of the Crossing

Among those who had recently crossed, the story of their own crossing was one of the first points of conversation they offered. These stories varied greatly, but most involved tales of walking, often at night, over long distances, with scant information about what to look for, or where to go. Many did not make the trip entirely on foot, often taking lifts on trucks, or buses or other local transport to a point close to the border post. Some had walked through the border post with or without papers, but most had not: they had either been smuggled through on trucks or, more commonly, had crossed the river and the many-holed fence. Some had met the dreaded '*maguma-gumas*'[2] (literally, 'those who take unfairly'), the bandits who operated freely in the border zone, on the veld either side of the river, attacking, mugging, robbing and raping illegal crossers; while others had paid for rides but were duped and dropped off at the side of the road before the border, stripped of their savings. These two groups were among the worst off. While some had crossed with the aim of heading for the farms, or even a specific farm, some had ended up there by default, their dreams of making it to Johannesburg shattered by the theft of money, cellphones and phone numbers, and sometimes certificates, their only evidence of the skills they hoped might earn them access to better jobs in South African towns and cities.

Most had crossed in small groups, often with friends, but also sometimes strangers met on the way. In this way, through force of numbers, groups of border crossers hoped they would be protected from the predations of the *maguma-gumas*. One group of 'walkers' we came across as they traversed this farming district told a much-repeated story:

> We met a person with a bakkie [pick-up truck] at the border after we had crossed the river. This person charged us R300 to take us to Makhado [a town about

80 km south of the border]. When we got to Musina [the northernmost town, about 10 km south of the border] he ordered us to get off the car and said the journey was equivalent to our money. We could not question because we were afraid the person was going to call the police, get us arrested and deported.

We are left with R10 [about US$1.50] and now we are just walking. (Tawanda, 2008: pers. comm.)

Herbert, a 26-year-old market researcher from Harare, having found that his salary could no longer cover the cost of basic food for himself, his mother, three sisters and brother, had left Harare a few weeks before we met him on a South African fruit farm in early 2008, and recounted his experience of crossing.

I left Harare, got to the bridge, got off the truck. I was afraid of going through the river and under the fence, so I went through the new bridge, walked over it, and crossed there. I went through the immigration from the Zimbabwe side. On the South African side, it was hard. On the South African side, there were some holes [in the fence], and I got through the holes and from there I had to run through the grass. On the way you meet these guys, the *maguma-gumas*, who demand money to let you pass. I was just dishing out money to each one as I went. I spent about R400. They can kill you – they have knives. When I had crossed, I was at the South African side, I thought it was over. Then the policemen came, chasing everyone. I ran to the road and stopped a car and they gave me a lift for free to Musina. (Herbert, 2008: pers. comm.)

There were specific and well-substantiated stories: farm workers fishing at the river had found a baby that had drowned.

Just last week people who were catching fish in the river picked up a baby; she had drowned. Nobody knows where the mother is. People are risking their lives. At the beginning of January we found three bodies here [in the river close by]. Further down there were seven or eight more that had been washed down. Nobody knows the true number [of people who are drowning as they try to cross] but we know it does happen. (Jake, 2008: pers. comm.)

We later heard from the white administrator of one of the farms what was probably the same story, but from another perspective: the story of a mother, her baby on her back, who had crossed the river in full spate as part of a group, holding hands, to get through the water – only to find at the other bank that the baby was no longer there, and had turned back by herself in distress, probably to her own death.

They get very hungry that side; even when the river is very full they are coming.

[A few weeks ago] a woman came through the river with a baby on her back and came out of the river and the baby was gone – and she turned back and then she was gone, she was swept away in the river. They care for their babies like that. It is very sad. (Eloise, 2008: pers. comm.)

The horror of anecdote had become the stuff of legend, as elements of truth and fiction became interwoven. Another farm worker, with greater experience of the migration route, had crossed many times, been deported several times, often crossing back into South Africa the same day. He had for the past couple of years been commuting between the two countries, working for six months in South Africa, during the harvest season, and returning to his own smallholding outside Harare for the rest of the year. His characterization of the river crossing and its dangers resonated with many others', but also held the hallmarks of exaggeration. It is striking that, despite having experienced being deported, in discussing the dangers of crossing back into South Africa, the police are not mentioned.

Crossing the river is very dangerous. Either you lose your clothing or your money or your life. The biggest danger is the *maguma-gumas*. Crocodiles are the second biggest danger, especially because the river is full now. [The third biggest danger] is the river itself; you can be washed away by the river. 70 people a day are washed away. Yes, it is true…. When we are deported from South Africa we are 200 in a group. Coming back over the river, we are in big groups so we can help each other – we use sticks, not ropes, and there are ladies and men together. (Simon, 2008: pers.comm.)

Perhaps the most poignant moment in our research was our meeting with Simba, a young man from Harare. His was a tragic story about the devastating loss of a list of phone numbers – the key to the network that could provide security and protection, food, a place to stay and onward contacts with the possibility of, ultimately, a job, income and hope for the future. This loss of the means with which to contact people was clearly more concerning to him than his wounds from being attacked with machetes. We met him on a farm road less than 100 km from the border, in February 2008, two days after he had been attacked, in the veld, on his first day in South Africa. The three men had taken the small amount of money he had been able to bring with him, as well as his documents, including his letter of reference from the Sheraton Hotel in Harare where he had maintained the boiler. They had stolen his shoes. Among his papers was his most valuable possession: a list of phone numbers, including that for his male cousin, living in Gauteng, and his 'sister' (actually also a cousin) living in Kimberley, and various other acquaintances and friends-of-friends dotted around northern and central South Africa. Only through exceptionally lengthy and expensive phone calls was he able to reconstruct this list and, eventually, to make contact with some of those from home who were already in the country.

Official patrolling of the border means that soldiers and police are also feared, though less than the bandits; at least the soldiers and police were most likely to arrest and deport people rather than rob or kill them – though that had allegedly happened too. Both were bribable. A security manager from one of the farms, who himself often arrests and hands over illegal crossers to the authorities (unless they are needed for employment on the farm), told us:

> We had two incidents whereby a person was found shot there where they cross. They are the border jumpers. We just assume it was soldiers. The last one was in November or December [three months previously]. We sometimes hear shots and we just assume they are [from the] soldiers. [Indeed, the bullet found in the body in this later incident was from an 'R5' standard army issue rifle, according to the police]. The *maguma-gumas* are here but they are not having a weapon – they may have a knife or sticks or a panga, but not a gun. The soldiers' camp is 800 metres away to the east and the next one is just over 1 km to the west, and there are some soldiers inside the farm. There is a camp in the bush next to the gate at [the next door farm]. They've been there two months now. They moved from a place next to the river but it was too obvious. (Jake, 2008: pers. comm.)

While many had crossed the border without visas, some had been lucky enough to be 'picked up' on the other side of the border by white farmers brandishing their corporate permits, and seeking Zimbabweans to fill their authorized labour quotas. Farm owners usually employed Zimbabweans as casual or seasonal workers and then organized corporate permits to allow them to work only for them. Those who crossed illegally could have their residence and employment on farms regularized by farmers – but this offered no protection once they left the farms, and so bound them to continued employment on the farm. Those who crossed illegally, without visas, indeed without passports or 'ETDs' (emergency travel documents), were often received by family members, friends, friends of friends, clan members, on the farms. But even those migrants without networks were often taken in by fellow Zimbabweans on the farms, sometimes sheltered under the pretence that they were family members, and sometimes sheltered illicitly, without the knowledge of either owners or foremen.

Arriving in South Africa was not the end of the journey, as many tried repeatedly and at great risk (and financial cost) to get their stay in the country legitimized. As a young man, Jabulo, told us, he and his friend had tried to do this:

> We heard about the asylum centre from six women who are working on the farm who had already managed to get their papers. They advised us that if you are from Zimbabwe you must tell the immigration authorities that you came to South Africa because of hunger and also because the ZANU-PF people were beating us. The six women said that we need to emphasize that even if the political parties in Zimbabwe are talking, things are still the same in the villages. Once we get asylum we [will] get back to [this] farm. And this time we will be able to walk freely. But right now we do not know what we will eat. The police officer at the roadblock demanded R50 [about US$7.50] from us in order to let us pass. We had to bribe him, otherwise we were going to be arrested and deported. (Jabulo, 2008: pers. comm.)

The danger of the crossing is founded on its illegality, and this is mirrored in the risks of crossing back – often carrying money. The quest for legality, then, is not only in order to get work (and is not a prerequisite for employment anyway), but also to limit exposure to violence or being robbed on the return journey(s). Patience, a young Zimbabwean living on a game farm with her Zimbabwean lover and their child, made the trip back to Zimbabwe to visit her parents legally, taking someone else's corporate permit and replacing her picture on the permit so that she can cross over the bridge rather than by the river. Although she had come via the river, crossing by the bridge was essential: she was taking her newborn baby with her to visit his grandparents.

It is challenging to think about how different the logistics of migration would have been if this period of economic crisis and the displacement it prompted had occurred in a pre-cellphone era. Despite enormous economic hardship, including widespread hunger and even starvation, people had cellphones – not everyone, but many, if not most. Airtime was one of the most prized commodities among migrants, short text messages could be sent cheaply and, for those crossing, the contact details of family and friends who went before them, who were better established, are their roadmap to security.

The last straw: the push factors

The main 'driver' of migration was overwhelmingly economic distress – the unaffordability and unavailability of food and other basic items – but some migrants we spoke to had been directly affected by farm occupations. For instance, on one farm we met a former commercial farm worker who had lost his job and, with his family, been displaced when their farm was targeted by war veterans and others; working with him, doing the same work as him, was Simon, a former farm manager, with a tertiary degree in agriculture. The horticultural farm he had managed outside Harare was owned by a white man with high-level ZANU-PF links, and so the farm had *not* been occupied during the Fast Track Land Reform programme. However, like many, despite having a job Simon had found that his salary did not keep pace with hyperinflation, and that he simply could not get enough food to feed himself and his family. Working as a general farm worker in South Africa was more profitable than managing a farm in Zimbabwe.

Simon's situation had been better than most of those we encountered, yet resonated with what most people told us: they came because they and their families could not afford food. Quite simply, many of the migrants were motivated directly by the fear of starvation, for themselves and their families. Toana from Masvingo explained what had finally prompted him to leave:

> My two children died in Gutu, Masvingo, last month. They were still in primary school in Grade 5 and Grade 6. They spent the whole week eating 'chakata' [figs] because we had no food and the government had banned CARE[3] to give us food. Our neighbours felt for our kids and gave them sadza [maize porridge]. Their system was no longer used to such solid food so they reacted badly and died. (Taona, 2008 pers. comm.)

Driving to a farm to meet with some workers one day in early spring, we came across four men walking on the gravel road towards us. From some distance it was clear that they were Zimbabwean: they were carrying their shoes, and they were carrying water bottles. These, we had come to learn, were the telltale signs of recent border-crossers. Traveling for several days on foot, and without any knowledge of when next they would come across a town, a river or a friend, they needed to have water, and they needed to arrive in town without having worn out their only footwear. Like many, they chose to follow one of the minor farm roads that runs north–south, parallel to the main arterial N1 route between Harare and Johannesburg. Two were friends, having walked all the way from Kariba, where they were at high school, but school was closed for the holidays. The other two they had met on the road: one from Harare and one from Masvingo. Like many, they knew exactly where they were going – a farm at a particular turn-off from the road – though none had been in South Africa before. They had received detailed directions by cellphone text message. On this farm, they were confident they could get short-term work, they would save money, return to Zimbabwe, some prioritizing food for their families, others planning to pay school fees.

Strikingly, political intimidation was seldom mentioned by Zimbabweans we interviewed on South African farms. It was not something that we probed adequately, and there may have been reasons for people to withhold this information if they feared they might be seen as politically active and thus a threat to the 'order of things' on the farms. While this was possibly underreported to us, Home Affairs officials told us that migrants are told by others who have already crossed that they should exaggerate the extent of ZANU-PF intimidation, and to claim to be MDC supporters in fear of their lives, when applying for asylum (Makatse, 2008: pers. comm.). We were, indeed, struck by the extent of knowledge of the border-crossers about the asylum process; from how much to pay as a bribe on your way there, at the police roadblock, and the need to mention being beaten up by ZANU-PF youth as well as hunger and facing certain starvation (since the latter is considered by authorities to be an inadequate reason) – and to emphasize that the political deal concluded in September 2008 between the MDC and ZANU-PF was not filtering down to the localities from which people had fled.

New Dimensions of Heterogeneity

Nationality is only one line of difference within these changing farming communities – and is not new. The movement of people across the border to work on South African farms has its own long history, shaped in large part by the apartheid government's preferential labour policies and its relaxation of immigration controls to enable white farmers to take advantage of available labour on both sides of the border (see Chapter 6 by Bill Derman, and others for more on the history of this 'zone of exception' and its utility to the Afrikaner nationalist government and its farming constituency). Among the Zimbabweans, what is new is the astonishing mix of backgrounds, in terms of location, class and education level. Economic collapse in Zimbabwe by the late 2000s meant that small-scale farmers from the communal areas of Masvingo rubbed shoulders with white-collar workers from Harare who had tertiary qualifications as they worked side-by-side on a citrus farm. Some spoke of these former lives as a matter-of-fact reality to which they aimed to return, and by others nostalgically and painfully as fading memories of a life no longer available to them. Among those we interviewed in one farm compound were a former barman, a hair-dresser, a mechanic, a boiler maker, a farm manager, a farm worker, a market researcher, a smallholder farmer and a high school student.

These differences – so key to their identities back home – were subordi-nated to the common experience of becoming a farm worker, and a foreign one at that. One Zimbabwean man, educated and formerly in a white-collar job, told us how painful it is to him not only that he felt compelled to flee his country and work, illegally, as a farm worker, but also that migrancy had been a homogenizing experience. Any reference to his former life, and his qualifica-tions, prompted the derision of his co-workers. Here, on a citrus farm just 50 km from the Beitbridge border post, the work is hard. His co-workers come from all walks of life, and his former identity is being stripped of much that mattered to him – leaving just his nationality:

> My hands have changed, they are now like lemon skins. I am afraid to talk about my papers [qualifications] there in the field – they say, don't tell us about your papers. We must all be the same here. We are only Zimbabweans down there in the field. (Herbert, 2008: pers. comm.)

This stripping of the multidimensionality of identity was also the product of how communities received the new migrants, in either accommodating or repelling ways. Stereotypes of Zimbabweans among the South African farm workers combined 'othering' discourses that 'they steal our jobs', in part because they were considered to be more docile, to work harder and not to ask ques-tions; that they were criminals and murderers, and adulterers who 'steal our women'; but also that they were educated, literate and more fluent in English. Despite this, they elicited a combination of pity and ridicule as 'people from the land of hunger'.

Typology of Situations

In this section we present a range of narratives that epitomize the varied situ-ations in which migrants have found themselves, and a range of ways in which they understand and explain their position within the realm of the commercial farms. Although schematic, and simplifying enormously varied and textured realities, this typology observes the different ways in which migrants were situated on farms, the terms and conditions on which they did so, and their subjective understandings of their trajectories for the future, on or off farm, on to Johannesburg, back to Zimbabwe, and so on. In this way, the purpose is to depict a combination of people's aspirations with their assessments of the realm of possibilities available to them.

Case study 1: Recent first-time migrants in distress

Perhaps most prominent in the media coverage of the migration across this border is the image of desperate Zimbabweans, crossing into South Africa for the first time, into a country they don't know, and being exposed to its many hardships – their willingness to do so evidence of the hardships they were fleeing. Many of the recent first-time migrants arrive on farms by default, unsure about a future on the farm or further within South Africa. Many expressed fears about crime in Johannesburg but were also frustrated with poor conditions on farms. This represents a new pattern of long-term, though often not permanent, migration. Although it existed before, this pattern is now more widespread, and whereas in the past many of those arriving to work on the farms were from nearby districts over the river, by the late 2000s most of those arriving were from further north in Zimbabwe – and from a wide array of backgrounds.

Calvin, for example, had been a boiler-maker in Harare, but his family home was in close-by Masvingo province. He first came to South Africa in 1999, worked on the farm where we met him nine years later, but in the interim had moved up in the world, getting as far as Pretoria, where he secured a better-paying job in the construction industry. Yet, because he was in the country illegally, his quarterly trips back home had exposed him to losing his savings, a total of R500 (about US$75.00), when he was robbed during the border-crossing on his return. As a result, he was unable to get back to his job and ended up returning to the farm he already knew. Here, he was frustrated that he was training South Africans to be boiler-makers, who would be paid for their specialist skills, while he was only paid as a general worker.

Case study 2: Long-term oscillating migrant workers

Many Zimbabweans on farms in this region have long been migrating across this border to seek work, often returning to the same farms on a seasonal basis, with some becoming more settled in South Africa than in Zimbabwe, returning to fetch their family members, and over time remitting less, sometimes marrying South Africans, and some eventually obtaining (legally or illegally) South African identity documents. Their experience of life on a farm is very different from that of the new arrivals. This is an old and established pattern of oscillating and quite localized migrancy. Most such migrants were Venda, came from close-by, and had kinship linkages with Venda people on the South African side of the border. Many were building kinship ties in South Africa and seeing a future for themselves in the country while also retaining links back home.

Snikiwe and his wife were both from Zimbabwe, married in 2003 and had a three-year-old son when we met them. His wife's younger sister (a teenager) was visiting them on the farm where they both worked, and helping them out with childcare, cleaning and cooking in return for food. Both he and his wife are using temporary work permits for which they have to re-apply every six months – but the farm management organizes this. Snikiwe got his first permit in 1998, but has never had possession of the permit himself and was unsure whether he would be able to get the copies of the permits from the farm to open a bank account. They occasionally send money to relatives in Zimbabwe, but not regularly. He has family in Beitbridge, about 15 km away. When his permit is in order he visits them, by crossing via the gate; when his permit is not in order, he goes via the river. He has a sideline enterprise as a tin-maker, making tea-pots and other items. 'I have to think about the future. I am thinking about what I might do next year. I am saving money. I want to buy something that takes me somewhere.' He wants to buy a car, if everything goes well, by next year, which would enable his family to visit Beitbridge. He has learnt much on the farm, has expertise in irrigation and feels he could initiate his own farming if he had the land and the money, but for now he cannot leave (Snikiwe, 2008: pers. comm.).

Case study 3: 'Passing-through' migrants

For some, the farms were a way-station for a period before they moved on. This may be understood as 'passing through' migrancy: these migrants saw a farm as a short-term stop-gap, a respite from the danger of the crossing, the river and the *maguma-gumas*, but also a space of exploitation and danger, particularly for young women (see also Chapter 10 by Poul Wisborg on the farm as 'refugee camp'). Shadrack, a former mechanic from Harare, appeared still to be in shock that he was living and working on a farm when we met him in 2008. He had no intention of staying.

I crossed three weeks ago, and I have been here [on the farm] for about two weeks now. At Beitbridge I met somebody who directed me to this farm. It was a Zimbabwean; he only mentioned this place. I [walked by] foot from Beitbridge to here; it is about 70 km. It took me nearly two days. [In all] my life I never walked such a distance. I never had any papers [official documentation] so I was afraid. Whenever I heard the sound of a vehicle I would jump in the bush. By the time I arrived here, I would take any job. So far I'm working in the field picking up lemons. I'd prefer going somewhere where I can feel my heart pumping blood. I've never been on a farm before in my life and I never thought I'd find myself here, with my hands looking like this. (Shadrack, 2008: pers. comm.)

Similarly, two young men, Johannes (24) and Jabulo (23) used to make radios in Zimbabwe but could not generate enough money as they were hit by hyperinflation. Together they crossed the Limpopo River and there met people who told them about a farm where the owner needed people to pick oranges. This is where we met them three months later, when they were about to move on. They explained:

We used to earn R500 [about US$75], per two weeks. At the end of June we were told that our services were no longer needed. We used to help a man who makes bucket tins in the compound, so we used to help him and he would give us R10. We need to get asylum papers and go to Johannesburg. We have no relatives on the farm so we hope to save our earnings from piece jobs. We need to save R200 each because the truck drivers told us that they would charge us that much. We have a half brother who is a security [guard] who promised to [give us a place to] stay once we get to Johannesburg. It's better to be a street kid in South Africa than in Zimbabwe because in South Africa its better you can pick food from the ground. In Zimbabwe there is hunger, in South Africa if you get R10 you can buy bread and juice and have a meal for a day. In June 2008 when I got paid I sent R600 home and some clothes and sugar to my family in Zimbabwe. (Johannes, 2008: pers. comm.)

Case study 4: Short-term savers

Some migrants were explicitly in South Africa for a short stay, hoping to hop in and out, accumulate enough cash to tide them over for a while and make essential investments back home – specifically in education, but also to buy stock or equipment to enable them to pursue some economic activity back home. This new pattern of seasonal migrancy involved people from further afield within Zimbabwe; this was in contrast to the well-established pattern of people coming from close-by for seasonal work. Among the short-term seasonal migrants were people from as far away as Kariba, on Zimbabwe's northern border. This is often intended as a once-off trip, to accumulate money for a passport, in order to gain a better job that would make better use of their skills and qualifications. Herbert, a former market researcher, recounted his story.

> I came three weeks ago, for the first time. I heard about it [the farm] from friends in Harare. Here we can get cheaper food. This is my first time to South Africa. I haven't seen much. This is the first place that I came to. On my first day, I was at Musina and I had nowhere to go. An old woman took me to her house and gave me food and money.... She gave me a bath and a place to sleep, because I told her of my ordeals, what had happened earlier that day. (Herbert, 2008: pers. comm.)

Legality was much prized – despite *illegality* being the norm among Zimbabweans on many of the farms. The unaffordability and near-impossibility of securing a Zimbabwean passport and a South African visa was one reason for migration: people crossed illegally to earn South African rands in order to save up, return to Zimbabwe, get official documentation and return legally, with the hope of securing a better job. We heard this story repeatedly. As Herbert explained:

> Next time, I won't come back here. From this work I will save to go back and get a passport and visa, and then come back and go further, all the way to Cape Town, and get a better job there. My aim is to finish my marketing degree and to get a [banking certificate]; it is your entry ticket into the banking world. It is only possible if I have a passport and a visa. (Herbert, 2008: pers. comm.)

Case study 5: New pattern of local theft

Owners and, in particular, the new stratum of middle management on farms occupied by 'security managers', identified for us a further category of migrants. According to them, thieves cross the border specifically to steal from the farms – to steal fruit and vegetables to eat, but also to steal copper piping, cables, pumps and other infrastructure to sell or use back home, and even resort to stock-theft – though no-one could tell us how they got the animals over the river, especially since it was flooding intermittently. As the young black (Namibian) security manager on a horticultural farm outside Musina told us, 'They come and steal tomatoes or watermelons. Some even go and steal the sheeps (sic). Some go back and some keep going (southwards) and perhaps sell those things to make money in order to proceed in their journey where they are going' (Jake, 2008: pers. comm.). He had recently arrested four Zimbabweans stealing; all were under the age of fifteen and claimed to have been commissioned by people back home to steal certain items and return the same night. He feared there may be collusion with Zimbabweans already living on the farm, and observed, 'I wouldn't mind if people were not coming to steal, but you never know who is and who isn't so you have to treat them the same' (Jake, 2008: pers. comm.).

Despite strong prejudices among people, including in the villages, and sometimes on farms, about Zimbabweans as thieves and criminals, widespread xenophobic violence was *not* in evidence in this part of the country, when it erupted in the major urban centres. There were, though, a few isolated instances of xenophobic violence, including the murder of a Zimbabwean in the provincial capital of Polokwane, but nothing on the scale evident in the metropolitan centres of Johannesburg and Cape Town. The extent of family ties and links across the border was the reason provided by the police for why the violence did not extend to this area, despite the scale of immigration, though as our study confirmed, only a proportion of Zimbabweans had such links.

Thematic Analysis

Living and working in the country illegally made Zimbabweans doubly vulnerable to exploitative practices by farm owners. In Limpopo there were reports of employers calling the police to deport workers just before pay-day, to avoid having to pay them at all. These stories circulated as legend, without detail, on the farms we visited (though no one suggested it had happened on those farms), but specific instances have also been recorded by NGOs, including Nkuzi Development Association. Here we address some of the structural factors, as well as subjective notions of 'belonging', which shape the experiences of migrants in their interactions with South African farm workers, owners and others.

Housing and family life

On each of the farms where we conducted research, there appeared to be a standard position on co-habitation being imposed by owners, managers and foremen: men could bring women to live with them on the farms, but women who were employed were not allowed to bring their husbands or boyfriends to stay with them. This denial of a right to family life had the effect of driving women's relationships underground, and in practice dictating that, without their own partner, they attach themselves to another man already resident on-farm. On one farm, the system of deductions for housing meant that men would hide their women so as not to have to pay additional fees for sharing their living space with a lover or wife. These practices compounded the ways in which migration had split families; most migrants were men who had come without their families, and while some aimed to supplement the incomes of their wives, children, siblings and parents back home, others hoped to bring their wives and children over to join them in building a new life together once they were settled. The forms of 'domestic governance' practiced by farm authorities, however, exacerbated inequalities between women and men and appeared to be promoting practices of people having multiple sexual partners.

These conditions presented women with excruciatingly difficult choices (see below). Not only the rules imposed by farmers, but also the absence of secondary schools in the farming areas, led many of the migrants to leave their family members behind. Those of secondary school-going age either stayed at home or were sent to live with relatives either in Zimbabwe or South Africa, or dropped out of school entirely, as was the case with unaccompanied minors. Legal status also affected the education life of learners. Children who had crossed the Limpopo usually missed substantial parts of the term during the rainy season, when the river was full. The white woman doing the farm accounts at one horticulture farm outside Musina recounted to us how and why a small child was sent home for her education, and crossed back by herself out of desperation for food:

> My nanny's daughter was going to the primary school next door.... I used to drop her off at school on the way to drop my daughter at school in Musina, and then fetch her again on the way home. It is about six to eight km for primary school kids if they are walking. One day my nanny went to the school and she was very upset because there were no teachers there. So she sent her daughter back to Zimbabwe, to stay in their village, for her education. Then one day she woke up to find her daughter had arrived back [at the farm in South Africa] on foot. She was a ten-year-old; she said, mommy there is no food at home. She came from Beitbridge by truck, she got a lift, until near the mine, and then she crossed through the river and the fence, and then walked to the farm. It was so dangerous! My nanny was very cross with her but what could she do? (Eloise, 2008: pers. comm.)

Survival strategies

Although the view of South African officialdom classifies Zimbabweans on farms as 'farm workers', our study suggested a much more variegated reality. Many of the Zimbabweans on the farms were not employed, nor were they family members of someone employed there. Some had crossed illegally and, in return for a place to stay, were performing menial services either for other Zimbabweans who were employed (especially those employed legally). For this reason, the picture of Zimbabweans on the farms is incomplete without some analysis of the secondary economy that operates in the villages and compounds on the farms, and the informal economy operated by some of its most vulnerable and sometimes even invisible members.

Despite appearing to be unemployed – or rather because of it – people living on farms were engaged in a wide range of micro-survival strategies. This constituted a secondary economy driven largely through the poorly paid work of illegal migrants living on the farms without the knowledge or consent of the owner and providing informal services to others whose tenure was more secure, including established and legalized Zimbabweans and South Africans. Given the gendered demographics of the farms and of the migration itself, transactional sex in return for shelter, protection or food was widespread. Because of the significance of this – for the right to protection from sexual exploitation, and for sexually transmitted diseases among migrants and others on farms – it is addressed separately below.

Other than farm work, the main form of informal work that Zimbabweans were engaged in on the farms was provision of childcare. Teenage girls and adult women were looking after babies, even running small crèches, to enable other women to perform farm labour. In addition, farm workers – both South Africa and Zimbabwean – were outsourcing their farm employment, subcontracting (illegal) Zimbabweans to complete their work quotas and paying them a small portion of their wages, sometimes in the region of R10 to R20 a day (about US$1.50 to US$3). Others were running *spaza* shops on behalf of established farm workers, brewing and selling traditional beer, running informal barber shops and hair salons and buying and selling cheap clothes. A few, better resourced and with more established social networks had developed businesses targeting not the farm population but rather the urban and tourist market: they used the farm as a base from which they would order small crafts, sculptures and other cultural artifacts from Zimbabwe to sell in nearby Musina or along the side of the N1 highway. More commonly, though, the character of informal work on-farm is insecure, poorly paid and highly gendered. One such example that typifies the complex choices being made about the shape and distribution of family members, and constrained innovation in the face of unpleasant alternatives, is that of Patience.

Patience (22) was from Beitbridge and first came to South Africa in 1992, at the age of six, with her mother, who worked on a farm east of Musina. Her mother was retrenched and returned to Zimbabwe. Patience later came to the farm where we met her, west of Musina, because her cousin worked there. She was employed to look after the cousin's child (whom she was carrying on her back) but complained that she is 'paid, but too little': R150 a month (about US$22.50). She had appealed, without success, to the farm owner for formal work on the farm and now lives openly in the compound. Meanwhile, her own two children (aged two and four) were with her mother 'at home in Zimbabwe'. Her mother will not let her have them on the farm, fearing that a man might take them away from her. Her own wish is to have them with her on the farm. She is separated from the children's father, who works in Johannesburg and provides some support for them. Patience says that if she had a job she could plead with her mother to get her children. She showed us her three-month temporary permit as an asylum-seeker, which she hoped would help her to get work. Her own employment as a nanny has its own expiry date: there is a crèche on the farm which is run by the farmer, it is clean and costs only R10 (US$1.50) per child per month, including meals, and her cousin will send the child there when it is old enough – once it can walk.

Sexual violence and transactional sex

As our research progressed, it became clear that one of the key survival strategies for Zimbabwean women on farms was transactional sex: sex in return for cash, but more commonly sex in return for food, for a place to stay, and for protection. At Makwembe farm, which reaches to the banks of the Limpopo River itself, we were told that this extended beyond the farm itself. Zimbabwean men on the farm had made arrangements for young women and teenage girls to have sex with the soldiers patrolling the border in return for allowing the men access to the river for fishing. Sex with soldiers was also paid for in food and sometimes in cash.

A lot of the soldiers come to the compounds on the farms and some of them have girlfriends there, and so they can let some of those people go in and out. A man can say: if you let me go in and out, I can organize a girl for you, and then I can go and catch fish. Some [girls] are given those Russian packs [army rations], the food, some are maybe given money too. I'm also a fan myself [of the Russian packs]. There is tinned stuff, viennas and chocolates, meatballs and you get some juice packets, you get sweets, those 'chappies', you get butter and sugar and milk and coffee. They [the soldiers] get them for free. (Jake, 2008: pers. comm.)

Married women on the farms – both South African and Zimbabwean – complained about the prevalence of single women, whom they accuse of 'taking' their husbands. There was widespread victimization of single women due to alleged prostitution, including the reporting of these women to managers and owners, in order to get them evicted. Allegations against single women of practicing witchcraft were also mentioned, though we came across nobody who would reveal details of these instances. The International Organization on Migration (IOM), which has an office in Musina, claims that its own research shows that, in the context of illegal cross-border migration onto farms, casual sex is the norm:

[Zimbabwean] women usually give sex to men in senior positions on the farms, those who have spacious apartments because of seniority in return for a place to sleep. Both the South African and Zimbabwean farm workers did not know the dangers of HIV. They had a general idea about the disease. The majority of the farm workers have had a sexual partner elsewhere. They use sex as sexual recreation because they usually have nothing to do after work and there is little entertainment around the farms. They always stay on the farm. Sex is used both as currency and as recreation. (Hassan, 2008: pers. comm.)

Also vulnerable are the 'gonyets', the women who travel with truck drivers plying this route between Zimbabwe and South Africa, providing sex and companionship in return for transport, food and protection. IOM explained how this practice has evolved.

Transaction[al] sex is common. Cross-border traders also give sex to the truck drivers for free transport and for a place to sleep. I saw it last night, it's not something we heard. When you see a 30-year-old woman with children back home, she will try to minimize the costs [of transport]. The wages are not equivalent to their inputs. (Hassan, 2008: pers. comm.)

But there is also rape, perpetrated on farms, but also in towns and villages, and in the bush – and little chance for successful prosecution, particularly if the victims keep being arrested and deported:

A woman was raped in Thohoyandou in October 2006. When she went to report to the police she was held in custody for two weeks and got deported. [In another case] a guy offered three women a place to stay, the guy took [one woman] to the bush and raped her. The procedure was to take the perpetrator to court. We are not winning the case because lots of evidence has been lost. When someone is raped they need to be taken to court. The courts are sympathetic but [there is] no evidence. (Hassan, 2008: pers. comm.)

The most poignant story about how economic vulnerability translated into transactional sex, and even violence, was told to us by a young pregnant woman on a vegetable farm bordering the river. Sarah (21 years) had been in South Africa for just three months when we met her at a vegetable farm where she was living without the knowledge of the owner or management. Coming from Mashonaland, she related how she had been 'chased away' from home due to a cultural clash, because her fiancé, an Ndau, did not provide lobola to her family, and her mother first refused to allow the match and then chased her away from her home on discovering that she was pregnant. When we met her, she was eight months pregnant with her first child.

Sarah was in an extremely difficult situation: pregnant, on her own, jobless, and about to lose her 'home'. Having been chased away from home, and without any income or any place to stay, she had crossed into South Africa with a woman friend and they had settled on the farm next to the one where we met her. After some time, she found she did not like the relationship her friend had developed with an older man – though she did not give details. She left, moved to a neighbouring farm (where we met her), and there had got a job as a nanny for a woman working on the farm, in return receiving from her R200 (approximately US$30, or seventeen per cent of the minimum wage) per month, but also a room and some food. She did not try to get other work, as she had no permit but she did apply for a three-month temporary asylum permit. The farmer was not aware that she was staying on the farm; her presence had been kept secret, as the owner of the house where she stayed would have to pay to the farmer an additional R20 per month for her.

The owner of the house had recently decided to employ a new nanny for her child, a young woman who comes from the same area as herself: Beitbridge. Sarah faced having to leave but did not know where to go: neither her mother nor her father will accept her back. Asked what she thinks of the farm, apart from her own dire situation, she says it is okay but one has to 'show a lot of self-control', and referred to there being a lot of 'beer pressure'. Men approach her for sex, either directly, or by sending messages via other women. They tell her that it is the only way to survive. Her friend, with whom she crossed the border, is doing this: having sex with men for food, money and shelter. She could not see a way out of her predicament.

Remittances: a foot in two places

By supporting their families back in Zimbabwe, migrants invested in sustaining linkages between their places of origin and places of arrival. As also observed in a study of remittance strategies among Zimbabweans in northern England (Magunha et al., 2009), remittances are a means of building social capital. Most of the migrant workers we interviewed remit money to their families in Zimbabwe. By 2007-08, the forms of remittances included food items that were unobtainable in Zimbabwe, for example, sugar and cooking oil. A few invested in larger household goods such as television sets and DVD players to send back home. Yet the migrants encountered enormous difficulties in taking money back home –they risked being robbed on the way out, and on their return. Remittances were being made through informal channels such as sending money through relations or, more riskily, via truck drivers plying the Zimbabwe–South Africa routes. Soldiers also received bribes to enable people to cross the Limpopo River close to the border post, where it is better patrolled. The need to rely on informal channels to transfer money back home was due to the fact that undocumented migrants had no access to formal financial services. Without passports and visas, they were unable to open bank accounts or navigate exchange controls. Even for those able to access formal channels, the fees involved were prohibitive for those remitting small amounts. Logistics, price and trust emerged as factors that made door-to-door delivery the preferred means of remitting.

The influential recasting of migration as a business, proposed by Salt and Stein (1997), has led many observers, policy-makers and academics to interpret the practice of migrants sending remittances back home as evidence of *entrepreneurial* rather than *survivalist* motives. As Herman (2006) observes in her account of Moroccan and Senegalese immigrants in Spain and Ghanaian and Egyptian migrants in Italy, the 'business model' of international migration fails to account for the significance of personal relations – rendering the decision-making that of 'entrepreneurs' rather than that of people embedded within family and friendship networks, under pressure to invest in continued relations of affinity. In the process, the personal stories and subjectivities of migrants may be misinterpreted. The business idiom pivots on a central belief in choice, whereas, despite there being agency, many of the situations and stories we encountered while talking to Zimbabweans on white-owned farms in South Africa centred on the opposite: extraordinarily circumscribed options in which agency involved navigating wholly unpalatable alternatives and facing outright coercion.

Identity and Citizenship

One line of enquiry in our study arose from an interest in acculturation and identity formation – and the possible implications of this for migrants' future decisions to stay or return, and for their ability to claim rights. We explored what kinds of identities these migrant workers (and non-workers) were assuming. Did they see themselves as new citizens or were they marking time, for example, in the expectation of a return to Zimbabwe? Why might some migrants see a future for themselves in South Africa (or on farms) while others might not? We were particularly interested in the ways in which the divergent positions and experiences of women and men might shape their perceptions and aspirations. What we found was far more variation than we had anticipated. Some of this related to the length of time people had been in the country, but there were many other contingent factors that seemed to shape whether or not people emphasized their identity as Zimbabwean, or preferred to aim at becoming South African, or prioritized other dimensions of identity. There were different views of what constitutes 'home' – and whether a South African farm could ever be home. Some of these themes are illustrated below with reference to particular people's stories.

Long-term oscillating (and particularly non-oscillating) migrants were steeped in a process of what Berry (2001) calls 'acculturation', learning South African vernacular languages, particularly Venda, and marrying South Africans:

> Berry and his advocates suggest that minority groups face two central issues within host societies: maintaining and developing their own ethnic distinctiveness; and formulating the terms of their relationship with the larger society, which depend on their adoption of values, norms, rituals, and so forth. Berry's acculturation model emphasizes the relationship between these two issues and offers four central strategies for dealing with the potential tension between the two: assimilation, integration, segregation, and marginalization. Whereas the

202

integration and segregation strategies involve an attempt to maintain the culture and language of origin, the assimilation and marginalization strategies involve their loss. (Tannenbaum, 2007: 148)

A young woman we met on a farm near Musina seemed to epitomize the process of acculturation through assimilation. Shoni (22) left school in Zimbabwe after Grade 6 and walked to South Africa with a group of border-crossers. When we met her in 2008, she was not working and had not worked since the previous year. She had not tried to be recruited alonside the new cohort of seasonal workers that January because she was not well – due to the fact that she is pregnant, she thinks. As a result, she was not entitled to any maternity leave, was not getting any income, but relies on income from her South African husband, who is employed. They are planning to build a house in his home, Ha-Makushu at Venda, which she has visited several times: 'It is now my home'. She may also visit her family in-law on her own. Asked if her in-laws accepted her, she says: 'My family was happy. They were saying I am a human being'. The farm is thus a 'workplace' home (where they have a mud house), while Ha-Makushu is now her 'proper' home, to which they will one day return (Shoni, 2008: pers. comm.).

Tensions between South Africans and Zimbabweans on farms led to feelings of marginality for others:

> [We are] free as South Africans, yes, as Zimbabweans, no. We are 80 per cent Zimbabweans, 20 per cent South Africans. But we are colonized here on the farm. They can tell us: hey, you are Zimbabweans and we shut up. Forget about the employer; we are talking about Zimbabweans and South Africans [living on the farms]. [The farm owner] did us a very good favour because he gave us a job. The (fruit) that is exported is marked 'South African packed'. Is that true? It should say 80 per cent Zimbabwean packed. (Edmond, 2007: pers. comm.)

Those who had acquired South African identity books identified themselves as citizens, and seemed more likely to refuse to do hard chores and more likely to claim land (and other) rights. There were a few Zimbabweans who considered South Africa as their permanent home, especially those now married to South Africans. As one observed, 'I will not go back to Zimbabwe, I will just continue to send money but going back means disturbing my children. I have already built a homestead in the village.' Many of the migrants we met, though, particularly those who were the most recent arrivals, identified themselves solely as workers with expectations of returning to Zimbabwe in the long term. As one man working on a fruit and vegetable farm outside Musina said, 'I just came here to work, accumulate money to buy livestock and return to Zimbabwe' (Tendai, 2008: pers. comm.). Yet plans for the future were constantly subject to change in view of perceived and actual opportunities and threats, and most people's life circumstances were a far cry from the intentions with which they had first set out for South Africa.

The different positions of long-term established migrants and recent migrants led to very different views about the roles of the state and farm owners in responding to migration. Joseph, a South African married to a Zimbabwean, explained that many migrants were passing through the farm where he lived and worked and, he complained, 'they break into houses and steal', particularly when workers like himself and his wife are at work (Joseph, 2008: pers. comm.). For this reason he did not feel secure and said that government and the farmer should be doing more to protect them. These discourses of migrant criminality, and the appeal to white farm owners and to the South African government for protection, seemed to be shared by South African farm workers and their Zimbabwean counterparts who were well established on the farms and saw a future for themselves there.

In contrast, a young woman, Flora, working on a livestock and game farm further south, outside Mopane, told us 'The farm will never be my home, it is just a workplace. Once the situation in Zimbabwe has improved I will pack my bags and go' (Flora, 2008: pers. comm.). Yet, while she described herself as Zimbabwean, she saw her child as South African. Indeed, she was able to obtain a South African identity book for her child, who was born in a South African hospital. She reconciled, then, a wish to retain her Zimbabwean identity and see a future for herself in her home country with a realism about economic opportunities in South Africa. Like the South African farm workers on this farm, she had another 'home' elsewhere: they had links to nearby (and not-so-nearby) communal areas, where their children were being looked after by grandparents, while she had her 'home' in Zimbabwe. As Moeletsi Mbeki observed, in Zimbabwean migrancy there are echoes of the economic structures of Bantustans and labour reserves, which themselves remain in evidence, despite their formal dismantling nearly twenty years ago (Ramutsindela, 2007).

In the course of this study, who exactly was South African or Zimbabwean became murky. Many people told how it was possible to get a South African identity book, and that some Zimbabweans had managed to do so. In fact some had 'non-citizen' ID books, which can be acquired after five years of being in the country legally (with permits) – but this is not how it was perceived on-farm. The next generation of children seems more likely to make the transition legally, with many children born of at least one Zimbabwean parent, in South African hospitals, being able to secure South African identity documents. This official sanctification of a hope for better opportunities for their children, together with the ability to open bank accounts and to receive South African child-support grants, were the most common hopes expressed by Zimbabweans we spoke to.

Finally, what new kinds of identity are emerging? Could it be that, for those now frequently moving across this well-trodden border, a new identity is evolving of being 'in the border zone', which is not so much a hybrid of Zimbabwean and South African identity, but one founded on common experiences of hardship, migration and survival?

Conclusions

This chapter draws attention to the variegated patterns of migration that have shaped who ends up where, how and why, and what have been their experiences on some of the commercial farms of northern South Africa. These narratives outlined above are products in large part of the policy context, in particular South Africa's policy towards Zimbabwe, and specifically the denialism of political and economic crisis in that country which characterized the Mbeki regime. This had produced a certain surreality in which the influx of hundreds of people per day – by any standards a case of large-scale displacement – was criminalized, rendering people all the more vulnerable and their experiences and suffering largely invisible. The easing of some restrictions from 2008 and 2009 opened possibilities for some people to move about with less fear, to make the onward journey to Johannesburg with temporary asylum-seeker permits, while others were able to make the return journey, bringing basic foodstuffs and cash in South African currency to their families, without having to endure the danger of another illegal crossing.

This chapter proposes a schematic way of distinguishing between (provisionally) five different types of migrancy and migrants, according not only to duration, but also the subjective ways in which migrants themselves characterize their plans, purposes and aspirations. It further offers three correctives to what is already known and documented about this remarkable pattern of migration. First, it emphasizes that this migration builds on historical precedents: observable on these farms is a mix of continuity in and new types of migration and migration networks. Social networks are key to understanding this mobility, perhaps less paramount as a reason to migrate and more as a survival strategy. Many of the stories of crossing and arriving related how people knew where to go and who to look for – not through direct contact, but indirect networks. Second, it draws attention to the specificities of the ways in which South African 'farm life' is governed through control and coercion, as well as being a place of community and, sometimes, reciprocity – and the often illicit informal economy on farms in which migrants provide cheap labour often to other farm workers rather than to the owner. Third, it focuses attention on the role of transactional sex as a survival strategy and more generally emphasizes the socially differentiated and gendered ways in which migrants experience their new, often temporary, homes and how their choices, hopes and fears reflect this differentiation.

Notes

1 The research reported in this chapter was conducted by a team comprising Shirhami Shirinda, Poul Wisborg, Phillani Zamchiya and the author. Fieldwork was conducted jointly and all team members contributed. Any errors or omissions in this text, though, are the responsibility of the author alone.

2 We do not know the origin of this term. It is sometimes spelled *maguma-guma*.

3 Food aid has been politicized since 2001, with increased abuses close to election times. MDC supporters, MDC sympathizers and those accused of being MDC were denied food assistance by local authorities. NGOs were forced out of certain areas to ensure that only ZANU-PF was distributing the available food aid.

8

Finding Shelter and Work in the Communal Areas of Limpopo
Zimbabweans in Rural South Africa[1]
Bill Derman, Anne Hellum and Shirhami Shirinda

Introduction

South Africa's communal areas have become the homes and work places for significant numbers of Zimbabweans. As elsewhere in South Africa, newly arriving Zimbabweans come in search of employment, housing and an escape from suffering and insecurity. However, the realities of life in the communal lands provide a different context for obtaining shelter, security and work.[2] We suggest that the life stories of inclusion of Zimbabweans in communal areas expand the range of narratives currently used to explore and understand how they have become part of a complex and highly differentiated South African nation. Currently, there are several co-existing narratives which attempt to capture how the situation of Zimbabweans in South Africa should be understood. These narratives include the human rights violations experienced by Zimbabwean asylum-seekers, the exploitation of undocumented Zimbabwean farm workers, and the xenophobia that exists in many parts of South Africa.[3] While academic research, human rights accounts and media reporting has been focused upon Zimbabwean immigration to the cities and commercial farms of South Africa, less attention has been given to those seeking shelter and work in the communal areas. There is a significant unknown and highly mobile number of Zimbabweans in Limpopo Province and in other communal areas throughout South Africa. This chapter describes how Zimbabweans seeking work and shelter in communal areas in the Elim area of northern Limpopo Province see themselves and their lives in South Africa. Despite the ongoing official hostility to undocumented Zimbabweans and human rights abuses toward them, they continue to make a life, if only an insecure one, in the communal areas.

The chapter is based on mixed methods. Aside from reading the history and studies of immigration, we visited the temporary offices set up by the

Department of Home Affairs in the showgrounds of Musina to observe and to interview Zimbabweans and Home Affairs officers from 2008-12. During this period, we visited and interviewed officials of the various organizations who were attempting to assist the tide of Zimbabweans (and others) coming across the border. These included the International Office for Migration (IOM), South African Lawyers for Human Rights (LHR), the United Nations High Commission for Refugees (UNHCR) and the Musina Legal Assistance Office. We interviewed farm owners and Zimbabweans living in the area, in addition to the 42 Zimbabweans living in the communal areas around Elim we interviewed on a more systematic basis in 2009. The latter interviews, upon which this chapter is based, took place at a special time; it was when Zimbabweans could apply for asylum and when deportations were brought to a halt during the southern winter of 2009. It is quite possible that the security that many then felt about building a new life in South Africa might not last. While Chapters 7, 9 and 10 in this book focus on Zimbabweans working on commercial farms in Limpopo, the location for this research is in and around Elim and the former homelands of Venda and Gazankulu.

The chapter proceeds from describing some general features of Zimbabwean migrants in South Africa to their passage through the border town Musina to illustrating life in the communal areas around Makhado and Elim. In adding to the range of experiences, we point to the lack of research concerning the communal areas of South Africa and the ways in which such research may deepen and enrich our understandings of the Zimbabwean diaspora. Lastly, we discuss the new immigration policies toward Zimbabweans (and other Africans) and our fear that these policies will fail to assist Zimbabweans in communal areas in their hopes of securing livelihoods, work and housing.

Zimbabweans in Limpopo Province

Of South Africa's provinces, Limpopo is the most rural. In addition to agriculture, there is forestry, mining (with substantial prospecting continuing), tourism and formal and informal trade. The major data for Limpopo Province comes before the great increases in emigration by Zimbabweans.[4] As a consequence, this data does not capture the Zimbabweans in the province.[5] The poverty rates of South Africa's nine provinces differ significantly, as do those of the urban and rural areas of the country. In 2005-06 the poverty rates ranged from 24.9 per cent in Gauteng and 28.8 per cent in the Western Cape to 57.6

per cent in the Eastern Cape and 64.6 per cent in Limpopo.[6] In a relatively poor country, Limpopo Province was the poorest.

The gateway into South Africa from Zimbabwe is through Musina, which has always been an important border town. It has, however, been transformed since 2000. Before then, it was mainly Zimbabweans close to the Limpopo River who sought work on the South African side, and South African Venda also maintained contacts with those to the north. Since 2000, the Zimbabwean population in Musina has rapidly increased. Most Zimbabweans use it as a point of departure, but an unknown number have stayed. In Musina itself,[7] Zimbabweans have become entrepreneurs, informal traders, micro-business operators, bricklayers, money traders, craft makers or sellers, vegetable and fruit hawkers, low-level employees in many businesses, guards and domestic servants.[8] More recently, some have been hired as teachers in rural schools, which are short of trained teachers or have none at all. Lastly, and before the termination of the Zimbabwe dollar, Musina was filled with hundreds of cross-border traders purchasing South African goods to sell back home or to exchange huge piles of Zimbabwe dollars for South African rand.

The next large town south of Musina is Makhado, or Louis Trichardt.[9] To the east are the communal areas of former Gazankulu and Venda, while to its west is part of what used to be Lebowa. Makhado/Louis Trichardt has served as an important transit point for Zimbabweans heading toward Pretoria and Johannesburg, but it has also been a stopping point for many others. There are numerous employment opportunities on the commercial farms, in the lumber mills, in the businesses and in the construction industry in the area. It is from Makhado that many Zimbabweans have sought work in the vast communal areas to the east. In 1994, there were approximately 7,000 whites living in Louis Trichardt, whereas now there are less than 3,000. As of 2012, even though the 2011 statistics are not yet available, the population of Louis Trichardt has changed from a white to a black majority. The reasons for this dramatic decline are unclear and require research.[10]

At least 35 per cent of Limpopo's area is in former homelands and is home to a high percentage of the province's population.[11] Apartheid is writ large on the landscape. The former homelands were pushed away from the best-watered and fertile areas and they still lack many of the services to be found in towns. Heading east from Makhado and the N1, there are two tarred roads – either north or south of the Luvuvhu (Levubu) River – which heads directly into the heart of commercial agriculture and to the communal areas. The Luvuvhu River and

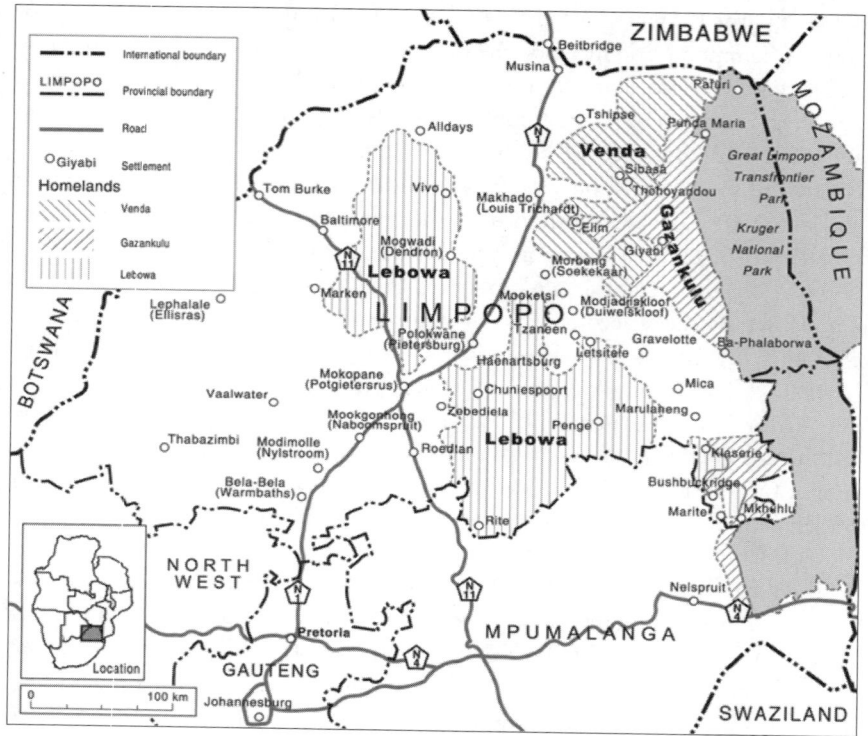

Map 5: Communal Areas/Former Homelands, Limpopo Province

Albasini Dam mark an intensely cultivated area, the building of which cut into the heart of earlier Venda and Shangaan communities, forcing them out of their fertile lands and river valleys during the 1940s and 1950s. The rich farming area was for exclusively white settlement and ownership. Large amounts of land were removed from indigenous ownership and are now the sites of land restitution claims. As one goes further east, one enters the former homelands of Gazankulu and Venda. Elim is located in former Gazankulu, close to the waters of the Albasini Dam, but its inhabitants could only work on the farm as labourers; their lands were inadequate for farming.

South Africa continues to have a dual tenure system whereby most of its territory falls under private landholdings, whereas a much smaller percentage, and quite variable between provinces, has communal tenure. Areas called 'communal' are those which had been the former homelands, and comprised

210

approximately 35 per cent of Limpopo Province. In communal lands, ostensibly, land cannot be bought and sold and its governance rests partly in the hands of the traditional authorities (kings, chiefs and headmen). Politically, residents are subjects of chiefly authority and the customary laws in existence, although these are not supposed to supersede national and provincial laws. In general, the communal areas are located in the lower and drier portions of Limpopo Province, but can provide employment opportunities in agriculture, building and construction, domestic labour and miscellaneous jobs. However, the labour market is unregulated and wages are far below national minimum standards. There is a double difficulty: residents typically cannot afford to pay minimum wages and Zimbabweans can't make complaints because of their undocumented status.

While communal areas are often described as places of underdevelopment or occupying significant parts of what has been termed South Africa's second economy,[12] they are far more diverse than these definitions suggest: there is substantial economic activity, including home-building, business and shopping centre construction, transport, agriculture, herding and trading, The multiple government services include police, postal services, health services, road building, etc. Spatial divisions remain of great significance despite formal political and developmental integration into the current government structures of provinces, municipalities and districts. This continuing duality stems from the apartheid era, where the homelands had government-appointed chiefs, headmen, native courts, police and clerks, and this system has continued. These functions are legitimated in a series of acts including the Council of Traditional Leaders Act, 1997, the Traditional Leaders Framework Governance Act (2003), the National House of Traditional Authorities Act (2009) and the existence of a House of Chiefs at national and provincial level. As a consequence, the governance system into which Zimbabwean migrants (documented and undocumented) have to fit varies greatly between urban and commercial farming areas.

Unlike many places in South Africa, the commercial farming areas and the former homelands in Levubu are in close proximity. In Levubu, the lands were taken relatively late from the black South African communities, beginning in the 1940s and continuing through the 1970s. With land restitution, the landscape of Limpopo Province has been changing rapidly, as what had been state lands or commercial farming lands are being returned to claimant communities (Derman, Hellum and Manenzhe, 2012; Derman, Lahiff and Sjaastad, 2009; Hellum and Derman, 2009).

Migration into Limpopo Province: Some historical dimensions

There is a long history of the use of Zimbabwean workers in Limpopo. As many historians have noted,[13] South African agriculture was heavily subsidized by the national and provincial governments throughout the twentieth century. In addition, the government made efforts to support commercial farms to obtain sufficient black African labour. According to Dan O'Meara (1983), profits from agriculture soared during World War II and continued to expand afterwards. Without detailing the complicated post-World War II labour debates, the election of the Nationalist Party and the creation of apartheid, they set new trends in motion, including the expulsion of labour tenants from white-owned farms and the expansion of area of the Bantustans. In Levubu, the government sold land to farmers at low prices with very low interest rates, and subsequently built a dam in the 1950s to supply water for irrigation. However, the local supply of labour for the farms was seldom sufficient. While the new Bantustans were to control the flow of labour out of the reserves into the towns and cities, black Africans preferred to work in the cities and mines, avoiding the harsh conditions on the farms (van Onselen, 1976; Jeeves and Crush, 1997; Krikler, 1993, among others). In Levubu, from the 1940s onwards, to increase labour the white farmers in the Transvaal (part of what is now Limpopo) doubled the number of days tenant farmers had to work for them from 90 to 180. This led increasing numbers of black South Africans to leave the farms. The farmers responded, in part, by substituting migrant labour for South African labour. This led to the (often forced) removal of the remaining black South Africans on the white farms to the homelands. Labour tenancy came to an end.

Labour conditions on the farms themselves, by most accounts, were awful. The workers were poorly paid, housing was sub-standard and the workers were often locked on the farms. And if the workers were not in South Africa legally, they could only disobey the owners and managers with great difficulty.[14] White South African farmers in Mpumalanga and Northern (now Limpopo) provinces were permitted to register their undocumented resident farm workers in order to escape prosecution. They did this by applying for a corporate permit.[15] However, the farmers had to pay for the corporate permits, which led many to not bother.[16] During the 1970s and 1980s, labour continued to cross the now fully militarized border but only for specific farms and employers.

Migration to Post-Apartheid South Africa

With the end of apartheid and the election of Nelson Mandela as South Africa's new president, expectations were high for a new future for southern Africa. While estimates for South Africa's unemployment level were around 40 per cent in the mid-nineties, still people from the region were coming for work. The International Labour Organization (ILO) suggested four interconnected reasons: 1. The actual unemployment level in South Africa was actually lower than the official figure, especially with opportunities in the informal sector or else contract labour; 2. The size of South Africa's economy and its diversity presented many more opportunities; 3. Pay levels for comparable work were much higher in South Africa than in surrounding nations; 4. The South African economy could absorb immigrants because of its size. What is harder to document in our view is employers' and industries' preference for migrant or foreign workers. In general, such workers are easier to discipline and harder to unionize and were not part of the anti-apartheid struggles. Many employers operated with stereotyped notions of the qualities of different ethnic groups or nationalities. Thus, they would choose certain peoples for farm worker jobs, or mining or forestry and for specific tasks within each industry.[17]

During the 1990s, South African workers and their labour unions contended that immigrants drove down wages and took South African jobs. In general, South African unions have a minimal foreign worker membership and try to maintain high wage levels in the face of labour over-supply and large numbers of unskilled and semi-skilled sectors. The current hostility has deeper roots. Migrants are afforded few, if any, social protections. The ILO report from 1998 noted that there was a lack of full protections for immigrants who stayed in South Africa after apartheid's end. A general amnesty from deportation was offered to SADC citizens if they had been living and working in South Africa. Those who applied for and were granted amnesty became eligible for unemployment insurance fund benefits, while coverage for state old age and disability pensions was restricted to South African citizens. In short, migrant workers were treated differently than other South African workers. The issues of job security, social services access, occupational health and safety for migrants were left unaddressed in South Africa and more generally in the region as a whole. And as is well known, the mining industry is dangerous with high risks for illnesses and accidents. However, forestry and agriculture also have multiple risks. There was then and there is now insufficient protection for migrant workers. Zimbabweans were able to benefit from this general amnesty but most arrived after its end. We have presented the details of recent immigration laws and policies in Chapter 6.

Migration to the Communal Lands in and around Elim

Here we turn to Zimbabweans who are living and working in the communal areas in and around Elim in Limpopo Province. This material is based upon interviews with Zimbabwean immigrants and provides a picture of why and how they have come, the kinds of employment they have been able to obtain, the conditions of their living and their views on life in South Africa and in Zimbabwe. Elim was selected because we knew the area from our research on land restitution (Derman, Lahiff and Sjaastad, 2010; Hellum and Derman, 2009). In the course of the land restitution research, we noted that a large number of undocumented Zimbabweans were employed by members of the claimant communities to work in their homes and fields in the communal areas. We were interested in the situation of Zimbabweans living and working in the communal areas around Elim because we assumed it would differ from those living on the border, who tended to be Venda and indigenous to the Limpopo Valley. Furthermore, we wanted to portray those who are relatively 'invisible' rather than those with formal, legal employment in the towns or on the commercial farms in the area. Our overall aim was to assess how these Zimbabweans thought they were being treated, and if they were indeed concerned about xenophobia or attacks upon them because they were Zimbabwean.

Elim

Currently, Elim is a transport hub and home to a new shopping centre, with a second one under construction. Under the post-apartheid government, paved roads, electricity and other governmental services were provided. It does not, however, house the agro-processing and transport facilities for the fruit, nut and vegetable industries that characterize the area. These are located in the nearby small farming centre of Levubu, which was part of the areas reserved for whites, Elim was selected because there had been a tradition of resistance to national authority and it had an important office of the Nkuzi Development Organization.[18] In 1969, the Minister of Bantu Affairs, M.C. Botha, declared that Elim and the population in the area would be moved about 60 km to the east, to the area known as Malamulele. The Elim Hospital, still run by Swiss

214

Missionaries at the time, refused to move. Because of the hospital's refusal to move, all capital grants were stopped and the Elim authorities were forbidden to make any extensions or improvements to buildings. Finally, around 1972, the government decided not to force the removal of Elim Hospital and the surrounding population, but it did take over the mission hospital. The government then began funding the Homeland authorities in Giyani, the new capital of Gazankulu, which permitted new capital projects (van der Merwe, 2002). While the missionaries have left and the Elim church is in local hands, their presence continues through the large and important hospital and the families descended from the early members of the church. And unlike many other black South Africans in the area, the residents of Elim did not have to move to a homeland but rather found themselves the new residents of a homeland that had expanded to include them.

Interviews with 42 Zimbabweans in the Elim area

We conducted 42 interviews with Zimbabwean women and men in August and September 2009. They were interviewed either at their work place or at home in the area around Elim. Their ages ranged from 15 to 45 (Table 2). Ages were self-reported, but the spread was as follows:

Table 2: Age of respondents

Age	Women	Men	Total
15-20	3	6	9
21-30	7	15	22
31-40	3	4	7
41-50	3	1	4
Totals	16	26	42

This age pyramid of mainly young adults in their twenties fits with the high degree of physical labour that characterized their jobs. Six moved freely across the border with passports, including three sisters who moved back and forth. Two others said they had passports, while there were two who claimed they had permits. Work permits in the corporate sector are time- and place-bound (see discussion in Chapter 6). That leaves 35 undocumented who have a variety of experiences in crossing the border, ranging from paying bribes to fear of being attacked and robbed by the *maguma-gumas*.

It is not possible to determine representativity for this group since we are dealing with an unknown number of immigrants. There is no recording at the communal area or ward level of the names and numbers of immigrants. The Zimbabweans who were first approached to be interviewed in turn assisted us in identifying others. In addition, Themba Maluleke and Shirhami Shirinda are from the area and knew many local Zimbabweans. While our interviews were carried out with those who were overwhelmingly undocumented and working in poorly paid, low-skilled jobs, this does not adequately capture the range of Zimbabweans who work in other parts of Limpopo.[19] And, it does not represent the Zimbabwean women who cross the border but seem to disappear according to LHR, IOM, and the UNHCR.[20]

Why did they come to South Africa and Elim?

The most frequent reason provided by our respondents was that they were unable to maintain a reasonable standard of living in Zimbabwe. Or, to put it more strongly, poverty or the inability of the family to feed itself forced them to leave. However, it could be put more mildly, as did interviewee number 6: 'In South Africa there are lots of jobs and it is very close to Zimbabwe compared to other countries, the value of the rand is also a factor in this case.'[21] Two younger women and a man emphasized the availability of consumer goods alongside wages that make it possible to buy them. Most people emphasized the need to provide food or assistance to their families in Zimbabwe. The underlying driver, however, seems to be the inability to earn a living and to provide sufficient support to one's family. It is also important to note that we were interviewing in August-October in 2009 and most migrants had left Zimbabwe before dollarization. They arrived in South Africa when inflation was very high and then when it reached an almost uncountable amount. The figures are worth mentioning to indicate how difficult it was to function economically. In 2006, the annual rate of inflation was 1,281 per cent, rising to 66,212 per cent in 2007. 2008 saw the Zimbabwe dollar lose virtually all value, with inflation percentage exceeding nine billion.[22] In short, there was an unprecedented set of difficulties faced by Zimbabweans, an important contributor to leaving home. On top of inflation was the increasing violence and the instability produced by the political conflict as ZANU-PF attempted to keep power.

In terms of 'knowing the place', most had no or little prior knowledge of Elim and the surrounding communal areas. They wound up in the Elim village area through contacts made on the commercial farms, or through family members who had earlier come to South Africa. Most Zimbabweans came with either friends or family across the border. They tended to come from Masvingo and Chipinge, with a few from Midlands, two from Harare and one from Gokwe in the far north. These are new patterns with migrants coming much further from the border. Some people's journeys to the cities were interrupted as they did not have the resources to go further, or they found a temporary job and opted to stay. As more Zimbabweans stay in the area, the social context for newcomers improves. There is now the possibility of greater social support as well as new churches catering to Zimbabweans, including services in Shona, the dominant language of Zimbabwe.

Remittances

A major purpose of living in South Africa for all respondents was to earn money to send home.[23] Like their counterparts throughout South Africa, Zimbabwean residents in the communal area of Limpopo either sent money or traveled back to Zimbabwe with money and commodities. In general, remittances have been a critical source of income for hundreds of thousands of Zimbabweans, especially before dollarization. To earn hard currency was an important way to control for the extreme inflation indicated above. For example, in a new report written for People against Suffering Oppression and Poverty (PASSOP, a South African-based NGO representing immigrants), David von Burgsdoff (PASSOP's researcher) surveyed 350 Zimbabwean migrants in the Western Cape, of whom 210 were urban and 140 rural. Of these, 46 per cent arrived after 2008, and 92 per cent reported that they had sent remittances to their families in Zimbabwe over the last twelve months. We found that among our interviewees, all sent remittances home in spite of their low incomes. In addition, PASSOP found that remittances (money and in-kind goods) made up approximately 31 per cent of the total annual income of Zimbabwean migrants (PASSOP, 2012: 15). In sum, the study found that remittances have been critically important for the economy of Zimbabwe. Crush et al. conducted a survey of Zimbabwean migrants in Johannesburg and Cape Town in 2010. In their analysis, they categorize this new group as the 'Third Wave' of Zimbabwean migration. They find, in comparison to earlier surveys, that the new urban migrants were younger, less educated and wanted to stay longer in South Africa. There were more women among them but they tended, in comparison to the men, to still be engaged in circular migration return to their homes, children and families in Zimbabwe. In comparison to older migration patterns, these new migrants (male and female) tended to have lower paying jobs and therefore their remittances were lower than had been sent by other Zimbabweans in South Africa.

Housing

Finding decent and affordable housing in the villages in and around Elim is a major issue and is complicated by the very low incomes the migrant workers receive. The respondents have attempted several different solutions to this ongoing problem. While the majority of Zimbabweans are living without family (spouse, parents, brothers and sisters), they do not usually live on their own. In several cases, individuals in Elim and surrounding villages work in Pretoria or Johannesburg and need someone to look after their home while they are gone. There were three or four who were living in Reconstruction and Development Programme (RDP) houses that had been left abandoned by their original owners. This was in the village of Bungeni. Houses were built outside the village and residents refused to move in. These Zimbabweans thus live rent-free. Others are given a hut by their employers, and some pay rent when they have more regular jobs and income. In general, because of low wages, Zimbabweans generally tend to seek non-market solutions or live with other Zimbabweans in order to save some money.

In comparison to village housing, the cost of house and flat rental in Makhado/Louis Trichardt for a two-bedroom apartment is around ZAR2,000 per month, whereas in a village it might be 50 to 400 rands a month depending upon if they were renting alone or sharing the space. One woman had a secretarial qualification from Zimbabwe and had worked as a secretary. She is now, however, working at a checkout supermarket in Makhado as a teller and earns more than ZAR3,000 a month. She rents a village house for 200 rand per month, so that she has money for her children who live with her. In addition, she supports her mother and sister, who remain in Gutu in Zimbabwe, which she couldn't do if she lived in Makhado, where she works. She was unusual in that she lived on her own and not with a man. Another man had accompanied his employer from Zimbabwe after he lost his farm. Unlike most other respondents, he thought he had purchased a residential plot by paying the chief 350 rand. His employer had assisted him to get a Zimbabwe passport, although he no longer had a work permit and has joined the ranks of the undocumented.

Education, skills and employment

As has been found in earlier studies, the Zimbabweans in this survey are relatively well educated (and better educated than South Africans in the area), with most having completed Grade 7 or higher. Very few, however, had the opportunity to pursue the profession or career in South Africa for which they had trained in Zimbabwe. There were a couple of exceptions, including one man who worked in veterinary services based on his veterinary degree from Zimbabwe and a woman who has a degree in computer science, taught in Zimbabwe. She now works in a computer shop in Makhado/Louis Trichardt. Given the young ages of many migrants, they had not been able to find jobs in Zimbabwe directly related to their education.

The employment that most of our respondents had found was short-term, informal, and low-paid. This is not an unexpected finding given that we were selecting village residents. However, there were some exceptions already mentioned above – the cashier in Makhado and the worker on a game farm. Most of the Zimbabweans had simply walked around the villages and asked if residents needed assistance with weeding, clearing, or repairing something, and would then negotiate a price for the job. Many Zimbabweans did this and then found housing in the area. Others were hired as part of a brick-making enterprise but without contract or formal agreement. This meant that the employer did not pay unemployment insurance and pension payments, which formal employers are required to do. Some were hired to maintain property in exchange for rent while they also sought other income opportunities.

A fairly typical response came from a younger man aged 27, who stated that he came to South Africa to find a job. Such a job would enable him to purchase goods that were not available or affordable in Zimbabwe. He heard from fellow Zimbabweans that jobs were available in a town known as Tzaneen, which was about a 75-minute drive from Makhado. Tzaneen is a centre for fruit farms and tree plantations. He found a job in forestry. Forest workers are paid at the same level as farm workers. He said that he found the job too difficult and left to join a friend in a village near Elim. Now he is doing piece jobs in the villages whereby he goes around and offers to carry out tasks including building a fence, clearing land, weeding gardens, getting straw for roofs, etc. He lives in a small room that was offered to him by a family for whom he does piece work. In exchange for the free room, he performs chores or jobs when requested by the house owners. He knew nothing about either Tzaneen or Elim before he came.

We interviewed a young eighteen-year-old woman who had left high school (secondary school) because her family had money problems. She had crossed the border illegally with her boyfriend and a friend. They reached a small town known as Waterpoort, where a woman hired her as a housekeeper and baby-sitter in Elim. For this job, she was paid 500 rand per month but left the job because her employer wouldn't let her boyfriend stay with her when he visited from Waterpoort. Walking around the Elim community to find alternative employment, a household offered her a job that pays ZAR500-00 (less than $80.00 U.S.) a month as a housekeeper and baby-sitter. She pays 150 rand for her rent. She is relatively well-educated, having completed Grade 11 at Mwenezi Secondary School in 2007.

In general, we chose not to ask the interviewees directly about how much they were being paid (unless they volunteered the information) since we did not want to arouse suspicion and cause anyone to lose their jobs. Nonetheless, we do know that black South African farm owners or managers in communal areas do not pay minimum wages in the communal areas, nor do those who employ Zimbabwean construction workers pay them anything close to a minimum wage. Black-owned farms and businesses can be exempt from the wage labour standards set by the Department of Labour. There are separate labour standards, which can be legally obtained for new black-owned businesses or those operating in communal areas. It is more likely, however, that the payment of sub-standard wages is due to employers ignoring regulations and the lack of unions in most of these businesses. Human Rights Watch (HRW) conducted interviews in 2006, responding to allegations of the mistreatment of Zimbabweans in the province. Most of their interviews were in Musina, but they also conducted a few in the communal areas of Limpopo Province. At one black-owned commercial farm, they found nine Zimbabwean workers. HRW wrote:

> The accommodation for the nine Zimbabwean farm workers was atrocious; the accommodation for the farmer was only marginally better. Eight of the nine workers shared a small room; the oldest, a 52-year-old, had his own room. The cardboard walls were wet and crumbling, the roof was of corrugated sheeting, and the window openings were filled in with scrap paper. The workers were destitute: they had no blankets and kept themselves warm at night with a fire in the room. (2006: 47)

Of all the Zimbabweans to whom HRW talked during the research for this report, they wrote that these were the only people who, when asked if their situation was better or worse than in Zimbabwe, uniformly responded, 'Ah, this is worse'. We don't doubt the truth of this report since there is much suffering on farms. However, there is a general lack of research on labour recruitment, pay and working conditions in the communal areas. It also means that generalizations about Zimbabweans in South Africa are difficult and highly contextual because there are diverse findings, including ours. However, the farm workers/gardeners whom we interviewed did not indicate the suffering described by HRW.

Governance Issues: Customary Authorities and Zimbabweans

There has been a long history of the flow of Zimbabweans in and out of communal areas. In general, they have been tolerated, since common ethnic identity and language were more important than nationality or citizenship. This has changed with the Zimbabwe crisis and the far greater numbers of people seeking shelter and work. In Musina, Makhado/Louis Trichardt, and in Tribal Councils, we had many encounters where respondents discussed the characteristics (usually negative) of Zimbabweans. There were, however, some who empathized with the difficulties faced by migrants in leaving their country and in attempting to find jobs in South Africa. In general, the arrest and deportation of Zimbabweans has not taken place in the communal areas. The communal areas have 'tribal police' along with national police. Both have accepted the presence of Zimbabweans, unlike in the commercial farming and forestry areas, where police would periodically raid compounds looking for undocumented Zimbabweans.

In light of many negative attitudes toward Zimbabweans, we were interested in finding out the ways in which undocumented and documented Zimbabweans sought to inform the customary authorities of their presence. Most respondents did not inform them or did not know if the chief or headman had agreed for them to be resident in his territory. We combined the two answers, since we could not know if the house-owners had consulted the headman or chief. In addition, since most Zimbabweans were already feeling very insecure, it was not something we wanted to increase. Thus, 32 either had not asked or did not know if the customary authorities had been consulted on their stay, while eleven had notified the chief and in a couple of instances had 'purchased' land. Purchased meant that they paid the chief or headman money for the right to hold property in his community, usually known as a Permit to Occupy. However, this could not be an official permit to occupy since it would not be recognized in court. In general, there is little incentive for the home-owners to either notify or seek approval from the customary authorities as this would officially make visible Zimbabweans who are undocumented and might make them responsible if the Zimbabweans were to commit any crimes.

While chiefs and headmen seek to know who is living in their areas, they have not sought to register Zimbabweans. There is no adequate local way to either block Zimbabweans from coming or to prevent individuals from hiring them. Chiefs have avoided getting into the business of checking the status of Zimbabweans. Some Zimbabweans have become South African citizens or have entered into long-term relationships (either formal or informal marriage unions) with South African men or women; in addition are the needs and preferences of employers. South African employers (black and white) vary greatly in their attitudes and practices from being sympathetic to highly exploitative. According to the respondents, many employers provide only food and/or shelter and no wages. Others are known for hiring undocumented Zimbabweans and then firing them and refusing to pay them because if they complain, they will be deported. One communal area employer threatened to shoot one of our researchers if he tried to interview his Zimbabwean brick-workers. And this person does indeed carry a rifle to his brick-manufacturing site.

In an effort to explore if there were norms which might underlie the reception of Zimbabwean immigrants by chiefly or customary authorities, we asked for a tribal council meeting to discuss the issue.[24] We asked if there were procedures or processes for finding out if Zimbabweans were living in their tribal territory. The response from the headmen was that there were not. The headmen said that they had no idea how many or where Zimbabweans were living, but they were not welcome. They went on to make claims about unsubstantiated stereotypes including the qualities and actions of Zimbabweans, naming their propensity for thievery, violence, taking advantage of South African women and their lack of truthfulness.[25] In this meeting, they advocated forcing all Zimbabweans back to where they had come from. This was more posturing than anything else. In contrast, when we asked about incorporating Zimbabweans into their families after marriage or birth of children, they agreed that this is what occurred and claimed that there was no discrimination against the children. An important dimension of Zimbabweans living with them was burial or the return of the deceased to Zimbabwe. In the meeting, the assembled headmen worried about not knowing the proper way to care for the deceased because they were unsure of the family traditions and faith of the families concerned. The headmen believed that if Zimbabweans were not buried correctly, their spirits could do harm to those who didn't perform the correct rituals. To indicate that there are large numbers of Zimbabweans now living among them, there was a portion of the cemetery now set aside for Zimbabweans even though the village leadership much preferred to send the bodies back to Zimbabwe for appropriate burial rituals.

One other dimension of this meeting deserves mention since it reflects current political and social practice. The meeting was male-dominated and neither of the two women who were present spoke. Power in rural Limpopo continues to be held in royal or chiefly families and with strong emphasis upon following customary norms. Royal families continue to dominate local governance and the ruling party, the ANC, does not challenge them. In general, it appears that royal families throughout the communal areas do not report undocumented Zimbabweans to either Home Affairs or to the police.

In contrast to this meeting, we interviewed a headman in the Nzhelele Valley and then the brother of the chief of a Venda village.[26] In each case, we received very different responses to questions about Zimbabweans. On the basis of this, we made assumptions that Zimbabweans, like other homeless people in the area – particularly those who had been chased off the farms – were seen as having a 'right' to basic livelihood resources – that there were customary norms entailing a right to livelihood and that they were not dependent on national background. And the importance of ethnicity and language would vary. This headman who had been very active in the Landless Peoples Movement in Limpopo Province contended that he could not refuse Zimbabweans who asked him for a residential plot. Implicit in his statement are male Zimbabweans. Undocumented Zimbabwean single women would have great difficulty in accessing a plot. He claimed that he was acting in the spirit of the area to welcome those who needed land if land was available.[27] At the same time, he complained bitterly about how his community had lost much of its farming land to residential areas because of overcrowding. It was also the case that he asked for approximately ZAR500 for permission. In the interview with the chief's brother, he expressed the shame that he felt that Zimbabweans were being deported and repatriated. He noted that Zimbabweans were entering South Africa due to the awful conditions in Zimbabwe. He maintained that the South African government was wrong to return them and to hold them at the showgrounds. We believe that there are a variety of responses to the presence of Zimbabweans in the communal lands, but that the recent increase and the rise of xenophobia in urban areas has led to an increase in national consciousness and assertions of nationality as opposed to other ethnic and regional identities.

Zimbabweans are stereotyped as thieves or potential murderers. The following incident describes how fragile the security of Zimbabweans in communal areas can be. In July of 2010, there was an incident of potential violence against Zimbabweans in a village next to Elim.[28] A Zimbabwean was accused of assault and the local chief used the occasion to demand the removal of all Zimbabweans from his area. A chief acting in this fashion raises significant concerns. The police took the side of those who accused the Zimbabwean of assault and the local Zimbabweans fled into the nearby hills. A traditional authority meeting was called, where many local people spoke against the Zimbabweans.[29] The crisis passed without any actions against Zimbabweans in general when the perpetrator turned out to be a non-Zimbabwean. At the same time, the local police moderated their actions at the behest of the local command in Levubu. The rapid identification by the police with local rumours rather than more objective police procedures was disturbing. However, the actions by more senior police calmed the situation.

In one village, because of rumours circulating about Zimbabweans carrying out illegal activities, a headman is seeking to register all Zimbabweans in his area. The purpose is to know who is in his jurisdiction for the mutual protection of Zimbabweans and the residents under his jurisdiction. It is unlikely that Zimbabweans will register themselves because of the climate of suspicion. In addition, it is even more uncertain that employers and landlords of Zimbabweans want public knowledge of their activities. Moreover, some Zimbabweans do not stay for long in one area. There is substantial mobility among them as they seek employment or housing with fellow Zimbabweans.

Reflections on Life in South Africa

Given the general insecurity of many Zimbabweans, we were interested in how the migrants felt they had been treated in South Africa and under what conditions they wanted to stay in South Africa or return to Zimbabwe. We were surprised at their emphases upon their overall positive experiences. Given the descriptions of xenophobic attacks, life at Lindela Centre in Johannesburg,[30] and life in and around the Musina showgrounds, we had expected the reverse.

Most respondents had, except for crossing the border, expressed satisfaction at some fundamental economic and political issues that were absent in Zimbabwe. They were all aware of the attacks upon immigrants in other parts of South Africa and of course they might change their feelings and plans if attacks were to break out in rural areas.

We asked all respondents if they wanted to stay in South Africa or return to Zimbabwe. Of these, 23 stated they wanted to stay in South Africa and 19 wanted to return home. We asked them what needed to change in Zimbabwe for them to consider returning. Here, there were a series of common answers, but taken together they indicate a failure in the Zimbabwean economy and hence piece or farm work in South Africa is considered preferable to staying at home. Even though four respondents reported attacks by the gangs collectively known as *maguma-guma* and six reported paying bribes to soldiers and police, 40 of the 42 respondents indicated that they were treated well by the government. Some were given clothes, others food, some blankets, those with children can receive child grants and free education. Of course, most of the clothes, food and blankets were provided by international organizations or local churches and not by the government, but this seems not to have influenced their views. In informal conversations, many respondents felt relief that the government had stopped deporting Zimbabweans at the time of the interviews in 2009. The cessation of deportation had meant a dramatic decrease in what they regarded as police harassment.

We found that most respondents had accessed South African health care. They had done this at hospitals and at clinics. In particular, one village clinic provided anti-retrovirals for those with HIV/AIDS. In fact, Zimbabweans from close to the border would come to the clinic just to get their medication. In general, access to medical care was something that distinguished rural life in South Africa from that in Zimbabwe. We found, in contrast to the HRW 2009 study, that Zimbabweans were accessing the health care system using networks in the communal areas. Thus, migrants staying in South Africa had complex reasons for doing so, including jobs, fear of ZANU-PF, new family in South Africa, access to health care or the sense that there were greater possibilities for the future.

Zimbabwean identities

In light of discrimination, stereotyping and vulnerability, we expected more Zimbabweans to try to hide their identity. While some Zimbabweans have sought to conceal their national identity, others chose not to do so. Zimbabweans have formed a number of Shona-language churches in rural Limpopo. Shona is the major language in Zimbabwe and while there are many churches and religions that transcend national borders, it appears that many do not feel comfortable, for example, in the Zion Christian Church, which is widespread in Limpopo.[31] Lastly, Zimbabweans in the Elim area have also begun to form Zimbabwean soccer leagues, the players on these teams being all Zimbabwean. Soccer games provide space and time for Zimbabweans to interact with each other.

Even so, not all Zimbabweans seek to remain apart from South African society. While it is unclear if this is a conscious strategy or an outcome of forming relationships, many Zimbabwean men had South African women as girlfriends or wives even if they had a wife in Zimbabwe.[32] When these men accepted responsibility for children with their wives and girlfriends, they became part of South African families. For women it was different. In Musina, we heard concerns expressed by UNHCR, LHR and IOM that many women who crossed the border then seemed to disappear. They hypothesized that they often became the wives or mistresses of South African men in order to guarantee their security as they were highly vulnerable. Such a situation would also provide access to employment in South Africa. However, it was the human rights organizations' belief that many of these women and girls were being trafficked.[33]

Do the migrants interviewed want to stay?

One of the central characteristics of past Zimbabwe migration to South Africa had been the phenomenon of circular migration. According to Crush et al., '70 per cent of migrants went to South Africa for less than one month in 1997, a figure that dropped to only 18 per cent in 2005. By 2005, half of all migrants were going for six months or more (an increase from only 16 per cent in 1997' (2012: 17). In light of this research, we were interested in whether or not the respondents wanted to stay in South Africa. And, if they did want to return to Zimbabwe, what needed to change there for them to consider returning. Because we were so close to the border, where it was relatively easy for Zimbabweans to return home, a desire to stay in South Africa might mark significant changes in attitude.

There was a linked set of answers on staying or returning. We did not ask about specific experiences with political violence, but it was named as having to end before many would return to their homes. One interviewee expressed the powerful sentiment that 'the Zimbabwe government must treat its citizens as human beings'. Another stated that 'People are forced to join ZANU or else they are killed.' One respondent left when ZANU war veterans were forcing young men to train as militia to harass members or supporters of the Movement for Democratic Change (MDC). There were others who called for political tolerance in Zimbabwe. Such expressions confirm the notion of 'mixed' migration which attempts to combine the concepts of economic migrants and political asylum-seekers, since the motives for leaving can be multiple. Given the close relationship between economic and political factors and the politics behind the economic decline of Zimbabwe (see Chapter 1), it is hard to distinguish between them.

Respondents who wanted to stay in South Africa included their emphasis upon the need for greater political freedoms in Zimbabwe, less harassment by ZANU-PF, with the availability of employment in South Africa also being important. However, since most came just before dollarization, the difference in rates of pay featured in their responses. Half of the respondents linked the two general issues. For example, a nineteen-year-old young man stated: 'South Africa is a good place, I would like to stay because there are lots of jobs and you can't sleep hungry like in Zimbabwe. I will visit Zimbabwe as a home but not to stay there.' In answering the question as to what needs to change in Zimbabwe for him to go back he said, 'Jobs must be created and the economy will be revived by calling back all the white farmers who were producing food in the country.' In probing further, the analysis is really political economy: the failure of the agricultural policies of the ruling party and thus the separation between the political and the economic evaporates. A young woman of only eighteen responded to these questions as follows: 'South Africa is a nice place because you cannot sleep hungry like what is happening in Zimbabwe. If I can manage to get my mother and her child to South Africa, I will leave Zimbabwe for good.' We asked her: 'What would need to change in Zimbabwe for you to go back?' She responded: 'If people can be employed and get paid with money that can buy unlike the Zimbabwe dollars which are not valuable. If Mugabe can be removed and put someone who is willing to save people [rather] than himself.' So, even in a relatively young person, direct links are made between the political situation and the long-standing economic crisis. One of the three sisters who travel between Masvingo and Elim responded as follows: She did not want to leave Zimbabwe to live permanently in South Africa because her husband

and children are there. And then she stated in terms of what would keep her permanently in Zimbabwe: 'The President has to change. The economy must improve and my husband who is a teacher must be able to earn enough money to support the family.' Another 33-year-old woman put it more bluntly: 'Life in Zimbabwe is hell.' Five respondents mentioned the need for MDC to govern in order to improve the economy and reduce the violence. An implication was that they wanted a sole MDC government without Mugabe as President.

In summary, there was a series of common answers which, taken together, indicate such a failure in the Zimbabwean economy that piece or farm work in South Africa was preferable to staying at home. There were four lines of explanation provided for under what circumstances would they return: the first was that the economy had to improve. Included in the broad notion of economy was the fundamental survival question of enough food to eat, along with a livable wage that would make it possible to purchase food, if available. The second was jobs. There was an enormous focus upon the lack of jobs in Zimbabwe. The third was the question of money. Zimbabwe dollarized its economy on 29 January 2009. Although we carried out the interviews in August and September and 2009, there was still a heavy focus upon Zimbabwe's weak currency. No one cited the need for education for their children, despite the difficulties in Zimbabwe's schools. We suspect that was because the ages of our respondents and their low incomes made it impossible for them to support dependents.

The fourth set of responses concerned the broadly political circumstances in Zimbabwe. Around 70 per cent of the respondents named political violence, political difficulties or the need for Mugabe to leave office as part of what they wanted to see change in Zimbabwe. We did not ask about specific experiences with political violence but it was named as having to end before many would return.

Freedoms and politics in South Africa

In another set of responses, we asked a related set of questions about how they had been treated by the South African government, and we asked them to give brief comparisons between life in Zimbabwe and South Africa. What we found most surprising in the responses was the degree to which South Africa was considered politically peaceful, with basic freedoms such as the freedom to join political parties and the ability to speak freely as practiced by South African citizens. This again reinforced the connections between the political and the economic. While most undocumented respondents reported fears and difficulty at the border, they did not attribute this to the government. They expressed acknowledgment of access to clinics or hospitals, to some child support if they were documented or had taken a South African spouse and in general to a more peaceful atmosphere than in Zimbabwe. In sum, all but three articulated the view that in South Africa there was a level of freedom that could not be found in Zimbabwe.

We also asked our respondents how they viewed the relationship between the South African government and the Zimbabwe government. All talked in one way or another about the closeness of the ties. However, there was a marked divergence in those who noted that the good relations between the two governments permitted them to stay in South Africa. This was true of five respondents. The majority emphasized that the relations between the two governments were poor because of Mugabe. The answers ranged from the opinion that ZANU-PF should learn from South Africa to the idea that South Africa should show Mugabe and the government how to run a country peacefully. Others emphasized that South Africa had to force change in Zimbabwe, otherwise things would continue to remain unaltered. In general, all respondents but two had very specific views on the broader political context which led them to be in rural Limpopo.

New immigration policies or a return to the past?

Despite the lack of a full policy toward Zimbabweans in particular, and refugees and immigrants in general, the South African government issued a call for all Zimbabwean nationals living in South Africa to be documented by 31 December 2010. A statement issued by the South African Government Minister of Home Affairs, Dr Nkosazana Dlamini Zuma, and supported by the Zimbabwean government, claimed that this process would legitimize all those living 'illegally' or undocumented in South Africa. Her remarks were supplemented by Mr Maseko, official spokesperson for the South African government, who also stated that the special dispensation for Zimbabweans (described in Chapter 6) would end on 31 December 2010. Thereafter, all Zimbabweans who had not had their presence in South Africa formalized would be deported. The deportation policy would not apply to Zimbabweans who had applied for asylum, but if their application was denied they would have to leave or be deported. In addition, the South African government was hoping to greatly reduce the time it took to process asylum applications.

In an effort to speed up the general documentation process for Zimbabweans, the South African government insisted on a short time limit, although many specialists, including the African Centre for the Study of Migration and Society at the University of Witwatersrand (formerly known as the Centre for Forced Migration), held that this is unrealistic and cannot be achieved with a reasonable degree of fairness.[34] Maseko went on to say that 'Those who are here illegally without any documents will be given a period between now and the end of December to sort out their documentation with the Zimbabwean authorities and with home affairs and after this date anybody who does not have any form of permit to be in the country will be deported.' He didn't ask if the Zimbabwean government was capable of acting this quickly. Maseko said the special dispensation was put in place during 'a time when there was a political crisis in Zimbabwe' to allow free movement. 'But we believe some form of stability has returned to Zimbabwe and therefore all Zimbabweans will now be treated like any other foreign nationals.' There has been a long history of the South African government arguing that there 'is no war in Zimbabwe' and that claims for asylum were therefore illegitimate.

According to Maseko (2010), Zimbabwean nationals working, conducting business or studying in South Africa would be issued with a working permit, business permit or a study permit provided they had valid Zimbabwean documents. 'I would imagine this would also apply to those doing informal work in the country,' he said. As part of the agreement to suspend free movement, Harare had undertaken to issue documents to all its undocumented nationals, he said. Where this was not possible, the Zimbabweans would be allowed to return home and fetch the necessary papers.[35] In fact, and over the past number of years, the Zimbabwe government has been unable to provide such documents. In addition, he claimed that there would be 'an amnesty' for Zimbabweans who might have obtained South African identity documents fraudulently, on condition that such documents were returned to Home Affairs with immediate effect. However, this would not mean that they would automatically qualify for regularization; Maseko said that they would then have to apply for permits that would enable them to legally reside in South Africa. He added:

> We are saying return these [illegal] documents.... Start making sure that you get your Zimbabwean documents and then when you've got your Zimbabwean documents, then we clarify what is your status in this country and we will then issue you with the relevant permit. So if you are in the country illegally and you have a job, you get a work permit. If you don't, you get deported.[36]

In sum, the South African government continues to believe that the crisis in Zimbabwe will soon be over. In light of this prediction, the government has returned to deportation and documentation as its strategy. We think that this is overly optimistic and ignores why large numbers of Zimbabweans will continue coming and why many will continue to avoid trying to change their undocumented status. It also ignores the varied and complex ways that Zimbabweans have inserted themselves into various sectors of rural Limpopo. We do not know, and can't anticipate, if and how the South African government will systematically attempt to root out the undocumented Zimbabweans in rural Limpopo. On the other hand, many Zimbabweans in the course of living out their lives can be caught without documentation and repatriated to Zimbabwe, causing them great difficulty. For those without proper documents of marriage, or birth certificates, they will have increased difficulty accessing basic services like schools and medical care.

Conclusion

In the long history of migration between Zimbabwe and South Africa, Zimbabweans have gone not just to the towns, cities and large-scale farms but also to the communal areas. Their comings and goings as traders, job seekers, relatives, etc. did not provoke much notice until the growing economic and political crisis in Zimbabwe led them to enter South Africa in increasing numbers. From a number of standpoints, Zimbabweans have not been particularly welcomed. On the other hand Zimbabweans coming to South Africa have brought new opportunities for some South Africans. For example, shops in Musina altered their stock and their bottom line by buying items in large amounts that Zimbabweans would take back with them to Zimbabwe to resell. Farm owners have had a large supply of part-time and full-time labour, as have had contractors. With increased contact between Musina and Zimbabwe, Zimbabweans faced with reduced prospects for urban employment have opted to remain in rural Limpopo Province. Many entered the more formal labour market of working on commercial farms. Others, but in much lower numbers, sought shelter and work in the communal areas. The position of farm workers has partly been addressed in Chapter 7 and many more observations will be presented in Chapters 9 and 10.

In this chapter, we have sought to introduce a different perspective on Zimbabweans in South Africa. The major research and enquiries have focused on Zimbabweans as victims of the economic and political situation in Zimbabwe. While we accept they have been victims and subject to rights abuses by the South African government and unscrupulous employers, we also find that there are multiple narratives involved in understanding Zimbabweans in South Africa. In interviewing and observing Zimbabweans around Elim in the communal areas of South Africa, we found a different narrative. And this narrative fits more closely with the experiences of many Zimbabweans who came to South Africa before 2000, despite existing xenophobia and some anti-Zimbabwean sentiments. The dramatically increased number of Zimbabwean migrants has, however, increased tensions throughout South Africa and led to the adoption of new policies by the government as it attempted to cope at multiple levels with hundreds of thousands of unexpected arrivals. We have discussed in Chapter 6 how Zimbabwean migration has revealed much about contemporary South Africa and its desires to keep 'aliens' or 'foreigners' out to protect the gains of the apartheid struggle. Nonetheless, the proximity of Limpopo Province to Zimbabwe, shared ethnicities and the crisis in Zimbabwe means that such a policy of exclusion will always fail.

In terms of the communal areas, the Zimbabweans we interviewed had relatively positive attitudes toward their life in South Africa compared to the suffering they described in Zimbabwe. Life for them was better in rural Limpopo than in Zimbabwe. Such results provide a window into the extent of their suffering and insecurity in Zimbabwe. This was a surprising finding, given the general lack of security in either jobs or housing in South Africa. Yet, the general peace that prevailed combined with income opportunities has meant that many Zimbabweans now think of making South Africa their permanent home. It reaffirms the idea that the Zimbabweans have come to South Africa for a mixture of political and economic reasons and that, for them, circular migration is no longer a straightforward choice.

Notes

1 We wish to thank the International Office of Migration (IOM), the Musina office of the United Nations High Commission on Refugees (UNHCR), the Musina Legal Assistance Office, the Musina Office of the South African Lawyers for Human Rights (LHR), selected Refugee Officers of the South African Department of Home Affairs in Musina, the Uniting Church of Christ, the We Love Jesus Church, and the Zimbabwean immigrants who were at the Musina showgrounds. We have chosen not to name those who assisted us, not knowing who might be subject to repercussions. We especially thank Mr Themba Maluleke, who assisted with the

interviews.

2 Communal areas are the former homelands or Bantustans. These are partly under the rule of customary authorities, who are part of South Africa's formal governance system.

3 The best-known attacks upon immigrants were in 2008. They are ongoing.

4 Income and Expenditure Survey of 2000 (Statistics SA a and b) and the Labour Force Survey of 2000.

5 Zimbabweans would be highly unlikely to supply information as they are afraid of being deported.

6 Statistics South Africa – the *Income and Expenditure Survey of Households (IES) 2005/06* and the *General Household Survey 2006*.

7 In 1994 there were approximately 33,000 people and in 2004 there were 44,000. The boundaries changed with the creation of the municipality. Zimbabweans are everywhere, mostly undocumented or traveling through. As they are undocumented, their number can only be roughly calculated.

8 This does not include multiple illegal activities.

9 There remains an unresolved conflict over its name. Louis Trichardt displaced the Venda from the new settlement dislodging Makhado's son Mphephu (in late 1898). Keeping the name of Louis Trichardt is viewed by many as celebrating apartheid. On the other hand, the name of Makhado is equally problematic. The Hlanganani Concerned Group, made up of some Shangaan, Pedi and Indian residents, argued that Makhado was an oppressor who subjugated surrounding communities until the arrival of the Voortrekkers. The Soutpansberg Chamber of Commerce, various Afrikaner groups and political parties such as the Democratic Alliance and Freedom Front have also spoken out against the name change.

10 http://en.wikipedia.org/wiki/Louis_Trichardt.

11 It is not possible to give an accurate number since the current political divisions for a census are not by communal areas but by municipalities, which are mixed.

12 There is not space here to explore the important debates around the concept of South Africa's second economy, which, according to the National Spatial Development Perspective, refers in part to those people who find themselves with little or no potential to develop, largely because of the designs of colonial powers or the apartheid state. Ironically, one report concludes that the most important constraint on transforming the second economy is that the vast majority of those who inhabit this economy are manifestly unprepared to make the transition to the first economy or to somehow link to it. This is, after all, why a number of government's second economy interventions have not had more impact. *Synthesis Report of the 2005 Development Report: Overcoming Underdevelopment In South Africa's Second Economy*. http://stepsa.org/resources/shared-documents/overcoming-underdevelopment-in-south-africas-*second-economy*.

13 Krikler 1993; Mulaudzi 2000; Murray 1995; van Onselen 1976.

14 We will not deal here with the competition in recruiting workers between the

mining and agricultural industries.

15 A corporate permit may be issued to a corporate applicant which will allow him/her to employ a predetermined number of skilled/semi-skilled/unskilled workers.

17 The Immigration Act (No. 13 of 2002) deals with immigration and migration. It repeals the Aliens Control Act of 1991 as well as the Aliens Control Amendment Act (No. 76 of 1995) and regulates the admission of people to South Africa and their right to live and work here. The Act uses a licensing fee to manage the process of allowing foreigners to work and live in South Africa. The idea is that if someone is willing to pay more to employ a foreigner than they would to employ a South African, then that foreigner is needed.

17 Donham (2011) describes the ethnic division of labour in the South African gold mines.

18 Nkuzi was a key player in lodging land claims and then in the restitution of lands. For a discussion of Nkuzi, see Langford and Derman et al. (2013).

19 They include teachers, professors, farm workers, hotel managers and many other professions.

20 Interviews in Musina, 2010.

21 The interviews were conducted just after dollarization but all our respondents had left before then. The issue of currency was thus very important for them.

22 Hanke, 2008, and Hanke and Kwok, 2009, found in Crush, Chikanda, Taowadzera, 2012: 13

23 Zimbabweans also had goals other than just sending back money. For example, in Chapter 9, Addison provides examples of how Zimbabweans (especially women) used their farm earnings to invest in Zimbabwe.

24 This was held in August of 2011. However, we choose to keep the village anonymous.

25 The Solidarity Peace Trust and PASSOP have parallel findings. 'The Musina-Beitbridge area is not a very large metropolitan area, and proportionally the number of foreign nationals in the towns is high. There are frequent and targeted raids of Zimbabweans and other foreign nationals, which are fostering Afrophobic tensions. In Musina, the word "Zimbabwean" is used by South Africans with a negative connotation; someone who does something socially unacceptable – stealing, smelling badly or begging is referred to negatively as being '*Zimbabwean*'. The severity of the anti-foreigner sentiment is shown in the formation of their anti-crime coalition that is responsible for conducting, among other things, immigration raids and arrests' (2012: 40).

26 The Nzhelele River originates in the Soutpansberg mountains, flowing mainly east through what had been the heart of the Venda Homeland and into the Limpopo River.

27 In our interviews around Elim, we only found two Zimbabweans who had approached traditional authorities for a homestead. We do not know if anyone was refused. We suspect that it was fear of denial or lack of resources that led many not

to ask.

28 Name of village withheld.

29 People who attended the meeting were interviewed by Shirhami Shirinda.

30 The Lindela Repatriation Centre is a detention centre in Johannesburg for undocumented migrants in South Africa. It has been the subject of claims of abuse from many who have been held there. There have been several reports published on human rights abuses, overcrowding and corruption. There were riots there against the harsh conditions in June 2012. http://www.timeslive.co.za/thetimes/2012/06/08/lindela-hell-ignored.

31 The founder of the church is said to be a man named Lekganyane who is believed to have received a revelation from God in 1910. The church was first established in his home village near Polokwane, the current capital of Limpopo Province.

32 This fits a long-standing pattern of building families in multiple places. However, there is no data on the longer-term outcomes for the survival of one or both families.

33 Interviews conducted in August 2011.

34 http://www.migration.org.za/press-statement/2010/fmsp-2010-many-individuals-will-be-unable-access-zimbabwe-documentation-process; Amit, 2011; Solidarity Peace Trust, 2011.

35 See Chapter 6 for the difficulties that this demand poses.

37 Themba Maseko's statement reported in Polityorg.za among many other places. http://www.polity.org.za/article/special-deal-for-zim-citizens-to-end-2010-09-02.

9

Factions in the Field

Social Divisions and Gendered Survival Strategies on a South African Border Farm

Lincoln Addison

'*Ndiyo Joni yacho*' (this is Johannesburg), a young Zimbabwean woman says to me when I ask her about sex work in the farm compound. Our conversation takes place on Heddon Estates, a large-scale tomato farm nestled along the banks of the Limpopo River. A torn plastic tarpaulin wrapped around stick poles cordons off the small fire-pit in front of her hut. I am seated on a plastic bucket in this enclosed space – the makeshift kitchens of farm dwellers – and she sits on the ground, rising periodically to stir a pot of boiling sadza. The dry Limpopo, the border between South Africa and Zimbabwe, runs contiguously with the compound and is the backdrop to our conversation. 'You just tell yourself that this is Joni.... The wages are low and the men don't want to be married.'

During our conversation, a dispute erupts outside her hut involving a group of men, one of whom is her boyfriend. I gather from the dispute that he is trying to avoid paying his *chimbadzo* – the debts he has acquired from other workers plus a hefty interest. Johannesburg itself is more than 500 km away, yet *Joni* seems everywhere. All at once, the term characterizes the farm environment by the hustle and desperate strategies of individual survival.

In this chapter, I explore how the shifting labour regime at Heddon Estates divides workers and promotes individualistic survival strategies, most prominently transactional sex and high-interest money-lending.[1] I argue that these strategies are responses not only to oppressive working conditions, but are also related to the way workers privilege aspirations for their Zimbabwean homesteads over improving material conditions on the farm. Money-lending and transactional sex tend to exacerbate divisions on the farm and, in the case of latter, threaten the long-term health of workers, as high rates of HIV/AIDS attest to.

In what follows, I first provide a brief history of Heddon Estates and the border territory it spans. As a relatively new farm, it exemplifies how the increased availability of Zimbabwean labour has facilitated an expansion in commercial agriculture near the border. In this setting, labour relations are guided not so much by paternalism as by a kind of authoritarian neo-liberalism that eschews welfare and espouses 'self-responsibility'. After explaining how this labour regime widens segmentation and reinforces existing divisions, I demonstrate how it is supported by Zimbabweans' own ambitions. I suggest that building a rural homestead and supporting family ties in rural Zimbabwe, encapsulated in the chiShona term *kuvaka musha*, express the central aspirations for most workers at the farm. Under the pressure of social expectation from home, and divided by the labour regime at work, most Zimbabweans feel compelled to pursue individualistic livelihood strategies. I illustrate how two of the most widespread strategies, transactional sex and high-interest money-lending, tend to reproduce divisions, thereby further undermining prospects for collective action among workers.

This chapter is based on twelve months of fieldwork in 2009/10, during which time I lived in the workers' compound of Heddon Estates, occasionally staying with a white manager on farm property. Being immersed in the farm environment helped me to gain acceptance by farm residents and provided many opportunities for discussions in informal settings. In addition to informal conversations and interactions, I also conducted over 100 semi-structured interviews with Zimbabwean workers and white managers. These interviews were wide in scope, ranging from general demographic and economic information to informants' perceptions of labour, gender, spirituality and the Zimbabwean crisis. To protect the identity of my informants, all names, including that of the farm, have been changed.

The Eastern Border and Heddon Estates

Heddon Estates is located along the Limpopo River in the vast bushveld between Musina and the Kruger National Park. It forms part of a distinct geographical area which I refer to as the 'eastern border'.[2] Most of the land along the border is owned by a few companies operating game farms, but there are also two enormous tomato farms (one of which is Heddon Estates). Historically, the land along the eastern border has not been conducive to large-scale commercial farming. During the 1980s, the border was inhabited by dozens of small-scale white farmers, some of whom had lived there for several decades, yet they practically disappeared after the apartheid-era subsidies were withdrawn.

The current large tomato farms are relatively new and were established in the post-apartheid era. Due to the hot climate, water source and good soil near the Limpopo River, these farms are among the largest winter tomato producers in the country. Yet the owners mention another decisive reason for their success: the unprecedented supply of cheap labour from Zimbabwe. In the following section, I trace the local history of the land occupied by Heddon Estates, focusing on the sourcing of labour as it has shifted over time.[3]

According to long-term residents in the area, the original inhabitants of the land were Venda agriculturalists living under the authority of Chief Manenzhe. The inhabitants of this territory appear to have maintained a high degree of autonomy from the colonial state and farmers well into the twentieth century. Interaction with hunters, ivory traders and other African migrants crossing the Limpopo in the early 1900s did not displace Venda from the land or undermine the local headmen's authority. Venda inhabitants ignored or refused to pay taxes required for living on 'crown land'. Likewise, the sale of much of the eastern border as part of the huge 'Scrutton's Lease'[4] for mineral prospecting appears to have had little effect on their lives (Mulaudzi, 2000: 67-8). There appear to have been no white settlers actually living in permanent settlement along the Limpopo until, at the earliest, the 1930s; most farms were owned by absentee owners engaged in land speculation (Ibid.: 161).[5] One elderly Venda woman explained that the 'first whites' to live on the land near Heddon Estates were involved in hunting and cattle grazing: 'they were only staying here, not farming'. Small fruit and vegetable farms were not established until the 1940s. These farmers ordered Venda inhabitants to work as labour tenants. According to the woman and some of her relatives, this demand made many Venda leave the lands, with only a minority remaining as tenants.

The meaning of 'tenancy' was variable and shifted over time. One descendant of the original Venda group explained that when the first whites came, people were required to work three months without pay in exchange for grazing rights and staying on the land. Yet another Venda informant claimed that during the same period (roughly 1940 onwards) some people stayed on the land without working. Farm labour in this period was subject to negotiation and conflict between Venda inhabitants and the white landowner. As Mulaudzi (2000: 250) suggests, many Venda subverted labour demands from farmers even as they remained on the land. Although whites technically 'owned' the land, they lacked enforcement mechanisms, especially given their distance from towns and lack of decent roads. They needed a cheap source of labour near the farm, and there were few other options.[6] It appears that some form of labour tenancy persisted along the eastern border up to the 1960s and 1970s.

During the 1970s, however, many of the remaining descendants of the original Venda inhabitants were evicted from or vacated the land occupied by small white farmers.[7] Although they moved away, many settled across the river in what was then Rhodesia and continued working on the farms as seasonal labourers. One former Venda farm worker explained to me that his family moved across the Limpopo because the 'laws on the farm became too difficult'. In particular, he claimed that the farmer at the time stopped allowing people to graze cattle and that people left in large numbers, establishing small settlements across the river under the authority of Venda headmen on the Rhodesian side. Other Venda informants told me that they moved to other larger commercial farms in nearby Tshipise and Nwanedi, while still others relocated within the newly formed Venda homeland. As was occurring throughout South African farms during the period of forced removals, it seems likely that the small border farmers – with the support of the state – also evicted tenants in order to maximize their own land utilization (Marcus, 1989: 1-7).

Thus, while border farmers recruited some labour from the homelands or across the Limpopo, their main source of labour remained the Venda who lived 'permanently' on the farm. These workers were 'full-time' employees and were deeply enmeshed in paternalistic relations with the farm owner. A former worker on the border farms said that 'in those days the farmer was the master … they could just shoot blacks, there was no one to stop them'. But another former worker suggested 'some were not bad … on Christmas we were given so much clothes, food and drums of beer … enough to throw away'. These statements exhibited how, under paternalism, benevolence and coercion existed in tension. Farm workers could expect certain entitlements, such as the provision of food and housing, yet they remained at the mercy of the farmer, who presided over them as a father figure. As Du Toit (1993) argues, farm labour relations were premised on a discourse of 'belonging' in which acceptance depended on being in good favour with the white farmer.[8] Paternalism constructed farms as 'families' in which black workers lived in tightly woven, intimate communities with their white employers. 'In those days,' a Venda man reflected, 'we would play together as children… if the white man sold the farm, he sometimes took his blacks with him to his new place. At least they remained employed'. By constructing farms as families, paternalism helped stabilize highly unequal and racialized labour relations.

From the onset of white farming in the 1950s extending up to the 1980s, paternalism flourished along the eastern border, in part because the farms themselves were relatively small, allowing for closer relations between workers and employers. Previous farmers in the area say that at its peak in the mid-1980s, the white farming community along the eastern border represented between 30 and 40 individual farmers. The largest of these farmers could, at most, have employed 100 workers during harvest season, but most employed less than twenty. This paternalistic world was bolstered by state subsidies for border farmers. During the 1980s, the latter received monthly stipends, military training and equipment from the government (in addition to other forms of state support available to all white farmers during apartheid) as part of the state's efforts to clamp down on anti-apartheid resistance. These 'incentives' were intended to attract white people to live and farm along the border, thereby acting as a buffer zone in which invading guerrillas could be detected and intercepted. Roads along the border were tarred and soldiers regularly camped at the farm during the 1980s (Davis, 1987).[9]

From Paternalism to Neo-liberalism?

By the end of the 1980s, and especially after 1994, land ownership records indicate that farmers were facing financial difficulty, with successive farmers selling their land to banks. It was after apartheid and in the environment of liberalization that the current owner of Heddon Estates, Philip, began acquiring land along the eastern border. He started the estate in 1995 on a 540-hectare farm, but now owns at least 3,000 hectares of land near the Limpopo River, though only one or two hundred are planted in a given season. Philip narrates the loss of an older 'farming life-style' in favour of large-scale commercial farming:

> This area has been inhabited by struggler farmers for years, before we came here… really guys that had been struggling. They were small farms [sic], there was a community, but they were known as strugglers…. They were just using the wrong technology and they could not experience economies of scale. The way farming is going now, which is sad in a way, the old farming lifestyle is being pushed out, unfortunately. Farming is becoming more and more of a business. When I was in university in 1990, they told us farming in this country was going to be taken over by conglomerates, that fewer and few farming entities will be

operating on larger and larger pieces of land. When we came here there was ten people farming in our immediate vicinity, and they have all disappeared.

Despite Philip's nostalgia, Heddon Estates represents this shift in South African agriculture. In 1995, the estate employed roughly 50 people, but by 2009, the farm employed over 600. Almost all workers on the estate are Shona-speaking Zimbabweans. This is a relatively recent source of labour for eastern border farms, which have been historically dominated by Venda. To understand how the employment of migrant labour further diminishes paternalistic relations, some details on migration patterns and conditions of employment are necessary.

At present, the majority of workers come from villages in southern Mberengwa. Approximately 10 per cent of workers are from Chivi, and another 10 per cent are from Venda areas across the Limpopo, especially Diti and Beitbridge. The remainder of the work force is from places such as Shurugwi, Zvishavane, Mwenezi, Maranda and Harare. Approximately 50 per cent of the workforce is composed of people who have worked on the farm in previous years. The other 50 per cent are people arriving on the farm for their first time. With the exception of the few individuals based in urban areas, every farm worker is engaged in smallholder agricultural production at their rural homes. At least 100 workers from Mberengwa have received land as part of Zimbabwe's Fast Track Land Reform programme since 2000.

The employment of these Zimbabweans is caused by many factors, not least of which is the country's economic decline. But shifts within South Africa are equally important, particularly the restructuring of agriculture (Rutherford and Addison, 2007: 627-30). The introduction of farm labour and tenure security legislation in the 1990s, alongside the removal of farm subsidies, precipitated mass evictions and retrenchments of South African farm workers across the country (Wegerif et al., 2005). In their place, many farmers employed migrant workers who are less able to claim protection under the law. Johnston (2007) argues that the employment of migrant labour is primarily due to the fact that migrants find it difficult to strike or unionize (although it must be added that few South African farm workers are themselves unionized). Philip offers the following rationale for employing Zimbabweans: 'Zimbabwean labour is very important to our farm. [Zimbabweans] are intelligent, better educated, better mannered.... You can have a conversation with them. The South Africans say, "we do what we want, we have the government behind us".' Though Philip praises the higher skill level and education of Zimbabwean labour, his main emphasis seems to be upon their greater docility: they are less likely to claim protection from the government or unionize. This last observation is important given the unlawful 'contract system' that pervades at Heddon Estates.

The farm operates according to a system whereby every worker is classified as a seasonal worker, as defined by South African labour law. The only exceptions to this system are the four white employees (two production managers, a workshop manager and an office manager) hired on a permanent basis. All black workers, including managers, are classified as seasonal workers. They are hired on one-month contracts that are constantly renewed. On the twentieth of every month, a new roster of farm employees is created, replacing the previous one. This system grants the farm considerable flexibility in terms of laying off workers. It also prevents workers from being classified as permanent, which happens automatically if someone works longer than three months. As a permanent worker, one is entitled under South African law to vacation and pension payouts. According to everyone I spoke to, this 'contract system' has never been challenged by any government official. Thus, the employment of Zimbabwean migrants supports the rise of neo-liberal logic within farm labour relations. This logic is characterized by at least three tendencies: diminishing paternalistic welfare, increased emphasis upon 'incentive-driven' production and devolution of authority to black farm managers.

While paternalism diminishes, it does not entirely disappear. At Heddon Estates, workers stay in the farm compound free of charge. In fact, the compound is a somewhat unregulated space, accessed not only by migrant farm workers, but also by villagers from across the river, border-jumpers from further afield and tobacco smugglers. There are no fences blocking the compound from the river, so people generally come and go as they see fit. Of course, the accommodation is not ideal: workers stay in crowded spaces, either self-constructed mud huts or one of the small brick rooms reserved for senior workers. Water is available at communal taps, but there is no electricity. Workers are allowed to eat tomatoes from the fields. Some of these 'perks' may, however, be on the decline. Philip states that in the next few years, he expects to charge workers for accommodation, once enough brick rooms have been constructed. In the first few seasons, Philip would provide sacks of maize to all workers on a monthly basis, but this privilege was withdrawn as the farm expanded. While Philip practically never enters the compound, he does make some interventions to regulate behavior among his workers. For instance, he bans the sale of alcohol. 'I don't mind someone sitting in his room with a six-pack,' he explains, 'but we have found that with people selling, this creates disorder and violence'. Although the sale of beer still takes place in the compound, especially of the home-brewed variety, it is less overt than would be the case otherwise, and people are occasionally fired for breaking this farm rule. Philip also evangelizes among his workers by ordering a Bible reading and prayer at the general morning assembly before work begins. While evangelizing may stand as an exception, the alcohol policy is meant to maximize productivity, not construct paternalistic bonds.

Moreover, with such a large labour force, it is difficult for personal relationships to develop between Philip and his workers. Instead of a paternalistic 'family', there is a proliferation of managers and foremen to oversee production. Philip's interactions are almost entirely confined to a small, elite group of white and black managers. Moreover, there is also a high turnover: each year, approximately 50 per cent of the work force is replaced, reinforcing the impersonal nature of labour relations from Philip's standpoint.

To the extent that paternalistic bonds are formed, these are made with only a few black managers who have worked with Philip since Heddon Estates was established in 1995. These few managers receive much higher wages than the majority of workers. Most workers earn between ZAR800 and ZAR1,000 per month, but the managers earn between ZAR4,000 and ZAR5,000. However, most of their pay comes from bonuses tied to achieving or exceeding 'performance targets' set in place by Philip. The prevalence of 'incentive-based' production places more emphasis on cultivating neo-liberal subjectivities than fostering paternalistic relations. Philip states:

> We have developed a strong work ethic at this farm, by using the people themselves to enforce norms and accepted standards of work…. They work better when their own people lead them. Work is not time-orientated on this farm, it is task-orientated, and I've tried to instil that into my managers. I kind of work easier with black people than with white people in that respect, because white people come here with their old baggage, where the black people are fresh, they've got fresh ideas, and you can actually mold them into the ethic of the farm. And one thing we believe in here is that you come, you do the task, and you can go when it's done, irrespective of the time it takes.

As Philip's comments imply, neo-liberal labour relations not only emphasize 'incentive-based' production, but also grant considerable authority to black managers. Consider how the farm hierarchy at Heddon Estates is organized. All workers are placed in a complex chain of command, with Steve and other white managers at the top, followed by black managers and a series of foremen. The majority of workers occupy the bottom of the hierarchy, in such positions as picking, weeding and general labour. However, this hierarchy does not function as a smooth, seamless directive of orders, originating from on top and filtering down. Although the farm owner sits at the top of the hierarchy, he is not always in control. He communicates exclusively with manager and senior figures within the structure; his authority is indirect and distant from the majority. Black managers become the effective 'face' of the farm. These senior figures take on a parasitic role at the farm, as they extort other Zimbabweans for financial bribes or sex in exchange for jobs or other favours. Virtually every new worker at the farm pays a bribe to a senior manager, usually between 100 and 200 rands.

I once asked Philip why he doesn't stop this system of bribing. He said: 'It's very difficult to prevent it – I think in every farm there is a certain politics, or a certain mafia that is prevalent – but you've got to ask yourself, that by changing that existing mafia, and replacing it with somebody else, it's only a matter of time where the same thing is going to be repeated, because this is what happens in Africa.' By rationalizing the bribery as being just part of 'Africa' the farm owner effectively relieves himself of responsibility for the situation. One Zimbabwean informant likened the power structure at the farm to the ZANU-PF regime in Zimbabwe:

> What Mugabe is doing, he is only pleasing his politburo and MPs; they are pleased if he is treating them well, they have cars and everything. They are not suffering the public pain. The same applies here. All those at the top, they are getting money, they get bonuses, if they face problems, if they need money they can go to him.... They are not facing our problems that we face in the audience.

On several occasions, I asked Zimbabweans why they don't organize a worker's committee to represent their interests. One worker I spoke to replied: 'He [Philip] does not want that thing. If you try to organize something like that, there is the problem of CIOs [central intelligence officers], people will tell to the manager and you will be fired'.

In what follows I explore the problem of spying in the context of other divisions.

Other Sources of Division

Although the compound is unregulated in the sense that people freely move through it, there is also a culture of surveillance whereby workers often report each other to management when farm laws are broken. This could include inciting people to strike, stealing farm property or selling alcohol. When someone reports information, it is done in secret, to avoid being labeled a *mutengesi* (sell-out). These activities can remain secret only in perhaps three circumstances: first, that there are only few people involved in the transgression, so that the activity remains secret. Second, that very many people are involved such that any potential *mutengesi* will be extremely ostracized or beaten, and so no one steps forward to report out of fear. Third, in cases where senior managers are involved, Philip is unlikely to intervene and reporters fear retribution. A good example of these dynamics is when many farm workers left the farm for days to work as occasional tobacco smugglers – trying to maintain two jobs, as it were. This story was relatively easy to report to Philip because it involved only a few dozen younger workers and managers were not implicated. People are eager to report stories, since it is practically the only way to advance on the farm. Some will even invent stories in order to gain favour with the owner. For instance, while I was living in the compound, I was the subject of several false rumours, including working as an undercover journalist or plotting to steal farm equipment. This tendency to report on one another is characteristic of paternalistic farms, illustrating how certain 'older style' methods of labour control remain necessary in the present context. Neo-liberal labour relations thus continue to rely upon illiberal practices.

Related to the seemingly ubiquitous presence of farm spies, white managers enjoy seniority strictly because they are white and thereby have 'trust' with Philip. In a sense, the farm is a microcosm of apartheid. The white employees are the only workers hired on a 'permanent' basis, that is, their names are not entered and re-entered every month on the roster. The white employees identify more with the interests of their employer, Philip, than with the black workers. In part, this may be because they are paid far more than black people. When a young white man was hired to supervise the pack shed, his starting salary was above the highest paid black manager. The latter complained, 'Boss Philip is not fair; I built this farm to where it is now.' The solidarity among whites is also based on racial ideology. Philip feels that he can only trust white people because blacks have stealing 'in their blood'. There are limits, in other words, to how much blacks can be 'moulded into the ethic of the farm', as Philip put it. Regardless of skill or qualifications, white people rank above blacks in the farm hierarchy.

In contrast to the racial solidarity among whites, blacks are divided along ethno-linguistic lines between Shona- and Venda-speaking people. Shona is practically the official language on the farm, yet there are dozens of Venda speakers who understand little Shona and form a distinct community separate from the Shona majority. Within the compound itself, mud huts constructed on the upper reaches of a hill are effectively reserved for Venda-speakers, while the Shona reside elsewhere in the compound. This area atop the hill is called *tshikwarani*, Venda for 'mountain,' a sort of signal to all residents that the place belongs to Venda people. Given the fact that the farm is located in a histori- cally Venda-controlled area, it is perhaps surprising that Venda workers do not express more animosity towards the Shona workers. One Venda man describes his attitude towards Shona speakers as follows: 'We get along okay, but what worries us is that we think this is our area, but it is not the case because we are fewer, but we know they will go home in the due course of time.' (It is notable that the Zimbabwean Venda recognize the farm as 'their area', even though it is on the South African side of the border. In any case, to my knowledge no restitution claim has ever been registered on the land now owned by Heddon Estates.) Another Venda states that she feels 'looked down upon' by Shona people because she is less educated than most of them. Indeed, several Shona speakers admit to thinking the Venda are intellectually inferior. One Shona supervisor remarks: 'It is difficult to work with the Vendas because they are slow to learn what we are doing.' While it is true that the Shona-speakers are generally more educated than the Venda-speakers, this is because more highly educated Venda migrants tend to go further south for employment, as they more easily pass as South African citizens. It is only the least educated among them who seek employment on the farm.

Ethnic divisions and the prevalence of spying inhibit farm workers from organizing against the interests of management, but added to these obstacles is a general sense of lethargy among workers in relation to broader politics. This lethargy became clear when I asked informants about the Zimbabwean crisis and its causes. Responses from workers could be grouped into three cat- egories: first, there is a pro-MDC narrative that blames Mugabe's policies for economic decline. It attributes the modest economic stability over the last year to the involvement of the MDC in the government through the Global Political Agreement (GPA). Second is a pro-ZANU-PF narrative that blames the West and sanctions for ongoing economic troubles.[10] Third, there is a narrative of indifference or consternation concerning the political situation. Most people espouse this third narrative, although the majority can also be described as MDC supporters (despite the fact that most people admit to having voted for ZANU-PF in the last election). Overall, few people appear to be passionate about politics. Apart from a former MDC activist and one war veteran who ardently supports Mugabe, people do not take political debates very seriously. Most discussions and debates are seemingly light-hearted and interspersed with laughing, as though their real value lies in distraction from tasks at hand or possibly to defuse underlying tensions.

Nevertheless, politics is a frequent topic of discussion among workers in the fields or relaxing in the compound. Many read newspapers and listen to radio reports with interest. The first and second narratives are counterposed and frequently manifest in debates among Zimbabweans. I witnessed a typical debate among Zimbabweans as they picked tomatoes:

Machezo:	Why do you support Mugabe?
Lyton:	Because if Tsvangirai comes the whites will come back.
Machezo:	But that will not happen.
Lyton:	Look at our country. We have freedom. There is no crime. It is the white countries that are giving us problems.
Machezo:	So you like this life of being a migrant?
Lyton:	Do you like this life of being exploited by a white man?
Machezo:	So what is better, being a migrant or being exploited?
Lyton:	(laughing) You are the kind of people we beat at home, it's only that we're not there!

Supporters of the second narrative can have a more nuanced perspective than might be expected. On one occasion, a debate over sanctions against Zimbabwe erupted during an interview. The MDC supporter explained that sanctions are not broad-based and only target select individuals in Zimbabwe. The ZANU-PF supporter retorted that because the 'targeted individuals' own such a large share of Zimbabwe's economy, sanctions against them inevitably impact the wider economy. The MDC supporter, on the defensive, conceded that this could be the case.

Those who espouse the second narrative tend to come from rural areas of Mberengwa and are often beneficiaries of Fast Track Land Reform. One informant explained that 'these people are grateful to Mugabe for giving them land, but they also see how the economy has improved since the MDC got involved in government'. Such people may long for political change, but experience genuine anxiety about losing their recently obtained land should the MDC come to power. But the second narrative is not always so ambiguous. One man claims that when he arrived at the farm he was an MDC supporter. But after working on the farm and hearing stories about how the white owner, Philip, can beat people, he now thinks 'Mugabe is right'. He states: 'What will happen if the white man comes back in Zimbabwe? We will get the same treatment over there.' However, several informants claim that people are more likely to convert to the MDC, rather than to ZANU-PF, when they are staying at the farm. The experience of migration, exposure to new people and new ideas can be determining factors according to them.

The third narrative, an expression of indifference, accounts for most people's view. In conversations with informants, politics-related questions provoke a common response: informants often turn their eyes to the ground and utter 'Aaahhh…', followed by silence or a despondent statement such as 'Mugabe will not go' or 'we don't know how to change our President'. This sort of reply, eschewing detail, conveys the indifference many Zimbabweans at Heddon Estates feel towards politics in Zimbabwe. It is not that people don't care about the political future of Zimbabwe, but rather that many see little benefit in speculating about politics. One informant put it like this: 'what is the benefit of politics anyway? The people at the top are enjoying the good life in nice houses, while we are the ones fighting each other. Why do we even get into it? I'm not going to deal with politics, I'm just here to work. I don't even want to vote'.

Another common refrain on the farm, 'everyone here is after money,' illustrates how people are too preoccupied with immediate survival to invest deeply in political concerns. Indeed, Zimbabweans seem to express more concern over rainfall at their rural homesteads than they do over political struggles. Many people understand the current political-economic moment as a time of 'waiting and seeing', a time of weathering the storm by working in South Africa and maintaining only a distant connection to politics in Zimbabwe.

The sense of resignation that animates the third narrative also characterizes how many farm workers perceive farm politics. Prospective labour action against management is limited not only by the fear of being 'sold out' by fellow workers, but also by a feeling of powerlessness as migrant workers. One worker commented, 'We are foreigners and have no rights. If you are against the manager you will be fired. Here it is every man for himself.' Widespread divisions promoted by the shifting labour regime encourage farm workers to channel their energies into survival or pleasure-seeking activities. Yet, these activities are also driven by Zimbabwean's own motivations and goals.

Kuvaka Musha

Most Zimbabweans at Heddon Estates have in their possession a small notebook, usually stored in their rooms or mud huts. Inside they keep track of money lent and borrowed, records of purchases and lists of 'targets', the objects they intend to buy. One notebook, for instance, lists such targets as a generator, television aerial, a cow, radio, shoes and various groceries. For each item an estimated price is noted beside it. On any given day, Zimbabweans can be seen referring to the targets in their notebook, checking off the items they have managed to obtain or perhaps just reminding themselves of their goals. For Zimbabwean migrants, much depends on these targets which are both a source of immense hope and anxiety – hope that 'results' (*mbairo*) will be achieved, and anxiety over the possibility of failure. The targets are, in effect, Zimbabweans' attempts to *kuvaka musha*, a dominant idiom on the farm that literally means 'building a rural homestead'.[11]

Kuvaka musha usually refers to supporting dependents at home, through paying school fees or providing food and other necessities, but also to physical improvements to a house or plot, and the accumulation of livestock. A closely related concept, *kugadzira ramangwana* (to prepare for the future) encompasses using farm income to start a business, attend college, pay bride service to a wife's parents, or, as in the case of some women, purchasing fashionable clothing to attract a husband back in Zimbabwe.[12] These practices are important to Zimbabweans in at least three ways. One, many Zimbabweans believe that to obtain prestige or maintain good standing with friends and relatives in the rural home, one must demonstrate improvements to the homestead. *Kuvaka musha* in this cultural context is the 'proper' use of wealth. Two, adding assets to the homestead or educating children are investments in future security. For instance, in a country where banks are unreliable, it is far better to buy a cow, which can be used for ploughing, or sold in times of difficulty. Three, as in many other contexts, the dominant notion of masculinity is tied to effective provision for one's family. I was told on many occasions that a man who arrives home without having acquired significant funds or goods can become the target of derision. For many migrant workers, *kuvaka musha* is linked to a broader objective: attaining enough rural assets to sustain a permanent livelihood in Zimbabwe, most often through small-scale farming or starting a small business. If the Zimbabwean homestead is neglected, the individual risks severing ties with family and not having assets to build upon if he loses his job.

On the farm, the term has an almost hegemonic status as it is reinforced in daily discourse and in church formations. *Kuvaka musha* orders a moral code among Zimbabweans in which, almost as a matter of principle, finances should be channeled towards projects back home. Many informants define happiness as experiencing 'success' with one's plans in relation to *kuvaka musha*. One strengthens and maintains bonds with relatives and has greater peace of mind regarding the future. Yet, it is happiness at a remove, mostly experienced away from the farm on which they are working. Moreover, as each worker tends to be so preoccupied with his or her plan to *kuvaka musha*, they are disinclined to engage in collective struggle to improve conditions at the farm. According to many informants, there is just too much at stake in achieving individual targets; it is better to accept low wages and poor conditions, than to risk losing one's job by challenging them.

While the idiom *kuvaka musha* may undermine worker unity, to some extent it does grant lower-status workers a sort of moral ammunition against senior workers. For example, the most senior black manager on the farm is often ridiculed in relative secrecy for failing to build anything substantial in Zimbabwe, despite earning a high salary and operating several businesses on the farm. The vast proportion of his income is spent on paying for innumerable girlfriends. While he is something of an extreme example, he is not alone in spending the bulk of his income on women. My data suggests that longer-term workers (those who have spent more than four years on the farm) in spite of their generally higher salaries, send less home in remittances than short-term workers. It is almost as if the longer one is on the farm, the more one's strategy of *kuvaka musha* begins to stagnate. There is higher consumption expenditure among longer-term workers, particularly on entertainment; such people are more likely to drink, smoke *dagga*, gamble and maintain one or more farm girlfriends or wives. The last of these, farm relationships, constitute by far the greatest expenditure among men. And it is partly on the basis of this, that women farm workers emerge as stronger homestead supporters then men. It is widely reported that most women return home with more money and/or goods than men.

Gender Relations and Transactional Sex

In terms of gender, Heddon Estates is in many respects a patriarchal institution par excellence. At any given time, women constitute close to half of the farm population, yet they occupy the lowest paid and lowest ranking positions: chiefly, picking tomatoes and weeding. Sexual exploitation appears widespread. The head manager often demands sex from women before employing them. In the period before they are employed, newly arrived women at the farm are compelled to move in with a male employee in one of the mud huts or hostel block rooms to avoid sleeping in the bush. In these relationships, called *kuchaya mapoto*,[13] women provide the bulk of domestic labour, such as cooking, washing and collecting firewood, in addition to sexual relations. Women find it difficult to stop their partner from paying for 'no strings attached' sexual encounters with other women, a practice known as *chiback*.[14] If a woman involved in a *kuchaya mapoto* relationship is caught engaging in *chiback* with other men, she is beaten with relative impunity.

The majority of men and women on the farm are involved in *chiback* and *kuchaya mapoto* relationships. There are three dominant categories of men: first, men who have wives in Zimbabwe from whom they may or may not try to keep their farm relationships secret; second, men who have divorced their former wives; third, unmarried men who are generally also younger than other men at the farm. Most women are divorcees or widows. For divorcees, their marriages have fallen apart for various reasons. For these women, marriage is a failed institution and it is unusual to marry again, except as a second wife, a position most are unwilling to accept. Most women do not expect to be married again – even if they wish it – and their primary focus seems to be on supporting children and their own homesteads in Zimbabwe. There is a minority of previously unmarried, younger women on the farm.

As indicated, *kuchaya mapoto* is a form of domestic partnership. It refers to a man and woman staying together, without the elders being informed. While relationships often begin because a newly arrived woman needs a place to stay, after she gains employment she is able to renegotiate the terms of the relationship. If the man does not pay, a woman can leave the relationship. Normally, the man pays the bulk of the monthly grocery bill in town. The woman provides sex and domestic labour for the man in exchange. The relationship becomes complicated if the man's real wife visits him. Normally he persuades the woman to temporarily vacate the hut, but farm gossip usually reveals the situation. Many wives tolerate such liaisons, as long as the other girlfriend does not stay in the hut or room while she is there. More rarely, the discovery of a girlfriend can lead to the break-up of a marriage. *Chiback*, in contrast, refers to a form of cash-and-carry prostitution. Men pay the on the spot for sexual intercourse at an agreed price. A man or woman can have any number of *chiback* partners. Men typically pay women roughly ZAR20 for sexual intercourse – sometimes the payment is in kind, such as cold drinks or chicken pieces.

In many cases the *kuchaya mapoto* relationship continues for consecutive seasons. For many women, the longer they remain in the relationship, the more difficult it becomes to leave it. The woman becomes recognized as the man's 'wife', making it difficult for her to strike up a new relationship with another man, because other men will seek to avoid offending her former partner. If the woman tries to leave the relationship, the man can demand financial compensation for all the expenses he has incurred during the months they were together. The example of one farm couple, Mai Cynthia and Robert, provides an illustration:

> Mai Cynthia and Robert have been staying together in one of the hostel block rooms since January 2009. Robert, 42, is a senior foreman in the irrigation team. Mai Cynthia, 34, is a tomato-picker in her first year of employment. Robert has a wife and two children in his rural home in Zimbabwe, and Mai Cynthia is a widow also with two children. When she came to the farm in January, she initially stayed in one of the mud huts with her sister, but she was proposed [to] by Robert and decided to move in with him. In each month they lived together, Robert has contributed R150 to the monthly grocery bill, and Mai Cynthia has paid only R50. On one afternoon in November, I hear Robert arguing with Mai Cynthia, as she refuses to give him money for buying marijuana. 'Why can't you just give me 50 rand,' he complains, 'You will go home with money, and I am left with nothing.' Robert will not go home in December when the farm closes, his friends tell me, but will look for a job in a distant town. He has spent most of his money on drugs, alcohol and women. Mai Cynthia is his *kuchiya mapoto* partner, but he has other *chiback* partners. I ask Mai Cynthia if she is happy in the relationship: 'At least it is better, I can save something to bring home to my children.' Yet one of Mai Cynthia's friends tells me she cannot leave the relationship, because people at the farm think they are married and Robert could speak against her.

Mai Cynthia's comments emphasize the instrumental aspects of the relationship, notably the ability to 'save something' by having it. Clearly, this is a relationship that circumstances largely compel her to accept. As with other informants, she justifies the relationship because it allows her to better 'support her children'. For his part, Robert views it as natural – even expected – that a man will stay with a woman while at the farm for most of the year. Yet, he hastens in an interview to point out that she is not his real wife, that he has a real wife and family at home. Perhaps he mentions this because he desires to project a masculine sense of respectability and responsibility, and to disguise his apparent failure to *kuvaka musha*. Men who, like Robert, spend most of their income on relationships and other gratification in South Africa, risk being ostracized by their (rural) community in Zimbabwe. In comparison, women risk being labeled as prostitutes by friends and relatives back home, which can undermine their social status. Christian churches on the farm condemn the sexual liaisons as sinfulness and 'backsliding'. Some people may feel a sense of personal shame. However, it must also be said liaisons of this sort can be positive for women apart from the income they gain. In *kuchaya mapoto*, there may be a companionship or friendship dimension even if the relationship is largely defined by the transaction. More broadly, it would be wrong to understand these women as mere victims of male desire and control. In many cases women instigate *kuchaya mapoto* and *chiback* relationships – albeit less frequently than men – as they demand payment in the form of cash and groceries and thus are able to supplement their income.

The fact that women tend to generate more income than men makes them targets of male resentment. Men characterize most women in the compound as predatory *mahure* (prostitutes); they view women as experienced divorcees seeking to lure young men as their sexual victims. One says: 'The problem is, if you look at the ages, we have smaller guys and the women are more mature. They are drawing them in.' Whereas most men blame women for promiscuity in the compound, women tend to attribute blame equally or blame men. An older female informant (in her late 40s) explains: 'Men are the initiators, they pretend as if they want to help you... we are trying nowadays to protect the young women, but after some months we may fail.'

Most male informants feel they have a right to beat their *kuchaya mapoto* partner if she sleeps with another man. Men derive justification for these beatings by emphasizing that they pay the women to stay with them. Interestingly, when a man catches another man sleeping with his partner, it is usually only the woman who is beaten, while the offending man escapes without punishment. Moreover, when a man beats his partner, other men will rarely intervene, out of 'respect' for another man's private business. One male informant states: 'guys on the farm respect each other… they won't step on another guy if he is beating his wife… the same with chasing after ladies, if she is being chased by another guy, you cannot chase'. For women, the situation is very different, as they are more likely to have conflict over men – including in one case burning down another woman's hut. Thus, male resentment directed towards women generates some patriarchal solidarity among men, but it simultaneously fractures the workforce along gender lines. *Kuchaya mapoto* and *chiback* can generate competition among women for men, leading to conflict between women.

Although some women benefit economically from transactional sex at the farm the question must be asked, at what cost are these gains achieved? The spectre of HIV/AIDS looms large. As much as migrants do try to compartmentalize their behaviour at the farm, many do return home with the condition. As a recent report from the International Organization for Migration (2010) makes clear, commercial farms in border areas have among the highest HIV/AIDS rates in South Africa. The prevalence of transactional sex on farms is related to a multiplicity of factors, such as low wages, the high degree of mobility among workers, shifting gender identities and declining marriage rates.[15] However, one must also include the role of predatory managers that are empowered by owners such as Philip. It is well known on the farm that many of the most promiscuous men, who are also the most high-ranking managers, are on anti-retroviral treatments. Most of these men are disdainful of condom use and use their powerful position to demand sex from women seeking jobs or in need of a favour. Thus, many women are exposed to HIV/AIDS in the course of farm relationships, and it becomes difficult to argue that women improve themselves through such relationships. As survival strategies, such relationships are reactions to an oppressive power structure and do little to undermine it. A similar dynamic emerges with high interest money lending, known as *chimbadzo*.

Chimbadzo

On the last Friday of every month, workers at Heddon Estates gather at the farm workshop to receive their monthly pay. Outside the workshop gate, a chaotic scene invariably unfolds. As each worker exits the gated area, having collected their pay, they enter a swarming mass of people, a mob frantic to settle their accounts. If a worker has incurred debts, the creditor encounters them in this mob, hoping to be paid back before other creditors find the debtor. Tense conversations and arguments ensue, with debtors desperately trying to negotiate down the amount owing. In most cases the creditors are money-lenders, a popular business in the farm compound known as *chimbadzo*. The standard interest rate for *chimbadzo* lending is 100 per cent and due at the end of the month.

Apart from money-lenders, some creditors are shop owners in the compound selling goods on credit; or women collecting money for sexual favours. Generally, the payments are made without too much physical resistance, with debtors finally agreeing to pay their debts. That said, each month there are some who are reluctant but do not manage to escape; the envelopes containing their pay are forcefully torn from their hands and the money divided up between the creditors. It is very difficult to escape the latter, for they can report cases to farm security when people refuse to pay their debts.

It is this aggressive settling up of accounts on pay day which, in the words of one informant, make it 'a day of stress… you see how little you are paid, and you are forced to give most of it away'. In effect, pay day renders visible a series of desperate economic transactions made in previous months – notably money-lending at extortionist interest rates – which transform the community of farm workers into an assortment of creditors and debtors, often sparking conflict and lasting tension between people. Moreover, these economic practices, in particular *chimbadzo*, reflect a form of moral compromise.

At least one-third of my interview participants claim to participate in *chimbadzo* as money-lenders. When asked if they view it as morally problematic or sinful, or if the practice causes them to feel guilty, most reply in ambiguous terms. A typical response is 'it is sinful but it is the only way to get money in this place', or 'the wages are too low here, you can get money with *chimbadzo*'. Another informant linked the practice directly to border-crossing: 'when people come this side (of the border) they just do things as they like'. Informants stated that money lending rarely occurs in Zimbabwe, and if it does, it cannot be with such high interest rates.

Apart from *chimbadzo*, economic practices among farm workers are characterized, as one put it, by a general 'stinginess' (*kuomera*). 'A guy can survive with five rand down here,' one informant states, 'so that he can save more to bring home'. But frugal saving also translates into less willingness to share with others. 'You do what you can to help somebody else, but you think about yourself here. I buy fish far away from where I stay, so that people will not see me eat it'. The economic environment in the farm compound is characterized by hustling, an environment where practically everything is for sale. It is similar to the crisis/inflationary economy of Zimbabwe itself, with the possible difference that people are less inclined to share with each other.

An exception to this stinginess is the hospitality shown to new Zimbabweans entering the compound, usually for the first time. As the compound is situated directly on the border, migrants frequently pass through it, even if they are seeking destinations further south. These migrants will often try to acquire food and accommodation for a few days. One informant said, 'Them [migrants] staying with us is not that big of a deal; no one harms them. It is about being Zimbabwean. We are the same people, we are in the same fight. It is just an act of humanity [to accommodate them]'. And yet, other informants suggest that a migrant can only be accommodated if you find someone from your home area or a relative. My own observations suggest that a migrant without connections or money will find accommodation in the compound, but only for one or two nights.

Apart from the above example of hospitality occasionally shown to new migrants, the farm community is characterized by deep divisions. Other social practices in the compound such as Christian worship and soccer generate a measure of unity among workers. However, these involve only a minority of workers and can reinforce the farm hierarchy. For instance, the leading preachers or church elders on the farm are also senior foremen. While workers engage in a wide variety of social practices at the farm, few are as widespread as transactional relationships and high-interest money-lending. These practices may support livelihood strategies, but they do little to challenge the structure of farm power.

Conclusion

In this chapter, I have outlined how workers at Heddon Estates are sharply divided along ethnic, linguistic, occupational, gender and political lines, among other markers of difference. These divisions are reinforced by the changing labour regime of the farm, characterized as an articulation between paternalism and neo-liberalism. The regime grants a small clique of black managers' vast powers over the rest of the work force. Competition is fostered between workers by 'incentivizing production'; paying piece rates and assigning bonuses to foremen and managers who exceed targets. Workers are encouraged to spy on one another, to report any subversive murmurings to management as a means to promote themselves. Within this divisive atmosphere, farm workers have few avenues to improve their livelihoods apart from individualistic strategies, such as transactional sex and *chimbadzo*. These practices increase income for some workers, but they also deepen existing divisions. In the case of transactional sex, many women receive cash or groceries, but participants risk exposing themselves to HIV/AIDS. Moreover, transactional sex fosters male resentment towards women in part due to the income men spend on such relationships. *Chimbadzo* lenders increase their personal income, but to the detriment of other Zimbabwean workers, encouraging animosity between lenders and borrowers.

While these strategies are situated by the labour regime and wider divisions on the farm, their prevalence – at least transactional sex for women and money-lending for both genders – is also connected to how Zimbabweans privilege *kuvaka musha* in Zimbabwe over improving conditions at the farm. Paradoxically, *kuvaka musha* can encourage discipline and frugality among workers, but it simultaneously individuates the workforce, whereby each worker has his or her own projects or plans in Zimbabwe for which much is sacrificed. Thus, management practices and the ideal of *kuvaka musha* work together to diminish the possibility of collective action, such as strikes, that could improve conditions on the farm for the majority of workers. If power imbalances were addressed, possibly through some form of unionization, women could at least be more selective in choosing their partners and have the right of refusal with senior managers. With higher wages, workers may feel less need to borrow from *chimbadzo* lenders.

Yet, if Zimbabweans are to organize and challenge labour relations in the future, the motivation of *kuvaka musha* will remain central to this process. Zimbabweans will not abandon their homesteads and are likely to continue viewing their time at the South African farm as a temporary sojourn. If future organizing is to be successful, the ethic of supporting one's homestead must be connected to transforming oppressive working conditions in South Africa. How this can be accomplished within existing migrant farm-worker communities remains a key question.

Notes

1 I am grateful to all of the workers and farm owners who spoke with me during the course of my research. I thank Christina Doonan, Ben Pauli and one anonymous reviewer who read previous versions of this chapter. I would also like to thank the Canadian Social Science and Humanities Research Council and the Department of International Environment and Development Studies at the Norwegian University for the Life Sciences for funding the research.

2 What I refer to as 'eastern border' constitutes the border-line east of Musina, stretching along the Limpopo until arriving at the Madimbo Corridor military base. I do not consider the area between Madimbo corridor and Kruger Park as part of this designation, since it has historically been communal land or mining areas and thus not as relevant for white farming.

3 In this historical section, I draw on archival sources, interviews with long-term Venda residents in the surrounding area (including former farm workers), local white farmers and secondary sources.

4 Scrutton himself was an active trader in the northern Transvaal in the 1880s and 1890s and had originally obtained the land from the Venda chief, Makhado, before the latter was driven out of the Zoutpansberg district by an army detachment from Pretoria (see Mulaudzi, 2000: 67-8).

5 The obstacles to white settlement along the northern frontier, in an earlier period, is also discussed by Wagner (1980). Mulaudzi (2000) discusses how conditions for white farming improved in northern Zoutpansberg District after 1930.

6 It is unclear if, and to what extent, farmers in the study area made efforts to recruit labour using recruiting agents, as was done by white farmers in the Tchipise/Nzhele-le area and others around the Soutpansberg. Farmers along the border were well positioned to 'intercept' migrants who were crossing the river en route to the mines near Johannesburg, much like Heddon Estates today. However, I have not found any archival or oral evidence supporting this possibility. It is likely that migrants avoided the farms given the poor wages. The farms depended, in the main, on Venda living on the farm or migrants from nearby villages across the Limpopo.

7 This was probably the second major exodus from the land. The first occurred when the first white settlers arrived and many Venda chose to leave at that time.

8 For discussions of paternalism on South African farms, see Du Toit (1993). For a Zimbabwean case, see Rutherford (2001). More recent analyses include Kritizinger et al. (2004) and Ewert and Du Toit (2005).

9 The extent of guerilla activity along the eastern border is unclear and needs further research. I was told by farmers and former workers that during the 1980s border farmers had the authority to shoot anyone they found crossing the Limpopo River.

10 Supporters of this narrative disguise their preferences from Philip. Informants claimed that Philip has been known to fire workers if they are Zimbabwe African National Union-Patriotic Front (ZANU-PF) supporters. I was told that on one occasion a few years ago, a group of Zimbabwean border-jumpers stood before Philip asking for employment. He asked the group who among them raises a fist, and who raises an open palm (the raised fist is associated with ZANU-PF and Robert Mugabe, while the open hand is related to the MDC and Morgan Tsvangirai). Those who raised the closed fist, suggesting support for ZANU-PF, were not given jobs.

11 The 'rural homestead' refers to land occupied by a Zimbabwean or his or her family in the communal areas of Zimbabwe, including the houses, huts, livestock and crops within the homestead boundary. It also refers to the extended family living in or around the homestead.

12 *Kugadzira ramangwana* is often pursued by Zimbabweans precisely so that they can more effectively attain *kuvaka musha*. For example, obtaining training or certificates from a college will enable one to get a better job, earn higher income, and thus support the rural home even better.

13 The Shona term *kuchaya mapoto* literally means in English 'to bang pots'. The reference to pots derives from the domestic labour that women perform in such relationships.

14 *Chiback* is a one-time sexual encounter that is typically paid for on the spot. It literally means 'from the back' because it is done secretly, 'behind the back' of your *kuchaya mapoto* partner or spouse.

15 See Hunter (2010) for a more detailed discussion of how these factors are implicated in transactional sex in South Africa.

10

Farms as Camps
Displaced Zimbabweans on commercial farms in Limpopo Province, South Africa[1]
Poul Wisborg

Introduction – To be in or out of the Camps

In J.M. Coetzee's (1983) novel *Life and Times of Michael K,* the protagonist walks through a South Africa torn by civil war, from Cape Town to Prince Albert in the Western Cape. Here he seeks freedom on an abandoned farm below the Swartberg mountains, getting by on a meagre living, scraping up the leftovers in livestock troughs or trying to grow pumpkins. He is then incarcerated at a labour camp but escapes and returns to Cape Town where, completely exhausted, he is interned at a medical relief camp. An empathic doctor believes he can hear Michael K's yearning to escape from both charity and camps:

> I am not asking you to take care of me, for example by feeding me. My need is a very simple one. Though this is a large country, so large that you would think there would be space for everyone, what I have learned of life tells me that it is hard to keep out of the camps. Yet I am convinced there are areas that lie between the camps and belong to no camps—certain mountaintops, for example, certain islands in the middle of swamps, certain arid strips where human beings may not find it worth their while to live. I am looking for such a place in order to settle there, perhaps only till things improve, perhaps forever.(Coetzee, 1983: 162-3)

The doctor interprets Michael K to be enthralled with an idea of freedom or dignity, to the point of fatally neglecting his own bodily needs: 'I slowly began to understand the truth: that you were crying secretly, unknown to your conscious self (forgive the term), for a different kind of food, food that no camp could supply' (163). Michael K himself tries to define his identity but always find himself out of place, a gardener in the city by the sea, an earthworm on a cement floor. Finally he defines himself by what he has escaped: 'Perhaps the truth is that it is enough to be out of the camps, out of all the camps at the same time. Perhaps that is enough of an achievement, for the time being. How many people are there left who are neither locked up nor standing guard at the gate? I have escaped the camps; perhaps, if I lie low, I will escape the charity too.' (182). Michael K regretted that 'everywhere I go there are people waiting to exercise their forms of charity on me' and refused to become 'an object of charity' (183).

The idea of escaping camps and charity contrasts with the role that refugee camps play in providing safety to human beings in distress. An employee of a Norwegian aid organisation working in conflict zones around the world said at a seminar: 'Everybody wants to be in a camp, because the camp makes them visible in the eyes of the world.' Such a desire contrasts with Michael K's quest for freedom and dignity outside any camp.

Such perceptions of camps, or 'the camp', came back to me when researching farm workers' and farm dwellers' issues in South Africa's Limpopo Province on the border with Zimbabwe. The political and economic disaster in Zimbabwe, unfolding with particular intensity with the turn of the millennium, has displaced people on an extraordinary scale (Hammar, McGregor and Landau, 2010). Many Zimbabweans went to South Africa for its job opportunities, despite the often harsh, living conditions. National and regional responses were characterized by denial (Chapters 1 and 2). The scale of displacement led to a discussion about the construction of refugee camps on the Limpopo border, a suggestion ultimately rejected by the ANC government. During the team's first research visit to Limpopo in 2007, we noticed the role which farms played in the survival and livelihood strategies of migrants as temporary places of abode or as centres of employment, shelter and services. Farms struck us as being ambiguous: as *enterprises* that utilized migrant labour, and as *camps* that provided the relief that neither the government, the United Nations, nor aid organizations offered, the latter unable to cover the vast landscape across which farms lie scattered.

The experiences on commercial farms in the borderlands of South Africa and Zimbabwe evoked Italian philosopher Giorgio Agamben's (1998) seminal analysis of 'bare life', biopolitics and camps which have inspired a 'sociology facing the camp', examining, for example, refugee camps and gated communities (Diken and Laustsen 2005). This chapter explores these experiences and ideas further. Agamben's key concepts are outlined in section 2. In section 3, I consider the 'zones of exception' over which displaced Zimbabweans move. Section 4 presents four different farms and their 'camp-like' functions related to *labour, relief, internment* and *protection*. I suggest that whereas official camps could have made the displaced, and the crisis, more visible in the eyes of the world, *farms as camps* contribute to containing and concealing the human impact of the Zimbabwean crisis, removing a thorn in the eye of rulers who seek to protect the public images of themselves and the region (see Chapters 2 and 3).

Bare life, biopolitics and camps

According to Agamben, life in camps is *nuda vita* – 'bare life' or 'naked life' – produced through transgression, humiliation, suffering and the violation of the universal human need for protection. Drawing on Hannah Arendt and Michel Foucault, among others, he suggests that the production of bare life is characteristic of how modern mass society exerts control over individuals. In early modern Europe, 'natural life begins to be included in the mechanisms and calculations of State power, and politics turns into biopolitics' (Agamben, 1998: 3), the politics of 'modern man' that 'calls his existence as a living being into question' (Foucault, 1998 [1976]). While Aristotle used *bios politicos* to refer to the political life that is unique for human beings (Agamben, 1998: 1, 7), Foucault and Agamben use 'bio-political' to refer to the situation where power works directly on the human body, in the absence of the spaces (*agora*), statuses (citizenship) and rights on which political life relies. Biopolitical 'techniques' exert control over human bodies and include methods of labour extraction, political control and surveillance, such as the Panopticon prison advocated by Jeremy Bentham (1995 [1787]). While biopolitical techniques make human beings objects without rights, democracy may make them the subjects of political power (Agamben, 1998: 6, 9, 181). However, with Nazism in mind, Agamben sets out to understand, 'why democracy, at the very moment in which it seemed to have finally triumphed over its adversaries and reached its greatest height, proved itself incapable of saving *zoē* [life], to whose happiness it had devoted all its effort, from unprecedented ruin' (Ibid.: 10). One reason, he argues, is that in 'post-democratic spectacular societies' grand performances and superficial appearances of success (growth on the stock exchange or large sporting events, for example) are valued more highly than the wellbeing of humans.

Camps can be seen as manifestations of modern biopolitical situations. Agamben refers to European camps such as those made by the United Kingdom in South Africa during the South African War (Boer War) and by other countries to contain communists and refugees (Ibid.: 167-8). In the Nazi camps human beings lost dignity in an unprecedented manner, and from a time-bound state of emergency they were extended 'until further notice'. A camp is 'the space that is opened when the state of exception begins to become the rule' (168-9), and suggests a 'hidden matrix and *nomos* [law] of the political space in which we are still living' (166). Camps create an 'absolute biopolitical space… where power confronts nothing but pure life, without any mediation', since citizenship is lost (171). Hannah Arendt observed that in the camps 'everything is possible'. The loss of status and rights by cross-border migrants at least makes more things possible, so they have to resort to their human rights (Albertyn, 2008) or to the civility and ethics of individuals and authorities (Agamben 1998: 174). Diken and Laustsen (2005: 88) suggest that 'the most basic characteristics of camp life' are: (i) living on small payments or vouchers, hindered from normal economic participation; (ii) being prevented from finding paid work; (iii) living according to the government's determination of residency; and (iv) having limited mobility.

The possible character of farms as camps may be examined with the use of such ideas and criteria. I note, though, that Agamben seems to assume a monistic and centralist law (dissolved in the camp), rather than plural normative orders. The concept of 'the sovereign' seems to be more suited to such state facilities as detention camps rather than farms with their many actors at considerable distance from the state. 'Bare life' also seems to emphasize victimhood at the expense of agency and resistance, which follow from an interest in politics. I approach the farms as camps with such reservations in mind.

Zones of exception

On a day in February 2008, driving along a back road in the Waterpoort area of Limpopo Province, we passed a young man carrying an empty water bottle and looking exhausted. We saw that he was bruised, with cuts on an arm and a leg, and gave him a lift and food and water. Themba told us a brief but powerful story. Twenty-one years old, he had left Harare two days previously. Until then he had worked in an international hotel. His salary had been ZD60 million per month; at the time a loaf of bread cost ZD5 million, a bag of maize meal ZD30 million, and a buffet lunch at his hotel ZD160 million, two and a half times his monthly salary, which had been eroded by hyper-inflation. He had lived with and supported his mother and two nieces. As he could no longer do so, he decided to look up his only sister, who had left Zimbabwe for South Africa in 1994.

Themba paid ZD60 million for a lift in a truck that was to take him and a couple of friends across the border and on to Johannesburg. After an early morning crossing at Beitbridge, the promised lift on the South African side did not materialize. Deceived, he and his friends started walking through the forested area between the border and Musina. Here they were attacked by the *maguma-gumas* (robbers), who stole his belongings, money, identification documents and cellphone. One robber demanded his new shoes and gave him an old, ill-fitting pair in return. Another inflicted a deep cut on his arm. The friends made a frantic escape and became separated. Themba took a back road in the direction of Makhado/Louis Trichardt, avoiding the more patrolled N1 Highway. He had his wounds dressed and received food and water at a rural clinic, and walked on. He was about 50 km south of the border when we met him, dehydrated, hungry, having had no food that day, and his feet hurting from walking in the oversized shoes. He had also lost all contact information with the loss of his cellphone. He remembered the number of his brother in Harare and phoned him using one of our phones, and learnt that his friends were walking on the railway track to Makhado. He failed to make contact with them and chose to come with the team to Johannesburg, where he met a relative at a construction company, and later joined his sister.

Within a few days Themba, a healthy young man, had been brought to the limit of human existence, or bare life, where one more unfortunate incident could be fatal: a deeper wound, an infection, missing a rural clinic; and where he had no control over small consequential acts such as the robber swopping his ill-fitting old shoes for his victim's newer ones. Themba said, 'Mr Mugabe is the one who is causing those problems. He is putting everyone's life in danger.' He credited Mugabe with supporting new farm owners, but said: 'Before, bread was cheap. The whites used combine harvesters. Now workers are using their hands. It is too hard for us to do that.' In direct and indirect ways the 'sovereign' was producing bare life, 'putting everyone's life in danger': the disruption of production, physical labour, lack of bread, the compulsion to migrate and, ultimately, the fear and mortal risk of an illegal border crossing.

At the time such stories of extreme exposure and danger were common in Limpopo. In this landscape, migrants crossed through 'zones of exception'. The first zone was Zimbabwe itself, a country shaped by a history of race and inequality, as the commercial farms manifested. Cousins et al. (1992) argued that landlessness and poverty had forced many workers onto these farms as places of survival. Rutherford (2001) estimated that more than two million people, almost a fifth of the Zimbabwean population, lived on the farms.

Many originated in surrounding countries and in the post-colonial period they were still 'viewed as belonging to the farms and therefore outside the ambit of state development and welfare policies' (Ibid.), experiencing contempt from others. Workers' semi-forced enrolment, limited economic participation, and exclusion from the public sphere could suggest that these farms were already camps in the analytical sense suggested by Diken and Laustsen. In the land invasions from 2000 an estimated one million farm workers and their families were displaced (IDMC/NRC, 2009), treated as objects and appendices of the (former) owners: 'We were told to get out of our homes within five minutes and follow our white masters' (Hartnack 2009: 355). A parliamentarian stated that dwellers could be 'shipped home' at short notice. The ZANU-PF war veterans and militant youth treated the commercial farms as exceptional places where owners and workers were deprived of rights, reduced to bare life. Even worse things became possible on the farms, suggesting that the severity of the camp character may vary.

While the Matabeleland massacres in the 1980s signalled that Robert Mugabe was willing to use extreme means to crush opposition (Alexander, McGregor and Ranger, 2000; Raftopoulos, 2000), from the turn of the millennium the exceptional became increasingly normal, with rural and urban areas being turned into zones of fear. The displaced farm workers studied by Hartnack went to an urban 'holding camp' of squalor and poverty, which they compared to a bus terminus, 'a place of limbo where there is no security, where people come and go but nobody puts down roots' (Hartnack, 2009: 371). Some of them were evicted again in 2005 when the authorities bulldozed the area in Operation Murambatsvina.[2] In 2006 and 2007 the homes of thousands of informal miners were destroyed in Operation Stop the Gold Panning. As discussed in several chapters of this book, 'Mugabe's ZANU-PF rolled out a campaign of violence… [of] extra-judicial executions, systematic use of torture, widespread population displacements, and a general campaign of terror' (Raftopoulos and Eppel, 2008: 369). Evictions of farm workers and urban dwellers continued in 2009, when the IDMC/NRC (2009) estimated that five to eight per cent of the population was internally displaced. Economic, political and health calamities made Zimbabwe a zone of fear and insecurity, or a place on fire, as the political opposition stated on a billboard just south of the Limpopo border, ironically greeting every migrant (see photographs 1 and 2).

The second zone of exception is the lawless Limpopo River border (see also Chapter 6). The two states appear to have given up enforcing order, and police, military and immigration authorities may even benefit from the situation (Coplan 2008). According to Vigneswaran (2010), human traffickers collaborated with police officers to exhort money from migrants, one of the traffickers saying, 'I am the border, I can do whatever I like across this border, and you just have to bring money.' We noted how the triple-rows of razor-blade fences on the South African side were cut open at regular intervals. Migrants who lack identity documents or permits might cross the Limpopo River, often at night, exposed to the powerful current and crocodiles. Physical need and the regulations compel them to enter a zone where their life is put at risk. Deportations combined with migrants' rapid return create a flow back and forth across the border, as a farm worker told us in 2008:

> They arrested 60 to 70 people last year [2007] in June, on a Sunday. The police and the army came into this place and those who did not have their papers were deported. The majority came back; less than twenty did not. You are taken to IOM[3] at Beitbridge on the Zimbabwean side. There you are given a bath, beans and mealie meal. It's not so bad, before we were just dumped there to make our way elsewhere.

An ephemeral third zone is the Musina showgrounds. Responding to civil society demands for facilities for assisting migrants, the Government of South Africa, in 2007, decided to offer rudimentary immigration services at this site, though with irregular attention to refugee law: while waiting to submit applications or receive answers, the displaced lived in rudimentary self-made dwellings, plastic covered frames leaning against the fence. The showgrounds offered different kinds of visibility: here organizations could find and service the displaced; the government could demonstrate action; the displaced either told their stories to visitors or resented cameras and attention, fearing that friends or family at home might see them in humiliating circumstances. The thesis that it is desirable to be seen in the eyes of the world is qualified: this camp imposed the humiliations of bare life (hunger, dirt, crowding) with only the marginal benefits of being seen by helpers. Importantly, farmers sent their labour consultants here to contact and negotiate with potential workers. Though most aimed for the cities further south, the showgrounds in some cases facilitated the recruitment of workers to the farms as labour camps, which in turn provided salaries, housing and services, perhaps as substitute relief camps.

Limpopo, just south of the border, is the fourth zone. As in apartheid years, the area between the Limpopo River and Soutpansberg is a zone of exception where farm owners may hold corporate permits that empower them to grant a defined number of individual work permits. Farmers and workers stress how common cross-border labour exchange is in this region. One commercial farmer said, 'the Limpopo supplies us with water, and Zimbabwe supplies us with labour' (Skjæraasen, 2008). The displaced cross the area by vehicle or by foot, depending on their resources and legal status. Facing exposure to crime, capture and extradition by the police, extreme weather, inadequate food and water, and dangerous animals, they balance these risks, as when they walk through game farms to avoid the inspections and crime on the roads. A manager of a large game farm told us that he regularly sent his staff to collect water bottles *inside* the farm's fence along the N1 Highway. Migrants walking here pull into the bush if necessary to avoid the police, while hoping to escape any lion, leopard or rhino by quickly jumping back across the fence onto the road. Access to the farms, a fifth inner zone, is controlled by landowners, managers and security personnel. Some of the displaced find refuge on the farms, as workers, dependants or servants, while their human rights may also be violated there (SAHRC,[4] 2003; FMSP and MLAO, 2007).

The sixth zone is the wider territory of South Africa, where employment, food and public facilities may sometimes be found in diverse spaces from communal areas to private farms and urban townships. Labour from the southern African region was pivotal in building South African mines and agriculture, but black mine- and farm workers entered the country subject to 'secret side deals' regulating labour migration (Peberdy, 1999; 2008). Although it remains central to the economy, immigration is governed as exceptional. Those among the displaced who cross the border of nations and the boundaries of farms traverse these perplexing and changing zones of exception.

Farms as camps?
Four farms

From May 2007 to March 2009, a team of South African, Zimbabwean and Norwegian researchers researched farm worker and farm dweller issues on four commercial farms in the Vhembe district of Limpopo Province.[5] Three of the farms are in the semi-arid lowveld between the Limpopo River border and the Soutpansberg mountain range, where grass and woodlands provide opportunities for livestock-rearing and game-farming and the climate excellent for vegetable and fruit crops when water is available for irrigation. Farms were selected to represent agro-ecological zones and types of production, but incidentally

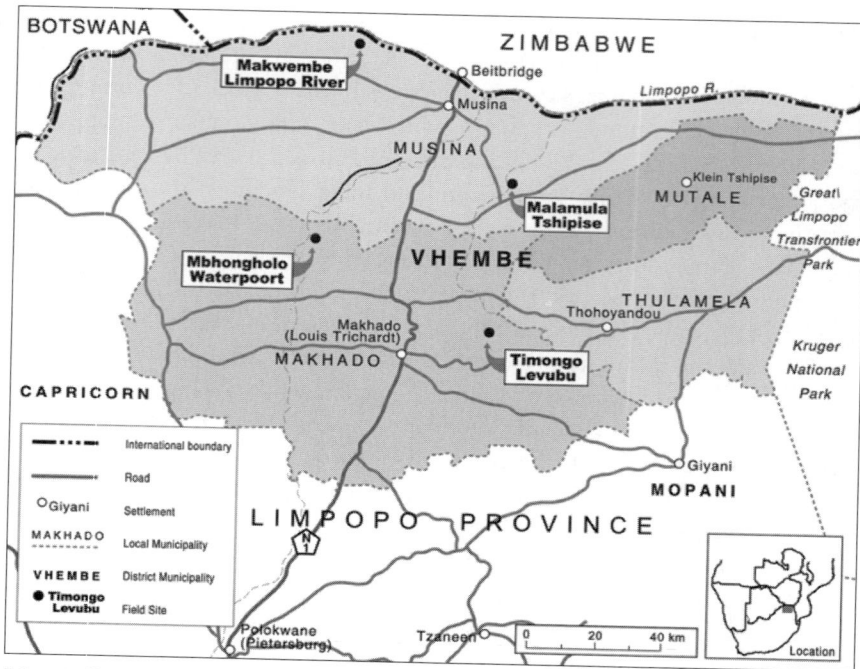

Map 6: Study sites in Vhembe District, Limpopo Province

show contrasting approaches to migrants. On *Makwembe,* a vegetable farm on the Limpopo River, and *Malamula,* a large citrus farm, migrant labour was central to the economy and social life. *Mbhongholo,* a small game farm, had no urgent demand for labour but two Zimbabweans had found refuge there. South of the Soutpansberg, in the fertile Levubu Valley, we studied the *Timongo* fruit and nuts farm, which strives to keep migrants off the farm.

Makwembe on the Limpopo: Labour, relief and gated community

'In Africa you cannot take a river as a border: a river valley is inhabited by people.' (Farm owner, Makwembe, 2007)

Having driven from Musina through the arid terrain along the border, with its triple-rows of razor wire fencing, the lush green garden of the homestead and the meticulously laid-out vegetable fields and greenhouses of Makwembe farm are striking. The family-owned farm was bought in 1982 and now exports vegetables to European supermarket chains in a highly competitive market. Its

265 hectares of specialized vegetable production is irrigated by water from the Limpopo, which is accessed via gates through the border fences.

Makwembe illustrates camp functions of labour, relief and internal security. In 2008, the work force comprised about 450 people, of whom about 300 were permanent, some 100 employed for the eight- to nine-month cropping season, and about 50 for the short term. In 2009, workers received the minimum wage of just over ZAR1,200 (about US$150) per month. Some of them praised Makwembe for relatively decent work conditions, for example, regarding work hours, labour inspectors found conditions compliant with South African law: it is not a place outside the law, though its protection has little reach for some of the unemployed, who also seek to make a living on the farm. When more workers are needed, the staff are asked to spread the word, which always secures sufficient labour. 'Africans are the best communicators in the world,' said the owner, but another view is that farms capitalize on the desperate underemployment on both sides of the border.

The key role of migrant labour on Makwembe is shaped as much by a history of labour migration as by the current crisis. The owner said that migration for trade and work is normal within the Limpopo basin, with ties of language and culture across the river, which was why he said that in Africa a river could not be a border and that this one was only respected during the war years in the 1970s. Thus, the border, not movement across it, is historically exceptional. The owner felt that 'the world had suddenly discovered' the Zimbabwean migrants in the area, leading to visits by journalists, the Human Rights Commission and researchers. Yet change is apparent on Makwembe as the first point-of-call for some of those who cross the river: 'They get very hungry that side: even when the river is very full they are coming,' a woman office worker said. Some seek employment but most continue to the cities or other farms.

Immigration governance displays characteristics of the camp, such as decentralized governance of the civil status of individuals, as the state has devolved to farm owners the authority to grant work permits. The owner said that most of his Zimbabwean workers have South African IDs, but that about 50 have permits as foreign workers (it increased from 45 in 2007 to 60 in 2009). They need to get a new permit in order to change employer, which workers say rarely happens; the low mobility, characteristic of camps, is accentuated by the isolation of the farm, the cost of transport and lack of mobile phone coverage, which workers say hamper their networking and job-seeking activities.

As a relief camp, Makwembe displays welfare aspects, particularly compared with life on the road or at the Musina showgrounds. There are incomes for about 450 staff, shelter, a subsidized milk supply, free firewood and affordable housing and services. However, relief provisioning is based on the owner's discretion about whether to employ or not, and the small rations that workers and their dependants live on is reminiscent of camps (Diken and Laustsen, 2005: 88). The farm owner said that he took pride in seeing workers progress but admitted that nobody could lead 'a decent life' on the salary he was able to offer – US$150 per month is just above a dollar a day per person in a family of four. Workers said that their salaries were being eroded by rising prices, particularly of food, their major expense. South African parliamentarians who, considering job-losses in agriculture and protests by farmer organizations, determined the minimum wage at only one fiftieth of their own package of over ZAR60,000 (US$7,500) per month. While included, migrant farm workers also experience the exclusion of the South African menial labour class from normal economic participation: inability to live with dignity is a characteristic of the camp.

Gender affects the power and work relations into which displaced men and women are incorporated. The majority of the permanent workers are male and the majority of temporary staff are female. Poverty is gendered and most severe among those who lack jobs; they are mainly women and may be there illicitly since the farmer charges for extra persons in the rooms. Some of them become servants or lovers of those with jobs and the right to stay, or they resort to transactional sex for rations or for protection from soldiers in the border area, despite the accompanying risks of violence and HIV/AIDS. Nannies for the children of workers earn about ZAR200 per month, one sixth of a basic labourer wage. A young, eight-months' pregnant woman was about to lose her position as nanny for a worker and therefore her temporary home (see Chapter 7). Men approached her for sex, telling her that 'it is the only way to survive'. She was giving up hope, the pain of bare life written in her face and words. Complications late in her pregnancy combined with her illicit status on the farm could have proven fatal. However, by getting connected with an aid organisation she managed to give birth at a hospital in Musina and to move on to a friend in Johannesburg, escaping from a place of gendered exposure to 'bare life'.

Makwembe has an ambiguous character as a home and as a camp. The worker residential area resembles a 'farm village', not the sterile compounds seen on other farms in the area. Many workers have built thatched mud houses decorated with geometric designs in brown and white and a yard with vegetables, trees and a few chickens. While some are at work, others are cleaning, looking after children and maintaining homes and gardens. Yet, the farm is not completely 'home', a worker told us, since everyone has to leave at retirement. Also at odds with the 'village' character is the entrance through a long narrow gateway with electric razor wire fences on both sides. Along this gateway is a crèche for farm-worker children, illustrating the intermixing of welfare, control and security. The fence encloses the village, a boundary to the rest of the farm rather than the outside world, with the double function of keeping workers and their families inside (away from tempting food crops) and hindering unwanted visitors. Some passers-by steal crops, equipment and workers' belongings. Reports to the police had little effect, said the owner, so he hired a security firm in addition to his own security staff. Compared to those who are passing by or are surviving in the secondary economy, workers have a position of privilege and power. They worry about security in the compound and crop theft, which threatens their production targets and bonuses. Thus, they too are gate keepers: 'How many people are there left who are neither locked up nor standing guard at the gate?' asked Michael K. Thus, the security functions of the farm show similarities to a 'gated community' 'where risks are sought to be minimized in secured zones of discipline, while outside in the "urban jungle", horror lies in wait' (Ibid.: 73). Yet, here the danger is rural and a product of the Zimbabwean crisis and the proximity to the exceptional border that 'cannot be a border'.

To summarize, Makwembe is a labour camp that relies on the workforce of the displaced. The merger of residence and work place, the isolation, the confinement and semi-public control over civil rights are camp characteristics. The owner, and I think many staff too, would object to the term 'labour camp', seeing employment as voluntary and even workers having sympathy for the enterprise. Yet, the context compels many individuals to remain or return. Secondly, Makwembe provides relief and livelihoods for the displaced: camps sometimes provide 'a paradoxical habitat of hospitality' (Ibid.: 13). Revealing of the contradictions between 'labour camp' and 'refugee camp', the relief relies on the ability of the farm to compete in a harsh economic environment. Low salaries and exploitation in the secondary economy of the farm produce bare life for the most exposed individuals. Finally, due to security concerns in an exceptional context of persecution, hunger and crime, the worker village has been fenced off like a gated community. The exceptional is normalized in the camp: Makwembe makes it easier for the governments of South Africa and Zimbabwe to reject requests for camps for the displaced, though larger political issues determined this outcome (see Chapter 2). The farm as camp is real and actually does something for the displaced, while 'society' is vague and remote, organizing its control of human bodies outside politics.

Malamula, Tshipise: Labour and detention camp

'They are bringing those laws from the Zimbabwean side and applying them here: it is not South African law that applies.'
(Zimbabwean worker, Malamula, 2008)

South-east of Musina the undulating lowveld is studded with baobabs and water from the Soutpansberg mountains which irrigates large citrus farms that produce for domestic and world markets. Malamula ('orange'), was bought by the present owner and manager in 1982 and has a total area of over 5,000 hectares. It is another labour camp, with about 800 workers (550 seasonal and 250 permanent) and with about equal numbers of women and men in both categories. Migrant workers, almost exclusively from Zimbabwe, constitute about 80 per cent of the work force and the owner-manager claims that not enough South African labour can be sourced. Workers may enter and exit the farm, and some keep returning to work in the picking season from February to September, although the lack of physical and political security in Zimbabwe compels many to do so. In the harsh conditions of the fields, manual workers experienced bodily humiliation under the biopolitical techniques employed to make them work harder: A worker described the system of rate payment, making workers pick twelve 25-kg bags of lemons per hour, his hands becoming 'like lemon skins'. Zimbabwean workers got the more arduous work, so relations with South African workers were tenser than on Makwembe. However, so were relations with the fifteen of eighteen field foremen who were Zimbabwean and who were 'bringing those laws from the Zimbabwean side and applying them here: it is not South African law that applies', as a worker said. Another said, 'we are paid the same, we are all farm workers... what is missing is the papers, passports and work permits': legal ambiguity and lack of documentation are typical of camps.

As a relief camp, Malamula helps some off the roads and into a livelihood: there are houses, vegetable gardens and shops run by workers; firewood and water is provided. However, the compound has little 'village' character, with its rows of grimy brick houses, dark and smoke-stained inside. They fall short of the official requirements as many lack windows, electricity and required standards of sanitation. In the late 1980s, the owner replaced farm-dweller-built thatched huts with constructed brick houses. But, having built them, the owner requires workers to stay in them and pay a monthly rent. From 2005, additional rent was added for a spouse or relative. During the picking season several people sleep in a single room, each being charged for accommodation: 'Four of us live in a tiny room but the farm owner deducts ZAR180 (US$22) from each of us… The owner – don't write my name – is greedy, he makes so much money from one room' (male worker, Malamula, 2008). With the impunity of farms as camps, some owners use illegal housing and deductions to compensate for the minimum wages introduced in 2003. A worker said: 'The salaries are too low. We just survive on sadza [maize porridge]. A woman worker complained that under-employed colleagues were 'stealing men'. The former teacher regretted the exposure of women and girls to transactional sex and domestic violence: 'HIV/AIDS on this farm is on the rise. Pandemic diseases and poverty work hand in hand. Nearly a hundred women are not working or are waiting for jobs… some sell sex' – gendered effects of the inadequate rations of the camp.

One may contrast 'camp' with 'home', a place of freedom and the escape from monitoring and control, as when Michael K was looking for 'spaces between the camps'. Workers and dwellers on Malamula are enrolled in the control of fellow human beings, a characteristic of the camp (Diken and Laustsen, 2005: 61-2). The owner paid a retired worker to regularly report on life: 'he is my ears and eyes in the compound'. Though tolerated, few stayed on the farm after retirement, probably due to the labour camp character and the payments imposed. A seasonal worker said: 'This farm is just a place to work, where we get our wages, and then build our homes elsewhere. You cannot plan to live here all your life, for the place belongs to the owner'. Three Zimbabwean women workers reflected on meanings of 'home', one saying, 'this place does not feel like home. My home is in Zimbabwe'. They agreed that they could only go back when jobs were back, prices down and schools re-opened. Home may be a place outside all camps but nevertheless depends on the economic and political context.

The enterprising and visionary owner-manager of Malamula argued that around the world agriculture offers entry-level and poorly remunerated jobs. He stressed that he is a 'player' operating within rules and conditions set by the market and the state, which controls central parts of the economy (water, electricity, transport).

One day we interviewed the owner in the morning and talked with workers and dwellers in the fields and compound in the afternoon. I remarked to a colleague that it felt odd that we had been studying one farm, and he said, astonished: 'You know what: I completely forgot that we were talking about the same place!' Reasons include the vast difference in socioeconomic positions of owner and workers and the dual geography of the farms, with the contrast being between a wealthy owner homestead and administrative centre and the fields and workers' compound of relative deprivation. Asked if it would not be good idea to encourage families to live together rather than encouraging split families, casual sexual relations and the risk of spreading HIV/AIDS, the owner explained that it would also be nice for him to take his family with him on European business trips but that costs did not permit it. His analogy over-looks the reality of semi-forced transactional sex and HIV/AIDS causing bare life. 'Camps come in twos' since the 'mirror image of bare life' is 'power in its positivity' (Ibid.: 101). The power of the 'sovereign' produces bare life, while also rendering it invisible. It also, argued the owner, reduces crime locally by offering livelihoods to desperate individuals, who again resort to crime when they leave for the cities. Thus Malamula is a labour camp, a substitute for a relief camp, and one which promotes public security like an internment camp – all this while putting orange juice on breakfast tables around the world.

Timongo, Levubu: 'Back to their mother country'

'This is not a military camp.' (Senior Manager, Timongo)

Timongo comprises several merged fruit and nut farms, about 2,000 hectares in total, in the well-watered and fertile Levubu Valley, and differs from the other farms in several respects. South of the Soutpansberg range, it is outside the zone of exception where farm owners receive corporate permits to facili-tate their employment of migrant labour. Historically, it has relied on labour from nearby South African communities who were dispossessed of their land from the 1930s but, under the post-apartheid land restitution programme, were given the land of 26 family farms. An estimated 40 per cent of the former workers and dwellers were evicted during this protracted process. At the time of study, the farms were managed in 'Strategic Partnership' between claimant communities and an agro-business company. The first, comprising mainly the former traditional landowners withdrew from the joint venture in 2007, and the second collapsed in 2009.

Timongo did not rely on migrant labour, so the function of farms in provid-ing relief to the displaced is based on managers' discretion. The main reason is workers from the new land-owning communities are prioritized. However, camp characteristics such as surveillance, deportation, and control were important for Timongo managers, since theft of equipment and crops was common and surveillance of the mountainous terrain of plantations and forests was challenging. Though many workers came from nearby communities, those living in poor dwellings scattered over the large property also worried about their safety and their belongings. A gated, monitored entrance to a single compound, as at Makwembe, was not possible. A security manager – a former policeman and community leader – working with four staff and five motorbikes was in charge of surveillance, control and evictions. He argued that workers as co-owners had to internalize the surveillance of co-workers and 'intruders', as in a camp: 'Each and every employee working on a farm must be the police of himself, he must take care of his property, because he might lose his job if they steal a lot; and then where are they going to work?' On one of the lush, green banana fields a gigantic billboard showed the watchful eyes of an eagle and the word *PLAASWAG*, 'farm–watch', inspiring the 'sentiment of an invisible omniscience' (Bentham, 1995 [1787]). 'Security' also arrested migrants, and the manager particularly remembered a Zimbabwean who was caught eating bananas, and who explained that he was hungry. The security staff told him: 'Well, you won't be hungry any more, because you will eat food at the police station.' The Security manager explained: 'We take them to the police station and then they are deported back to their mother country.'

This somewhat draconian approach was extended to other groups who were seen as 'intruders', including those who were not employed but only came to stay. Even farm-worker children old enough to go to school were not wanted on the farm. The security manager said, 'Today I instructed my people to go around to the hostels, to find out if there are [any] little children, those who are above six years.' He tried to convince parents that they should 'not keep them here on the farm, because I don't see them having a good future'. As the only nearby school had recently been closed down by the government, children were sent to extended family in sometimes distant rural areas. One South African worker could not have her two children living with her for lack of space or childcare, and her salary only extended to cover monthly bus ride to see them. Asked about this, a senior manager explained the boundaries between company control and family life. He said, 'we don't allow families to stay for a period of time in the compound' but that 'visits' by a grandmother for three to four days was different, as he would not 'interfere in a person's private life'. He concluded that the farm was 'an environment in which we want everyone to be happy, and staying nicely, working nicely ... This is not a military camp.' Neither, however, does it provide a permanent home; retired workers are expected to return 'to their former homelands with their houses and their pensions and they will stay there'.

Timongo has no Zimbabwean migrant labour and reports those who come its way to the police. In this respect it undermines the theory that capitalist farming is primarily interested in creating labour camps to exploit the displaced. Camp characteristics, however, derive not from the inclusion of the displaced but from the exclusion of a variety of groups, including children and the elderly, to secure or incarcerate the community/corporate hybrid created under the land restitution programme. In justifying this hybrid, the manager felt a need to mark the boundary between a modern farm and 'a military camp'.

Mbhongholo, Waterpoort: Precarious refuge

'He is willing to work and to learn, he does not know anything about the law, he comes to work, he brings no livestock.' (European manager of Mbhongholo about a Zimbabwean worker.)

Mbhongholo is a game farm in the semi-arid northern area of the Soutpansberg. Its border runs along a back-road frequently used by migrants walking south with their water bottles, shoes sometimes in hand. It was here that we met Themba, wounded and exhausted.

In 2003 a European investor bought six mixed livestock farms, took down the fences between them, and created a large 4,300-hectare farm. It was first managed by a young European man, then a South African middle-aged manager. Some ten workers and their families (remnants of the many dwellers and workers who lived on the former constituent farms) could supply the necessary labour, so there was no great need for Zimbabweans. In one corner of the farm a single family had secured a fenced area for housing and gardening. The owner and the manager feared this homestead might provide a base for poaching and an entry point for outsiders. Concerns about security were not unwarranted: In 2008, a violent robbery had left the manager and his wife severely injured. Although some of the workers were involved in a restitution claim on the land, they had little confidence in it. Indeed, some of them were building a second home in a communal area, something their parents did not have, in case they were forced to move: the concept or quality of the farm as 'home' was declining.

Mbhongholo did not have the material basis to be a large-scale labour or refuge camp. Ten worker families, a middle-aged manager and a few displaced individuals found refuge there. A Zimbabwean man had gained employment, representing what South African farm owners and managers found attractive in Zimbabwean workers. As the young white manager said bluntly: 'He is willing to work and to learn, he does not know anything about the law, he comes to work, he brings no livestock.' The second manager said that having fewer ties to workers and neighbours he could be trusted. In the shift from home to camp, bonding is kept minimal and persons without relations are preferred. He quickly became promoted to the position of guard residing in the good house at the entrance. He gave water to migrants passing along the road, but did not let them in, 'standing guard at the gate' of this relatively benign camp. A woman who left Zimbabwe because of hunger joined him. She had first found a job on a neighbouring farm, but the manager abused her verbally and physically. She escaped to Mbhongholo and the house at the gate. Now with a baby but no job her refuge was precarious and the couple were considering their options. Their agency and choices contradict the passive suffering that the term 'bare life' may suggest. She observed dryly that, 'if you are poor and you follow the law, you die', confirming that, 'for the exile, breaking rules is not a matter of free choice, but an eventuality which cannot be avoided' (Bauman 2000: 208).

The Significance of Farms as Camps
Labour, relief, internment and gated community
People's movement across the borders of southern Africa is part of cross-border trade, labour and cultural relations, but the intensity of the current crisis has reshaped the zones across which people are moving and the patterns of hardship, hospitality and exploitation that they encounter. Considering these farms as camps, I did not note a single, hidden biopolitical logic of bare life but rather certain functions that are shaped by social context and political economy: as labour camps organizing work and production; as relief camps, providing shelter and livelihoods; as internment camps promoting security locally; and as gated communities promoting the safety of those who live there.

As labour camps, the farms displayed contrasting strategies towards displaced Zimbabweans, who are pivotal to the economy of Makwembe and Malamula but not to Timongo and Mbhongholo. As in the past, migrant labour is incorporated in a combined inclusion and exclusion, employed but often denied the freedoms that come with a work and residence permit. Contemplating 'the most basic characteristics of camp life' (Diken and Laustsen, 2005: 88), (i) workers and dwellers live on meagre wages, which hinders normal participation in society and access to health services, savings and credit; (ii) while not prevented from finding paid work, as in refugee camps, many of the displaced individuals on the farms lack employment contracts and rely on short-term or piece work; (iii) migrants have some limited choice of where to work and reside, but this is controlled through a permit system authorized by the state and partially governed by employers according to their labour needs; and (iv) workers have limited mobility, as in a camp, due to the isolation of farms, the nature of the permits (or lack of them) and the costs and dangers of travel. The conditions of the exceptional zones compel many to remain or return to farms. While farms only fit certain of the 'camp' criteria, – contract-based and time-bound employment does suggest 'normal' modern, capitalist relations – arguably, the definition of 'camp' has become normalized in a context where the 'freedom of contract' has become somewhat meaningless.

In circumstances of distress, the farms in the Limpopo region of South Africa serve as relief camps, providing (some) livelihoods, basic housing, services and secondary economies, and thus protection against the reduction to bare life. Protection, in the form of minimum wages, services and labour inspections, are significant compared to what many had to make do with north of the Limpopo or when in limbo at the Musina showgrounds. A relative loss of legal and social protection is managed and normalized on the farms – as in camps. Thus, in some respects farms substitute for refugee camps on the Limpopo border. They also provide a vital flow of goods back to families in Zimbabwe, which is an advantage over conventional camps. Yet, relief is discretionary: a security manager sent Zimbabweans caught in the fields back to their 'mother country'. Also, their salaries hardly sustain a decent living and those without a job are even worse off: the relief function is not governed according to the human rights of children, women and men but the biopolitics of extracting labour without enabling the workers to sustain full lives, as during colonialism and apartheid.

Farms to some extent serve as detention camps that promote public security by giving migrants an alternative to criminal activity, as Malamula's owner argued. This may overlook the fact that farms (i) also attract those in search of livelihoods; (ii) unlike camps, have no obligation to provide for any one; and (iii) are only moderately effective, evidenced by the high and rising level of crime and insecurity reported by workers and owners alike. Even if they have certain public security functions, farms cannot replace the army personnel and police officials in protecting public safety, and neither can replace resolution of the causes of instability and crime.

Violence and insecurity affect both workers and managers, as seen when an attack at night left Mbhongholo's senior manager and his wife traumatized. Some of the farms contain gated communities, i.e. fenced interior zones that promote the security of workers and dwellers, as is the case in Malamula's compound and Makwembe's 'farm village', each of which is surrounded by a high, electrified, barbed-wire fence. Timongo in the Levubu Valley could not have a gated community since dwellers live in compounds scattered across the estate or away from the farm. While some managers dreamt of establishing planned farm villages with enhanced security and services for all, the strict security measures currently focused on the protection of crops and equipment. In a context of displacement and crime, both managers and the relatively privileged farm workers participate in security efforts, becoming co-creators of the farms as camps that at once protect and reduce freedom.

Camps, homes and gender

Farms as camps stand in contrast to homes. The displaced seek places where one can lead a normal life: find a job, buy goods, marry, and raise a family, but for the most part the farm is not 'home' but rather a place to stay 'till things improve, perhaps forever', as Michel K said (Coetzee, 1983: 163). They resemble a bus terminus, a metaphor expelled farm workers in Zimbabwe used to describe their new township settlement, 'a place of limbo where there is no security, where people come and go but nobody puts down roots' (Hartnack, 2009: 371). Limpopo farms as camps contradict notions of home and belonging partly because their owners and managers reject workers and dwellers from seeing them as such. Families were often split, partners and children lived at a distance, and retired people were generally compulsorily released – a reason why Makwembe's pretty farm village could not truly be 'home'.

While Agamben and Diken and Laustsen appear to imagine bare life as gender neutral, on these farms 'the sovereign', including layers of 'middlemen', wears a masculine face while bare life is feminized. Women's weaker access to full-time employment exposes them to hunger and want. A number of women used sex to obtain food, housing and security. A pregnant nanny was effectively evicted when her worker-employer laid her off. Both men and women tried to keep intact a patchwork of relations within and between households on the farm, and with people elsewhere, women appearing particularly skilful in socializing and articulating problems. Thus, power and bare life on farms as camps reflect gendered family situations, life histories and strategies (Addison analyses these from a different standpoint in Chapter 9).

A place for politics?

It would be surprising if there were no scope for challenging oppressive camp features. Whereas Agamben's analysis appears to play down agency, Diken and Laustsen (2005: 151, referring to Hardt and Negri, 2000) contrast bare life – 'constituted through human passivity' – with what they call 'multitude' – agency, politics and resistance. Individuals use strategies of escape, evasion and co-operation and cellphones to network, plan and share. Workers use farms, and fight against their owners and managers, to resist the reduction to bare life. Despite the hazards of the border, most of the Zimbabwean workers we interviewed managed to visit and bring supplies to family and friends fairly regularly. Many came back repeatedly for employment in the cropping season: migrants represent not merely displacement and escape but the 'refusal to disappear' (Diken and Laustsen, 2005: 153). Expressions of mutual sympathy and assistance were common although 'solidarity' might be too strong a word, true even of the fragmented, disorganized farm worker relations in general. During the time of the study, Zimbabwean-South African relations on the farms were marked by some tension and jealousies but the xenophobic violence that marred other parts of South Africa, particularly in May 2008, did not affect this area. Diken and Laustsen (2005: 163, 170) claim that 'the camp is the enemy of politics' and identify a 'disappearance of the link between knowledge and politics'. Although farms south of the Limpopo probably have more space for politics and rights than the abandoned zones of fear in Zimbabwe, the space is severely curtailed. The knowledge base of well-educated Zimbabweans is rarely applied, as former market researchers and teachers, now turned manual labourers, were well-placed to point out. A former teacher aged 27 said that he had left Zimbabwe because he could no longer afford life, 'education was going down' and teachers were looked down upon, as people asked, 'where is the need for education when teachers and doctors are dying of poverty?' Now he argued that the farm should:

> Equip people with training. Make a school where people can get skills related to agriculture. Cater for those with education and special knowledge from outside. This will improve the whole farm. On the compound, give electricity to everyone. We are living in the world of technology and the poles are passing by just

next to the farm. There should be radio and television for the workers. Newspapers will make people more aware. Research should be shared: researchers just come, interview, go, pass their exams or earn money and submit their research to the international community.

The absence of such facilities on the farms we studied confirms that 'the camp is the enemy of politics' (Diken and Laustsen, 2005: 163). Farms lack an *agora*, a public place where debates take place and workers become organized and political. Zimbabweans on these farms were seeking opportunities in a South African city or a normalized Zimbabwe rather than on politically reformed farms. Coupled, however, with the South African labour unions and civil society, their knowledge could have made the farms less the enemy of politics than the camps they are today.

Camps, capitalism and violence

Farms as camps reflect exceptional circumstances of the Zimbabwean crisis but also the normal workings of capitalism. Commercial farms were bricks in the construction of a southern Africa that was controlled by white minorities; the state relegated many members of the majority into the mega-camps of 'native reserves', 'homelands'/'Bantustans' or the smaller camps of commercial farms. If the reserves may be seen as 'classical camps' of exclusion and abandonment, the commercial farms are prototypes of 'contemporary camps' of adverse inclusion, the camp as rule, the camp as a way of doing business. Both classical and contemporary camps construct spaces and boundaries that reduce the status and rights of individuals. According to Žižec (2009: 12), systemic violence 'is inherent in the social conditions of global capitalism, which involve the "automatic" creation of excluded and dispensable individuals from the homeless to the unemployed'. While it is not clear that global capitalism drove the Zimbabwean crisis, its effects may be observed on South African farms. Here there have been massive displacements of dwellers and workers from farms in recent decades – 1.8 million individuals displaced in the decade prior to 1994 and 2.3 million in the decade after (Wegerif, Russell and Grundling, 2005: 43-4). Reflecting, among other things, the increased exposure to global capitalism, farms have changed from places where workers live, have homes, livestock and burial grounds to places where they work and have temporary and inferior rights, to farms as camps that disregard tenure legislation with impunity (RSA, 1997; Hall, 2003; Wegerif, Russell and Grundling, 2005; Wisborg, Hall, Shirinda and Zamchiya, 2013).

Power and visibility

Farms' current role in converting the displaced to a productive resource and supplying security, internment and relief functions assists neo-liberal governance and the ability of states to 'govern at a distance' (Duffield, 2001). Yet, the agro-food-industrial complex, of which farms as camps are part, captured most of the surplus value created. And the patrolling, internment and extradition was costly for the state, so political concerns appeared more important than (neo-liberal) economic ones. Agamben defined the camp as the place where a state of emergency is normalized. Farms contributed to normalizing a national and regional emergency. As they normalize the exceptional, farms conceal power and responsibilities by blurring distinctions between farmers, family-business-es, managers, corporations, conglomerates, strategic partnerships and global agro-business. The camps studied here did not appear subject to a unitary, sovereign power but by providing economic benefits, relief and security, they facilitated the policies of silence and the invisibility of its human consequences. They concealed suffering, not least because they reduced it. Humanitarian interventionism can challenge the sovereignty of leaders (Duffield, 2007). At the time of our study, the respective presidents of Zimbabwe and South Africa, Robert Mugabe and Thabo Mbeki, expressed sovereign power by rejecting a (societal) state of emergency; indeed, Mbeki argued that Zimbabwe's main problem was fiscal imbalance caused by past over-expenditure on public services (Mbeki, 2003). Official refugee camps in the borderlands of South Africa would undermine the position that there was no major crisis in Zimbabwe. Victims of hardship may seek refugee camps, which make them visible in the eyes of the world while these 'sovereigns' preferred farms as camps that did not.

Places beyond Camps

In common with Michael K, displaced Zimbabweans sought survival and dignity in South Africa. The farms as camps in Limpopo offer better prospects than the militarized labour camps from which Michael K escaped to find a spot of land of his own, beyond the control of employers and fences. Part II discusses Zimbabweans in Mozambique who found themselves in an environment without 'camps' in the sense discussed here. Michael K also remained convinced that there exist 'areas that lie between the camps and belong to no camps... I am looking for such a place in order to settle there, perhaps only till things improve, perhaps forever' (Coetzee, 1983: 162–3). The displaced look for places with more freedom than camps, sharing Michael K's yearning for freedom and dignity but they do not, I think, share his tentative conclusion: 'Perhaps the truth is that it is enough to be out of the camps, out of all the camps at the same time' (Ibid.: 182). They are more pragmatic, less prone to choose emaciation over any challenge to dignity. The South African farms were often better than what the displaced left behind, and certainly better than the road. Yet the vast country still remains with few 'areas that lie between the camps and belong to no camps'. There is no equitable society and sharing of the land as yet. Both Zimbabweans and South African dwellers and farm workers experience hardship and frustrated life-plans. One option is to make 'better camps' by promoting the interests of workers, but given the biopolitics of exploitation and deprivation and the economic policies that seem to lead inexorably towards farms with fewer people. Farmers are constrained in what they can pay and workers have few options but to accept wages that cannot provide for a life of dignity and opportunities for themselves and their children. Some workers and farm dwellers will need, and ought to get, the opportunity to acquire their own land, through creation of a more diversified countryside and support for ownership, production and employment at different scales. Smaller farms for these populations can provide additional livelihoods, a better basis for negotiating employment on commercial farms, or be steppingstones to other sectors and careers. And yet, a form of land redistribution in Zimbabwe was integral to the crisis that contributed to the problematic situations discussed here: peace and respect for rights has to accompany the redistribution of resources. Perhaps we may even see new senses in which 'in Africa a river cannot be a border', so that certain opportunities for access to land, public support and employment are widened for everyone. There is need for more farms and fewer camps – to recreate the sense that Zimbabwe and South Africa *are* really large and *do* offer places of freedom outside the camps, places 'for a different kind of food, food that no camp could supply'.

Notes

1 Acknowledgements: I am thankful to farm-dwellers, workers and managers for conversations during visits to farms in Limpopo during 2007, 2008 and 2009. The research on farm workers and farm dwellers was part of the collaboration between the Institute for Poverty, Land and Agrarian Studies (PLAAS) of the University of

the Western Cape and the Department of International Environment and Development Studies, Noragric, at the Norwegian University of Life Sciences and funded by the Norwegian government through the Norwegian Centre for Human Rights, the University of Oslo. I am grateful to Ruth Hall, Shirhami Shirinda and Phillani Zamchiya for their co-operation and discussions during field research and beyond, and for the use of shared material in this chapter.

2 'Throw Out the Filth' (Hartnack, 2009: 358), an operation which made an estimated 570,000 poor urban dwellers homeless (IDMC/NRC 2009).

3 International Organization for Migration.

4 South African Human Rights Commission.

5 The names of the farms and individuals have been changed to protect respondents' anonymity.

11

Home away from Home

Land, Identity and Community on the Mkushi Farm Block

Espen Sjaastad, Thomson Kalinda and Fabian Maimbo

Introduction

Just after the turn of the millennium, a series of farm invasions began in Zimbabwe that would eventually see some 150,000 farm workers and an unknown number of commercial farm families flee the country.[2] Most of the farm workers crossed, legally or illegally, into South Africa, Mozambique, or Malawi. The farm owners and their families, most of European descent, faced a different set of options. Some gave up farming and settled in Britain or South Africa. Others started afresh in Australia, Brazil, Mozambique, or Nigeria. Over a period of seven years, around 250 families found their way to Zambia. Thirty-one of these settled on the Mkushi Farm Block in Central Province.[3]

The links between Zimbabwe and Zambia have historically been strong. In 1888, Cecil Rhodes and the British South Africa Company sought permission to negotiate concessions for mining rights throughout the territory between the Limpopo River in the south and Lake Tanganyika in the north. Known as Zambesia, the area was divided into two management units: the area south of the Zambezi River became Southern Rhodesia and the area north of the river Northern Rhodesia. The former would officially become a self-governing British colony in 1923. The latter was governed as two separate units – North-Western and North-Eastern Rhodesia – until 1911, when it became a protectorate and remained so until 1953. Together with Nyasaland (Malawi), Southern and Northern Rhodesia formed a federation from 1953 to 1963. This period saw a steady northbound stream of migrants, as natives of Southern Rhodesia fled from the destocking and land dispossession that followed in the wake of the Native Land Husbandry Act (Thompson, 2004).

The original division along the Zambezi transected tribal and kinship units, but the border has, throughout its history, been permeable. Between Zambian

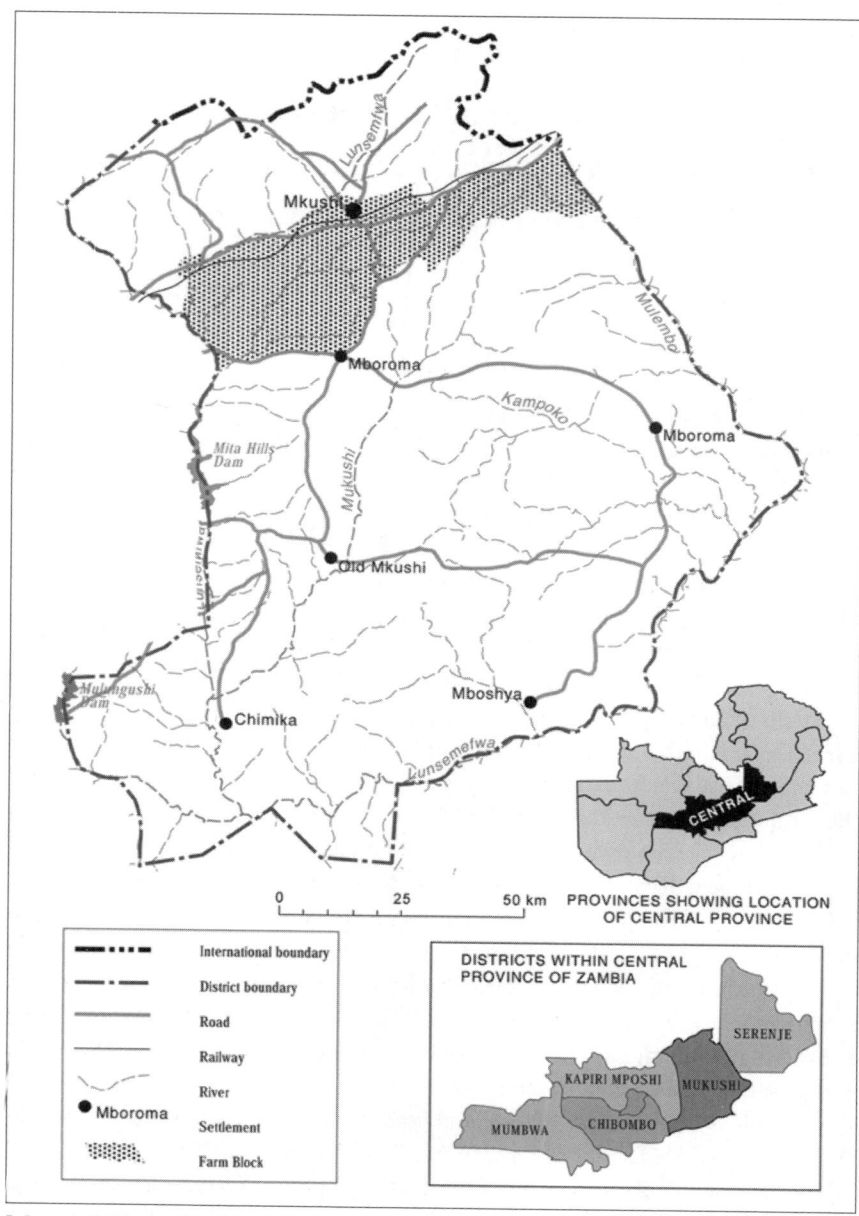

Map 7: Mkushi District in Central Province, Zambia

independence in 1964 and Zimbabwean independence in 1980, a series of small migrations resulted in a handful of enclaves of black Rhodesians scattered across Zambia. Even today, despite some political tension in recent years, crossing the border at the three official border posts is but a formality for citizens of the two countries. Nor is the recent migration of commercial farming families from Zimbabwe into Zambia the first such event. Throughout colonial history, there have been waves of white migration across the border. In the 1950s, many of the migrants were farm managers who wished to strike out on their own and found land more easily available further north. Later, others migrated to escape the mounting tensions in Rhodesia through the late 1960s and 1970s. This history, as well as the climatic and environmental similarities between the two countries, made Zambia an obvious destination for commercial farmers leaving Zimbabwe following the farm invasions of the 2000s.

Zimbabwe is, however, not the only country to provide a sporadic influx of commercial farmers into Zambia. Over the last 50 years or so, the Mkushi Farm Block (hereafter MFB) has been the recipient of an intriguing mix of farmers from a wide variety of backgrounds. They arrived alone, in pairs, or in groups, with or without finance, having left their old farms for a multitude of reasons. Some stayed for only a short while, others are still there. One aim of this chapter is to assess the impact of the recent Zimbabwean troubles on a community of commercial farmers in Mkushi. The recent settlement of Zimbabwean farmers must be examined within an extended local context, however, so we also look into the broader history of this area and the question of how African commercial farmers created a space for themselves in the natural, economic, and political environments of Zambia. In particular, we look at the dynamics of the relationship between recent settlers and Block veterans and the long-term prospects for Zimbabweans in the area.

The study is based on interviews with 44 farmers on the MFB, of whom 26 were recent immigrants from Zimbabwe. Interviews, both of a formal and open-ended nature, took place between November 2007 and May 2009. We also had conversations with representatives from local authorities. These included: the district administrative officer, immigration, agriculture, police, courts, the labour office, and the national pension scheme. We also interviewed members of the local banking community, farm workers, farm managers, and settlers from the Southern Province on farms surrounding MFB.

A Brief History of the Mkushi Farm Block
Mkushi in colonial times

Today, if you drive some 200 kilometres towards the north from the capital Lusaka, you reach the junction at Kapiri Mposhi. If you continue north from there, you soon reach the Copperbelt, the main source of the country's wealth, both past and present. If, instead, you turn towards the east on the Great North Road and drive for about one hour, you reach Mkushi (see Map 7, p. 286).

At the close of the nineteenth century, however, the British South Africa Company was running its operations in north-eastern Rhodesia from Fort Jameson (now Chipata, Eastern Province). A further station had been established at Fort Hargreaves, now inside the South Luangwa National Park. With the war against the Ngoni won, the company decided to expand operations by sending two men to 'the Hook of the Kafue,' the very large bulge in the Kafue River that now forms the eastern border of the Kafue National Park. One of those men was a young telegraphist from Fort Jameson named J.E. Stephenson, who said that 'I was to accompany Jones to the Hook of the Kafue. If all went well, I should then return to some suitable place, and there build a Station of my own' (Stephenson, 1937: 22).

That suitable place turned out to be Mkushi. The story of how Mkushi, its surroundings, and its people were colonized makes, as do many such tales, for fascinating reading (Ibid.: 63):

> Jones spoke. 'Tell them,' he said, 'tell these great ones of the Lala nation, that we come from the Great White Queen. We are fresh from conquering the Angoni. We have three things to say. First, in this country there shall be no more war. Secondly, in this country there shall be no more witchcraft. Thirdly, in this country there shall be no more slavery. In regard to all other things, men shall do as they have done, and as their fathers have done before them.

> And the above comprises all the negotiations, all the conditions, in connection with the 'occupation' of the copperbelt of Northern Rhodesia. We made no treaty; we referred to no treaty; we compiled no treaty. We walked in; we laid down those three rules; and we forthwith started to 'administer' the country. That, in a few words, is the history of the annexation of the copper-belt of North-western Rhodesia.

Stephenson later adds that in the absence of a treaty with the Lalas and

Lambas, the colonial authorities apparently encouraged Barotse king Lewanika to claim their lands all the way east to the Luangwa River. The authorities already had a treaty with, and concessions from, Lewanika, so if his kingdom were suddenly to envelop those areas for which no treaties existed, it might save them some trouble (Ibid.: 136): 'So Lewanika claimed the lands of the Lalas and the Lambas – and the copper, which belonged no more to him than to the man in the moon – where his name was never even heard, and where his writ had never run. And his claim was accepted.'

Although the first copper concession in the Katanga Region of the Belgian Congo was awarded in 1906, exploration in the Copperbelt of Northern Rhodesia only got underway in 1921. In 1928 two mining companies were formed; the Rhodesian (later Roan) Selection Trust, a South African company, and the Rhodesian Anglo American Corporation, a British company. These two would control the mining industry until 1969 (Cunningham, 1981).

The development of mining in the Copperbelt rendered Mkushi an interesting location. Although it was not situated along the Livingstone–Copperbelt line of rail, its proximity to the mines established its potential as a supplier of both labour and food to the industry. In the 1940s, the area was sparsely populated but already contained a handful of European settlers.

The eventual mapping and alienation of land on the MFB appears to have come about as a compromise of sorts. In 1928, following a Northern Rhodesia Order in Council, the land settled by white farmers, and the land originally set aside for future settlement (Trust Land), was deemed Crown Land, whereas the land originally retained by the indigenous population became known as Native Reserves. The non-occurrence of the expected influx of European settlers led to vast areas of unused Trust Land, which became known as 'silent lands', while some of the Reserves became crowded and degraded. The 1938 Pimm Commission stated that the official land policy in Northern Rhodesia had been disastrous (Bruce and Dorner, 1982). A formal reversal did not occur before 1947, however, when a Northern Rhodesia Order in Council made Trust Land available for resettlement by the indigenous population, albeit with certain restrictions on land use (Hellen, 1968; Wood et al., 1978-79).

Against this, the colonial authorities had for some time harboured concerns about the inability of commercial farmers to meet domestic demand for agricultural produce. Furthermore, the authorities wanted a relatively wide distribution of settlers throughout the country, since these were seen as a stabilizing influence. The perceived lack of quality locations within the remaining Crown

Land also caused disaffection among existing European settlers:

> Thus, designation by the Land Commission in 1947 of Mkushi Block as an area suitable for alienation may be seen as a sop to settler interest. Certainly it was the only major economically viable commercial farming area to be confirmed as Crown Land at this time, and so became the last major area of European agricultural settlement in Northern Rhodesia. (Woode et al., 1978-79: 3)

The mapping and surveying of the MFB was carried out by Unwin Moffat, who was Senior Agricultural Officer at Broken Hill (now Kabwe). The exercise was completed in 1951. In summary, MFB lies at altitudes between 1,200 and 1,400 metres above sea level, with average monthly temperatures ranging from between 15 and 24 degrees centigrade. Rainfall at Old Mkushi, south of the block, averages 890 millimetres and the natural vegetation is open *miombo* woodland. While three perennial rivers transect the area, groundwater is scarce. Soils are moderately acidic but regarded as suitable for tobacco and maize cultivation (Woode et al., 1978-79). Troupe (1954) also recommended cattle ranching. The total area of 176,000 hectares was originally divided into 163 farms (Woode et al., 1978-79).

Settlement of the MFB was initially slow. In 1942, when the Land Commission made a visit to the area, they found two active and six abandoned farms.[4] In 1951, subsequent to Moffat's surveying of the area, 42 farming units were advertised in the *Government Gazette*. Yet by 1956, according to figures in Woode et al. (1978-79), only twelve farming families were present on the Block, one of these being Moffat himself. In the meantime, however, establishing a pattern that seems to have lasted until the present, a number of other farms had by this time already been settled then abandoned. Incentives were given to ex-servicemen from the Second World War during this early period, and while more than a dozen of these settled in Mkushi, none stayed for long. Of those twelve families that had settled by 1956, only the descendants of Moffat remain to this day.

From 1957 until Independence in 1964, however, settlement accelerated, with 59 new farming families arriving. Woode et al. (1978-79: 6) provide an explanation:

> Consideration was thus given to ways in which settlement could be encouraged in Mkushi. As a result, in 1956, the Federal Department of Conservation and Extension (Conex) undertook a land capability survey of the Block and reconsidered the farm units into which it had been proposed to divide the Block. New

farms were laid out, each of approximately 1,700 acres (700 ha.) with at least 500 acres (200 ha.) of Class I and Class II land.... Farmers who took up these farms were assisted in a number of ways...

According to Woode et al. (Ibid.), this assistance included assured water supply, land clearing, land capability plans, erosion control, access roads, and finance. The terms varied, however, depending on nationality and whether or not you were an ex-serviceman. One of the early settlers, arriving in 1957 from South Africa, has the following recollections:

> I settled in Mkushi in 1957. To get a farm, one needed to have a tractor and machinery; £1,500 worth of machinery minimum. I paid six shillings and eight pence per acre for the land. I also had to build six tobacco barns and two tobacco sheds and had to deposit £2,000 in the Land Bank at Broken Hill. I needed a clerk of court from my home country to verify these sums for the machinery, and a receipt from the bank for my deposit. Before I could plant my first tobacco, I needed to stump 40 acres. Then an inspector came the next year to check that investments and crops were satisfactory. If the inspector was happy, the Land Bank would give you a loan equalling £1.10, at three per cent interest, for every £1.00 you had invested.

The farms were alienated on 30-year leases, and intensive tobacco production was a contractual requirement. While tobacco previously had been followed by pasture, however, tobacco and maize rotations became more common in the late 1950s and 1960s (Woode et al., 1978-79: 7):

> The proportion of the territory's tobacco produced in Mkushi rose from under 1 per cent in 1950 to over 18 per cent in 1964 and 24 per cent in 1965, while the Block's share of the territory's maize production reached 7.3 per cent in 1964 and 16.2 per cent in 1965. This was despite the fact that Mkushi farmers accounted for less than 10 per cent of the commercial farming community and, with their relatively recent establishment, had limited capital resources and equipment.

The moderate amount of cattle ranching was explained by lack of market access (Woode et al., 1978-79: 8):

> This very limited diversification of the farm enterprise was probably also influenced by poor communications and distance from the main markets.... Until the end of the 1960s the Great North Road from Kapiri Mposhi to Mkushi was untarred.... Farmers tried to make as few trips to market as possible and as a result their choice of enterprise was constrained.

Despite challenges related to infrastructure and markets, and despite the presence of vacant farms, the Block housed a vibrant and productive farming community by the time liberation came to Northern Rhodesia. Vibrant and productive enough to allow Unwin Moffat to write in 1963 that:

> For a settlement scheme to succeed it is now accepted that certain basic principles must be recognised and applied. There must be a close linkup between the Government and the settler-farmer. The Government must show its confidence in the scheme by accepting a large portion of the risk, and by supplying the necessary technical and advisory services. In return the settler must be a picked man, sufficiently trained and experienced in the type of farming to be undertaken to ensure that he will make a success of his farm. He must also provide his share of the finance... The Mkushi settlement scheme owes its success to the practical application of these principles. (Moffat, 1963: 16)

The Kaunda era

At Independence in October 1964, when Kenneth Kaunda and his United National Independence Party (UNIP) assumed control of government, there were 72 farmers on the Block, mostly cultivating tobacco and maize. Independence brought with it a host of agricultural parastatals and one of these, the Tobacco Board of Zambia, would influence development on the Block from the late 1960s onward.

Partly because of a scheme organized by the Tobacco Board, the farming population on the Block continued to expand after Independence. As part of the national push for increased tobacco production, the Board purchased around 60 farms on the Block between 1968 and 1970 and then rented these out on five-year leases. The scheme coincided with the exodus of European farmers from Tanzania. In particular, a contingent of farmers of Greek origin migrated from Tanzania to Mkushi during these years following the nationalization of commercial farms by Nyerere's post-independence government in Tanzania. At its peak around 1969, there were some 30 farming families of Greek origin in the 'Greek Corner' of the block, but only six of these remain today.

According to Woode et al., the tobacco scheme was no great success. Steep slopes were cultivated, windbreaks were chopped down for fuelwood, and soil conservation structures were allowed to fall into disrepair:

> Some 'shifting' cultivation has occurred with farmers changing farms after they have despoiled one farm during a five-year lease. The insecurity of five-year leases, which in the case of the Greek farmers was heightened by their recent

investment loss in Tanzania, meant that many T.B.Z. farmers tended to look for short-term benefits and quick returns rather than farming carefully and investing time and capital in the land. (1978-79: 9-10)

Other challenges were afoot. In the early 1970s, the Zambian government embarked on a policy of intervention in agricultural markets. Despite the dedicated efforts of the World Bank and the International Monetary Fund (IMF), this strategy has since been only partially abandoned (Aarnes et al., 1998; Øygard et al., 2003). A massive, government-controlled effort to promote maize cultivation among African smallholders was accompanied by pricing changes that led to deteriorating terms for commercial growers of maize. At the same time, labour-intensive tobacco production became less profitable due to an increase in minimum wages and a gradual decrease in real prices during the 1970s. Improved terms for crops like cotton and sunflower failed to entice most of the commercial farmers. With the 1975 Land (Conversion of Titles) Act, which vested all rights to land 'in the President on behalf of the Zambian People', freehold titles were converted to 100-year leases and – in theory though not in practice – the sale of farmland was prohibited.[5]

These developments, along with the collapse in the price of copper in 1974, spawned an exodus of experienced maize and tobacco growers from the Block: 'Whereas only some 20 farms changed hands in the 1960s, 94 (more than half the farms on the Block) had a change of farmer during the 1970s.' (Woode et al., 1978-79: 11). This naturally also led to changes in the composition of the farming community on the Block. Families of 'British' or 'Afrikaans' origin dropped from 71 in 1964 to 51 in 1972, falling to 33 by 1980. Also by 1980, half the Greek families had left. These farms were largely taken up by native Zambians, who by 1980 owned exactly half of the occupied farms on the Block, although three families of 'Indian' origin had also settled there by this time (Ibid.).

Woode et al. state that 'These changes in ownership had an impact on production as they generally involved the replacement of experienced farmers with considerable capital resources by persons with limited experience and capital' (Ibid.: 11). The difficult farming conditions caused substantial reductions in cultivated area, with only 30 per cent of the cleared area of the Block devoted to crops by 1980. But diversification also resulted. There was a marked shift during the 1970s towards ranching, with stable prices for beef during this period. Vegetables, citrus fruits, soya beans, and potatoes were also tried, in many cases successfully.

Because of shortfalls in domestic maize production arising from the policies of the 1970s, the government tried a new tack in the early 1980s: producer prices and fertilizer subsidies were raised in successive years; tax on farm income was reduced and favourable depreciation rates were introduced; new incentives were put in place to encourage more investment; regional pricing was introduced to encourage regional self-sufficiency; the crop-marketing system was liberalized, with traders encouraged to operate in competition with government agencies.[6] The 1980s generally provided a favourable economic environment for Zambian commercial farmers, and, as a result, crop cultivation on the Block expanded, vacant units were purchased, and farms again changed hands.

The new farming families came from far and wide. One of them was the Fullers, who came to manage a German-owned farm. They arrived in Mkushi in 1983, by way of Rhodesia, England, Rhodesia again, Zimbabwe, and Malawi. Their story has been engagingly told by Alexandra Fuller (2003: 272):

> We have driven hundreds of kilometres and each kilometre brings land more beautiful and fertile and comforting and with each passing kilometre the air clears and the sky appears wider and deeper. And then, when it feels as if the land could not have settled itself more comfortably for human habitation, there it is – Serios Farm – lying open like a sandy-covered, tree-dotted blanket. Softly, voluptuously fertile and sweet-smelling of khaki weed, and old cow manure and thin dust and msasa leaves.

But, as she goes on to say, 'The farm has been without proper management for years. Even before the Germans acquired it, a series of alcoholic, occasionally insane *mazungus* (mostly burnt-out Rhodesians) have run the place into the ground' (Ibid.: 276).

The combination of beautiful landscape and a run-down farm is what many settlers in Mkushi would have met on their arrival. And the wheel of fortune that is the Mkushi property market would soon be engaged in new revolutions.

Democracy

In 1991, Kenneth Kaunda and UNIP lost to Frederick Chiluba and his Movement for Multiparty Democracy (MMD) in Zambia's first free elections. The new government, somewhat reluctantly, adopted the structural adjustment policies recommended by the World Bank and the IMF. Many of the Zambian government's agricultural policy interventions through the years have been reviled by commercial farmers. But the *laissez faire* approach of the first Chiluba government was not a popular winner either.

Liberalization of the Zambian economy had several effects. Of these, the most significant, as far as commercial farming was concerned, was the great increase in interest rates which took place in the early 1990s. Agriculture is sequential; between planting and harvesting, returns are slow, making the sector particularly vulnerable to high interest rates. Predictability – especially in the form of reasonable expectations about output prices – is also a key factor, but exposure to free market policies made agricultural producer prices volatile throughout much of the 1990s.

Zambia's honeymoon with democracy brought a government-led drive for increased foreign investment in agriculture, and this coincided with the unravelling of apartheid in South Africa. In the early 1990s, some 50 or 60 farmers made their way to the MFB from various parts of South Africa, having been offered land by the Chiluba government (Keller, 1992: 1):

> Driven by drought, debt and dread of South Africa's future under black rule, Mr. Van Niekerk and others of his white tribe are scouting new frontiers…. This time the frontier that has captivated the white farmers is, of all places, Zambia, where they will have their first experience of submission to a black Government.

Of these South African farmers, only two remain today, and most had left before the end of the millennium. A difficult economic environment no doubt contributed to the mass exodus. Veteran farmers on the Block,[7] however, also emphasize the lack of farming experience and commitment among the South African settlers, variously dubbing them bureaucrats, fishermen, miners, sailors, chancers, or crooks. Some had financing, others not, but few survived: 'They would load their bakkies in the middle of the night and take off, leaving behind a run-down farm and a large debt.'

The contempt with which many of the veterans on the Block portray these 'chancers' –South African or otherwise – is not only a reflection of the way that stayers might generally feel about quitters, but also springs from the effects that the exodus had on the commercial farming economy; these failures gave Mkushi farmers a bad reputation, generating a lack of trust among traders and bankers.

Interestingly, this period also saw a large influx of commercial Tonga farmers to farmland surrounding the Block. After successive droughts and a collapse in the livestock population in the Southern Province in the early 1990s, several hundred Tonga farmers found their way to Mkushi. Many negotiated land deals directly with customary leaders in the area, others took advantage of the land made available by the Zambian government along the TAZARA Corridor.[8]

Land in the TAZARA Corridor was subject to size restrictions, and acquiring title for customary land is often a long and cumbersome process, making loan capital inaccessible and investments uncertain during the first years of settlement. This, in part, is why land on the Block is so attractive. Yet these surrounding lands represent an alternative for settlers who cannot afford the price of land on the Block; and some of today's Block veterans initially started out in Mkushi by acquiring customary land.

Some of the earliest settlers from Southern Province had worked as farm managers on the Block, others had been teachers or bureaucrats in Mkushi. Most of the native Zambian farmers who settled on the Block in the 1970s have now disappeared,[9] as have the majority of foreigners who came in the early 1990s. Most of the 1990s Tonga settlers, however, have survived and some have thrived. While their operations are generally less capital-intensive than those found on the Block, they are commercial in nature and some of these Tonga farmers now utilize farmland exceeding 1,000 hectares. And after some initial difficulties between the Tonga settlers and the indigenous population – mainly related to grazing practices – the Tonga community now appears to be well integrated, with frequent inter-tribal marriages among the younger generations.

Towards the late 1990s, interest rates dropped and prices improved. By the time the new millennium dawned, and the Zimbabwe land invasions gathered pace, the conditions for commercial farming in Mkushi had again become favourable.

Land and Identity
Zimbabwean stories

Mkushi farmers who fled from the farm invasions came from a number of different farming areas in Zimbabwe: Shamva, Darwendale, Goromonzi, Mvurwi. There is some clustering, as early settlers paved the way for neighbours and friends from their home areas.

More important than place of origin, however, is the time at which they left. A few of the Zimbabwean farmers on the Block anticipated the Zimbabwe troubles to the extent that they had time to make extensive preparations. One had his Zimbabwean farm invaded as early as 1998. He heard about the Mkushi Farm Block in 1999, but first checked out Mozambique and Australia:

The language in Mozambique is different and the infrastructure is not good enough. In Australia the competition is fierce and the margins are small; you need big equity to make it there, and we don't have that, since we received nothing for our farms.'

He made his first trip to Mkushi in 2001: 'When they got to know about the trip, my own workforce turned against me, they now thought it was certain that I would leave. So my own security people gave me a curfew. Then I knew I would have to leave.'

Another of the early settlers states: 'What I liked about Mkushi was that it wasn't isolated; there were commercial farmers already present on the Block. And there was a good school, good tobacco land, and it wasn't that far from Zimbabwe where I still have family and friends.' Several of the early settlers had contacts in Mkushi or elsewhere in Zambia, having gone to school with white Zambians in South Africa or knowing them through the trade. The earliest settlers from Zimbabwe arrived in Mkushi in 2002. Most of these received full financing from Standard Chartered Bank through Harare and London when building their new farms, loans that mostly ranged between US$1-3 million. A few received similar terms from Barclay's Bank.

Many of the early settlers suffered humiliation before leaving Zimbabwe, for example:

I had 50 or 60 guys camping at my gate, with sticks and machetes, drugged and drunk, demanding food and meetings and other things. They searched me at my own gate when I wanted to leave my farm. Then I got a notice from government, a Section 5, announcing expropriation of my farm. And then a Section 8, giving me 90 days to leave.

As they will readily admit, however, the early settlers were fortunate in comparison with those who had to leave later. The early settlers were able to look around before deciding on where to go and, in some cases, brought with them machinery and even financial capital. Some of those who left at a later stage witnessed atrocities on their farms and some were given as little as one or two hours to pack up and leave. They were also able to take advantage of the window of opportunity with respect to fully financed investments on their new properties in Mkushi, one which was not open to later settlers. At the height of the commercial farmer exodus from Zimbabwe in 2004 and 2005, there were at least four companies in Harare and London that were offering assistance in terms of relocation and financing. None of these, however, could offer terms comparable to Standard Chartered's deals.[10]

The majority of the Zimbabwean farmers on the Block, early and late settlers alike, farm more or less along the same lines that they did in Zimbabwe. If they grew tobacco and maize in Zimbabwe, they grow tobacco and maize in Mkushi. They may have dropped a secondary crop, for example cotton, from their operation, but by and large there is a great deal of symmetry between their old and their new operations.

Of the established farmers on the Block, most have experimented extensively through the years and have dropped established crops and sought out new ones as prices dictated. Many now successfully cultivate wheat and soya beans. As the Zimbabwean farmers settle in, however, their ability to experiment will be constrained by their often sizeable capital investments and long-term trade commitments.

Most of these farmers are experienced but still young enough to take on the challenge of building another business.[11] Those who received the favourable loan deals belonged, we can assume, to a very capable segment of Zimbabwean farmers. Most have already committed serious amounts of capital to their holdings in Mkushi. And while some of the Block veterans point out that the financial risk is borne by the commercial banks rather than the Zimbabweans, the latter are risking their reputations as farmers and future borrowers. Anything but a committed effort at making their farm businesses viable and sustainable seems highly unlikely. 'We are farmers, we didn't come here for a holiday.' The survival rate to date would seem to confirm this.

Land and identity

As Alexandra Fuller's father noted when debating the merits of moving to Mkushi, 'It's the bloody League of Nations' (Fuller, 2003: 268). The Mkushi Farm Block harbours, and has harboured, farmers from origins as diverse as Croatia, Greece, England, Hungary, Scotland, South Africa, Sweden, Yugoslavia, Zambia and Zimbabwe. Black, white, and coloured farmers, some of whom have been farming all their lives, others who have not.

One of our initial ambitions was to enumerate farmers according to such origins. As our conversations with the Mkushi farmers progressed, however, the categories we had constructed disintegrated before our eyes. Many of the 'Rhodesians' who arrived in Mkushi in the late 1950s and early 1960s were Englishmen who had spent only a couple of years as farm managers in Rhodesia. Another farmer may ostensibly be of British origin. However, if he was born in Africa, ejected from the Congo in the 1960s, fled Rhodesia in the 1970s, and left a liberated South Africa in the mid-1990s before settling on the Block, then origin becomes a complicated matter. Is a 'Greek' farmer really Greek if he was born in Tanzania and moved to Kenya before ending up in Mkushi? Does the answer depend on whether most of his family lives in Greece or Australia?

The number of farmers on the Block who 'feel Zambian' is very low. It includes a couple of the very early settlers who are now Zambian passport-holders, and, more decisively, their offspring, now farming their own units on the Block. If one asks a farmer who settled in the 1970s or 1980s whether he feels Greek or Zambian, European or African, he is prone to shrug his shoulders and say, 'take your pick'. These are survivors of a tough farming environment who are mostly dependent on themselves as individuals. Identity is focused and honed around occupation, personality and family rather than around citizenship or nationality.

Nor is this identity particularly attached to land. While the earliest settlers and their offspring may have developed a sense of belonging, most of those who settled during the last 30 years or so have a distinctly utilitarian and opportunistic relationship to land. Some of these settlers have lost or traded half a dozen farms or more in their lifetime. Volatile markets, an unstable regional political environment and the experience of seeing others come and go have taught many of these farmers that a strong emotional attachment to a place is something they cannot afford. While most go about their farming, and indeed their home building and ornamentation, as if they will be staying indefinitely, there is also a certain detachment; an awareness that they may one day have to leave. Making a living is more important than making a home.

The formation of place attachment is partly a temporal issue. Those Zimbabweans who arrived in Mkushi after the turn of the millennium naturally represent a local extreme. They may possess a strong sense of attachment to land, but this attachment concerns the land they left behind in Zimbabwe rather than the land they settled on in Mkushi. And this attachment also informs their feelings of identity.

The Zimbabweans we talked to in Mkushi feel both Zimbabwean and African, with no exceptions. A typical statement is: 'We are Zimbabwean. We were born there, our parents were born there. How could we be anything else?' While much has been made, by Mugabe and others, of the dual English–Zimbabwean citizenship enjoyed by many of these farmers, some of the younger generation of settlers in Mkushi possess only Zimbabwean citizenship. And the strength of the emotional attachment to land and country can perhaps be summed up by the following statement: 'How do I explain to my son that he no longer has any identity?'

Some Zimbabweans also use their Zimbabwean and African identity to distinguish themselves from white Zambian farmers who, as the Zimbabwean story goes, all hold dual citizenship, do not invest or reinvest on their land, and generally act like expatriates. One of the Zimbabwean farmers, however, saw this strong sense of attachment as one of the reasons for their downfall, implying that it provided them with a sense of invulnerability: 'We thought we were citizens – that was the whole problem'.[12] As Lafraniere (2004: 1) states, 'some transplanted farmers say they have learned from their experience in Zimbabwe that they need to integrate, not just prosper, if they want to be accepted'.

Identity, of course, looks different from the perspective of the local workforce and the black Mkushi community. A century of colonial history is difficult to erase. Zambia has a history of benign race relations compared to most other countries in the region, and the peaceful reputation has traditionally been a factor in the decision of white farmers to resettle there (Keller, 1992). But many Zambians have an ambiguous attitude towards recent events in Zimbabwe (Geloo, 2004), and locals in Mkushi have a hard time accepting white farmers as 'Africans'. European, and particularly British, reactions towards Mugabe are to some extent taken as evidence: although violations of human rights are difficult to rank, the feeling is, for instance, that there are worse abuses of power taking place in Africa than those committed by Zimbabwe's president. Yet the Europeans, it is said, only seem to react when whites are involved.

Conflict and community

'We're always quarrelling.' This is a sentiment that is repeatedly expressed by farmers on the Block, both old and new.

Much of what they quarrel about is water for irrigation. The rules, such as they are, say that older dams should be filled before newer dams. Regardless of upstream or downstream location, more recent structures should remain open until older structures are full. However, between rivers, new owners, expansions of older dams, discreet use, and friends in the local bureaucracy, there is a lot of room for conflict. These disputes are as much a part of the older history of the Block as they are a feature of the meeting between the veterans and the recent settlers from Zimbabwe.

Some of the recent settlers have already been in such disputes, one of which involved the building of a dam without any notice given to downstream farmers. They insist, however, that the problem lies in the lack of a proper system of water allocation rather than ignorance or ill will. The current system is, according to the Zimbabweans, medieval compared to what they are used to and to what it should be. Yet there is today no legal mandate for the establishment of a catchment area committee and a more detailed and efficient allocation of the area's water resources.[13]

More generally, the Zimbabwean invasion of Mkushi did not unfold without incident. Many of the Block veterans perceived the Zimbabweans to be boastful about their farming proficiency and insensitive to established rights and customs. The former also increased local competition for labour, particularly skilled labour, and there was undoubtedly some envy with regard to the favourable financing enjoyed by many Zimbabwean settlers.[14] Some of the latter, on the other hand, were shocked at the poor state of local farming infrastructure and the perceived inefficiency of farming operations.

Two opposing narratives emerged. In the 'Zambian' narrative, (most of) the Zimbabwean farmers were arrogant, pampered by their big soft loans, ignorant of how to survive in a more hostile political and economic environment and overcommitted in terms of farm investments: 'The Zimbabweans arrived during a period of unprecedented growth in Zambia, when conditions were ideal. All the roads were good, the prices, the dollar, the Zambian open-arms policy; they had a real easy time of it with their loans and everything. Now that it's back to normal, many of them are struggling.'

In the 'Zimbabwean' narrative, (most of) the local commercial farmers were weak, under the thumb of the authorities, unwilling to stand up to their workers, afraid to take up loans, and therefore unable to make long-term commitments to their farms and their existence as Africans.

When the Zimbabweans arrived, there was little that joined the Block farmers together as a community beyond their trade. They generally acknowledge this themselves. This can, in part, be attributed to the individualist bent of most of the veterans on the block. Farmers we talked to could, for example, only recall a single instance of intermarriage between young people who had been raised on the Block. According to a couple of the earliest settlers, however, community spirit on the Block tends to fluctuate with the agricultural economy. Difficult times are attended by turnover in the Block population and investments in community are not foremost in the minds of farmers struggling for economic survival. During good times, however – notably the 1960s and the

1980s – the communal spirit was apparently good, as manifested in an active Mkushi Country Club and regular, organized tours of each others' farms.

With respect to the Zimbabweans, it seems natural that a group of recent immigrants from a similar – and to some extent entrenched – background, having been through similar and harrowing experiences, would want to re-establish a sense of community upon arriving in a new location. This could stem from both social and business motivations, in part banding together for a sense of familiarity and comfort, in part wanting to recreate some of the economic environment they had lost. A risk in this regard could be the formation of a Zimbabwean clique and enduring conflict. The Zimbabweans, however, insist that after the initial birth pains of their entry into Mkushi, they have tried hard to avoid conflict.

Many of the veterans on the Block have previously gone through ordeals of a similar nature to those experienced by the Zimbabweans, albeit in other locations and under somewhat different circumstances. On the one hand, this makes it hard for the Zimbabwean farmers to garner a great deal of sympathy. On the other hand, a feeling of shared predicament might, in the long run, contribute to a sense of community.

Most of the divisive issues were apparently resolved after a series of meetings between the Zimbabwean settlers and the Block veterans and relations are today quite benign. While some veterans remain ambiguous, most of them admire the farming proficiency displayed by the Zimbabweans. Some also compliment the Zimbabweans' willingness to share farming knowledge and see in the Zimbabwean presence an inspiration to improve their own farming efforts. The attitude among the oldest families on the Block is generally one of unqualified approval. The Zimbabweans, it is emphasized, have brought a much-needed sense of community to the Block, exemplified by their resurrection of the neglected and run-down Mkushi Country Club and its golf course, the establishment and running of a community-wide internet server and their engagement in community health and education matters. They have also, according to this view, improved the economic environment for all the farmers on the Block by making finance more accessible, by attracting traders, by establishing a professional workshop for repair and maintenance of machinery and by their overall contribution to agricultural production in Zambia and the attendant goodwill that this generates for the Block.[15]

There are also ambiguities with respect to the wider Mkushi community. In Zimbabwe, the commercial farming sector was a co-ordinated and well-oiled machine along the entire supply chain, from input production to marketing of processed goods. This machine included a highly paternalistic and authoritarian approach to labour, with workers and their children living in on-farm settlements. In Zambia, few workers live on the farm and employer–employee relationships are traditionally less hierarchical. Upon arriving in Mkushi, the settlers, to varying degrees, tried to duplicate the Zimbabwean approach with some unfortunate but predictable consequences.[16] While the settlers invariably complain about the local lack of work ethic and discipline, Zambian workers invariably complain about draconian rules and working hours. And if a farm business is suffering from liquidity problems, workers complain that their wages always seem to be at the end of the pay-out queue.[17]

Again, these problems have to some extent been ironed out, but not without incident. Walk-outs, no-shows, and rampant theft were common during the early period and at least one farmer was beaten by his workers on his own farm. And the Labour Office in Mkushi states that cases brought against Zimbabwean farmers still outnumber those brought against all other farmers. On the other hand, most of the Zimbabweans are still in a precarious position with respect to their immigration status in Zambia. The local National Pensions Scheme Authority (NAPSA) states that 'We follow them up quite vigorously' and both NAPSA and the Labour Office admit that the Zimbabweans are quick to comply once a legitimate complaint is lodged.

In Zimbabwe, farmers also met little resistance from local authorities. In contrast, in Zambia the red tape flows freely and often in proportion to the resistance with which it is met. One Zimbabwean farmer said, 'Anyone within the state with even a sniff of an interest will hassle you non-stop.' Another insisted he had been 'hounded by every possible government department you could name'. For an Mkushi farmer, this might include departments and agencies associated with customs, agriculture, veterinary services, immigration, tax, the environment, labour, water, as well as a host of other fringe departments. While the Block veterans have found ways of dealing with a local bureaucracy, most of the Zimbabweans still find it hard.

The Zimbabweans have, however, also had obvious and substantial positive effects on the local community. They employ a fixed force of around 4,000 workers, and almost the same number is called in as seasonal labour during peaks. Most of this can be seen as job creation, as few farms employed significant numbers of workers at the time they were purchased. Local bank officials confirm that the Zimbabweans have had a stabilizing effect on the local banking environment through their large outstanding loans and regular debt servicing. The fall in local unemployment has also had positive effects on crime in Mkushi, according to the Zimbabweans, although this is not unequivocally confirmed by official statistics from the local police.[18]

The overall picture, seven years after the first of the latest wave of Zimbabweans arrived, is that their relations with both the Block veterans and the surrounding Mkushi community is relatively stable and amicable.

Concluding Remarks

Although the perceived stability of rural communities may be an illusion, the relatively young Mkushi Farm Block has had more than its share of turbulence over its comparatively brief existence. Of the families who settled there prior to Zambian independence in 1964, only a few remain. Between then and now, the Block has seen multiple replacements of almost its entire community. Greeks, Zambians, Indians, South Africans and others have come and gone. But from each new wave of farmers that has spilled onto the Block and then withdrawn, at least a few families have remained. Whether the Block, in the long term, faces increased stability is in part a matter of agricultural and economic policy.

To be a commercial farmer in Zambia – whether big or small – is to harbour a continuous apprehension towards the future of input prices, output prices, interest rates, exchange rates, government rent, export bans, wages and taxes. Perhaps more important than facing any particular combination of these would be some sense that the combination could be expected to remain stable over time, rendering farming investment decisions predictable. The turnover of land and the ups and downs of farming on the Block through the years can in large part be ascribed to unstable government policies towards commercial farming. One Block veteran feels that this is due to a misguided focus: 'The government looks only at consumers, not producers. But if you took care of your producers, you wouldn't have to worry about your consumers.' In addition to economic concerns, however, there are political concerns.

The contingent of Zimbabweans that settled in Mkushi since 2002 faced mostly favourable frame conditions for farming. In late 2004, President Mwanawasa met them at the Mkushi Country Club and promised them a profitable future in Zambia as long as they behaved well, respected Zambian law and stayed away from politics.[19] In presidential elections in 2006 and 2008, however, Michael Sata of the Patriotic Front lost narrowly on both occasions.

In the run-up to these elections, he blamed many of the country's ills on the behaviour of 'foreigners' and made favourable noises about Robert Mugabe. Sata's statements were largely directed towards Chinese investors. As Larmer and Fraser (2007) emphasize, Sata is also an opportunist rather than an ideologue; his statements about foreign influence on the Zambian economy reflect genuine concerns among the Zambian electorate related to increasing inequality and the failure of a technocratic state to acknowledge popular aspirations. Nevertheless, his utterances – blown up in the press and toned down by his political allies – certainly had an effect on the white farming community; and not only the recent Zimbabwean immigrants but also the very early settlers.[20]

Since Sata's victory in the September 2012 presidential election, his close relationship with Mugabe has been on display (see, for example, Kawadza and Maodza, 2012), but the first few months of his term has otherwise not given the Zimbabwean farmers in Mkushi any greater cause for concern. The apprehension that Sata's earlier comments generated perhaps reflects a more general feeling of insecurity among white farmers in the region, a feeling fuelled by the recent troubles in Zimbabwe but with roots that go back beyond the end of apartheid in South Africa to the wave of liberation that swept the continent in the 1960s. As noted, many of the farmers on the Block have fled from, or been thrown out of, one African country or another in the past. Their fear is possibly that the search for a home on this continent could ultimately prove futile. And despite the contribution that white commercial farmers make to the Zambian agricultural sector, and despite Zambia's reputation as a peaceful nation, this fear is perhaps given weight by the fact that Zambia's economy – founded as it is on mining rather than agriculture – would be unlikely to implode in a manner similar to Zimbabwe if indeed a purge of white farmers were to take place.

Against this background, do the Zimbabweans in Mkushi plan to stay? It would appear so, at least for a while. All of them have bad memories of the Zimbabwe troubles. And while some are plainly unhappy in Mkushi, others seem relatively upbeat. Common to all is a lack of alternatives. In a sense, they are all in Mkushi against their will but have nowhere else to go. Options such as England and Australia have been discarded, in part because they are 'not Africa'. Few are optimistic about a rapid solution to Zimbabwe's problems, and some insist they would not return even if they were offered their old farms back, hoping only that the title deeds, which they still possess, might someday provide them with a financial windfall.

As Somers (1994) has pointed out, narratives are important drivers of identity, and the Zimbabwean settlers in Mkushi share powerful and dramatic narratives related to both their distant and immediate past. As noted earlier, however, the Zimbabweans – as individuals and as a group – also share powerful narratives with many of the Block veterans. The stories told by farmers, old and new, on the Mkushi Block differ in their specifics, for example with regard to country of origin, time of settlement and reasons for leaving the previous location. At a more general level, these stories also often converge around fluctuating economic fortunes, political change and a willingness to take a gamble. Most clearly, the recent arrival of Zimbabwean farming families on the Block – despite the obvious differences – shares important parallels with the Greek settlement in the 1960s with respect to their forced removal from existing farms in a neighbouring country, their European origin, the relatively benign economic frame conditions they met upon their arrival and the number of families who migrated.

Of the 30 Greek families who originally settled on the Block, four decades later only six remain. Although predictions of this nature are speculative, it is not unthinkable that as we approach the middle of the present century, we may find a similar number of survivors among recent Zimbabwean settlers. These are likely to be those farmers who successfully adapt not only to the peculiar community of commercial farmers already present on the Block – with its rugged individualism and businesslike approach to both land and its cultivation – but also to the surrounding social environs, exemplified by Zambian labour relations and a tradition of local government scrutiny.

From a short-term perspective, the recent settlement of Zimbabwean farmers on the MFB represents a dramatic development, with immediate and diverse impacts on land use conflicts, labour conflicts, commercial crop output, banking, employment and community spirit. From the perspective of the area's history, however, the Zimbabwean settlement is just the most recent in a long line of similar dramas and the story line, as it unfolds, is likely to trace an already familiar trajectory.

Notes

1 The authors wish to thank Webster Banda and Felix Moyo for their invaluable assistance during fieldwork in Mkushi, all the farmers, workers, and government officials who took time to answer questions, and David and Christine Moffat who provided insightful comments on an early draft and who drew the authors' attention to some key references.

2 See FCTZ (1999), FCTZ (2003), and Utete (2003). Estimates of the number of commercial farmers that left generally range from 1,500 to 4,000.

3 Five of these have now left, while others who originally arrived as farm managers have been able to strike out on their own. As of May, 2009, there were 29 farms on the Mkushi Farm Block that were operated by recent Zimbabwean immigrants.

4 Five of these eight units were later attached to the Farm Block (Woode et al., 1978-79).

5 Sale of improvements to land was still allowed, so the value of bare land was naturally subsumed into the prices for improvements. The 1975 Land Act was replaced by the 1995 Land Act, after which sales of land again were permitted. Nearly all the recent Zimbabweans settlers purchased land on the Block – only in a couple of cases did Zimbabwean settlers lease land on an annual basis from other owners.

6 Continued pressure from multilateral donors would eventually lead to reduced subsidies, which at one point caused a 100 per cent increase in maize-meal prices. This resulted in food riots, and in May 1987 the government broke with the IMF (Wood, 1990: 21).

7 We use the term 'veteran' loosely, in the sense of all farmers already settled on the Block before the recent wave of Zimbabweans arrived.

8 This was land alienated on either side of the Tanzania–Zambia line of rail, which runs through Mkushi, as part of the Chiluba government's promotion of investment in agriculture in the 1990s.

9 There are today six native Zambian farmers active on the Block, one of which is the Block's largest employer and perhaps its most successful farmer. All of these settled between 1972 and 1980. A further five properties are owned by native Zambians but are not farmed.

10 One of these companies was, apparently, a complete hoax: 'they just took the money and ran'. Another scheme, involving Zambia Leaf Tobacco, aimed to relocate Zimbabwe farmers to Southern Province. Although ill-fated, about two dozen farmers involved in that scheme are now renting land in the Southern Province on their own terms.

11 Their ages ranged from the 20s to the 60s, but most Zimbabwean farmers were between 30 and the mid-50s when arriving in Mkushi.

12 In Southern Africa, the degree of 'African-ness' among people of European decent can apparently be measured along a scale that incorporates both time and space. The first areas to be settled, in the seventeenth century, were around the Cape. The most recent, in the twentieth century, were in Zambia. In between is an almost mythical history of voortrekkers, adversity and civilisation. So while a tenth or fifteenth generation of South Africans may reflect with disdain on a third or fourth generation Zimbabwean's feeling of continental attachment, the Zimbabwean may express the same type of scorn towards his Zambian neighbours.

13 A new act that should provide such a mandate is, however, in the pipeline.

14 A popular conjecture among Block veterans is that the Zimbabwean farmers' loans ultimately are underwritten by the British government, since 'no commercial bank would offer such terms without having their backs covered'. Gossip abounds under circumstances such as these. One early rumour, allegedly spread by Mugabe's propaganda machine, identified Mkushi Zimbabweans as ex-military officers trying to set up a resistance force in Zambia; another suggests that the Zimbabwean business loans were squandered on expensive cars and holiday trips.

15 The favourable economic conditions that met the Zimbabweans have already been mentioned. One of the Block veterans also points to the conjunction of the Zimbabwean arrival with the arrival of mass access to electricity on the Block. Where most of the farmers previously had to rely on generators, a new powerline to Mkushi around the turn of the millennium transected the Block, with beneficial effects on equipment maintenance, irrigation, fencing and morale more generally. The revitalization of the Block in recent years may thus have multiple sources.

16 The Zimbabwean farmers insist that the only workers brought along from Zimbabwe were top management and those who already possessed immigration rights to Zambia through ancestry. In 2009, however, a Mkushi immigration officer was suspended for furnishing false residence permits to Zimbabwean workers. We do not know the extent of such activities.

17 From a foreign exchange perspective, wages paid to Zambian workers are roughly twice those paid to Zimbabwean workers before the farm invasions. From a purchasing power perspective, however, the relationship is almost the opposite, and this may explain some of the conflicts between farmers and workers. Zimbabwean farmers also focus more on output than the hours of work put in.

18 According to these statistics, the number of crimes reported in Mkushi over the last six years were as follows: 2003 – 525; 2004 – 461; 2005 – 546; 2006 – 422; 2007 – 409; 2008 – 513. These crude statistics may, however, disguise variations in the seriousness of crimes and in unreported crimes.

19 Mwanawasa died of a stroke in August 2008. After a close election, Mwanawasa was succeeded by Rupiah Banda, who was born in Zimbabwe. President Banda visited the Mkushi Country Club in March 2009, complimenting farmers on their efforts and addressing worries over cheap imports of wheat.

20 The protection afforded by a Zambian passport would probably be scant consolation if the commercial farming community and agro-industry were to crumble all around you.

12

The impact of the Zimbabwean crisis on informal cross-border trade with Zambia

Thomson Kalinda, Diana Banda, Priscilla Hamukwala, Fabian Maimbo and Espen Sjaastad[1]

Introduction and Background

The economic crisis in Zimbabwe in the past decade has led to extraordinary growth in informal cross-border trade (CBT). Within the informal economy lies informal cross-border trade, which is unrecognized and often deemed illegal. For the purposes of this chapter, 'informal cross-border trade' is defined as trade where the movement of goods and services across borders is, by and large, not officially recorded. It is characterized by under-invoicing and under-declaration of invoices. At times, it may even be outright illicit and of a contraband nature. It characteristically involves 'the frequent movement of people across borders with small consignments' (Ndlela, 2006: 8). This study does not, however, deal with informal cross-border trade of an officially illegal nature such as the sale of stolen goods and proscribed drugs.

Informal traders are often viewed as 'smugglers', while women traders are frequently portrayed as 'prostitutes' (Muzvidziwa, 2005: 51; 1998). This perception can be attributed to the fact that most trade is undocumented and unregistered, and thus unaccounted for in national trade statistics. This perception is prevalent, moreover, because the informal economy is understudied. The level of trade in the Southern African Development Community (SADC) is understated due to the non-inclusion of informal CBT into official trade statistics. SADC states obtain revenue from duties and taxes charged to small informal traders who operate across borders, although this sector is not officially recognized. Available statistics suggest that informal trade within SADC contributes an average of over US$17.6 billion per year (Peberdy, 2000; Musonda, 2004).

Poverty is pervasive in the region and has been aggravated by the negative effects of structural adjustment programmes prescribed by the International Monetary Fund and the World Bank as a means of achieving economic recovery (SADC, 2000). In the case of Zimbabwe, the chaotic land reform programme, poor governance and a polarized political climate took its toll on the country's economy as foreign currency reserves dried up, exports declined and foreign direct investment dwindled to zero. As a result as local authorities allowed various economic activities to flourish, ranging from flea-markets, tuck shops and street vending to mushroom-growing, resulting in a significant shift from formal to informal sector activities (Ndlela, 2006; Solidarity Peace Trust, 2006).

Informal economic activity spiraled as a result of the high unemployment, inflation, shortages of foreign currency, goods and commodities, high levels of poverty and food insecurity that followed fast-track land reform (Chari, 2004; Solidarity Peace Trust, 2006). The growth of the informal sector was further fueled by a thriving black market, buoyed by the differential in foreign currency rates, and the collapse of health care and education services. The HIV/AIDS pandemic exacerbated the situation (Chari, 2004). The informal sector provides people with a source of income and employment. For many economic destitutes, informal CBT has become a means of survival, a source of income and employment. It is also a dynamic sector in which small traders or small exporters and importers make a profit (Muzvidziwa, 2005).

Historically, informal CBT in Zimbabwe dates back to pre-colonial times. People carried out barter trade without the need for formal registration. At independence, many African states adopted the artificially created borders, which led to the emergence of tariff and non-tariff barriers. This, in turn, disrupted informal economic activity (Nyantaga et al., 2000). Goods were sold internally within Zimbabwe and across the border to neighbouring countries. Informal CBT was often associated with low-income earners.

Cross-border traders are confronted with a hostile policy environment at both national and regional levels. However, SADC governments can gain from informal CBT by creating an enabling environment in which informal traders can operate and in turn generate revenue (Mpande, 2004). Furthermore, informal CBT facilitates regional integration through the sharing of ideas and experiences at grass-roots level. The formal sector cannot be studied in isolation from the informal sector. Informal CBT not only benefits the traders themselves, and government, but it also provides employment opportunities in industries such as transport, manufacturing, production and revenue institutions at border posts. In this way, the informal sector is closely linked to the formal sector (Mpande, 2004).

This study focuses on informal trade by Zimbabweans who operate across the border to Zambia. The major thrust of the study was to capture the many narratives with regard to the way Zimbabwean traders go about their cross-border trade activities, with emphasis on reasons for participating in CBT; sources of initial capital; types of goods traded; types of clients; mode of transport and frequency of visits; networks and help received while in Zambia; views of the border-post officers; and future aspirations of the traders.

Research Methodology

There is very little information available about Zimbabwean cross-border traders living and working in Livingstone, Zambia, their numbers, what economic activities they are involved in or in which parts of the city they live and work. Given that some Zimbabweans do not want their whereabouts to be known, establishing a sampling frame would be a long and costly, if not impossible, exercise. Due to time and resource constraints, the research team decided to concentrate on those Zimbabweans working in public spaces in the informal economy in the city. Although the sample is not representative, it provides a profile of people involved in CBT or survivalist activities on the streets of Livingstone. It is acknowledged that even within this segment, cross-border traders represent only one point in a chain of activities. There are, for example, less visible value-adding activities and supply relations that are not included in this study, in particular, the more established traders who supply shops and wholesalers with high-value durables and consumables in the major interior markets such as Lusaka and the Copperbelt. In order to arrive at a more complete picture of Zimbabweans' involvement in informal activities in Zambia, it is important that further research be conducted on these and other issues.

A total of 149 interviews were conducted with Zimbabweans working in public spaces in the Livingstone central business district and in Dambwa, a low-income and high-density residential area. Interviews and field observations were conducted between November 2008 and March 2009. The interviewers focused on an area locally referred to as 'Zimbabwe Market' in the central business district, the border crossing point at Victoria Falls and the Dambwa area. Zimbabweans were initially identified by sight and/or by the language they spoke. A snowballing technique was then used whereby interviewees identified other Zimbabweans who could be interviewed. Given the legal status of the traders, the questionnaires were anonymous and no questions were asked about the interviewees' official status. However, questions were asked about why the interviewees came to Zambia.

Interviewers reported that, on occasion, some of the cross-border traders were reluctant to be interviewed – some refused, others pretended they could not speak English and some told interviewers to return but could not be found when they did so. This did not happen frequently enough to be of serious concern, with the interviewers noting that the majority of the Zimbabweans who were approached were willing to be interviewed.

A number of interviews were also conducted with government officials, particularly those from the Immigration Department, to ascertain how the city currently deals with the issue of CBT, how this has changed over time, and in order to understand some of the issues that the officers have to deal with as regards the Zimbabwean cross-border traders.

The study primarily yielded qualitative data. The data obtained from the interviews and key informants was edited and verified while in the field. Transcripts of all field notes and interviews were checked for accuracy. The data was analyzed following a thematic procedure. First, to ensure completeness, the data was checked for any gaps. A summary was then made to obtain trends and meaningful typologies and associations (Detels, 1997). This information is incorporated within the narratives contained in this paper.

Overall Effects of the Zimbabwe Crisis on Border Crossings

The study team collected quantitative data on border crossings from the Livingstone and Siavonga borders (on the Zambian side) from January 2003 until September 2008 (the team was unable to access reliable data from Chirundu, the third border post). The data collection time coincided with a period of rising political, economic and humanitarian problems in Zimbabwe.

Officials at the borders distinguish between 'international travellers' and 'day-trippers'. The latter are Zimbabweans and Zambians who are given a pass to cross the border (usually early in the morning) on the understanding that they will return to their country of origin before the border closes at 6 p.m. on the same day. They need only show identification and sign an official list at the border post. International travellers represent all other travellers. The vast majority of traders who sell their goods in the Livingstone and Siavonga areas are day-trippers. Long-distance traders will be found among the international travellers, but these were not captured in the surveys.

The data shows a clear and significant increase in entries to Zambia from Zimbabwe over this period. The rise is especially marked from the middle of 2005. It is noteworthy that the entire increase can be attributed to an associated surge in the entry of day-trippers (see Fig. 1). From a low point of 1,517 in November 2003, entries reached a peak of 16,671 in July 2008. The average monthly number of day-tripper entries in 2003 was 3,280; this had increased to 11,155 in 2008. There was no significant change in entries of international travellers during the same period.

If, as seems reasonable, the increase in day-tripper entries cannot be explained by tourism or labour commuting, and if each trader makes roughly twenty entries per month, daily CBT provided around 400 Zimbabweans with a livelihood option at these border posts between 2003 and 2008 (see Fig. 1).

Interestingly, while there is a significant downward trend in the number of 'tourists' in Siavonga (all border crossings of neither Zimbabwean nor Zambian nationality), no such trend exists in Livingstone, by far the more popular destination for international visitors. This, of course, does not mean that tourism in the Victoria Falls area of Zimbabwe has not suffered, by all accounts it has. But crossings by internationals would remain stable if tourists chose to visit the Victoria Falls from the Zambian rather than the Zimbabwean side. This has implications for CBT, i.e. Zimbabwean traders who target tourists would have to become day-trippers in order to keep their turnover from falling.

Demographic Profiles of the Cross-border Traders

The socio-demographic characteristics of the cross-border traders presented in Table 3 (overleaf) show that of the overall sample of 149 cross-border traders interviewed, 53 per cent were female and 47 per cent were male. The estimated mean age of the traders in the sample was 33 years, with ages for both men and women ranging from 20 to 59 years. The traders, who are usually the heads of households, have mean family sizes of eight members. In terms of ethnicity, 62 per cent of the cross-border traders were Shona, 26 per cent were Ndebele, while a further 12 per cent said they belonged to other ethnic groups. While it is generally believed that people who engage in CBT have a humble educational background and belong to marginalized groups that seek survival strategies (being excluded from the normal channels of employment), this study found

Table 3: Socio-demographic characteristics of sampled cross-border traders

	Gender					
	Male		Female		Total	
	No.	per cent	No.	per cent	No.	per cent
Educational level						
Illiterate	0	.0	1	100.0	1	0.7
Primary school	2	15.4	11	84.6	13	9.2
Secondary school	44	48.4	47	51.6	91	64.1
Post-secondary school	22	59.5	15	40.5	37	26.1
Total	68	47.9	74	52.1	142	100.0
Marital status						
Single	32	54.2	27	45.8	59	42.1
Married	27	48.2	29	51.8	56	40.0
Divorced	4	40.0	6	60.0	10	7.1
Separated	1	25.0	3	75.0	4	2.9
Widowed	1	9.1	10	90.9	11	7.9
Total	65	46.4	75	53.6	140	100.0
Ethnic group						
Ndebele	20	52.6	18	47.4	38	25.5
Shona	41	44.6	51	55.4	92	61.7
Other	9	47.4	10	52.6	19	12.8
Total	70	47.0	79	53.0	149	100.0
Employment status						
Self-employed	55	43.7	71	56.3	126	84.6
Government employee	6	66.7	3	33.3	9	6.0
NGO employee	8	61.5	5	38.5	13	8.7
Other	1	100.0	0	.0	1	0.7
Total	70	47.0	79	53.0	149	100.0

Source: Survey data, 2008

that a majority of the cross-border traders were well-educated. The majority (64 per cent) had secondary school education and some had attained a qualification at tertiary level. Others reported that they were raising funds to improve their educational qualifications.

In terms of marital status, most of the cross-border traders were either single (42 per cent) or married (40 per cent), with the remainder being divorced or widowed. Over 70 per cent of the respondents attested to having been involved in varied forms of employment prior to being involved in informal CBT. Some in formal institutions as secretaries, office administrators/managers, teachers and civil servants; some in construction work as builders, foremen, carpenters and so on; others had been variously self-employed for most their working lives. In terms of their current employment status, the majority (85 per cent) indicated that they work only for themselves as cross-border traders, while the remainder indicated that they also have some form of formal employment in NGOs, government institutions, and so on. They constituted 9 per cent, 6 per cent and 1 per cent of the respondents respectively.

Reasons for Participating in Cross-Border Trading

Respondents were asked to identify their reasons for engaging in CBT. The majority gave financial reasons (either economic push/poverty or economic pull). Seventy-eight per cent mentioned the need for extra cash as the major prompt for entering into CBT. The need for additional cash arose out of particular circumstances, for example, the death of a breadwinner, the loss of a job, poverty and survival.

Loss of a breadwinner – especially a husband – was mentioned by a number of female traders as the major driver for them to engage in CBT. From an oral interview carried out with a widow who identified herself as Otillia, it is evident that poverty and the deteriorating economic situation in Zimbabwe were major push factors that had fuelled CBT:[2]

> Following the death of my husband, life became tough for me and the family. When the situation worsened, we slept on empty stomachs with only one meal per day. By then, I and my family were under the care of my late husband's relatives, because culture demanded that I should stay with them waiting to be inherited or married to the brother or cousin of my late husband. I refused to be married off to the brother of my late husband and that is how my elder brother offered to take care of us. Unfortunately, he also died. But before he passed

away, he gave me enough money to enable me to travel to Livingstone. I arrived in Livingstone in May 2003 with nothing on me, not even a *ngwee*, as you say it in Zambia. I started piece work such as washing clothes and cleaning house-surroundings. With the money raised from such piece works, I would go and buy sweets and chocolates from Zimbabwe and resale [sic] in Zambia at a profit. That was then, but prices shot up in the recent past and it became unprofitable to buy things from Zimbabwe. As if that was not enough, availability of most commodities became an issue in Zimbabwe as most shelves have become empty. Since the economic situation in Zimbabwe has become bad, I now buy biscuits and sweets from wholesale shops in Zambia and resale [sic] on the streets as the only means of survival.

Poverty, political instability and its associated problems were given as reasons for engaging in cross-border trade as Sandra Hindi, a nineteen-year-old Zimbabwean woman noted:

Persistent problems which I used to face forced me to make my first trip following my stepmother to Zambia in May 2006. Before I made my first trip to Zambia, I was at school doing my O levels, but due to the continued political instability and the effects of the land reform programme all the schools were closed, including private schools. Therefore, instead of waiting for the unknown I had to find a way out of my desperate situation, and raise money for school fees, which is my major task here in Zambia. Despite all the constraints encountered, I managed to raise enough capital and started selling sweets and biscuits. Through this business I raised about K650,000 [equivalent to US$186]. I went back home in 2006 and paid my exam fees and managed to write my exams and I passed all my theory papers, but failed the practical papers because I didn't have time to prepare for my practicals.

Another respondent Shamiso, a 29-year-old woman from Harare with one child, mentioned that the need to raise money to support her family became an urgent issue and since 2006 she has been in the business of selling ice-cream in Zimbabwe. She observed that:

I am here in Zambia mainly because I have a child to take care of. I cannot watch my child die of hunger while doing nothing about it. There was no need for me to come to Zambia until the Zimbabwean Company producing ice-cream cones folded up its operations. I couldn't stop my business because I also look after other relatives. This prompted me to look for alternative sources of ice-cream cones. Ice-cream cones can easily be bought from Botswana, South Africa and Namibia at a relatively low price, but the treatment that I receive from South

Africa and Botswana made me to operate in Zambia where people are friendly and they treat us like human beings.

The loss of formal employment was mentioned by only six per cent of the respondents as the reason they decided to engage in CBT. Moses Moyo, a 36-year-old from Victoria Falls is one such case:

> Before coming to Zambia, I had a very well-paying permanent job with a Zimbabwean Construction Company. Everything was okay until the land reform programme started. Our employer received eviction threats from government agents and from then on everything changed. We worked without pay for two months, until finally he was evicted and he managed to pay us our three months salaries and that was it. The next thing we heard was that he had relocated to Zambia. That news prompted me to visit Zambia for the first time in 2005 and I hoped to find my former employer with a view of getting employed again, but to my disappointment my former employer was only engaged in farming in Kazungula District. I simply decided to start to get into cross-border trading to earn some money for myself and my family.

With loss of employment, some interesting job switches have occurred. The cross-border traders have had to switch from being secretaries and office mangers to selling ice-cream, sweets, biscuits, CDs and DVDs, as well as engaging in commercial sex work. A number of the female Zimbabwean cross-border traders have entered into prostitution to survive whilst they are in Zambia.

Sources of Initial Capital

Various sources of initial capital to facilitate cross-border trade were mentioned by the respondents and included, in order of importance, own savings (81 per cent), gifts (13 per cent), retirement packages (2 per cent), loans (1 per cent) and others (3 per cent). Among the latter is commercial sex work, into which some women are forced as a result of the hard economic challenges they face. Joyce is a typical example of a woman in this situation who engages in both CBT (she sells women's suits, blankets and duvets) and commercial sex work. In terms of CBT, she pointed out that 'the business… is very difficult because of too much competition from Zambian traders dealing with the same merchandise'. This is how she explained her situation:

> I have to be here in Livingstone for a maximum period of three weeks per trip to sell my merchandise but I also have commercial sex with as many clients as possible in order to make some extra money to go and buy more merchandise,

pay school fees and buy food for my child back home in Zimbabwe. If the day has good business, I manage to raise up to as much ZMK200,000 per day. I don't enjoy what I'm doing, but because of the situation I'm in, I have no choice. I am actually a professional hairdresser and I am respected back home. They can't even imagine I am doing this business here in Zambia. I used to work as a hairdresser at one of the beauty parlours owned by a white commercial farmer. Unfortunately, it closed down when the owner was evicted from his farm and left the country during the land reform programme in Zimbabwe. Otherwise, even if things were to improve in Zimbabwe, it would be difficult for me to make money because the economy is not performing well.

Joyce was also quick to explain that making money through commercial sex work is risky, particularly if her clients take her away from her usual residence:

Some men take advantage of us and sometimes they want to force us to do it without any form of protection and sometimes if they don't want to pay us, they falsely accuse us of having stolen their cellphones. There was a time I was beaten and had to run for my life to my room naked because I left all my clothes in this terrible man's room. I couldn't report him to the police because the business I do is illegal and I would have been deported. We also have problems with the local women here in Livingstone. Sometimes conflicts do erupt between us Zimbabweans and Zambian sex workers. The Zambian sex workers accuse us that our charges are very low and that they are losing business because men shun them and come to us.

Clients and Types of Goods Traded

Cross-border shopping and trading ranged from the purchase of low-end consumer goods to the buying and selling of manufactured goods. The respondents were asked to list the major goods bought in Zambia for sale in Zimbabwe and vice versa. The Zimbabweans were mainly interested in purchasing basic food items such as cooking oil, sugar, sweets, biscuits, mealie-meal and bread, all of which were in short supply in Zimbabwe at the time of the study. This was commonly done by the so called 'daily trekkers' who travel to Livingstone almost every day to purchase these items for own consumption and sale back home in border towns such as Victoria Falls. Those who are away for longer purchase assorted merchandise including DVDs, CDs, second-hand clothes (*salaula*), lotions and beauty accessories. Items brought by traders from Zimbabwe for sale in Zambia included assorted liquors, curtains, duvets and blankets.

Items brought into Livingstone by Zimbabwean traders are generally sold in the central business district at a market now popularly known as the 'Zimbabwe market' in Livingstone.

The main clients for the Zimbabwean traders that we interviewed are individual consumers, but a few sell to wholesalers. Similarly, although most of the transactions involve small volumes and values, bulk transactions do occur. One female Zimbabwean said:

> The major clients for my business are members of the local church I go to when I am in Livingstone. The business of duvets and blankets is very difficult because there is a lot of competition from Zambian traders who also deal in the same items. To overcome this, I usually price my goods slightly cheaper than the Zambians and offer discount for bulk buyers.

One trader spoke of the clandestine ways in which she manages to smuggle or avoid paying taxes for some of the goods she brings into Zambia:

> I used to carry four second-hand knitting-machines in sacks and connive with the truck drivers to hide them amidst their goods and then we would meet in Zambia after crossing the border. I would then pay the truck driver for this service. It's quite risky, especially if the truck driver used is a crook but it was worth the risk. I used to sell these second-hand knitting-machines each at K2.5 million [equivalent to US$500]. I only experienced delays when collecting the money from my customers who had to pay in five installments, starting with a deposit of K500, 000 or the US$100 equivalent.

Mode of Transport and Frequency of Visits

For the majority (83 per cent) of the respondents, the most common mode of transport into Zambia is public. They use buses or taxis that operate between Victoria Falls town in Zimbabwe and Livingstone in Zambia. Some traders also use buses to go as far afield as Lusaka. Own vehicles were used by about 9 per cent of the traders and 7 per cent walked across the border check-point from Victoria Falls town into Livingstone. The latter usually purchase low-end consumer products such as mealie-meal and bread for re-sale in Zimbabwe. The rest (1 per cent) use alternative means such as hitchhiking.

Many respondents regularly travelled to Zambia and this formed a central part of their occupational activities. On average, 41 per cent of the respondents travelled there every month; 29 per cent every week; 9 per cent every day; 8 per cent three times a year and 13 per cent once or twice a year. The duration of their stay in Zambia ranged from one day to one month. Were there no limits to the number of days permitted per visit, some traders indicated that they would like to stay longer. Moyo expressed his feeling thus: 'For me, Zambia seems to be home away from home, if only I could get a work permit, I would stay longer and I would even be more than willing to shift all my family to Zambia.'

Some Zimbabweans stay illegally in Zambia for longer periods of time, especially those who travel further afield, others attempt to find work without permits, while some survive through commercial sex work. Zambia's by-laws, enforced by local authorities, do not have provision for foreigners to access vending licenses. The tendency is to encourage Zimbabwean cross-border traders to sell their merchandise wholesale to locals who have market stalls or vending sites. In Zambia, registered or unregistered locals are generally not harassed, while foreigners risk deportation, even when dealing with registered business counterparts. This also provides fertile ground for the corruption of police and immigration officials.

Networks and Help Received while in Zambia

Over the many years that Zimbabwean traders have commuted into Livingstone and elsewhere in Zambia, bonds or affiliations have been forged. Of the respondents, 60 per cent told us they had friends or relatives in Zambia, 40 per cent said otherwise. With the exception of 20 per cent of the traders who told us they lodged with Zambian families while on business, the majority of respondents arranged their own lodging and accommodation:

> We rent a single-roomed house to stay as a group, with each one of us making a contribution of K25,000 to K60,000 for monthly rentals, payable two months upfront in Dambwa township within Livingstone. The rooms are usually overcrowded as some of our colleagues fail to go back home in good time. As a way of cutting costs for accommodation, we even mix with males in one room.

Some of the Zimbabwean cross-border traders find paying for accommodation a major challenge. One commented on the monthly rental of K100,000 that required each of them to contribute K25,000:

> It looks cheap, but you appreciate the real cost when you experience how difficult it is to get that money. Sometimes I stay the whole day with no food. I pay for the rented house here in Livingstone and I also have to pay rent back

home in Zimbabwe at US$35 per month. I am too busy trying to make money. Even as you are interviewing me, I am losing out. We do this to avoid sleeping in bus stations following the fateful accident which happened some time back at the station where innocent lives of suffering Zimbabweans were lost. They were sleeping at the station when a minibus ploughed into them, killing them. Up to now nothing has been done to the minibus driver.

Another made this observation:

Whilst in Zambia, sleeping arrangements are a challenge. To cut down on the cost of lodging, I work illegally as a watchman at night by spending nights within some incomplete building under construction, because buildings take long to finish. If I were to lodge elsewhere, it would mean spending all the money and I would end up going back home with nothing.

Further discussions with Zimbabwean traders revealed that they depend on family connections in Livingstone and other towns in which they trade for their housing requirements. Long-term, non-kin connections are usually established through the traders' own initiative, particularly introductions from regular clients or through other Zimbabwean cross-border traders with whom they have friendships. Most traders who were interviewed indicated that they usually lodged at the same place every time they went to Livingstone or Lusaka and that this enabled them to develop a relationship with their Zambian hosts as known and trusted suppliers of goods. Some of them activated the kin networks of close or distant relatives resident in Zambia to facilitate their CBT. The accommodation issue around families is based on networks that have been developed over a century of migrant labour in the region.

As foreigners in Zambia, the Zimbabwean cross-border traders cannot negotiate for trading spaces in their own right. In this case, the traders hire local people, who then find market stalls. Alternatively, the Zimbabwean traders simply sell their merchandise to local informal traders. Zimbabwean traders are thus constrained through municipal by-laws and complex licensing procedures from reaching the consumer markets directly. In order to circumvent Zambian legalities, Zimbabwean cross-border traders have developed connections with domestic buyers of their products who hold a trading licence to sell their wares at street corners, at officially designated flea markets, or informal shops. They either collaborate with local informal networks in Zambia, which act as bulk buyers and retailers of their products, or resort to selling their merchandise illegally as street hawkers, thus risking arrest and deportation. The most organized cross-border traders deal with established contacts who buy their merchandise with cash or on credit. For many Zimbabwean informal cross-border traders, this is the only way of doing business. As foreigners in Zambia with no possibility of being granted permits to trade legally, they present themselves as either tourists or visiting friends and relatives.

Views from the Border Post

The large number of Zimbabweans crossing into Zambia has obviously been noticed by immigration or border post officials, as manifested by comments made by a senior official:

> We are overwhelmed by the large numbers of Zimbabweans crossing the borders into Zambia for trade in different merchandise. On some days we record as many as 1,000 Zimbabweans coming to Zambia. These cross-border traders like carrying their merchandise in small packages of luggage. The partitioning of merchandise in small packages of luggage by many people makes it difficult to formalize cross-border trade into formal market channels and most taxable commodities pass through the border tax-free. However, even with this challenge, our estimates show that tax revenues have increased by as much as 75 per cent over the period 2006 to 2008.

For Zimbabweans, there are no visa requirements to enter Zambia. When the cross-border traders enter into Zambia, they immediately engage in informal trading activities. Thus, it is obvious that they will be breaking the law, even though they have passed through the customs points and paid duties for their merchandise: this is most often officially recorded as being for 'personal use and not for resale'.

Zambian immigration officials indicated that they understand the serious economic crisis prevailing in Zimbabwe, one which has forced most Zimbabweans into destitution, and in the spirit of 'good neighbourliness' they do not usually follow the law to the letter and rarely arrest or deport the Zimbabweans. It is only in a few instances that they conduct 'clean up exercises' to arrest and deport Zimbabweans who overstay. As an immigration officer observed:

> Any foreigner staying illegally in Zambia is liable to prosecution and deportation and a few Zimbabweans have been charged and deported. [However,] the relationship between Zimbabwean traders and our officers has generally been very good. There is no victimization as long as correct border passes are pre-

sented. Our officers are also aware of the difficulties Zimbabwe and its citizens are experiencing and we try to accommodate them to the best of our abilities as long as they do not involve themselves in criminal activities. There have been unconfirmed reports of some of the Zimbabwean women involving themselves in commercial sex work here in Livingstone. These cases are difficult to deal with as immigration officials. Perhaps our colleagues in the Police Service can handle these, but I know they also do not find it easy to deal with such cases if they do not receive any complaints from members of the public.

It is difficult to determine the extent to which Zambian police and immigration officials have involved themselves in corrupt activities when dealing with Zimbabwean cross-border traders. Discussions with some of the immigration officials seem to indicate that most local officials such as the police, local authorities or immigration simply turn a blind eye to the presence of Zimbabweans involved in illegal trading and other activities.

Future Aspirations

The majority (80 per cent) of the cross-border traders who were interviewed indicated that they would like to continue to engage in this business and the rest (20 per cent) that they would rather obtain formal employment in Zimbabwe as and when the situation improves. One trader who intends to continue to trade in Zambia had this to say:

Even if things in Zimbabwe have improved slightly, as they seem to be, after the power-sharing deal, I will not stop doing this business because Zimbabwe has nothing to offer in terms of business. I have traded on the Zambian soil for more than six years now. I don't go to another country apart from Zambia because Zambians generally are friendly, except for a few instances when some drunken people harass and shout at me and kick my merchandise. However, as most of my fellow Zimbabwean traders will tell you, these incidents are very rare in Zambia but more common in South Africa, Namibia and Botswana.

Another trader observed that:

Even if the power-sharing government has brought a little hope for some people, up to now the majority of us are not yet settled. Maybe things will be better after the elections, of course, depending on who will be the leader. One of my daughters has dropped out of school because I can't afford to pay the US$300 school fees being charged at schools. There are no jobs since most of the companies, which were run by the whites, collapsed after being taken over by black Zimbabweans. Without jobs, even if shops are stocked with merchandise there is no money to buy. Most of us will simply continue with our cross-border trading to bring goods to our Zambian clients.

Summary and Conclusion

From 2006 to 2008, the Zimbabwean economy experienced a sharp decline. Along with unemployment, loss of livelihoods more generally, and production falls in virtually all sectors, the economy also suffered severe hyperinflation. Small-scale trade between Zambia and Zimbabwe became an important source of income for a large number of Zimbabweans with few livelihood options, and trade across the major border posts increased steeply during this period, as indicated by data on border crossings from Livingstone and Siavonga.

As revealed by our informants, this trade included an array of commodities, ranging from foodstuff to clothes and manufactured products. Due to hyperinflation, the preferred form of trade was one where goods brought into Zimbabwe were rapidly exchanged for a different set of goods which were then taken back into Zambia. Goods brought back from Zambia by day-trippers typically included basic food items such as cooking oil, sugar, sweets, biscuits, mealie-meal and bread, all of which were in short supply in Zimbabwe. Traders who habitually stayed for more than a day in Zambia would purchase more durable and higher value-to-volume commodities such as DVDs, CDs, clothes and beauty accessories. Goods taken into Zambia from Zimbabwe included liquors, curtains, duvets and blankets.

Trade in Zambia was perceived as difficult due to competition from Zambian merchants, and prostitution in particular carried additional risks. Some Zimbabwean traders did, however, emphasize that the treatment they received in Zambia was superior to that which they met in Botswana and South Africa, where Zimbabwean 'immigrants' are stigmatized to a greater degree. When selling their goods in Zambia, Zimbabwean cross-border traders would regularly try to aid turnover by undercutting local Zambian market prices. Most goods were sold directly to Zambian consumers but a few traders did manage to trade in bulk to wholesalers, and would then offer bulk rebates. While the normal, petty trade could be affected through use of public transportation, bulk trade requires risky dealings with truck drivers and the like and/or substantial bribes. Also, while petty trade on the Zambian side would typically take place in outdoor markets such as the so-called Zimbabwe market in Livingstone, bulk trade normally demands an established business relationship with a wholesaler. Kinship networks and prior acquaintances could aid in this, but some Zimbabweans had been able to establish more solid business relationships after a period of petty trading.

Day-tripping is attractive for two reasons: it is legal and a higher frequency of visits permits lower volumes and values to be taken across the border. Longer stays demand accommodation and also run the risk of deportation. In terms of accommodation, some of the Zimbabwean traders were able to rely on family or friends on the Zambian side, others would form groups where everyone chipped in for the lease of a home.

Zimbabwean cross-border traders face difficult conditions; while the range of goods they can bring back to Zimbabwe from Zambia generally is in high demand, their commerce on the Zambian side faces stiff competition. Those who stay more than a day, some of whom travel to Lusaka or other more distant markets, face risks related to deportation and transportation. They must often also deal with costs related to accommodation and bribes. Under such terms, it should be clear that the increase in CBT by Zimbabweans first and foremost represents a coping mechanism for people adversely affected by the economic difficulties in Zimbabwe – a temporary solution to serious livelihood problems rather than a lucrative window of opportunity opened up by circumstance. Stabilisation of, or, better yet, recovery in the Zimbabwean economy will undoubtedly have positive effects on the terms under which Zimbabwean traders carry out their business; four of five respondents indicated that they would like to continue trading also after a Zimbabwean recovery.

Nevertheless, it is equally clear that much of the recent trade was facilitated through the long history of cross-border migration and commerce between the two countries and associated kinship, friendship, and business networks already established. To many traders, such networks represent not only an entry point into the Zambian market but also an invaluable source of affordable accommodation and credit.

Notes

1   The authors would like to thank Mr Thomas Simfukwe for invaluable assistance during fieldwork in Livingstone. We are also grateful to all the cross-border traders and immigration officials who took the time to answer our questions. During the

course of the study, the authors benefited from constructive contributions from one anonymous reviewer and two reviewers from the University of Zambia. The views expressed in this paper are those of the authors and do not necessarily reflect the views of the authors' institutions. The usual disclaimer applies and the authors are responsible for any remaining errors and inferences.

2   The names of all the respondents have been changed to protect their identities and for reasons of confidentiality.

Bibliography

Aarnes, D., G. Scott and E. Sjaastad, 1998. *The Potential for Market-Based Agricultural Development in Zambia*, Report to NORAD, Lusaka.

Adelmann, M.,2004, 'Quiet Diplomacy: The Reasons behind Mbeki's Zimbabwe Policy', *Africa Spectrum, 39, (2)), pp. 249-276*

Addison, L.,2007, 'Zimbabwean Farm Workers in Northern South Africa', *Review of African Political Economy*, Vol. 114, pp. 619-635.

Afrobarometer, 2010, Tolerance in South Africa: Exploring Popular Attitudes toward Foreigners. East Lansing: Afrobarometer Briefing Paper No. 82.

Agamben, G., 1998. *Homo Sacer: Sovereign Power and Bare Life (Meridian: Crossing Aesthetics.* Palo Alto: Stanford University Press

Åkesson, G., A. Calengo and C. Tanner, 2009. 'It's not a question of doing it or not doing it – it's a question of how to do it. Study on Community Land Rights in Niassa Province, Mozambique'. SLU Report, Sweden.

AIM, 2006. 'Manica: miracle or mirage?', *Mozambiquefile* No. 360, July.

Albertyn, C., 2009. 'Beyond Citizenship: Human Rights and Democracy'. in S. Hassim, T. Kupe, & E. Worby, *Go Home or Die Here: Violence, Xenophobia and The Reinvention of Difference in South Africa.* Johannesburg: Wits University Press.

Alexander, J., 1997, 'The local state in post-war Mozambique: political practice and ideas about authority', *Africa*, 67(1), pp. 1-26.

Alexander, J. and G. Kynoch, 2011. 'Introduction: Histories and Legacies of Punishment in Southern Africa', *Journal of Southern African Studies*, Vol. 37(3), pp. 395-413.

Alexander, J., J. McGregor and T. Ranger, 2000. *Violence and Memory: One Hundred Years in the 'Dark Forests' of Matabeleland.* Portsmouth, NH: Heinemann.

Allina-Pisano, E., 2003. 'Borderland, Boundaries, and the Contours of Colonial Rule: African Labor in Manica District, Mozambique, c. 1904-1908', *International Journal of African Historical Studies* Vol. 3,(1), pp.59-82.

Amit, R., 2011. 'The Zimbabwean Documentation Process: Lessons Learned',

African Center of Migration Studies, Research Report, pp. 1-29.

Balibar, E., 2010. 'At the Borders of Citizenship: A Democracy in Translation?', *European Journal of Social Theory*, Vol. 13(3), pp. 315-322.

Balsan, F., 1970, 'Ancient gold routes of the Monomotapa kingdom', *The Geographical Journal*, 136 (2), pp.240-246.

Bannerman, J. H., 1993, 'Bvumba. Estado pré-colonial Shona em Manica, na fronteira entre Moçambique e o Zimbabwe', *Arquivo, Boletim do Arquivo Histórico de Moçambique* (13):81-98.

Bannerman, J., 2007. *An Historical Background to the Bandire Mine and Environs from about 1000 AD to the Present*. Baobab Mining Company.

Baumann, C.M. 2010. *A Legal and Ethical Analysis of the South African Government's Response toward Zimbabwe Immigrants*. MA thesis, Stellenbosch University:.

Bauman, Z., 2000. *Liquid Modernity*. London: Polity Press.

Bayart, J.F. 2009. *The State in Africa*, second edition. London: Polity Press.

BBC, 2006. 'Profile: Zambia's "King Cobra"', *BBC News Online*, 29 September.

— 2007. 'Zimbabwe Crisis "Like Titanic"', *BBC News Online*, 21 March 21.

Beekman, P.W., 2011, 'PROIRRI consultancy, identification of the irrigation potential for smallholder horticulture in the uplands of Manica and Sofala Provinces, Final report', Consultancy study undertaken for the World Bank sponsored PROIRRI programme, Chimoio, Mozambique.

Bentham, J., 1995 (1787). 'Panopticon', in M. Bozovic (ed.), *The Panopticon Writings*. London: Verso.

Berry, J.W., 2001. 'A Psychology of Immigration', *Journal of Social Issues*. Vol. 57(3), pp 615-631.

Bertelsen, B. E., 2010, 'Violent becomings. State formation and the traditional field in colonial and postcolonial Mozambique'. PhD thesis, University of Bergen.

Blair, D., 2002. *Degrees in Violence: Robert Mugabe and the Struggle for Power in Zimbabwe*. London and New York: Continuum.

Bolding, A., 2004, 'In Hot Water: A study on intervention models and practices of water use in small-holder agriculture, Nyanyadzi catchment, Zimbabwe'. PhD thesis, Wageningen University.

— 2007a, 'The dynamics of smallholder irrigation furrows along the Mozambique-Zimbabwe border: A resilient force of agrarian modernization or last resort for marginal communities?' Paper presented at the AEGIS conference in Leiden, The Netherlands, July 11-14.

— 2007b. 'Methodological problems associated with the MARRP 1991 re-study', mimeo.

— 2008, 'Going for (liquid) Gold. The differentiated impact of the Zimbabwe crisis on gold panning and furrow irrigation in central Mozambique'. Paper presented at a CERES-IWE research seminar, 'Good news from Zimbabwe? Promising initiatives emerging from the crisis', 12 November, Wageningen.

Bolding, A., N.C. Post Uiterweer and J. Schippers, 2010. 'The fluid nature of hydraulic property: a case study of Mukudu, Maira and Penha Longa irrigation furrows in the upper Revue river, Manica District, Mozambique', in *Water rights in informal economies in the Limpopo and Volta basins*, CGIAR Challenge Programme Project 66,.

Bolt, M., 2010. 'Cameraderie and its Discontents: Class Consciousness, Ethnicity and Divergent Masculinities among Zimbabwean Migrant Farmworkers in South Africa', *Journal of Southern African Studies*, Vol. 36(2), pp. 377-393.

Bond, P., 1998. *Uneven Zimbabwe: A Study of Finance, Development and Underdevelopment*. Trenton, NJ: Africa World Press.

Bond, P and M. Manyanya, 2002. *Zimbabwe's Plunge: Exhausted Nationalism, Neoliberalism and the Search for Social Justice*. Pietermaritzburg and Harare: University of Natal Press and Weaver Press.

Borras Jr, S.M., R. Hall, I. Scoones, B. White and W. Wolford, 2011. 'Towards a better understanding of global land grabbing: an editorial introduction', *Journal of Peasant Studies*, Vol. 38(2), pp. 209-216.

Bruce, J. W. and P. P. Dorner, 1982. 'Agricultural Land Tenure in Zambia: Perspectives, Problems and Opportunities', University of Wisconsin, Madison: Land Tenure Center Research Paper no. 76.

Bulawayo 24, 2012. 'Zambian President, Sata Answers Zimbabwean Critics', *Bulawayo 24*, 7 June.

Buur, L., 2011. 'Mozambique Synthesis Analysis. Between Pockets of Efficiency and Elite Capture'. Unpublished research paper.

Carmody, P. and S. Taylor, 2003. 2. 'Industry and the Urban Sector in Zimbabwe's Political Economy', *African Studies Quarterly*, Vol. 7(2/3), pp. 53-80.

Carter, D., 2011. 'Sources of State Legitimacy in Contemporary South Africa: A Theory of Political Good'. East Lansing, MI: Afrobarometer Working Paper No. 134.

CCJP, 1997. *Breaking the Silence, Building True Peace: A Report on the Disturbances in Matabeleland and the Midlands 1980 to 1988*. Harare: The Catholic Commission for Justice and Peace in Zimbabwe and the Legal Resources Foundation.

Chari, U., 2004. 'Informal Cross-border Trade and Gender'. Report of the Regional Workshop for SADC Informal Traders, 11-12 February, Harare.

Chifuwe, S., 2003a. 'Zimbabwe's Sovereignty Should Be Defended – Levy Mwanawasa', *The Post*, 11 May.

— 2003b. 'President Opposes Zimbabwe's Suspension from Commonwealth', *The Post*, 4 December.

Chinaka, C., 2007. 'Crumbling Economy Threatens Mugabe's Grip'. *Mail & Guardian Online*, 30 August 2007.

Chingono, M.F., 2001, 'Mozambique: war, economic change and development in Manica Province, 1982-1992', in F. Stewart, and V. FitzGerald (eds), *War and Underdevelopment, Volume 2: Country experiences*. Oxford: Oxford University Press.

Coetzee, J. M., 1983. *Life & Times Of Michael K*. London: Penguin Books.

— 2001. *The Lives Of Animals*. Princeton: Princeton University Press.

Compagnon, D., 2011. *A Predictable Tragedy: Robert Mugabe and the Collapse of Zimbabwe*. Philadelphia: University of Pennsylvania Press.

Consortium for Refugees and Migrants in South Africa (CoRMSA), 2009. *Report to the Government of The Republic of South Africa on the Humanitarian Crisis in Musina, South Africa*. http://www.cormsa.org.za/wpcontent/uploads/Resources/Crisis_in_Musina.pdf Accessed on September 24, 2010.

Coplan, D., 2008. 'Crossing Borders', in S. Hassim, et al., *Go Home or Die Here*.

Cousins, B. (ed.), 2000. *At the Crossroads. Land and Agrarian Reform in South Africa into the 21st Century*. Cape Town: PLAAS and NLC .

— 2002. 'Legislating Negotiability: Tenure Reform in Post-Apartheid South Africa', in K. Juul, and C. Lund (eds), *Negotiating Property in Africa*. Portsmouth, NH: Heinemann.

— (2003). 'The Zimbabwe Crisis in its Wider Context: The Politics of Land, Democracy and Development in Southern Africa', in A. Hammar, et al., *Zimbabwe's Unfinished Business*.

Cousins, B., D. Weiner and N. Amin, 1992. 'Social Differentiation In The Communal Lands Of Zimbabwe', *Review Of African Political Economy*, Vol.53, pp. 5-24.

Cravinho, J., 1995. *Modernizing Mozambique: Frelimo ideology and the Frelimo State*. DPhil thesis, Oxford University.

Cramer, C., 2001. 'Privatisation and Adjustment in Mozambique: A 'Hospital Pass'?', *Journal of Southern African Studies*, Vol. 27(1), pp. 79-103.

Crush, J., 1999. 'Fortress South Africa and the Deconstruction of Apartheid's Migration Regime'. *Geoforum*, Vol. 30, pp. 1-11.

Crush, J., 2000. 'The Dark side of Democracy: Migration, Xenophobia and Human rights in South Africa', *International Migration*, Vol. 38(6) pp. 103-133.

Crush, J. and B. Dodson, 2007. 'Another Lost Decade: The Failures of South Africa's Post-Apartheid Migration Policy', *Tijdschrift voor economische en sociale geografie*, Vol. 8(4) pp. 436–454.

Crush, J. and B. Frayne, 2007. 'The Migration and Development Nexus in Southern Africa', *Development Southern Africa*, Vol. 24(1), pp. 1-23.

— 2010. *Surviving on the Move: Migration, Poverty and Development in Southern Africa*. Pretoria: IDASA.

Crush, J. and D. Tevera (eds), 2010. *Zimbabwe's Exodus: Crisis, Migration, Survival*.

Cape Town and Ottawa: Southern African Migration Programme and International Development Research Centre.

Crush, J., A. Chikanda and G. Tawodzera, 2012. *The Third Wave: Mixed Migration from Zimbabwe to South Africa*. Cape Town: Southern African Migration Programme.

Cunningham, S., 1981. *The Copper Industry in Zambia: Foreign Mining Companies in a Developing Country*. New York: Praeger.

Cusworth, J., 2000. 'A Review of the UK ODA Evaluation of the Land Resettlement Programme in 1988 and the Land Appraisal Mission of 1996', in T.A.S. Bowyer-Bower and C. Stoneman (eds), *Land Reform in Zimbabwe: Constraints and Prospects*. Aldershot: Ashgate Press.

Da Costa, M.A., 1940. *Do Zambeze ao paralelo 22*. Beira: Imprensa da Companhia de Moçambique.

Danso, R. and D. McDonald, 2001. 'Writing Xenophobia: Immigration and the press in post-apartheid South Africa', *Africa Today* Vol. 48(3) pp. 115-137.

Davis, S. M. 1987. *Apartheid's Rebels: Inside South Africa's Hidden War*. New Haven: Yale University Press.

Dashwood, H.S., 2000. *The Political Economy of Transformation*. Toronto: University of Toronto Press.

Derman, B., R. Odgaard and E. Sjaastad (eds), 2007. *Introduction to Citizenship and Identity: Conflicts over Land and Water in Contemporary Africa*. London: James Currey.

Derman, B., A. Hellum, and S. Shirinda, 2010. 'Land to the Tiller: A Case Study of the Nkuzi Development Association, Limpopo Province, South Africa'. Unpublished manuscript.

Derman, B., E. Lahiff and E. Sjaastad, 2010. 'Strategic Questions about Strategic Partners: Challenges and Pitfalls in South Africa's New Model of Land Restitution', in C. Walker, A. Bohlin, R. Hall and T. Kepe (eds), *Land, Memory, Reconstruction, and Justice: Perspectives on Land Claims in South Africa*. Athens, OH: Ohio University Press.

Desai, A., 2008. 'Xenophobia and Cape Town'. Cape Town: Media Monitoring Project for the Centre for the Study of Violence and Reconciliation.

De Schutter, O., 2011. 'How not to think of land-grabbing. Three critiques of large-scale investments in farmland', *Journal of Peasant Studies*, Vol. 38(2), pp. 249-80.

De Soto, H., 2000. *The Mystery of Capital: Why Capitalism Triumphs In the West and Fails Everywhere Else*. New York: Basic Books.

Detels, R. 1997. *Methods of Public Health*. Oxford: Oxford University Press.

De Wit, Paul, 2000. 'Land Law Reform in Mozambique: Acquired Values and Needs for Consolidation'. *Land Reform/Réforme Agraire/Reforma Agrarian*, 2000/2. Online version.

Diken, B. and C. B. Laustsen, 2005. *The Culture Of Exception: Sociology Facing The Camp*. London: Routledge.

Dondeyne, S., E. Ndunguru, F. Cesario, P. Jantar, F. Nhaca and P. Rafael, 2007. *Em busca do ouro. Implicações ambientais e socio-economicas para uma politica de desenvolvimento sustentável'*. Centro de Desenvolvimento Sustentável de Recursos Naturais (CDS), Chimoio.

Dondeyne, S., E. Ndunguru, P. Rafael and J. Bannerman, 2009, 'Artisanal mining in central Mozambique: policy and environmental issues of concern', *Resources Policy*, 34(1-2), pp. 45-50.

Donham, D., 2011. *Violence in a Time of Liberation: Murder and Ethnicity at a South African Gold Mine, 1994*. Durham and London: Duke University Press.

Dorman, S., D. Hammett and P. Nugent, 2007. 'Introduction: Citizenship and its Casualties in Africa', in S. Dorman, D. Hammett and P. Nugent (eds), *Making Nations, Creating Strangers: States and Citizenship in Africa*. Leiden: Brill.

Duffield, M., 2001. 'Governing the Borderlands: Decoding The Power of Aid', *Disasters*, 25(4), pp. 308–20.

— 2007. 'Development, Territories, and People: Consolidating The External Sovereign Frontier', *Alternatives: Global, Local, Political*, 32(2), pp. 225–246.

Dugger, C.W., 2009. 'Zambia: A Reversal on Anticorruption Efforts', *New York Times*, 27 August.

Durang, T., 2004, 'Annex 10 – Planning with regards to land and the management of natural resources', in T. Durang, 'Natural resources management support, Manica and Tete province, Mozambique'. DPADR Manica, Chimoio.

Durang, T. and C. Tanner, 2004. 'Access to land and other natural resources for local communities in Mozambique: Current Examples from Manica Province'. Presentation to Green Agri Net Conference on 'Land Registration in Practice', Denmark, 1-2 April.

Duri, F.P.T., 2009. 'Informal negotiation of national borders for survival: The foray of Mutare's marginalised people to and from Mozambique, 2000-2008'. Paper presented at colloquium, 'Exploring the Hidden Dimensions of the Zimbabwe Crisis', Wits University, Johannesburg, 1-2 July

— 2010. 'Informal Negotiation of the Zimbabwe-Mozambique Border for Survival by Mutare's Marginalized People', *Journal of Developing Societies*, Vol. 26(2), pp.125-63.

Du Toit, A., 1993. 'The Micro-Politics of Paternalism: The Discourses of Management and Resistance on South African Fruit and Wine Farms', *Journal of Southern African Studies*, Vol. 15, pp. 287-305.

Eriksen, S.S., 2000. 'Close Links and Blurred Boundaries: Council and Community in a Tanzanian and a Zimbabwean District'. PhD thesis, University of Oslo.

Ewert, J. and A. du Toit, 2005. 'A Deepening Divide in the Countryside: Restructuring and Rural Livelihoods in the South African Wine Industry", *Journal of Southern African Studies*, Vol. 31, pp. 315-332.

FCTZ, 1999. Unpublished Survey. Harare: Farm Community Trust of Zimbabwe.

— 2003. 'The Situation of Commercial Farm Workers in Zimbabwe after Land Reform'. Report prepared for the Farm Community Trust of Zimbabwe, Harare.

Felix, B., 2007. 'Zimbabweans Flee To More Misery In SA'. *Mail & Guardian Online*, 31 August.

Ferguson, J., 2006. *Global Shadow: Africa in the Neoliberal World Order*. Durham, NC: Duke University Press

First, R. 1983. *Black Gold: The Mozambican Miner, Proletarian and Peasant*. Brighton and New York: Harvester Press and St Martin's Press.

Forced Migration Studies Programme and Musina Legal Advice Office, 2007. 'Special Report: Fact Or Fiction? Examining Zimbabwean Cross-Border Migration Into Limpopo'. Johannesburg: Forced Migration Studies Programme, Wits University.

Foucault, M., 1998 (1976). *The History Of Sexuality Volume 1: The Will To Knowledge*. London: Penguin.

Freeman, L., 2005. 'South Africa's Zimbabwe Policy: Unraveling the Contradictions', *Journal of Contemporary African Studies*, Vol. 23(2), pp. 147-172.

French, H. W., 2010. 'The Next Empire', *Atlantic Magazine*, May.

Fuller, A., 2003. *Don't Let's Go to the Dogs Tonight*. London: Picador.

Gava, J., 2007. 'Zimbabwe: Mugabe Blasts Mwanawasa', *Zimdaily.com*, 7 September.

Gavin, C., 2010. 'The Role of SADC in Managing Political Crisis and Conflict: The Cases of Madagascar and Zimbabwe'. Maputo: FES Africa Security Policy Network Peace and Security Series No. 2.

Geloo, Z., 2004. 'Nation Reaps Benefit from Zimbabwean Farmers', Inter Press News Agency, 2 January.

Gevisser, M., 2007. *Thabo Mbeki: The Dream Deferred*. Cape Town and Johannesburg: Jonathan Ball.

Goebel, A., 2005. 'Is Zimbabwe the Future of South Africa? The Implications for Land Reform in Southern Africa', *Journal of Contemporary Africa Studies*, Vol. 23(3), pp. 345-70.

Gould, J., 2007. 'Zambia's 2006 Elections: The Ethnicization of Politics?' *News from the Nordic African Institute (NAI)*..

GoZ, 2003. 'Report of the Presidential Land Review Committee' (Utete Report), Vols. I and II. Harare: Government of Zimbabwe.

Gumede, W., 2005. *Thabo Mbeki and the Battle for the Soul of the ANC*. Cape Town: Zebra Press.

Hall, R., 2003. 'Farm Tenure', in R. Hall (ed.), *Evaluating Land and Agrarian Reform In South Africa. An Occasional Paper Series; No. 3*. Cape Town: Institute for Poverty, Land and Agrarian Studies (PLAAS), University of The Western Cape.

— 2004. *Land and Agrarian Reform in South Africa: A Status Report.* Cape Town: Programme of Land and Agrarian Studies

Hammar, A., 2008. 'In the Name of Sovereignty: Displacement and State Making in Post-independence Zimbabwe', *Journal of Contemporary African Studies*, Vol. 26(4), pp.417-34.

Hammar, A., 2010. 'Ambivalent Mobilities: Zimbabwean Commercial Farmers in Mozambique', *Journal of Southern African Studies*, Vol. 36(2), pp.395-416.

— forthcoming 2013. '"Becoming Mozambicanised": Reflections on Zimbabweans Adapting to "Disorder" in Mozambique', in V. Dantas e Sá, P. Gupta, F. Noa and E. Rodary (eds), *The Mozambique Reader.* Johannesburg: Wits University Press.

Hammar, A., B. Raftopoulos and S. Jensen (eds), 2003. *Zimbabwe's Unfinished Business: Rethinking Land, State and Nation in the Context of Crisis.* Harare: Weaver Press.

Hammar, A. and G. Rodgers, 2008. 'Introduction: Notes on political economies of displacement in southern Africa', *Journal of Contemporary African Studies*, Vol. 26(4), pp.355-70.

Hammar, A., J. McGregor and L. Landau, 2010. 'Displacing Zimbabwe: Crisis and Construction in Southern Africa', *Journal of Southern African Studies*, Vol. 36(2), pp. 263-283

Hanke, S., 2008. *Zimbabwe: From Hyperinflation to Growth.* Washington, DC: Cato Institute.

Hanke, S. and A. Kwok, 2009. 'On the Measurement of Zimbabwe's Hyperinflation', *Cato Journal* 2009 (2), 353-64

Hanlon, J., 2004. 'Renewed Land Debate and the "Cargo Cult" in Mozambique', *Journal of Southern African Studies*, Vol. 30(3), pp. 603-626.

— 2010. 'Prefácio', in C. Serra (ed.), *A construção social do Outro: Perspectivas cruzadas sobre estrangeiros e Moçambicanos.* Maputo: Imprensa Universitária.

— 2011. *Understanding Land Investment Deals in Africa. Country Report: Mozambique,* Oakland: The Oakland Institute.

Hanlon, J. and T. Smart, 2008. 'O Milagre de Manico acabou', in J. Hanlon and T. Smart (eds), *Há Mais Bicicletas – mas há Desenvolvimento?* Maputo: Missanga/CIEDIMA.

Hanlon, J., and T. Smart, 2008. *Do Bicycles Equal Development in Mozambique?* Oxford: James Currey.

Hanlon, J. and M. Mosse, 2010. 'Mozambique's Elite – Finding its Way in a Globalized World and Returning to Old Development Models'. UNU-WIDER Working Paper No. 2010/105. Helsinki: UNU-WIDER.

Harber, A., 2012. *Diepsloot*. Johannesburg and Cape Town: Jonathan Ball

Hardt, M. and A. Negri, 2000. *Empire*. Cambridge, MA: Harvard University Press.

Harris, B., 2001. 'A Foreign Experience: Violence, crime and xenophobia during South Africa's transition'. *Violence and Transition Series*, Vol 5. Centre for the Study of Violence.

— 2002. 'Xenophobia: A new pathology for a new South Africa?' in D. Hook and G. Eagle (eds), *Psychopathology and Social Prejudice*. Cape Town: University of Cape Town Press.

Hartnack, A., 2009. 'Transcending Global and National (Mis)Representations through Local Responses to Displacement: The Case Of Zimbabwean (Ex-) Farm Workers', *Journal Of Refugee Studies*, Vol. 22(3), pp. 351–377.

Hassim, S., T. Kupe and E. Worby (eds), 2008. *Go Home or Die Here: Violence, Xenophobia and the Reinvention of Difference in South Africa*. Johannesburg: Wits University Press.

Hellum, A. and B. Derman, 2004. 'Land Reform and Human Rights in Contemporary Zimbabwe: Balancing Individual and Social Justice through an Integrated Human Rights Framework', *World Development*, Vol. 32(10), pp. 1785-1805.

— 2009. 'Government, Business and Chiefs: Ambiguities of Social Justice through Land Restitution in South Africa', in F. and K. von Benda Beckmann and J. Eckert (eds), *Rules of Law and Laws of Ruling*. Aldershot: Ashgate.

Herman, E., 2006. 'Migration as a Family Business: The Role of Personal Networks in the Mobility Phase of Migration', in *International Migration*. Vol. 44(4), pp. 191-230.

Holtzclaw, H., 2004. *The Third Chimurenga?* 'Political Violence and Survival in Zimbabwe's Commercial Farming Communities'. PhD thesis, Michigan State University.

Hughes, D.M., 1999. 'Refugees and Squatters: Immigration and the Politics of Territory on the Zimbabwe-Mozambique Border', *Journal of Southern African Studies*, Vol. 25(4), pp. 533-52.

— 2006. *From Enslavement to Environmentalism: Politics on a Southern African Frontier*. Seattle: University of Washington Press.

— 2010. *Whiteness in Zimbabwe: Race, Landscape, and the Problem of Belonging*. New York: Palgrave Macmillan.

Human Rights Watch, 2005. 'Zimbabwe: Evicted and Forsaken: Internally displaced persons in the aftermath of Operation Murambatsvina'. New York: Human Rights Watch.

Human Rights Watch, 2006. 'Unprotected Migrants: Zimbabweans in South Africa's Limpopo Province'. New York: Human Rights Watch.

— 2008. 'Neighbors in Need: Zimbabweans Seeking Refuge in South Africa'. New

York: Human Rights Watch.

— 2009. 'No Healing Here: Violence, Discrimination and Barriers to Health for Migrants in South Africa'. New York: Human Rights Watch.

Human Sciences Research Council, 2008. 'Citizenship, Violence and Xenophobia in South Africa: Perceptions from South African Communities'. Pretoria: Human Sciences Research Council.

Hunter, M., 2010. *Love in the Time of AIDS: Inequality, Gender, and Rights in South Africa*. Bloomington: Indiana University Press.

Huo, T., 2010. 'Analise estatística de percepções em Maputo, Maputo Beira, Nampula e Pemba', in C. Serra (ed.), *A construção social do Outro: Perspectivas cruzadas sobre estrangeiros e Moçambicanos*. Maputo: Imprensa Universitária.

ICG, 2005. 'Zimbabwe's Operation Murambatsvina: The Tipping Point?' International Crisis Group Africa Report No. 97.

— 2008. 'Negotiating Zimbabwe's Transition'. International Crisis Group Africa Report No. 138.

IDMC, 2008. 'The Many Faces of Displacement: IDPs in Zimbabwe'. Geneva: Internal Displacement Monitoring Centre.

IDMC/NRC, 2009. 'Zimbabwe: Quick Facts'. London: Internal Displacement Monitoring Centre and The Norwegian Refugee Council.

IDMPAIM, 2006. An Interview with Joseph Hanlon. IDMPAIM News (Maputo), May 17.

Ikdahl, I., A. Hellum, R. Kaarhus and R.A. Benjaminsen, 2005. 'Human Rights, Formalisation and Women's Land Rights in Southern and Eastern Africa'. Ås: Noragric Report No. 26.

Insider, 2011. 'Mwanawasa Accused Mbeki of Being Insincere about Zimbabwe', *The Insider*, 19 December.

Instituto Nacional de Estatística, 1999. *II Recenseamento Geral da População e Habitação 1997*, (Resultados Definitivos). Maputo: Estatísticas Oficias.

International Labour Office, 1998. 'Labour Migration to South Africa in the 1990s'. Policy Paper Series No. 4. International Labour Office: South Africa Multidisciplinary Advisory Team.

International Finance Corporation, 1996. 'Mozambique – Administrative Barriers to Investment: The Red Tape Analysis'. Washington: Foreign Investment Analysis.

International Organization for Migration, 2003. 'Mobility and HIV/Aids in Southern Africa: A Field Study in South Africa, Zimbabwe and Mozambique'. Pretoria: IOM, CARE and SIDA.

— 2009. 'Migrants' Needs and Vulnerabilities in the Limpopo Province, Republic of South Africa, Report on Phase One November-December 2008'. Pretoria: IOM.

— 2010. 'Integrated Biological and Behavioural Surveillance Survey in the Commercial Agricultural Sector in South Africa'. Pretoria: IOM.

Ikdahl, I., A. Hellum, R.Kaarhus, T.A. Benjaminsen, P. Kameri-Mbote, 2005.'Human rights, formalisation and women's land rights in southern and eastern Africa'.*Studies in Women Law* No. 57, Institute of Women's Law, University of Oslo.

IRIN News, 2008. 'Zambia: Rising Levels of Resentment towards Zimbabweans', *IRIN News*, 9 June.

Jeeves, A., 1985. *Migrant Labour in South Africa's Mining Economy: The Struggle for the Gold Mines' Labour Supply, 1890-1920*. Montreal: McGill-Queen's University Press.

Jeeves, A. and J. Crush., 1997. *White Farms, Black Labor: The State and Agrarian Change In Southern Africa, 1910-50*. Portsmouth, NH: Heinemann.

Jeeves, A., J. Crush, and D. Yudelman, 1991. *South Africa's Labor Empire: A History of Black Migrancy to the Gold Mines*. Boulder: Westview.

Johnston, D., 2007, 'Who Needs Immigrant Farm Workers? A South African Case Study', *Journal of Agrarian Change*, Vol. 7(4), pp. 494-525.

Juergensen, O. and H.P. Krugman, 1997. 'Paradise Lost? A Blueprint for Niassa', *Southern Africa Report*, Vol. 12(2).

Justice for Agriculture. 2008. 'Destruction of Zimbabwe's Backbone Industry in Pursuit of Political Power: A Qualitative Report on Events in Zimbabwe's Commercial Farming Sector since the Year 2000'. Report prepared by the Justice for Agriculture Trust and the General Agricultural and Plantation Workers Union of Zimbabwe.

Kaarhus, R. and P. Rebelo, 2003. 'CSOs and SWAPS: The role of civil society organizations in the health sector in Mozambique'. *Noragric Report No. 16*. Ås: Norwegian University of Life Sciences, UMB.

Kaarhus, R., R. Haug, J.P. Hella and J.R. Makindara, 2010. 'Agro-Investments in Africa – Impacts on Land and Livelihood in Mozambique and Tanzania'. *Noragric Report No. 53*. Ås: Norwegian University of Life Sciences, UMB.

Kaarhus, R. and P. Woodhouse, 2012. 'Development of National Producer Organizations and Specialized Business Units in Mozambique'. *Noragric Report No. 63*. Ås: Norwegian University of Life Sciences, UMB.

Kaarhus, R., with S. Martins, 2012. 'How to Support Women's Land Rights in Mozambique? Approaches and Lessons Learnt in the Work of Four Main Organizations'. *NORAD Report: Discussion 3/2012*. http://www.norad.no/en/tools-and-publications/publications/norad-reports/publication?key=390188

Kawadza, S. and T. Maodza, 2012. 'Mugabe Describes Zambia, Zim as Siamese Twins', *The Post Online*, 28 April.

Keller, B., 1992. 'Bloemfontein Journal: Path of the "Trekboers" Skirts Africa's

Realities', *New York Times*, October 31.

Kelsall, T. and D. Booth, with D. Cammack and F. Golooba-Mutebi, 2010. 'Developmental Patrimonialism? Questioning the Orthodoxy on Political Governance and Economic Progress in Africa'. Africa Power & Politics Working Paper No. 9. London: Overseas Development Institute.

Kinsey, B., 2000. 'The Implications of Land Reform for Rural Welfare', in T.A.S. Bowyer-Bower and C. Stoneman (eds), *Land Reform in Zimbabwe: Constraints and Prospects*. Aldershot: Ashgate.

Kiwanuka, M. and T. Monson, 2009. 'Zimbabwean Migration into Southern Africa: New Trends and Responses'. Johannesburg: Forced Migration Studies Programme, Wits University.

Krikler, J., 1993. *Revolution from Above, Rebellion from Below: The Agrarian Transvaal at the Turn of the Century*. Oxford: Oxford University Press.

Kritzinger, A., S. Barrientos and H. Rossouw, 2004. 'Global Production and Flexible Employment in South African Horticulture: Experiences of Contract Workers in Fruit Exports', *Sociologia Ruralis*, Vol. 44, pp. 17-39.

Lafraniere, S., 2004. 'Zimbabwe's White Farmers Start Anew in Zambia', *New York Times*, 21 March.

Lahiff, E., 2003. 'Land and Livelihoods: The Politics of Land Reform in Southern Africa', *IDS Bulletin* Vol. 34(3), pp. 54-63.

— 2003. 'The Politics of Land Reform in Southern Africa'. Sussex: Institute of Development Studies Research Paper No. 19.

Lan, D., 1985. *Guns and Rain: Guerrillas and Spirit Mediums in Zimbabwe*. Los Angeles and Berkeley: University of California Press.

Landau, L., 2010. 'Discrimination and Development? Migration, Urbanization and Sustainable Livelihoods in South Africa's Forbidden Cities', in J. Crush and B. Frayne, *Surviving on the Move*.

— 2011. 'Postscript: Positive values and the Politics of Outsiderness', in L. Landau (ed.), *Exorcising the Demons within: Xenophobia, Violence and Statecraft in Contemporary South Africa*, Johannesburg: University of Witwatersrand Press.

Landau, L. and A. W. Segatti, 2009. *Human Development Impacts of Migration: South Africa Case Study*. UNDP Human Development Reports Research Paper.

Langford, M., B. Derman, T. Madlingozi, K. Moyo, J. Dugard, A. Hellum and S. Shirinda, 2013. 'South Africa: From Struggle to Idealism and Back Again', in G. Crawford and B.A. Andreassen (eds) *Human Rights, Power And Civic Action*. London: Routledge.

Larmer M. and A. Fraser, 2007. 'Of Cabbages and King Cobra: Populist Politics and Zambia's 2006 Election', *African Affairs*, Vol. 106, pp. 611–637.

Lerner, A., S. Roberts and C. Matlala, 2009. *Race and Migration in the Community Media: Local Stories, Common Stereotypes*. Pretoria: Media Monitoring Africa.

Li, T.M., 2011. 'Centering Labor in the Land Grab Debate', *Journal of Peasant Studies*, Vol. 38(2), pp. 281-98.

Little, P.D. and M.J. Watts (eds), 1994. *Living Under Contract. Contract Farming and Agrarian Transformation in Sub-Saharan Africa*. Madison: University of Wisconsin Press.

Lodge, T., 2004. 'Quiet Diplomacy in Zimbabwe: A Case Study of South Africa in Africa'. Paper delivered to the African Studies Centre, Leiden.

Lubkemann, S.C., 2008. *Culture in Chaos: Anthropology of the Social Condition in War*. Chicago: University of Chicago Press.

Mabvurira, V., T. Masuka, R. G. Banda and R. Frank, 2012. 'A Situational Analysis of Former Commercial Farm Workers in Zimbabwe, a Decade after the Jambanja', *Journal of Emerging Trends in Economics and Management Sciences*, Vol. 3(3): pp. 221-228.

Magaramombe, G., 2001. 'Rural Poverty: Commercial Farm Workers and Land Reform in Zimbabwe'. Paper presented at the SARPN Conference on Land Reform and Poverty Alleviation in Southern Africa, Pretoria.

Magaramombe, G., 2010. 'Displaced in Place: Agrarian Displacements, Replacements and Resettlement among Farm Workers in Mazowe District', *Journal of Southern African Studies*, Vol. 36(2), pp. 361-375.

Magunha, F., A. Bailey and L. Cliffe, 2009. *Remittance Strategies of Zimbabweans in Northern England*. School of Geography, University of Leeds.

Makina, D., 2010. 'Zimbabwe in Johannesburg', in J. Crush and D. Tevera (eds), *Zimbabwe's Exodus*.

Makumbe, J. M., and D. Compagnon, 2000. *Behind the Smokescreen: The Politics of Zimbabwe's 1995 General Elections*. Harare: University of Zimbabwe Publications.

Malupenga, A., 2009. *Levy Patrick Mwanawasa: An Incentive for Posterity*. Grahamstown: NISC.

Maphosa, F., 2007. 'Remittances and Development: The Impact of Migration to South Africa on Rural Livelihoods in Southern Zimbabwe', *Development Southern Africa*, Vol. 24(1), pp. 123-135.

Marcus, T., 1989. *Modernizing Super-Exploitation: Restructuring South African Agriculture*. London: Zed Books.

Marini, A., 2001. 'Partnership Between Local Peasants and Large Commercial Investors: The Case of the Sugar Sector in Mozambique', *Land Reform/Réforme Agraire/Reforma Agrarian*, 2001/2. Online version.

Martin, D. and P. Johnson, 1981. *The Struggle for Zimbabwe: The Chimurenga War*. New York: Monthly Review Press.

Mattes, R., 2011. *The 'Born Frees': The Prospects for Generational Change in Post-Apartheid South Africa*. Afrobarometer Working Paper No. 131. Pretoria: IDASA.

Mazula, B. (ed.), 2004. *Mozambique: 10 Years of Peace*, Maputo: Center for Democracy and Development.

Mbeki, T., 2003. 'The People of Zimbabwe Must Decide Their Own Future', *ANC Today*, 9-15 May.

McDonald, D. and S. Jacobs, 2005. '(Re)writing Xenophobia: Understanding Press Coverage of Cross-Border Migration in Southern Africa', *Journal of Contemporary African Studies* Vol. 23(3), pp. 295-325.

McGregor, J. and R. Primorac (eds), 2010. *Zimbabwe's New Diaspora: Displacement and the Cultural Politics of Survival*. New York and Oxford: Berghahn Books.

McKinley, D., 2004. 'South African Foreign Policy towards Zimbabwe under Mbeki', *Review of African Political Economy*, Vol. 31(100), pp. 357-364.

Ministério da Administração Estatal (MAE), 2005. *Perfil do Distrito de Manica, Província de Manica, edição 2005*. Ministério da Administração Estatal, República de Moçambique.

Misago, J.P., 2009. 'Xenophobic Violence in South Africa: Reflections on Causal Factors and Implications', *Synopsis*, the Policy Studies Bulletin of the Centre for Policy Studies. Vol. 10(3), pp. 3-9.

Moffat, U., 1963. 'Settled Investors,' *The Central African Examiner*, May.

Mohapatra, S., D. Ratha, and E. Scheja, 2010. 'Impact of Migration on Economic and Social Development: A Review of Evidence and Emerging Issues'. Washington, DC: World Bank.

Monyae, D., 2006. 'South Africa in Africa: Promoting Constitutionalism in Southern Africa, 1994-2004', in V. Federico and C. Fusaro (eds), *Constitutionalism and Democratic Transitions: Lessons from South Africa*. Florence: Firenze University Press.

Moore, D.S., 2005. *Suffering for Territory: Race, Place and Power in Zimbabwe*. Harare: Weaver Press.

Moore, D., 2010. 'A Decade of Disquieting Diplomacy: South Africa, Zimbabwe and the Ideology of the National Democratic Revolution, 1999-2009', *History Compass*, Vol. 8(8), pp. 752-67.

Moore, D., 2012. 'Two perspectives on Zimbabwe's National Democratic Revolution: Thabo Mbeki and Wilfred Mhanda', *Journal of Contemporary African Studies*, Vol. 30(1), pp. 119-38.

Moyana, H., 1987. *The victory of Chief Rekayi Tangwena*. Harare: Longman.

Moyo, S. and P. Yeros, 2005. 'Resurrecting the Peasantry and Semi-Proletariat: A Critique of the New Marxist Analyses of Land Occupations and Land Reform in Zimbabwe: Towards the National Democratic Revolution', in Moyo and Yeros (eds), *Reclaiming the Land: The Resurgence of Rural Movements in Africa, Asia and Latin America*. London and New York: Zed Books.

Mpande, S., 2004. 'Overview of SADC and COMESA Protocols and their Impact on Informal Traders'. Report of the Regional Workshop for SADC Informal

Traders, 11-12 February, Harare.

Mtwana, N. and W. Bird, 2006. *Revealing Race: an analysis of the coverage of race and xenophobia in the South African print media.* Johannesburg: Media Monitoring Project.

Mulaudzi, M., 2000. 'U Shuma Bulasi: Agrarian Transformation in the Zoutpansberg District of South Africa, up to 1945'. PhD thesis, University of Minnesota.

Murray, C., 1981. *Families Divided: The Impact of Migrant Labour in Lesotho.* Johannesburg: Ravan Press.

Murray, M., 1995, 'Blackbirding at Crook's Corner: Illicit Labour Recruiting in the Northeastern Transvaal, 1910-1940', *Journal of Southern African Studies,* Vol. 21(3), pp. 373-97.

— 2003. 'Strangers in our Midst', *Canadian Journal of African Studies,* Vol. 37 (2/3).

Musonda, M. 2004. 'Overview of Informal Trade in the SADC Region-Where are we now?' Regional Workshop for SADC Informal Traders, 11-12 February, Harare.

Mustapha, A.R., 2011. 'Zimbabwean Farmers in Nigeria: Exceptional Farmers or Spectacular Support?', *African Affairs,* Vol. 110(441), pp. 535-61.

Muzondidya, J., 2008. 'Majoni-joni: Survival Strategies among Zimbabwean migrants in South Africa'. Paper presented at the International Conference on the Political Economies of Displacement in Zimbabwe, Johannesburg.

Muzondidya, J., 2009. 'From Buoyancy to Crisis, 1980-1997', in B. Raftopoulos and A. Mlambo (eds), *Becoming Zimbabwe: A History from the Pre-Colonial Period to 2008.* Harare: Weaver Press.

Muzvidziwa, V., 1998. 'Cross-Border Trade: A Strategy for Climbing out of Poverty in Masvingo, Zimbabwe', *Zambezia,* XXV(i), pp. 29-58.

— 2005. 'Women without Borders: Informal Cross-Border Trade among Women in the Southern African Development Community Region'. Organization for Social Science Research in Eastern and Southern Africa (OSSREA).

Mwitu, J.C., 1999. *Situação Linguística de Moçambique.* Maputo: KEPA – Centro de Serviços de Cooperação para o Desenvolvimento.

Ndlela, D., 2006. 'Informal Cross-border Trade: The Case of Zimbabwe'. Occasional Paper No. 52. Johannesburg: Institute for Global Dialogue.

Ndlovu-Gatsheni, S., 2011. 'Reconstructing the Implications of Liberation Struggle History on SADC Mediation in Zimbabwe'. Occasional Paper No 92. Johannesburg: South African Institute of International Affairs

Newitt, M. 1981. *Portugal in Africa: The last hundred years.* London: Hurst & Co.

— 1995. *A History of Mozambique.* London: Hurst & Co.

Nhamaleze, Cristóvão, E.Q., 2008, 'Estudo do desenvolvimento dos sistemas de irrigação de pequena escala utilizados pelo sector familiar no posto administrativo de Machipanda distrito de Manica'. BSc thesis, Universidade Católica de

Moçambique.

Nhantumbo, I. and A. Salomão, 2010. *Biofuels, Land Access, and Rural Livelihoods in Mozambique.* London: IIED.

Nyamnjoh, F., 2006. *Insiders and Outsiders: Citizenship and Xenophobia in Contemporary South Africa.* London and New York: Zed Books.

Nyatanga, P., S. Mpofu and M. Tekere, 2000. *Informal Cross-border Trade: Salient Features and Impact on Welfare – Case Studies of Beitbridge and Chirundu Border Posts and Selected Households in Chitungwiza.* Harare: Trade and Development Studies Centre.

O'Meara, D., 1983. *Volks-kapitalisme: Class, Capital and Ideology in the Development of Afrikaner Nationalism 1934-1948.* Johannesburg: Raven Press, 1983.

Ouden, J.H.B., den, 1989. 'A three generation perspective: its importance for ethnographic research in development studies: case studies from Cameroon and Benin'. Paper presented at the 88th annual meeting of the American Anthropological Association, Washington DC, November.

Øygard, R., G. Garcia, A. Guttormsen, R. Kachule, I. Mwanawina, A. Mwanaumo, E. Sjaastad and M. Wik, 2003. 'The Maze of Maize: Improving Input and Output Market Access for Poor Smallholders in Southern African Region - The Experience of Zambia and Malawi'. Report prepared for NORAD, Oslo.

Peberdy, S., 1999. *Selecting Immigrants: Nationalism and National Identity In South Africa's Immigration Policies,* 1910 to 1998'. PhD thesis, Queen's University, Kingston, Ontario.

— 2000. 'Mobile entrepreneurship: Informal sector cross-border trade and street trade in South Africa', *Development Southern Africa,* Vol. 17(2), pp. 201-219.

— 2008. 'The Invisible Woman: Gender Blindness and South African Immigration Policies and Legislation', *Signs: Journal of Women In Culture and Society,* Vol.33(4), pp. 800–807.

— 2010. *Selecting Immigrants: National Identity and South Africa's Immigration Policies.* Johannesburg: Wits University Press.

People Against Suffering Oppression and Poverty (PASSOP), 2012. 'Strangling the Lifeline: An Analysis of Remittance Flows from South Africa to Zimbabwe'. Johannesburg: PASSOP Report

Phimister, I., 1988. *An Economic and Social History of Zimbabwe, 1890-1948: Capital Accumulation and Class Struggle.* London: Longman.

Phimister, I. and B. Raftopoulos, 2004. 'Mugabe, Mbeki and the Politics of Anti-Imperialism', *Review of African Political Economy* Vol. 31(101), pp. 385-400.

Pitcher, M.A., 2002. *Transforming Mozambique: the Politics of Privatization 1975-2000,* Cambridge: Cambridge University Press.

Platteau, J.-P., 1996. 'The Evolutionary Theory of Land Rights as Applied to Sub-Saharan Africa: A Critical Assessment', *Development and Change,* Vol. 27(1), pp.

29-85.

Polzer, T., 2008. 'A Foot in the Door: Access to Asylum in South Africa'. Migration Studies Working Paper Series 41. Johannesburg: Forced Migration Studies Programme, Wits University..

Polzer, T. and L. Hammond, 2008. 'Invisible Displacement', *Journal of Refugee Studies*, Vol.25(2), pp. 417-431.

Pophiwa, N., 2010. 'Smuggling on the Zimbabwe – Mozambique Border', in J. Crush and D. Tevera (eds), *Zimbabwe's Exodus*.

Post Online, 2010a. 'Strangulation of Zimbabwe', *The Post Online*, 31 January.

— 2010b. 'Will Mugabe Go Down with ZANU-PF', *The Post Online*, 9 March.

Potts, D., 2008. 'Displacement and Livelihoods: The Longer-term Impacts of Operation Murambatsvina', in M. Vambe, (ed.), *The Hidden Dimensions of Operation Murambatsvina*.

— 2010. *Circular Migration in Zimbabwe and Contemporary Sub-Saharan Africa*. Woodbridge and Rochester, NY: James Currey and Boydell & Brewer.

Quingstone, F., 2006. 'Estudo da gestão e aproveitamento do sistema de regadio por gravidade pelo sector familiar na Bacia do rio Púnguè no distrito de Báruè'. Trabalho de Licenciatura em Ciências Ágrarias, Universidade Cátolica de Moçambique.

Raftopoulos, B., 2004. 'Nation, Race and History in Zimbabwean Politics', in B. Raftopoulos and T. Savage (eds), *Zimbabwe: Injustice and Political Reconciliation*.

— 2009. 'The Crisis in Zimbabwe, 1998-2008', in B. Raftopoulos and A. Mlambo (eds), *Becoming Zimbabwe: A History from the Pre-Colonial Period to 2008*. Harare: Weaver Press.

Raftopoulos, B. and T. Savage (eds), 2004. *Zimbabwe: Injustice and Political Reconciliation*. Cape Town: Institute for Justice and Reconciliation.

Raftopoulos, B. and S. Eppel, 2008. 'Desperately Seeking Sanity: What Prospects for a New Beginning In Zimbabwe?' *Journal of Eastern African Studies*, Vol.2(3), pp. 369-400.

Ramutsindela, M., 2007 'The Geographical Imprint of Land Restitution with Reference to Limpopo Province, South Africa', *Tijdschrift voor Economische en Sociale Geografie*. Vol. 98(4), pp. 455-67.

República de Moçambique, 1991, '*Study of Small Scale Irrigation in the Manica District*'. Draft Final Report prepared for Mozambique Agricultural Rural Reconstruction Programme, Chimoio, Mozambique.

Reitzes, M., 2009. 'Xenophobic Triggers Situated in the History and Legal Provisions of Domestic and International Migration Policies in South Africa', *Synopsis*, the Policy Studies Bulletin of the Centre for Policy Studies, Vol. 10(3), pp. 9-14.

Reitzes, M. and S. Barn, 2000. 'Citizenship, Immigration and Identity in Winterveld, South Africa', *Canadian Journal of African Studies* Vol. 34(1), pp. 80-100.

Rønning, H., 2009. 'The Influence of the Media', in H. Rønning and K. Orgeret (eds), *The Power of Communication*. Oslo: Unipub.

RSA, 1997. Extension of Security of Tenure Act (ESTA), Act 62 Of 1997. Pretoria: Republic of South Africa.

Rupiya, M., 2012. 'Zimbabwe-South Africa Foreign Relations: A Zimbabwean Perspective', *Alternatives: Turkish Journal of International Relations*.

Rutherford, B., 1997. 'Another Side to Rural Zimbabwe: Social Constructs and the Administration of Farm Workers in Urungwe District, 1940s', *Journal of Southern African Studies*, Vol. 23(1), pp. 107-26.

— 2001. *Working on the Margins: Black Workers, White Farmers in Postcolonial Zimbabwe*. London and Harare: Zed Books and Weaver Press.

— 2003. 'Belonging to the Farm(er): Farm Workers, Farmers, and the Shifting Politics of Citizenship', in A. Hammar, et al., *Zimbabwe's Unfinished Business*.

— 2007. 'Shifting Grounds in Zimbabwe: Citizenship and Farm Workers in the New Politics of Land', in S. Dorman, D. Hammett and P. Nugent (eds), *Making Nations, Creating Strangers: States and Citizenship in Africa*. Leiden: Brill.

— 2008. 'An Unsettled Belonging: Zimbabwean Farm Workers in Limpopo Province, South Africa', *Journal of Contemporary African Studies*, Vol. 26(4), pp. 401-415.

— 2008.' Zimbabweans Living in the South African-Border Zone: Negotiating, Suffering and Surviving', *ACAS Bulletin 80*, pp. 36-42.

— 2001. *Working on the Margins: Black Labour, White Farmers in Postcolonial Zimbabwe*. London and Harare: Zed Books and Weaver Press.

Sachikonye, L., 2003a. 'From "Growth with Equity" to "Fast Track" Reform: Zimbabwe's Land.

Question', *Review of African Political Economy*, No. 96, pp. 227-40.

— 2003b. 'Land Reform for Poverty Reduction? Social Exclusion and Farm Workers in Zimbabwe'. Paper prepared for the conference, 'Staying Poor: Chronic Poverty and Development Policy', Manchester University.

— 2003c. 'The Situation of Commercial Farm Workers in Zimbabwe after Land Reform'. Report Prepared for the Farm Community Trust of Zimbabwe, Harare.

— 2006. 'The Impact of Operation Murambatsvina/Clean Up on the Working People in Zimbawe'. Report prepared for the Labour and Economic Development Research Institute of Zimbabwe, Harare.

— 2011. *When a State Turns on Its Citizens – 60 Years of Institutionalized Violence in Zimbabwe*. Johannesburg: Jacana Media.

SADC, 2002. 'Zimbabwe Parliamentary Election Report 2002'. *Harare: SADC*.

SAHRC, 2003. 'Inquiry Into Human Rights Violations In Farming Communities'. Johannesburg: South African Human Rights Commission.

Schippers, J., 2008, 'Making the water(net) work: Towards an Understanding of Water Management Practices in Farmer-Managed Irrigation in Manica District, Mozambique'. MSc thesis, Wageningen University.

Scoones, I., N. Marongwe, B. Mavedzenge, J. Mahenehene, F. Murimbarimba and C. Sukume, 2010. *Zimbabwe's Land Reform: Myths and Realities*. Woodbridge: James Currey; Harare: Weaver Press; Johannesburg: Jacana Media.

Scott, J., 1985. *Weapons of the weak: Everyday forms of peasant resistance*. New Haven, CT: Yale University Press.

Selby, A., 2006. 'Commercial Farmers and the State: Interest Group Politics and Land Reform in Zimbabwe'. DPhil thesis, Oxford University.

Sender, J., 2002, 'Women's Struggle to Escape Rural Poverty in South Africa', *Journal of Agrarian Change*, Vol. 2(1), pp. 1-49.

Sender, J., C. Oya and C. Cramer, 2006. 'Women Working for Wages: Putting Flesh on the Bones of a Rural Labour Market Survey in Mozambique', *Journal of Southern African Studies*, Vol. 32(2), pp. 313-33.

Serra, C. (ed), 2010. *A construção social do Outro: Perspectivas cruzadas sobre estrangeiros e Moçambicanos*. Maputo: Imprensa Universitária.

Sichone, O., 2008. 'Xenophobia', in N. Shepherd and S. Robins (eds), *New South African Keywords*. Johannesburg and Athens, GA: Jacana Media and Ohio University Press.

Sigsworth, R., C. Ngwane and A. Pino, 2008. 'The Gendered Nature of Xenophobia in South Africa'. Cape Town: Centre for the Study of Violence and Reconciliation.

Silota, G. de J.L., 2007, 'Práticas do uso da terra e da água e a necessidade de reabilitação dos sistemas e esquema de irrigação dos produtores de pequena escala no distrito de Báruè'. BSc thesis, Universidade Católica de Moçambique.

Sims, B., S. Masamvu and H. Mirell, 2010. 'Restrictive Measures and Zimbabwe: Political Implications, Economic Impact and a Way Forward'. Report written for IDASA, Pretoria.

Sjaastad, E. and D. Bromley, 1997. 'Indigenous Land Rights in Sub-Saharan Africa: Appropriation, Security and Investment Demand', *World Development*, Vol. 25(4), pp. 549-62.

Skjæraasen, M., 2008. 'Velgerflukten [Flight Of Voters]'. *A-Magasinet*, 28 March, pp. 24–32.

Solidarity Peace Trust. 2003. 'National youth service training – "Shaping youths in a truly Zimbabwean manner"'. Harare.

—2004. 'No War in Zimbabwe: An Account of a Nation's People'. Johannesburg: Solidarity Peace Trust.

— 2006. '"Meltdown" – Murambatsvina one year on'. Johannesburg: Solidarity Peace Trust.

Solidarity Peace Trust and Passop, 2012. *'Perils and Pitfalls – Migrants and Deportation in South Africa'.* Johannesburg: Solidarity Peace Trust.

Somers, M. R., 1994. 'The Narrative Constitution of Identity: A Relational and Network Approach', *Theory and Society,* Vol. 23, pp. 605-49.

South African Lawyers for Human Rights. 2006. 'The Documented Experiences of Refugees, Deportees and Asylum Seekers in South Africa: A Zimbabwean Case Study'. A written submission prepared by civil society organizations working on the refugee and asylum seekers' human rights issues in South Africa presented to the Minister of Home Affairs.

South African Lawyers for Human Rights, 2010. 'Submission to the European Union on the Occasion of the South African Human Rights Dialogue'.

SouthAfrica.info, 2008. 'Postpone Zimbabwe Elections: SADC', *SouthAfrica.info,* 23 June.

Southern African Development Community (SADC), 2000. 'SADC Regional Human Development Report 2000: Challenges and Opportunities for Regional Integration'. Harare: UNDP and SAPES Trust.

Sparks, A., 2003. *Beyond the Miracle: Inside the New South Africa.* Chicago: University of Chicago Press.

Spiegel, S.S., O. Savornin, D. Shoko and M.M. Veiga, 2006. 'Mercury reduction in Munhena, Mozambique: homemade solutions and the social context for change', *International Journal of Occupational Health,* 12, pp. 215–221.

Statistics South Africa, 2002a. 'Income and Expenditure Survey'. Pretoria: Government of South Africa.

—2000b. 'Labour Force Survey', Pretoria: Government of South Africa

— 2005. 'Labour Force Survey of September 2005'. Pretoria: Government of South Africa.

Steinberg, J., 2005. 'An overview of South African Border Control: 1994-2004'. Institute for Security Studies Occasional Paper 103.

Stephenson, J. P., 1937. *Chirupula's Tale: A Bye-Way in African History.* London: Geoffrey Bles.

Sumich, J., 2010. 'The Party and the State: Frelimo and Social Stratification in Post-Socialist Mozambique', *Development and Change,* Vol. 41 (4), pp. 679-98.

Tannenbaum, M., 2007. 'Back and Forth: Immigrants' Stories of Migration and Return', *International Migration.* Vol 45(5), pp. 147-174.

Tanner, C., 2002. 'The Reform and Implementation of Land Policy in Mozambique – A Case Study of FAO Support', *Land Reform/Réforme Agraire/Reforma Agrarian,* 2002/2. Online version.

Taylor, S.,1999. 'Race, Class, and Neopatrimonialism in Zimbabwe', in R. Joseph (ed.), *State, Conflict, and Democracy in Africa.* Boulder, CO: Lynne Rienner Publishers.

—2007. *Business and the State in Southern Africa: The Politics of Economic Reform.* Boulder, CO: Lynne Rienner Publishers.

Tekere, E. Z., 2007. *A Lifetime of Struggle.* Harare: Sapes Books.

Telegraph, 2008. 'Obituaries: Levy Mwanawasa', *The Telegraph*, 19 August.

Tendi, B-M. 2010. *Making History in Mugabe's Zimbabwe: Politics, Intellectuals and the Media.* Oxford: Peter Lang.

Tevera, D., J. Crush and A. Chikanda, 2010. 'Migrant Remittances and Household Survival in Zimbabwe', in J. Crush and D. Tevera (eds), *Zimbabwe's Exodus.*

Thaler, K., 2010. 'Mozambique in 2010: strength on the surface but fissures emerging', *IPRIS Lusophone Countries Bulletin 2010 Review*, pp. 25-9.

Theting, H. and B. Brekke, 2010. 'Land Investment or Land Grab? A Critical View from Tanzania and Mozambique'. Unpublished report, Spire, Utviklingsfondets Ungdom, Oslo.

Thompson, G., 2004. 'Cultivating Conflict: Agricultural "Betterment", the Native Land Husbandry Act (NLHA) and Ungovernability in Colonial Zimbabwe, 1951-1962,' *Africa Development*, Vol. 29, pp. 1-39.

Thornycroft, P., 2010. 'ANC Youth Leader: South Africa Will Seize White-Owned Farms'. VOA News, 3 April.

Tibaijuka, A., 2005. Report of the Fact-Finding Mission to Zimbabwe to assess the Scope and Impact of Operation Murambatsvina by the UN Special Envoy on Human Settlements Issues in Zimbabwe. New York: United Nations.

Times of Zambia, 2008. 'Zim Political Situation Embarrassing', *Times of Zambia*, 23 June.

— 2012. 'Sata's Anti-Nationalisation Stance Wins Kudos', *Times of Zambia*, 23 May.

Tornimbeni, C., 2004, 'Migrant workers and state boundaries. Reflections on the transnational debate from the colonial past in Mozambique', *Lusotopie*, pp.107-120.

— 2007. '"Isto sempre foi assim": The politics of Land and Human Mobility in Chimanimani, Central Mozambique', *Journal of Southern African Studies*, Vol. 33(3), pp. 485-500.

UNDP, 1999. 'Mozambique: Economic growth and human development'. National Human Development Report. Maputo: UNDP.

— 2004, 'Youth: a new voice in the Millenium Development Goals'. Leaflet published on the occasion of the award of the 2004 Poverty Eradication Award, United Nations Development Programme, New York.

— 2008. 'Comprehensive Economic Recovery in Zimbabwe'. New York: UNDP

UNHCR, 2008. 'Map of Zimbabwe situation (Detailed map)', 23 June, available at: http://www.unhcr.org/refworld/Zimbabwe [accessed 19 July 2012]

— 2010. 'Mozambique: 2010 Regional Operations Profile – Southern Africa'.

Available at: http://www.unhcr.org [accessed 29 January 2010, removed by July 2012]

Vale, P., 2003. *Security and Politics and South Africa: The Regional Dimension*. Boulder: Lynne Rienner.

Utete, C. M. B., 2003. *Report of the Presidential Land Review Committee*. Harare: Government of Zimbabwe.

Valji, N., 2003. *Creating the Nation: The Rise of Violent Xenophobia in the New South Africa*. MA thesis, York University, Canada.

Vambe, M. (ed.), 2008. *The Hidden Dimensions of Operation Murambatsvina in Zimbabwe*. Harare and Pretoria: Weaver Press and the Africa Institute of South Africa.

Van der Merwe, C.F., 2002. 'Elim Hospital: The First 100 Years, Part 2', *South African Medical Journal* Vol. 92(1), pp. 75-78.

Van der Zaag, P., 2003. 'The bench terrace between invention and intervention: physical and political aspects of a conservation technology', in A. Bolding, J. Mutimba, and P. van der Zaag (eds), *Interventions in smallholder agriculture. Implications for extension in Zimbabwe*. Harare: University of Zimbabwe Publications,

— (ed.), 2010. *What role of law in promoting and protecting the productive uses of water by smallholder farmers in Mozambique?* Unpublished report of the Water rights in informal economies project. CGIAR Challenge Programme on Water and Food.

van Donge, J. K., 2009. 'The Plundering of Zambian Resources by Frederick Chiluba and his Friends: A Case Study of the Interaction between National Politics and the International Drive Towards Good Governance', *African Affairs*, Vol. 108(430), pp. 69-90.

Van Onselen, C. 1976. *Chibaro: African Mine Labour In Southern Rhodesia, 1900–1933*. London: Pluto Press.

Vermeulen, S., and L. Cotula, 2010. 'Over the heads of local people: consultation, consent, and recompense in large-scale land deals for biofuels projects in Africa', *Journal of Peasant Studies*, Vol. 37,(4), pp. 899–916.

Vigneswaran, D., A. Tesfalem, C. Hoag, and X. Tshabalala, 2010. 'Criminality Or Monopoly? Informal Immigration Enforcement In South Africa', *Journal Of Southern African Studies*, Vol.36(2), pp. 465481.

Vollan, K. 2002. 'Zimbabwe: Presidential Elections 2002'. NORDEM Report 05/2002. Oslo: Norwegian Institute of Human Rights.

Von Holdt, K., M. Langa, S. Molapo, N. Mogapi, K. Ngubeni, J.Dlamini and A. Kirsten, 2011. 'The Smoke that Calls: Insurgent citizenship, collective violence and the struggle for a place in the new South Africa'. Cape Town: Centre for the Study of Violence and Reconciliation.

Wagner, R., 1980. 'Zoutpansberg: The dynamics of a Hunting Frontier, 1848-

1867', in S. Marks and A. Atmore (eds), *Economy and Society in Pre-Industrial South Africa*. London: Longman.

Wegerif, M., B. Russell, and I. Grundling, 2005. *Still Searching For Security: The Reality of Farm dweller Evictions in South Africa*. Pretoria: Nkuzi Development Association and Social Surveys.

Willems, W., 2005. 'Remnants of Empire? British media reporting on Zimbabwe', *Westminster Papers in Communication and Culture*, Special Issue on Zimbabwe, October, pp. 91-108.

Willen, S., 2007. 'Exploring 'Illegal' and 'Irregular' Migrants' Lived Experiences of Law and State Power', *International Migration*. Vol 45(3), pp. 2-7.

Wilson, F. 1972. 'Migrant Labour: Report to the South African Council of Churches'. Johannesburg:The South African Council of Churches.

Win, E., 2004. 'Sisters, You Let Us Down'. *Mail & Guardian Online*, 10 March.

Wood, A.P., 1990. 'Agricultural Policy since Independence,' in A.P. Wood, S.A Kean, J.T. Milimo and D.M. Warren (eds), *The Dynamics of Agricultural Policy and Reform in Zambia*. Ames, IA: Iowa State University Press.

Woode, P., I. Condliffe and A. Wood, 1978-79. 'Mkushi Farm Block: The Development of a Commercial Farming Area in Zambia', *Zambian Geographical Journal*, Vol. 33-34, pp. 1-16.

World Bank, 2006. 'Mozambique: Agricultural Development Strategy: Stimulating Smallholder Agricultural Growth', Report No. 32416-MZ. Washington, DC: World Bank.

— 2010. 'World Development Indicators 2010'. Washington, DC: World Bank.

Wuyts, M., 2001. 'The Agrarian Question in Mozambique's Transition and Reconstruction'. World Institute for Development Economics Research, Discussion Paper No. 2001/14. Tokyo: United Nations University.

Zapiro. 2011. *Do You Know Who I Am?* Johannesburg: Jacana Media.

Zambian Watchdog, 2012. 'Sata Slams Sanctions, Supports Grabbing of White-Owned Farms in Zimbabwe', *Zambian Watchdog*, 27 April.

Zimbabwe Mail, 2010. 'Mugabe Fingered in Mwanawasa's Death', *Zimbabwe Mail*, 19 May.

ZIMOSA, 2009. 'Zimbabwean migrants in Mozambique and their perceptions regarding Government of National Unity'. Report by Zimbabwe–Mozambique Solidarity Alliance in partnership with Christian Council of Mozambique.

Žižek, S. 2009. *Violence*. London: Profile Books.